A Novel by
Tom Gauthier

A
Voyage Beyond
Reason

An Epic of Survival
Based on the Original Journals
of Benjamin Wade

Outskirts Press, Inc.
Denver, Colorado

This book is based on the personal, handwritten journals of Benjamin Wade, recorded as he traveled over 6,000 tortuous miles of open ocean in his kayak. His infrequent meetings with "civilization" along the coast of Baja California and Central America, record interaction with real people. Some people have been partially fictionalized in their dialogue and identity. All events from the journal are true.

To Marlene, Ray, Denise, and, of course, Benjamin
The Keepers of the Tale

Foreword

A Voyage Beyond Reason

J ournal (jûr'n☐l) *n*. A personal record of occurrences, experiences, and reflections kept on a regular basis; a diary.

Within this definition, the key word for me is *personal*. When I first discovered and began to read the journals of Benjamin Wade, I couldn't shake the feeling of being somehow voyeuristic; peering too deeply into very private corners of his mind. The water-stained and tattered notes revealed a young man who was keenly focused on his goal, even as it drove him to places of loneliness, fatigue and fear, that he could never have imagined in the beginning.

It's not just the words. His handwriting ebbs and flows with the days. An open bold hand one day, or a tight, sweat smeared scribble, telling of a day of fear. Marginal drawings on the pages were crude, but an obvious attempt by Ben to add an exclamation point to a particularly unique experience; a kind of ghost of the day. If the journal mirrors the life he experienced, it would seem a miracle that he survived at all.

My wife, Marlene, joined me in the reading. She too felt drawn into the struggle. And *struggle* is the only word that can begin to describe the minute by minute, hour by hour, day by day, matching of young muscle to old sea, and young mind to old sources of madness.

It was Marlene who insisted that other people needed to hear Ben

Wade's story. At first I wasn't sure. It was so private to me, so personal. But then the questions began to bubble up; questions that haunted me. Why did he do it? Did he complete his voyage?

I found his journals some 6,000 miles from the launching that he recorded so poetically. Did the man make it all the way with the journals? Was it he who buried them? Why would he do something like that?

This book is my humble attempt to share the contents of the treasure I found with all of you. You will be the judge of how well I've done. Sometimes I try to interpret Ben's thoughts, but mostly I share them with you directly from his notes and journals (printed in italics).

The descriptions of the world he discovered, and the people he met, are his. His journals drive the story, and reveal the pain and sorrow, sadness and suffering, euphoria and ecstasy, and triumph and discovery, as the boy struggles to become a man.

His journey began in 1996. My quest began in 1998. But it was not until 2003 that Marlene and I learned the true fate of Ben Wade.

And what was that fate? Read on.

Tom Gauthier

Prologue

Near Choco Bay
Columbia, South America
January 1998

W e had been working on a survey project near the Rio San Juan in Colombia, South America. The river is in Chocó state. Its upper reaches are rugged boulder strewn rapids, but its lower flow ends in a magnificent delta with many jungle laden islands and mangrove swamps.

Our team had taken a "mental health day off" from the tedious and sometimes dangerous project. This area of Colombia has a notorious history of drug trafficking and violence. Only the week before, we'd been held at gunpoint by a gang of drug runners who were bringing their cargo down river in two canoes. It was just our bad luck to be eating lunch on a sandbar when they rounded the bend and confronted us. It cost us a few pesos, and a couple of cheap watches, before they decided we were neither a threat nor a source of great wealth. We all carried some Colombian pesos (it was about 2,000 to 1 US$), and wore only cheap watches, for just such an event. We called it our 'mugging money'.

The rest of the team had gone into the town of Buenaventura to blow off some steam in a "fine cantina". Me? I needed a little solo time. So, after a short jeep ride and a medium hike, there I stood on the cliffs at Punta Charambira in Colombia, looking out over Chocó Bay toward Panama. The sun was warm, but there was enough sea breeze to keep my khaki sleeves rolled down. Clouds played on the horizon, promising more rain during the night. Rain is an integral part of the experience in these parts.

I sat on a rock outcropping that seemed to fit my medium wide, not too padded, backside, and enjoyed a lunch of leftover tamales and a thermos of tinto.

As I stood up to stow my trash in the little backpack that's always at my shoulder, a reflection of some sort caught my eye. I peered down into the jagged rocks to my right. There, again, I saw a sort of sparkle. As I looked, I caught sight of something else that I'd missed. It was faded blue, a shaped piece of wood. A handle to something?

Curiosity ruled, and I set the pack down and picked my way through the rocks toward the edge of the cliff. What looked like the handle of an old, weather worn paddle with a jaggedly broken tip, protruded from the soil between two sharply cleaved rocks. At its base, a bit of sun-yellowed plastic flapped in the breeze. My sparkle. The blue wood took an extra tug to free it from the crevasse. It was a handle, broken off. Then I pushed aside the loose soil and carefully revealed a plastic packet of papers.

I took the treasures back up to my rock roost and sat down. Carefully opening the mysterious packet, I read the meticulously hand-printed cover page:

My Journal
Ben Wade, Kayak Extremist
Solo Sea Kayak Expedition
1996/97

Who was Ben Wade? Was it Wade who buried this packet? Why would he bury his Journal? Had he passed this way, or someone else? Did he run into drug runners too? Did he survive? Questions, questions.

I poured another beaker of tinto, and began to read. Some hours later, I re-emerged to my surroundings, feeling the late afternoon chill, my legs cramped from sitting unmoving against the rock. I gathered up the journal, and carefully replaced it in its protective bag, picked up the paddle shard, and retraced my steps back to the jeep. I felt the need to share this with others. The intimacy, intensity, and real mystery, of the journal had to be interpreted by others smarter than me.

Before I went back to the jeep, I stepped to the edge of the cliff and stared hard around its base and up and down the darkening beach. I knew there was a kayak, and a man, connected to these writings.

Where are they?

The next morning during breakfast I told the others of my find, and my strong feelings about it. No one actually read the journal that day, but there was plenty of speculation around the table about what might have happened.

Did the fellow Wade meet up with the drug runners as we had?

Did he survive the encounter?

Was it he who buried the journal, or someone hiding the evidence of a tragic encounter?

No one really had a clue.

Our survey work was near completion, and everyone was focused on finishing their part, and getting packed up for the trip home. Not much more attention was paid to my find, other than occasional idle speculation and theories.

On the plane ride home to Mississauga, Ontario, Canada, I used the time to continue reading Ben Wade's journal.

Mississauga, Ontario, Canada
The home of Tom and Marlene Gauthier
February 2, 1998

My wife, Marlene, picked me up at Pearson International Airport in Mississauga, outside of Toronto. As the twenty minute drive brought us to the front of our home, a brick cube that is the Toronto suburb's *de rigueur* architecture, I still couldn't stop talking about my find. But it was a couple of days later before Marlene made the mistake of picking up Ben's journal and starting to read. I say 'mistake' because I'd already learned that you don't begin to read it, and ever expect to lay it down until the end.

"Tom, this is intense," Marlene tossed out to me. "Are you sure it's all real? I mean this guy Ben Wade really did this stuff?"

"I've got no reason to doubt it," I replied, fingering some of the stained pages. "No reason at all."

"It's sad that he never got to tell his story. Do you suppose he didn't want to, or he couldn't? I mean like something happened to him," Marlene said as she idly flipped the pages she held in her hand. A few grains of sand launched from a page. She didn't wait for my answer. She sat pensively for a short moment, then said, "Tom, you've got some time now. Why don't you see if you can write this young man's story? I don't know why, but it has to be told."

As I studied the first stained and crumpled sheets of the journal, trying to decide just where to begin, I kept coming back to the young man's state of mind. Even with my education and training I refuse to accept that one man can truly see into the mind of another with more than assumptions and educated guesses. Therefore, I proceeded with *my interpretations* of the thoughts of this young man as he faces his self-imposed trial by water.

Physically, we know he is young, just 24 years old. We can assume he is strong, and determined, from his training. He would never have attempted this venture without training. As I read, I see also that he sees himself as fearless, yet fearful; and competent, yet careless. Here I see both the dichotomies of youth – and, that Ben Wade is honest with himself.

I can work with that.

Sitting back in my chair, eyes closed, I visualize this fellow sitting in his one-man kayak, bobbing on the waves, the occasional splash hitting the journal in his hand. He pens fast, because the words come fast. He writes of leaving San Felipe behind, fading away with the images of the people on the beach. In short order, he writes of the loneliness of the open ocean with no one to talk to, nothing to look at save a vast expanse of water.

It's no wonder he wrote fast, sometimes furiously.

I, and eventually my readers, can try to feel this solitude, this emotional pain, but it will be a miracle if any of us can truly imagine just what this brave, and foolhardy, young adventurer went through on this voyage that seems to crash, and slog, and prevail beyond reason.

But who establishes the boundaries of reason? Certainly this young man has challenged any accepted limits of what is survivable, physically and mentally.

Miracles do happen.

I can work with this.

I lean forward, position my hands on the keyboard, and glance once more at the stained and battered sheets beside me.

Part One

The Sea of Cortez

Chapter 1

Don't walk behind me, I may not lead. Don't walk in front of me, I may not follow. Just walk beside me and be my friend.

Unknown

A Beach near San Felipe
Baja California, Mexico
September 13th, 1996

The tall, tanned, and fit, twenty four year old, stood holding the rudder lines of his one man kayak firmly in his left hand, looking out over the Sea of Cortez. While he gazed intently, he wasn't focused on the scene before him. Deep in thought, he wondered just what it was that had enticed and possessed him to attempt what he was about to do.

Wondering without questioning, anticipating without fearing, he let the prospects of his near future slosh around in his mind, imitating the water around his feet. His next step would launch him into shark infested waters, a sea passage known for its lawless drug smugglers, dangerous surf, and rocky coasts. Launching his tiny craft would start the journey. A journey that would not end before six thousand miles had passed beneath its keel.

Or perhaps, much, much, sooner.

Some thought him crazy to plan his departure date to coincide with the hurricane season in Mexico. Just as inexplicable, his planned arrival in a few months will coincide with the monsoon season in the Southern Hemisphere. But today, standing at the edge of his future, this was not on his mind.

These were decisions he would live to regret.

But first he had to *live* – before he could *regret*.

The young man's mind swirled with every thought imaginable, all pointed at excitement and a burning desire to succeed. With emotions running high, his body grew tense and rigid. Raw anticipation clutched at his throat. His breath was coming in short, ragged gasps. Drawn to this ocean, and the real dangers it promised, he saw this moment as what he'd been waiting for, and preparing for, for the past six months. Indeed, he felt like this was the time he'd been waiting for his whole life.

A few feet behind him, up on the dry hot sand, were the few people who came to see him off. People who loved him, and people who hated his decision to follow his dream. They were the same people. In front of the rest, his father stood, quietly resigned to the scene that unfolded around his son. His own last words to his son rolled around in his head, "Ben, you're going off half cocked. You don't know what you're getting into. People get killed out there on the ocean. It's a very dangerous place and you don't know the first thing about it." In the classic struggle of the ages between fathers and sons, he feared that his attempt to discourage may have only driven the stake for success higher and deeper into his son's soul. Quietly, silently, the father prayed for the son, *God speed, my boy, God speed.*

Standing apart from the small group on the shore stood a young lady. She was tall and beautiful with golden hair that shone in the desert sun as it fell halfway down her back. Her name was Heather, and Ben had known her only two weeks. But it was an intense two weeks, that found them emotionally entwined, and sweetly conflicted. Her arms hung limp and helpless at her sides, the expression on her face a mixture of admiration, sorrow, and fear.

All eyes were on the young man. At 6'1" tall, with piercing brown eyes, his shaved head showing pale contrast to his tanned, broad shouldered body, Benjamin Wade stood waist deep in the blue green waters of Baja California's Sea of Cortez. His heavily laden kayak floated faithfully at his side. The sun beat down hard on his brow. He squinted against its glare, and peered out across the sea to a world that seemed to open its mouth and swallow him whole. He stood there, pitiful like, in a valiant attempt to look confident, chest puffed out and jaw set tight. Slowly, his mind calmed, working its way through the pall of a feeling of complete and utter loneliness that had begun to shallow his breathing.

Now he drew a deep breath.

This is it! It's time! Now we put all the words to rest. I'll live up to my expectations – or damn well die trying. They may not believe, but I do – and that's what counts now!

This is it!

With a final push, and a yell that was harsher, more primal, than he or anyone expected, Benjamin Wade shoved the kayak into the waves. He climbed nimbly into the cockpit, thrust his paddle deep into the blue-green water, and began his journey. On the beach, people who cared watched him grow smaller and smaller, as the distance and the sea swallow him into his future.

On the sea, Ben did not look back.

Time is relative at sea. Especially so, when one is alone in a small craft, and learning as one goes. In only a couple of hours, but all too soon, Ben received his first shock – the stark realization that his training, and mental preparation, was nothing compared to what the ocean now hinted that it had in store for him.

He had expected the waters in the Sea of Cortez along the Baja California coast, to be fairly calm, and protected from the path of the hurricanes and the stronger swells of the Pacific Ocean. His plan was to hug the Baja coast down to La Paz, nine hundred miles to the south. Then he would *simply cross over* to the mainland of Mexico, a good month's journey away. Ben figured that this "*little cruise down to La Paz*" would give him plenty of time to adjust to a life of solitude on the water - and the prospect of increasing danger. He figured that after this first month into the voyage, he would be fit to tackle the twenty foot waves, the strong gales, and the continuous storms of the open ocean.

He was wrong, maybe dead wrong.

The currents in the Sea of Cortez were stronger and more unpredictable than he had anticipated. At the end of the first day he was more tired than he had been in his whole life.

Sunset
On the Sea of Cortez
September 13, 1996

This is my first entry in this journal. The sun is setting, but I have light to see as I stop for dinner, and to write this.

I have always been drawn to the ocean; transformed by its beauty, afraid of its power, changed by its pleasures, and totally mesmerized by its mysteries.

These massive living bodies of water that surround us have a magnetic passion, a dynamic energy that defies all logic. With a mind of its own, the ocean gives us but a fleeting glimpse of its storied and oft told past.

I have seen its raw power myself in the churning surf and raging swells that reshapes the land beneath our feet, and with seeming indifference, destroys anything foolish enough to defy it. So too have I experienced its serene beauty and splendor on a quiet night in a secluded cove, reflecting the moonlight, its waves gently pattering on a soft sandy shore.

With all of the focus back there in the world on man's so called progress and achievement, the ocean gives us a glimpse, a small example, of how ruggedly beautiful the hand of God can be.

These thoughts have been rolling around in my mind all day. I'm anxious to write them down, for me, or for whoever might find them. I will keep a record of everything that happens to me on this voyage. Some see this as a shot at the world's record for a solo voyage in this craft, but for me this is my search for who I am, what I am, and if I'm a quitter or not.

Too often of late, I accuse myself of being a quitter.

I WILL prove myself wrong.

The bottom of this page is smeared, apparently by a splash of seawater. The top of the next page continues, and the hand writing reflects the words.

For the past six months I trained every day, six hours a day, seven days a week. I knew I was prepared. But now as I sit here, a tiny speck in this endless and powerful sea, I know I am not prepared for this, my first day. The grueling agony of hours of aching muscles is pure torture. Even as I sit here watching the sunset, my hands have not stopped shaking. I can barely read my own writing!

Back home, I used to sit in my kayak on my living room floor, lights out, and listening to soothing music, while I tried to visualize what it will be like to sit in the darkness of the wilderness, miles from any human being.

I truly believed that my mental toughness was awesome; the better of any man or situation.

Well, I was wrong.

On all accounts, I was wrong!

I am tired, hungry, thirsty, and . . . God knows, lonely.

Oh, how I wish I had someone to talk to, to share this moment with. I feel that I'm on the verge of something great. But, there is a chasm of fear and doubt that has welled up in front of me.

Will I make it? I must!

Will I die? I cannot!

There is a scribble here. Like a pause in his thinking.

(Here this writer goes again; trying to interpret another man's inner turmoil. It's tempting, and I know I shall fail again as we progress.)

Ben continues.

I will write more in my journal later. For now I will set down this pen and paper, and concentrate on the majestic sunset that sweeps as a panorama before me. The water is gently lapping against the hull of my tiny craft; the seashore is a phantom, several miles in the distance; and I am content to sit here, and let this dream of mine encompass all that is in me and around me.

September 14, 1996

The second day at sea repeated the challenge, and the drain of energy, as the rough current seemed to make the miles and the minutes drag by. Doubts began to sneak into his thoughts.

The craft that had seemed so strong and up to the task back in California, now took on a very fragile and Lilliputian dimension in the face of the vast sea. Eighteen feet long and two feet wide at its widest point, the gray Kevlar hull of the kayak was strong. But the egg shaped cockpit that was Ben's 'hearth and home' was only three feet long by fifteen inches wide. The depth of the hull was twelve inches, which meant that Ben's exposed body was never more than six inches above the water – and any sea creatures that chose to explore this intruder. An outrigger pontoon, eight feet long by eight inches wide and deep, completed the craft that would be Ben's home, refuge, and life raft, for the months to come.

The potential fragility of craft, of body, and of mind, crept into the picture now, framed by a blue, brown, and green, restless sea.

5

On the Sea of Cortez
September 15, 1996

It was early on his third day on the water. Ben woke from a fitful slumber with a start. He stretched limbs, stiffened from the night of cramped sleep on the kayak. With a brief look around, he began to paddle at an even pace. The water was calm, and his spirits rose with the sun. The warming rays eased the stiffness in his back. *Okay, this is how it's suppose to be*, he thought, reveling in the smooth movement through the water. As the morning progressed, he could tell that he was making substantial headway. Occasionally he looked over to the passing shore, and sighted landmarks that he could identify on his map. His spirits as buoyant as his little craft, he settled into a decisive rhythm. He focused on the bow of the kayak, eight feet in front of him, that parted the small rolling swells, and sent glinting fragments of water rushing by.

Yes, this is how it's supposed to be.

Gliding along in a state of peaceful bliss and concentration, Ben was only mildly surprised when a sandbar emerged from the calm waters directly in front of him. It stretched out toward the kayak like a knife. He calmly pressed his right foot down on the rudder and steered around the obstacle. Then another one appeared, and yet another. Somewhat confused, and pondering what it might mean, Ben stopped paddling.

I know I'm far enough out from shore.... there shouldn't be any outstretching piece of the coastline....

He looked around, suddenly becoming aware of dozens of little islands that he hadn't seen before. They stretched across the horizon. Now he realized that he was floating in only a few inches of water. His paddle occasionally scraped bottom sand.

Good God, could the tide have gone out this rapidly?

He felt jerked back into the reality of how unfamiliar he was with the Sea of Cortez, and how suddenly the water along this stretch of coast can change.

The water level must have dropped over thirty feet!

Ben shook his head, smiled sheepishly at his own ignorance, and resigned himself to what was happening, as the sand islands slowly connected to each other until he was surrounded by one continuous ring of sand. Soon, the crystal clear waters receded so much that his now useless paddle buried itself in the bottom, and he was stuck in the sand miles from any shore. He climbed out of the kayak to stand in only a few inches of puddling water.

Benjamin Wade laughed out loud,

Lunchtime, I guess.

*O*pening the front storage compartment he retrieved some dried fruit, and sat down on the wet sand with his feet resting in a puddle of cool water. It was surprisingly peaceful, sitting a few miles out from a desert shore, eating a light lunch, and taking a break from the monotony of the morning's paddling. He smiled and leaned back against the boat, soaking up the sun and stretching out his weary back. *"This isn't so bad,"* he said aloud. Popping another morsel into his mouth, he drifted into thought.

It's so quiet here. I think I like being alone. The stresses of my old job, friends, bills, they all seem to float by carelessly. Hey, just like those clouds up there. They're part of another world.

Sometimes I really want – intend – to go back to it all. But now, I don't know. Alone, rested, and miles from the nearest human interference, I'm thinking that I can forget my past - for a while at least.

He laid his head back against the little craft and drifted into a peaceful sleep. The peace ended all too abruptly. At first the distant sound of waves crashing was barely audible, more like a buzzing sound that was far away, and intertwined with the dream-visions that swirled through his head.

As Ben lay there basking in the sun, he was oblivious of what was to come that day, as well as the next six months.

Had he truly known the ferocity of the ocean, he might have thought twice about confronting her power. But naiveté and stubbornness refused to allow him the luxury of "stop and think." Now he was going to pay the price for that stupidity of youth. Like many of the lessons learned in life, he was about to learn the hard way. But, out here where he had ventured, unlearned lessons can cost him his life.

The northern coastline of the Sea of Cortez is affected by extreme levels of tide. The water comes rushing up along this slender area between Baja California and the mainland of Mexico with vicious intensity and force. Second only to the Bay of Fundy, the distance between high and low tide can fluctuate as much as forty yards near the northern tip, where the Colorado river once dumped its mighty contents into the Sea. At low tide the water hesitates at this level for only fifteen minutes. It then begins to work its way up the beach, sometimes at a speed of more than fifteen miles per hour. Each day, the time for high and low tides advances one hour in accordance with the travel of the moon around the earth. During a full moon the difference between high and low tide is the least, the water often becoming tranquil, almost lazy, offering a perfect time to travel on its surface. But after this short period of rest, the gap between high and low tide widens steadily for fourteen days. During this time the ocean becomes more and more restless. Without warning, vicious storms, winds, and currents, can arise in a manner of minutes. In some areas along the Baja peninsula, the tide can be overwhelming. It can capsize and consume small craft, swallowing their human cargo with little or no remains.

Experienced fishermen and boaters know well the dangers on this perilous sea. Their sailing schedules coincide strictly with the tidal flow and, during some seasons such as the one approaching, they would not be caught dead in the middle of the Sea. Unfortunately, Ben was to learn most of this by dangerously experiencing the power and tenacity of the Sea of Cortez.

Once again his naiveté and stubbornness had placed him in peril.

The buzzing of the tide caused him to get up and look around. With relentless force the water moved in, rapidly rising up past his knees, and then higher. Ben calmly climbed into the kayak's cockpit, finished swallowing his last bite of lunch, and dipped the paddle into the water. At first there was no place to go, no specific direction to take. But then, up ahead he could see an area of deeper water angling out toward the main part of the Sea. It seemed to flow between the mysterious sand islands. The kayak headed straight toward it, and then banked hard to the port side to pick up the current.

Suddenly, Ben distinctly heard a distant crashing.

Looking out, he saw several huge sets of breakers battering the sand of an island not too far ahead. Hardly believing his eyes, he watched as the water continued to rise at an alarming pace. Islands of sand were disappearing without a trace. The tide was roaring in.

It waits for no man - and it's sure as hell not waiting for me.

Before he could react, waves leapt among the sand banks, and pounded over the kayak's bow and into his lap. Ben jammed the rudder into the direction of each new wave, avoiding when he could the water that wanted to turn the kayak sideways. There were hundreds of waves crashing in front, to the sides, and on top of him. Several of the waves towered over seven feet tall from trough to crest. He began to worry that he would make one mistake and capsize.

The kayak's cockpit was half full of water, adding another hundred or so pounds to the already heavy, supply laden craft. Though not full of enough water to make it sink, Ben wasn't going to take any chances. He could already feel the strain in his arms as he tried to pull not only the weight of the kayak and its supplies, but the added weight of the water inside. He steadied the kayak, aimed it at the next wave, and reached behind his seat for the automatic bilge pump. Quickly grabbing the soft foam handle, he sat it between his legs and pushed.

Damn, there must be a hundred pounds of water . . .

It was well past his stomach, sloshing around and making the boat all but unmanageable. His physical training had not prepared him for such additional weight. He feared that his muscles could not keep up with this added strain, and now the pump was not keeping up with the incoming water. He tried to splash some of the water out by hand. That didn't work. Every time he stopped paddling, the kayak would spin sideways in the crashing waves. He could feel the strength of the current forcing him backwards. Every few seconds a new wave would roar over the combing and threaten to completely flood the cockpit.

How much more weight can it bear without sinking?

He looked around the cockpit, desperate to find a faster method of bailing. The handle of an aluminum cooking pot was sticking out from behind the seat to his left side. He picked it up and began to bail the water out. He felt the conditions about to overwhelm him. His mind balked at reality. He was forgetting again about the strength of the current - and forgetting one of the elementary rules at sea.

Never take your eyes off of the ocean, shit . . .

He felt the boat suddenly surge forward and down. He looked up and saw another towering wave about to crash against him. Throwing all of his weight against the side where the wave was breaking, he thrust his paddle into the water for balance. Angry water poured into the cockpit again, filling it almost three quarters of the way full. The water level soon neared

9

what he knew would be disaster. The kayak was sinking. He had to do something fast.

Holding the paddle in one hand, and the aluminum pot in the other, he began to bail and paddle at the same time. With an effort born of urgent fear, he was able to bail enough water out of the kayak in a short period of time to give it more stability and lighten the load. His effort was enough, at least, to make it easier on his aching muscles. The easing on his muscles corresponded with an easing of his tensions.

I might be getting ahead of this thing . . .

He now had enough time, finally – if not tragically too late – to put on his spray skirt; the device he should have been using to keep water out of the boat. He pulled it tight around his waist, and checked to be sure it was sealed to the cockpit's edges. All was secure. There were still several inches of water in the bottom of the cockpit, but at least for now he wouldn't take on any more.

For the next three hours, with the tide continuing to come in unabated, Ben battled the wind and the waves. The muscles in his arms, back, and legs, ached beyond belief. He could feel the blisters on his hands swell where he gripped the paddle too tightly. His legs, having to steer the kayak's rudder in so many directions at once, were cramping. Now his breath was coming in short, rapid gasps. He wondered how long he could hold up without heading for shore.

As the sun began to set over the desert brown hills of Baja California, he realized that he did not want to spend another night out on the open water.

Chapter 2

I show you doubt, to prove that faith exists.
Robert Browning (1812-1889)

U p to this point, Ben had considered it a waste of time to look for a cove, and to head for shore before dark. Doing this meant paddling three or four miles to reach the beach and, once ashore, taking more time to pitch the tent and lay out a sleeping bag. Then it must all be undone the next morning. He was too impatient. The overwhelming thought that kept passing through his mind was to travel as many miles as humanly possible in a day – and to do this every day, every week, every month, until "*I end this ridiculous trip.*"

These feelings would change gradually over the next several months. But for now he was too tired to rationalize them, or even to care.

A small cove came into view on his right, and Ben headed for the quiet waters as quickly as he could maneuver the craft. He realized as the night air grew colder, stiffening his relentlessly tired muscles, that he had spent five and a half hours fighting a losing battle against the current. He didn't know how much progress he'd made, but assumed that it wasn't much. The kayak scraped against the ground in a small, nameless bay that would be uncharted on any map.

It was not a pretty place. Not pretty enough to sit and admire in quiet wonder, as he was wont to do in his previous life. Pretty or not, he could care less at that moment. Wearily he climbed out of the boat, happy to be on solid ground. He had not seen another person or boat for the last two days. But, as a precautionary measure, he strapped a knife around his leg and another around his waist. He had been warned by far too many people of the bandits that roamed the wilds of Mexico, and he wasn't about to take any chances.

By the time dusk had fallen, and the light around him dwindled, and then blew out like an extinguished candle, he was wet, exhausted, and frustrated. Frustrated because he'd gained such a short distance during the day, especially this near the beginning of his journey. He looked back toward the sea and thought,

For all the effort and energy I spent over the last twelve hours I should be halfway to Central America by now. Surely it has to get easier. Yeah, right.

He lit a candle, and climbed stiffly with it into the tent that he'd managed to erect on the rocky shore. Settling into this warmer environment, he brought out a map to study the next day's course. It wasn't a very good map. A landlubber would have smiled politely, and a boater would have laughed out loud, had they seen the absurd little map that Ben pulled out that night. He squinted his eyes a little to adjust to the light of the candle, and found himself looking at an AAA road map.

Can you believe this? Beginning a six thousand mile journey across vast stretches of ocean and alien shores, and I didn't even bring a decent map.

He shook his head and laughed, remembering a line he had heard once in a movie,

Assumption is the mother of all screw ups.

Then he thought, *was that a premonition?*

He lay restlessly awake on the hard sand that night, and tried to keep himself from becoming discouraged. He'd figured that the kayak had gone twenty-one miles in two days. This wasn't bad, but it wasn't good either.

The weather has to get better, and the tides have to weaken. Surely, tomorrow will give me calmer seas.

Then sleep began to overtake him. As he slipped into that place between full alertness and full slumber, his mind took him back to a few weeks past.

Heather. . .

Maybe one of the last people to see me alive, my last connection to the life I've grown accustomed to in Southern California. We met only two weeks ago, introduced by a mutual friend. She is a beautiful girl. Just twenty years old, but with more class than most women will ever possess, even later on in life. Heather is very independent. She works at a modeling agency in Hollywood and has her own place - just my type. Since I didn't want to get involved with anybody before I left, I figured no harm would be done if I asked her out. Indeed, I'd even gone so far as to sever a current relationship the day after I started training.

We were sitting in a restaurant across from each other when she decided to broach the subject that she had heard so much about in the last few weeks. "I can't believe you're actually going to kayak to South America," she said, her eyes looking intently into mine. Her eyes. . .

"Its something I just have to do. I've been training for it the last six months," I replied. I lowered my eyes in feigned modesty - then looked back into her steady gaze. "I love going into challenges like this," I continued. "I feel, well, I feel that meeting a challenge makes me a better person. But, you probably think I'm crazy, like everybody else." She nodded slightly and smiled. I smiled back. "It's just too bad that we had to meet so close to the departure."

Her smile broadened, and she slipped her hand into mine. The attraction I felt toward her troubled and confused me. But I brushed off the emotions welling to the surface by reminding myself of the task at hand. In the back of my mind, though, I knew that this would be more complicated than I had originally thought. "Listen," I continued, "I'm having a going away party on Sunday. I think you know about it. I thought maybe, well, that you would join me, you know, be my date. What do you say?"

"I'd love to," Heather replied, adding, "I was hoping you would ask."

And with that simple question, I took a step that put me in way over my head.

Ben was fully asleep now. But the memories morphed into a dream that flowed before him like a view from another dimension.

Heather arrived at the party, and joined about fifty of my close friends and family in southern California. Very few of the people there could believe that I was actually following through on my plans. They'd heard me talking about it for six months, but most dismissed it as a crazy plan, and doomed to fail. They thought that sooner or later I would come to my senses. Although most questioned my sanity, their love and concern was overpowering.

I was sad that I was about to leave all this behind, but looking around me at the smiling faces of my friends, I felt a beautiful warmth spread through my body. It felt good.

But it also felt right that I was leaving on my quest, and it strengthened my courage, knowing that these people, agreeing with me or not, were standing behind my decision.

There were plenty of drinks to go around, and the party was getting pretty loud as the night progressed. Slapping me on the back, people were offering me too many drinks as they enjoyed the comradery. I purposely kept my wits, and sobriety, about me. As it grew too warm in the house, I wandered out to the patio in search of new guests. Merriment abounded.

The two paddles that I would use on the trip were being signed by everyone, as they continued to voice their shared concern about my sanity. One paddle was double ended with white tips and a blue handle. People used a permanent marker to write their thoughts and wishes. "Don't be shark bait." "Come back alive." "Viva Mexico, Viva Ben Wade."

The festivities grew as the night progressed. There was laughter all around. But the glowing warmth I'd felt earlier began to fade away, and I began to wonder just what it would be like to be alone for the next six months. The faces of my friends remind me that I was loved; love and attention I knew that I needed, and longed for.

I remember the exact moment it all hit me. I was standing outside on the patio of the house, wondering just how difficult this task that I had chosen was going to be.

I guess I'm finding out.

Then, pushing those thoughts from my mind, I went back inside and made my way over to where Heather stood, surrounded by several ogling, testosterone filled, males who were hovering over her like circling birds of prey. I was jealous, and it was time to make the move. Certainly, this young woman's companionship would cheer me up.

I turned my eyes to the beautiful lady who now stood in front of me. "Can I have a moment of your time, pretty lady?" I asked quietly into her ear. "Of course," she said. I led her to a more secluded place, to one of the bedrooms in the house. "I know it's difficult to talk right now," I began, sitting down on the bed and facing her squarely. "I can't ignore all these other people. . .," I stammered, ". . . could you hang around until after everyone leaves? I'd like to talk to you for awhile."

"No problem," she said demurely. She looked down and smiled. I could feel my insides twist in a flurry of jubilation. And talk we did, until four in the morning. The party, the people, and even the trip, seemed to

fade out, and I couldn't help feeling just plain lucky sitting beside this magnificent lady. On this late night, or early morning as it was, I perched on one of the most triumphant and disastrous times of my life.

And the dream, the memory, faded away.

On a Beach
The Baja California Shore
September 16, 1996

The faint orange glow that crept across the eastern sky was like a mother awakening her child. Ben stirred and rolled over to look at his watch. It was 5:15. Brushing the sleep from his eyes, he climbed out of the tent, stood up, and cried out in pain as he tried to extend his limbs. He quickly retracted into a little ball, and gently rubbed his sore arms.

Every muscle aches with a fire that burns not only on the outside, but deep inside my tendons and joints that had borne so much work the day before. If someone had taken a sledgehammer to my bones, I don't think I would have fared much worse. I try to stretch, try to loosen up, but nothing is working. I ease myself down onto the sand, and, through gritted teeth, I say as loud as I can, "Stop whining about it, you big baby. It ain't gonna get no better!"

The sand beneath was cool to the touch. Ben laid back gingerly, now slowly stretching his back and allowing his body to relax. The morning air was already starting to warm as he listened to the small waves pattering against the shore. Beyond the gentle sound of the water, silence and solitude sank in and surrounded him with peace and tranquility.

Truthfully, I have no idea where the hell I am - or when I'll reach the next town. But, at this moment, I don't care.

After a while, he sat back up and looked out at the sea that he would soon have to face.

Maybe I'll take it easy today. What's the rush anyway?

He couldn't quite put a finger on it, but there was a dangerous undercurrent in his mind that wouldn't let him heed his wish to slow down. This

15

undercurrent drove him onward, relentlessly in pursuit of success – it always had. He shrugged his shoulders and stood, gingerly stretching painfully taut muscles. The pain was so great that he wondered whether he could last even a couple of hours out there. But, as he looked again at the calm sea, it beckoned him forth. There wasn't a whitecap in sight. He smiled at the prospect of the progress he would soon make. Even the wind, scarcely stirring, tickled his ear and beckoned him forward. With a few deep breaths to calm his nerves, Ben quickly packed up his tent and belongings, and shoved off, hunched over in the cockpit to seek a position to ease the pain that lingered.

The water was as calm and serene as a huge lake. Yesterday's plight seemed like a bad dream. But, knowing that the ocean would probably not keep its peace for long, he began to paddle at a faster pace than the previous day. He wanted to gain as much ground as possible in case the weather decided to turn sour. Gritting his teeth against the intense ache of his abused muscles he paddled on.

By the time the sun was overhead, his muscles had warmed and relaxed enough to put the pain out of mind. The rhythm of the paddles, and the passing water, had a hypnotic effect, as he let mind and body meld together. Ben guessed his travel that morning to be around fourteen miles. Reaching the desert village of Puertocitos was a distinct possibility by nightfall. His frustrations were dwindling as his muscles increased their pace. He felt stronger, mentally and physically, with every stroke.

Of course the weather would not remain calm.

His luck did not last long.

In fact, it had run out before he began.

To have a completely uneventful day would be a miracle.

Chapter 3

Pray that your loneliness may spur you into finding something to live for, great enough to die for.

Dag Hammarskjold (1905-1961)

S hortly after 9:30 that morning the wind began to pick up. In the distance Ben could see whitecaps as the tide returned. The sky above was a perfect topaz blue, with not a cloud in sight. Seagulls adjusted slightly to the increasing wind, and continued to swoop in search of fish as if nothing were the matter. Everything around him was unchanged and unmoved, as it should be on any normal day. Everything, that is, except the exceptional strength of the incoming tide.

Unlike the one before, this day was not going to catch Ben off guard or unprepared. Immediately after seeing the waves crashing several hundreds yards ahead, he set about putting on and adjusting the spray skirt. It was lucky that he had reacted quickly. Within minutes the first of the whitecaps began smacking the bow of the kayak.

The waves were a little smaller than the previous day, and Ben was now confident that he could maneuver past anything the sea had to offer. Although the waves continued to toss him about like a mere speck on its surface, he wasn't too worried. The spray skirt was doing its job, and the cockpit was relatively dry. But the current was so strong that at times he felt like he was paddling up a river. The pull was so great that he decided to chart his progress to be sure he was still *making progress*. Looking over his right shoulder toward the shore, Ben spotted a lighthouse perched on the rocks. He made a slight indentation with his fingernail on the road map –

17

the only way he had to mark it - where there was a little blip the size of a pin point. He assumed that was the spot.

From experience, he knew that the distance he traveled would not be noticeable at first. At about three miles off shore, the water created an illusion that he had stayed in one spot – even though he may have covered two or three miles. Also, he knew that he would be paddling at a slower pace now that he was going against the tide. Earlier that morning, when the tide was going out and acted like a 'tail wind', the miles seemed to fly by. He looked at his watch and silently counted the hours, telling himself that he would not sneak a look over to the shore until two o'clock, still four hours away. It was hard to avoid a glance over to the land, but he didn't want to be discouraged by the seeming lack of ground gained.

After an hour he felt his head lower slightly, and his eyelids droop. He squeezed them tightly and squinted to keep some vision, staying so focused on the waves ahead that he could only see one at a time. For the next three hours he paddled without stopping, or even looking around. He kept his head bent slightly forward, lulling himself into an almost trance-like state by the continuous rhythm of his arms' motion. Ben's mind began to wander. He was thinking of other things - friends, home, and family. The water ahead began to go slowly out of focus. Then, gradually, the scenery, the sky, the sea, even his kayak, faded out like a dimmer switch on a light bulb. First gray, then hazy, and then black. He kept one eye subconsciously on the sea. By now it was a reflex. But his mind was on his past.

He had practiced this trick of mind versus body while making trial runs on the Pacific Ocean off the California coast. It proved a good way to pass the monotonous time, while allowing him to reflect on certain memories that pushed their way to the surface of his mind.

I remember one spring, 1979 I think. My brother, Peter, and I are standing on top of a grassy sand dune on the coast of Florida. Funny that I remember this. We are just standing there holding hands, and feeling real proud of our new matching shorts and shirt outfits.

What am I, maybe 8 or 9 years old?

We're looking out over the vast waters of the Atlantic that stretch as far as we can see in any direction. Dad had taken us out of school for a week of vacation. Ha, what excitement – playing hooky and being able to see the ocean! Hey, we're from Tennessee – this is special stuff. The ocean. Even then, I could sense that it carried with it a soul, a mind, even a personality. This was a living, breathing, powerful being.

Was I really that poetic at 8 years old?

I must have been. The memory is vivid. I remember the wind whispering to my ears, beckoning me to partake of its challenges. I remember the surf roaring through my soul, and daring me to ride its thunderous currents. I don't think I could describe it like this back then, but that's what I felt.

I remember looking at my brother and my dad. They both seemed to be struck with the same sensations. "Daddy," I said, "what countries are on the other side? I mean, if you took a boat and headed straight from here where would you land?"

"Actually," my dad replied, after a moment of thought. "It's not too far from Cuba. Once you get past Cuba you can go all the way to South America. Colombia maybe."

Dad knew the answers to everything.

"Are there sharks swimming around out there?" I pressed on with my questions. "There sure are," he answered. "But they won't bother you if you stay close to the shore."

A rogue wave swirled across the bow, slapping Ben in the face and stinging his eyes. Jolted, he looked ahead and strained, blinking, to bring everything back into focus. His arms still moved forward, one long stroke after another. The art of paddling had become as natural as walking to Ben, requiring only a fraction of his brain to transmit the signals to keep going at the same pace, at the same rhythm and strength. He looked at his watch and saw that another three hours had passed. He took a break, letting tightened muscles relax. He set the paddle across his lap, resting just inches above the swirling water.

Casually, he looked over toward the shore. He was surprised to see a lighthouse slightly ahead of him. He shook his head and wondered, *another lighthouse?* He looked over his shoulder to see how far back the previous lighthouse was.

With a shock he realized,

The one in front of me is the same one I'd set my bearings on three hours ago!

Ben had not only failed to gain ground, he'd gone backwards. Indeed, in the few minutes of rest that it took to figure this out, the tide had already pushed Ben and the kayak backwards a couple of hundred more yards!

Now greatly discouraged, he hung his head in disbelief. Grabbing the paddle tightly with both hands, he shook it in the air over his head, but resisted his urge to scream out loud in frustration and anger. Finally, he slapped the paddle onto the water in a futile gesture to make a point with nature.

God, give me strength to overcome the current with new vigor.

He looked up at clouds beginning to billow and tower on the horizon. Below them were the unmistakable streaks that spoke of rain. With no more thought, he put his head down and paddled as hard as his weary muscles would allow. Blisters that had formed during the first few days now popped. Blood and puss greased his raw palms and mixed with salt water, but he didn't feel the sting of the open sores. For another hour he battled the current as it mercilessly continued to come at him with a force he refused to comprehend. At long last, Ben gave it up, utterly exhausted by his efforts. He looked over again at the unmoving shore. He had still not reached the lighthouse which had been so near - almost behind him - that morning, some five hours earlier.

It was now obvious that, with the storm pushing up from the south and increasing the tide's strength, Ben would be foolish to stay out in the middle of the Sea. Continuing on with this madness would only increase his frustration and waste precious strength. For the second time in two days, Ben reluctantly headed for the shore. For once, the waves were breaking in the same direction he was headed, and he neared the shore more quickly than he expected. He was preoccupied and distraught with the lack of progress he'd made that day.

The distraction nearly proved disastrous.

At the very last moment, he looked up to see angry white foam dashing up and over the jagged faces of the rocky shore. Had it not been for the abrupt difference the sound of breaking waves made on the shore, he would have crashed onto the rocks that now loomed ominously in front of him.

He fought the urge to panic and jump overboard.

He knew full well, that if the kayak were dashed upon the rocks, his trip, and possibly his life, would be over.

With all of the force he could muster, he swung the kayak around, pressing hard against the rudder until it would turn no more.

His paddle dug furiously into the sea in the opposite direction, aiding the movement of the rudder.

The waves thundered against the rocks.

The sound rang raucously in his ears, announcing danger, and warning of death.

The taste of salt on his lips joined with the bitter taste of fear.

The cold sweat on his brow spoke of terror.

The bow of the kayak sliced through the charging breakers.
It looked at first as though the adjustment had been too late.

But, as the tide continued to push the craft toward the rocky shore, it seemed as if the hand of God Himself had opened up a small stretch of sand among the rocks.
This scrap of safe harbor was only ten yards wide.
Just wide enough.
Ben maneuvered his kayak through with only a couple of jostling bumps.
As he felt the sharp nose of the kayak cut through the soft sandy bottom, he clambered out of the cockpit. Grabbing the front end, he hauled it safely above the tide line. Shaken but not hurt, and thankful for his escape, he looked out over the ocean. He could only see the white tops of the waves that thrashed about like a devil possessed. Out there was no place to be in a small boat, alone, and miles from anyone who could help.

I hate to admit it, but I've been wise to turn in to the shore.
No, not wise. I've just been lucky.

He secured the kayak, and sat down on the sand beside it. The saltwater that covered his body began to dry. The sun reflected sharply off the sand and, despite its heat, a chill crept up his spine. Whether it was from his close brush with death, or the stiff wind that evaporated the small drops of water from his arms, Ben didn't care.
Stunned by a sudden flood of loneliness, the fury of the sea, and the thought of never returning home, Benjamin Wade put his head in his hands and cried. Once the tears began streaming down his face, his macho pride sluiced away. He drew his tired legs to his chest in a vain attempt to feel secure, and wept like a baby. Giant sobs wracked his body. He shook like leaves in a cold November wind - lone, frail, withered, and utterly used up – leaves tossed about by the mighty hand of nature, powerless to stop their imminent fall.
In the throws of his despair he heard the taunting words of his friends chanting, "You'll be back in a week. You can't make it!" Doubts of frustration welled up from deep within him.

Maybe the voices are right. Maybe I have no business being out here on the ocean. I feel like I've already failed. Nothing is working out as planned. I surely don't have the strength to travel for another week, let alone the next five months.

He began to hate himself for being so proud – so damn cocky proud.

Taking on this miserable and lonely trip...what in the world was I thinking?

For a moment he wondered what would happen if, when he made it to the next town, he would just call home and have one of his friends come and pick him up.

Why not? This trip sucks! I thought it was going to be different. I stayed out there all day and kayaked my ass off – and I went backwards! Six months? Hell no, more like six years at this rate! But . . . but what would my friends say . . . if I quit this soon. I couldn't even show my face around them without hearing their thoughts . . . quitter, quitter, quitter.

Who gives a damn what they think! Just get me off this damn ocean! It's not worth it. I can be home in a week, in a warm shower, in a comfortable bed . . . with people again!

Then a stronger voice cut through the weaker one, and pressed up through his consciousness.

I am not a quitter! I began this trip and aim to finish it, no matter what the cost. I can't throw in the towel after just four days. Quitting now would prove everybody else right.

I began this journey to search my soul and regardless of the time, the sacrifice or the pain, there is NO TURNING BACK!

He stood and wiped away the tears and snot that mixed with sand and clung to his cheeks. He let out a yell, and shook his fists at the sea, and then pounded them furiously against his chest.

No way! You're not going to get the best of me yet. I'm not going to give up now!

Ben forced himself to see clearly through the tears that still clouded his eyes.

You're acting like a baby. Blubbering all over the damn place like a two year old. Are you some kind of a quitter?"

The unilateral conversation continued,

Absolutely not! I pride myself in mental toughness. Now is the time to put up or shut up.

He became quieter, more serene.

I can do this. I just need to pray.

He quoted from the Bible.

I can do all things through Christ who strengthens me.

In this manner Ben was able to get a firm grip, and to refocus his strength and resolve.

I think about the positives. I'm alive and well. My boat's still in one piece, and, even if it takes me two years, I'm gonna complete this expedition.

Wiping away a final tear that had somehow loosened itself from his eyelid and was warily making its way down his cheek, Ben managed a half-hearted smile. He wiped the sand from his legs, and looked around at things he hadn't noticed before.

His eyes wandered up from the jagged rocks to the lonely dunes above.

Then he saw them.

Chapter 4

One must be poor to know the luxury of giving.
George Elliot (1819-1880)

On top of the sand hill behind the kayak, stood half a dozen houses. Most of them were boarded up for the hot summer months. Ben was still feeling lonely and in need of some companionship, and he felt the urge to see something familiar. He began to climb up the steep sand dunes in hope of finding someone to talk to. As he suspected they were all empty.

As he turned to leave, a flash of something shiny caught his eye. Three houses down from where he stood an old station wagon pulled up in the driveway, the sun glinted off its windshield. With a muffled cry of joy, Ben walked down the small cobblestone lane that connected the houses. He wondered what kind of people he was about to meet. Certainly they didn't speak any English. But, with, at best, a two word vocabulary of Spanish that he could remember, Ben could really care less. These were the first people he had seen since he set out. He yearned for some kind of companionship. Whether they could communicate or not, he was confident that it wouldn't matter. Yelling out a greeting in badly accented Spanish, "Buenos Dias," Ben took the small Mexican family totally by surprise.

At least they didn't run away!

There were four people, an older man and woman, who Ben presumed were the parents, and two teenage boys. They stood and watched, exchanging apprehensive glances, as he approached. Ben greeted each with a handshake, and told them as best as he could - by pointing at the ocean and then to the kayak - that he was in the beginning stages of an expedition. They returned blank smiles and stared at him politely.

Finally, after a few minutes of complete and utter miscommunication, Ben took out a laminated newspaper clipping that showed him kayaking in the harbor of Newport, California. At last, a big grin passed over the old man's face, and he grabbed Ben's right arm as if testing the strength needed for such a voyage. *Whether he was making fun of my puny arms or not*, Ben smiled back and flexed a little. He wondered why this family was out on such a hot day, but it didn't really matter.

One of the sons motioned that they all sit down on the front porch, out of reach of the scorching midday sun. He spoke directly to Ben, "Siéntese, señor. El Sol es caliente." Ben smiled, nodded and understood. *Sit. Sun is hot. Close enough.*

The invitation was obvious. There were no tables or chairs, just the hard stone floor that felt cool to the touch. The little group spread out across the area in a random, haphazard way. With initial suspicions now fading, the older son spoke again to Ben, "Me llamo es Abraham." He pointed to his chest, then said, "¿Cómo te llamas?" He pointed at Ben. This too was obvious. Ben began to think he could remember more Spanish than he thought. "Benjamin. I am Benjamin," Ben said, a little too loudly. The boy replied, speaking slowly, "Ben – cha – min," then smiled, and offered his hand. Ben shook it and reveled in the warmth of the moment. The boy gestured around the group. "Presento mis padres, el Señor y la Señora Jiménez. Y mi hermano, Carlos," he said slowly enough that Ben understood the introductions. "A pleasure to meet you," Ben said. Everyone smiled.

He could see the boys looking curiously at his white skin, and the dark blue tattoo of a crown of thorns representing Jesus on the Cross that snaked around his right arm. The two boys looked to be about eighteen and twenty years old, with mahogany skin and broad smiles. Their clothing was worn, but modern, and their bellies were beginning to show signs of mama's good food.

Ben had stumbled across a middle class Mexican family on a simple outing to the beach, and their warm companionship was just what he needed right now.

Mrs. Jiménez wore a long dress of heavy cloth that must have been unbearable in the heat, though she showed no sign of discomfort. She smiled meekly at Ben every time their eyes met, and he could tell she was growing more comfortable with his presence. As was Mr. Jiménez, who wore a once white cowboy hat that shadowed most of his dark, weathered face. Brown stains along the sweat band told of countless hours of perspiring hard work in the hot sun. His hands, now folded calmly around his knees, were knurled and callused, and deeper lined than even his foreboding brow.

Ben had heard all sorts of stories and warnings about the natives of Mexico. Bloodthirsty bandits. Liars. Filthy fragments of human beings that were unfit for the civilized world. But, as he found out that day, and in the months that followed, these were some of the nicest, and most generous, people he would ever meet. If an entire family had only one piece of bread, they would divide it equally among the members present, including any strangers or guests, and give each an ample amount.

I'm going to have a long talk with some of my bigoted friends when I get home.

When he had stepped out of the kayak an hour before, Ben had reflexively strapped one of the knives he carried for safety to the back of his leg. It was, of course, all for naught. His experiences during the next few months would destroy Ben's stereotypes of this country, and teach him to love this land and its people. Meeting the Jiménez family proved to be the first stepping stone in the journey his mind would take to release its stronghold of fear and disdain for a society he knew little about.

The first thing that Abraham did, after Ben sat down on the patio, was to reach into the back of the station wagon and pull out an ice cold quart of Tecáte beer. "Algo para beber?" the boy asked. (Ben wondered if beber meant 'beer'. Later he learned it meant 'to drink'.) Ben could still taste the salt water on his lips and tongue. Cold, fresh water would have been preferred, but he didn't refuse the offer. He didn't want to appear rude, and start off on the wrong foot. They all settled down with backs to the house, and looked out over the sparkling blue ocean. The whitecaps continued their magical dance, and Ben was thankful that he didn't have to participate in any of the sea's festivities for the rest of the afternoon.

After about an hour, Abraham's mother opened up the ice chest from which Abraham had earlier gotten the beers, and pulled out a grocery bag. It was filled with tortillas, carne asada, onions, and salsa. The father pulled out a grill, from where Ben couldn't tell. For all he knew it was from the front of the station wagon. It looked to Ben like something off of a '57 Chevy!

Feeling idle, Ben jumped up and helped Abraham and his father haul the steel grill over to the sand in front of the house. They worked together to light the fire. Soon the smell of the meat cooking made Ben's mouth water in hungry anticipation. He had not eaten a hot meal in four days and could not wait to begin. There was plenty of food for everyone, as they washed down the spicy meat with another quart of Tecáte. Ben knew that delicious meals on the kayak were going to be few and far between. He easily decided to thoroughly enjoy the ones that came his way.

Aside from his other supplies, the food carried in the front compartment of the kayak made up more than two thirds of the load. There was enough food to last for three months, give or take a few days, and, in order to keep it from spoiling, it had all been dried. Ben could never stomach the freeze dried stuff that a fellow wilderness buddy had insisted on bringing to those grueling hikes in the Sierras. He knew better than to bring the tantalizing packages of Sweet and Sour Pork, Beef Enchiladas, and Spicy Jerk Chicken, that would not be so bad, if only the food tasted half as good as the names printed tantalizingly on the cartons.

The food that he did bring consisted of one hundred and sixty Power-Bars, sixty-four Pop tarts, one hundred servings of dried mashed potatoes, three pounds of trail mix, a pound of animal crackers, several bags of dried fruit, beef and turkey jerky, one loaf of bread to be eaten immediately before the mold set in, Tiger's Milk bars, an occasional candy-bar, and a gallon of powdered Gatorade. Even on the first day of the expedition, after eating three consecutive meals of the above mentioned delicacies, Ben had found himself dreaming of home cooked meals, steaming with savory flavors.

This meal with his new friends lived up to its expectations – and to Ben's dreams. Further enhanced by the scenery and the company, Ben was happy to keep his share of the leftovers that Señora Jiménez offered him. After they'd all finished with their plates, she cleared away the remains. The father went over to the station wagon and, to Ben's pleasant surprise, pulled out an old guitar. He sat down next to Ben and, after tuning up the strings, began to play. His voice was deep and rich and powerful. Ben found himself lost in the chords of the lilting Mexican ballads and songs. His foot involuntarily tapped to the rhythm that filled his lonely soul, and comforted his frustrated and worn-out body. The mood in the air, stirred by the gentle breezes of the sea, was relaxed. Everyone was full of good food and good cheer, and the music seemed to blend in with the rhythm of the waves below.

As the sun began to set, we all sat on that stone porch and watched the breakers wreak havoc on the rocks below. The sound of the waves sent its own message of joy to me as it went frothing about, and licked greedily at the niches on rocky tops.

I looked far out to the horizon, and saw it meshing together in perfect harmony with the sea. It struck me again how the simplest parts of nature could make me happy. I thought back to the times near Los Angeles where the water had been my haven, and how it had quieted my soul. Now I felt its gentle pull again, beckoning me back into the relationship we had once shared; a relationship of joy, not of grief.

I was quickly learning though, that, like most relationships, one of the two - joy or grief - would sooner or later have to take an arrogant bow. They both needed humbling.

Now Ben found that it was he that needed the humbling. Although it was a new found position, he accepted his role with a renewed mind.

It was past the lingering dusk when the Jiménez family packed their car and bid Ben farewell. Brazos, great masculine hugs, were given to Ben with genuine affection by Señor Jiménez and his two sons. A demure smile, and curtsey, with equal affection from the Señora, completed the farewells.

Ben waved, "*Adios – go with God*," then turned toward the beach, hurrying to get to his craft while he could reasonably see in the fading light.

Chapter 5

There is no cure for birth and death, save to enjoy the interval.
George Santayana (1863-1952)

The variance between high and low tide on September 17th was still over twenty yards. Before he'd climbed the dunes, and enjoyed the afternoon with the Jiménez family, Ben had tried to pull the kayak above the high water mark. But it was heavy with over four hundred pounds of food and gear, and, as much as he struggled, the kayak moved only a few inches. Leaving it where it finally lay, Ben unloaded the tent and pitched it farther up on the sand.

He looked around in vain for a tree or large boulder to tie off the safety line that ran from the nose of the kayak to the rudder in back. All he could see was barren desert sand. He had no type of anchor, and was worried that the tide would sneak up at night and steal away all that he now possessed. Finally, with no apparent alternatives, he ran the safety rope from the front of the kayak up to his tent. Inside the tent, he tied the end of the rope around his leg. It was all he could think of to do.

If the tide comes up suddenly tonight while I'm asleep, it'll pull me out to sea with the kayak, ha, ha!

Indeed, that night the tide did come up past the original water line. It woke him slowly at first, and then with a start, as he realized the source of his pain - the rope cutting into his ankle. He slipped out of the tent and pulled the now floating boat several more feet above the tide. Then he sat

31

down to wait, and watch the scene by starlight. In thirty minutes the water had risen substantially higher, and he moved the kayak once again. This continued for a couple of more hours, until the tide finally began to recede. Now he went back to much needed sleep, the rope still tied around his ankle.

Pre-dawn light filtered into the tent as Ben awoke. Slowly he became conscious of a strange sensation over his entire body. At first he thought it was a dream, or his imagination.

It was a tingling sensation.

Maybe my arm is asleep, he thought, his eyes still closed.

He lazily raised his hand up to his neck – and recoiled in wide-eyed horror.

Hundreds, maybe thousands, of tiny insects were crawling all over him.

Ben grappled with the tent flap as he fled his sleeping place in a panic. Finally free of the tent, he ran to the water's edge and dove in. Submerged in the cold morning water, he scratched and rubbed his entire body. Insects crawled over his head, emerged from under his arms, and scattered in small groups across his chest. Again he dove completely under water, grasping at ears and scalp. Rafts of wriggling creatures floated away from him. It took long moments before he assured himself that he had gotten rid of them all. Grimacing in disgust, Ben repeatedly checked his arms and legs for any sign of the pests that had probably slept better than he had, nestled warm and dry in the various crevices of his body. He spat on the sand, and grimaced again, as he tried to erase the memory of the invasion of bugs. He couldn't shake off the slinky feeling that still tingled his skin.

At that moment Ben decided that he hated insects.

He waded from the water and walked back up to the tent. Gingerly, Ben moved the flap and peeked inside. Thousands of little black bugs, only slightly larger than a flea, crawled over everything. His sleeping bag seemed to be the most concentrated area for their nesting. He assumed that they were some sort of sand tick, but he couldn't be sure. Actually, he didn't care. Squeamishly, Ben shook out the sleeping bag and the inside of the tent. Some insect infested food had to be discarded.

I hope the hell I've seen the last of them!

From that day on, Ben was very careful about not leaving a gap in the zipper flap of the tent. He'd find another way to get the rope from the kayak to his ankle. After presumably getting rid of the bugs, Ben shoved off, with the ocean once again smooth and calm.

He reached the small village of Puertocitos about 11:00 that morning. The wind once again blew steadily from the south, and the sea began to grow restless.

During the seemingly endless time sitting here in the cockpit, I've begun to dream and fantasize about everything around me. I look out at the ocean, undulating to her own music, and imagine myself asking her to dance. I've been with her for many days now, and I see her grow restless, as if asking me for the next dance. I feel that we have forged a relationship. Now I bow to her and shake my head, trying to politely tell her that this night she must dance alone. Tonight she will show off her power and majesty without me. I am going ashore.

The kayak pulled in among the jagged rocks surrounding the entrance to the bay. Ben climbed on shore. It had been a short paddle, but the waves had incessantly sloshed and sprayed him the whole way. Everything in the cockpit was soaked with seawater. He spread what he could reach, out on the rocks to dry.

Saltwater had penetrated the supplies that were strapped along the insides of the exposed cockpit. But, thankfully, the two waterproof compartments performed well and were dry.

He inspected each piece of equipment that lay on the rocks to see if anything had been damaged. In the end he had to throw away a safety manual, some batteries and food, two flashlights and one of the useless AAA road maps. Unfortunately, Ben found that the loss of supplies would be a common occurrence throughout the trip. He was now more careful about what was left exposed.

If it could get wet, it would get wet.

I am learning to accept the give and take required as an offering of peace with this powerful environment of the sea.

He sat under a large palm tree, letting his back rest against its graceful trunk. He gazed out across the tiny beach to the small u-shaped cove that stretched a half mile to the ocean. Jagged rocks enveloped the calm waters within the bay. Atop these protective guardians sat the winter villas of Americans, each positioned for best views of the sea. The quaint little town was quiet as the natives awaited the return of the tourist season.

A warm breeze ruffles the branches of the palm tree, and the sea laps quietly against the shore. These are comforting sounds that have long since become part of my surroundings. I barely acknowledge the gentle noises that are always there. The wind and the sea, always reassuring and comforting, always peaceful and serene.

The wind continued to blow from the south, but the sea had grown calm. It was as if the sea was disappointed by Ben's lack of participation this day. He acknowledged the silence by nodding slightly in her direction, telling himself that tomorrow would be another day. Today was rest.

Naturally, the first day that he took to the shore early would be the day that she, as he termed the sea, decided to grow silent. He resisted the urge to throw everything back into the kayak and shove off.

Now Ben took advantage of this brief access to civilization by deciding to make a few phone calls back to the States. He figured it was time to reassure everyone, who might be anxious to know, that he was still alive.

Now that I've made this decision I hope there's a phone in this small town.

But, he didn't move right away from his comfortable seat. As he relaxed more, he had lingering doubts about his decision to stop this early. He took out another map of Baja California, and studied the next hundred miles of coastline. The map showed some detail, and he could make out that the coast ahead was rocky and barren. The next town, Gonzaga Bay, was fifty miles to the south. If the weather remained calm, and the tides receded somewhat, he figured he could make it there in three days. The next nearest phone he knew was in Bahia de Los Angeles - another five days south from Gonzaga Bay. A long 'road' ahead with few beaches to rest on, and fewer towns for water.

He was losing the argument with himself about returning to the sea right away.

Better to wait, stock up on water, and get an early start tomorrow.

He sat up and looked toward the village.

Surely there's a phone nearby.

But, for the time being, he just remained where he sat and enjoyed the comfort of his resting place beneath the palm. He switched on a small portable tape player he'd brought along, listened to the music, and closed his eyes. *Just for a moment.*

After Ben took his little nap beneath the palm tree, he strode off down the small dirt road. The first person he found was a man fixing a flat tire on an ancient rusty yellow school bus with cracked windows. The man, Jay Panama, was the only English speaking resident in the village of Puertocitos.

Jay was quite a character, loud, lively, and sometimes obnoxious. He was also the only mechanic for a hundred miles around, so everybody knew the name Panama.

That day, Ben learned all about how, and why, Jay Panama came to live in this tiny town. "T'was eleven years ago," Panama began his story, as he and Ben sat on stacks of old tires. "I came down on vacation to visit my Grandma. She owned one of those villas overlooking the bay. Now, sir, after seeing the beauty and the tranquility around here . . ., well, I just never left." A machinist by trade, it was only a matter of time before Jay found a niche. Working on the local school busses, and an occasional broken down automobile, his place soon became known as the local *taller*, or workshop. He picked up the language, and the women, and settled into the community, building a small shack from the remains of an old trailer to live in. The garage, where he now worked on hundreds of cars a year, was in the front of his *casita*. Out back was an open patio where he slept, drank, and ate.

Everyone in the town knew Panama, and where he lived. It was just up the street from the beach where Ben was camping. The house was the place to go for gossip, a drink, or of course, a broken down vehicle.

He'd seen a lot. I could tell it in his eyes that sometimes twinkled, and spoke of some merriment that he saw, even when others didn't. Once in a while, Panama would drift off into another world, perhaps in some faraway place he had ventured before. At one time he'd traveled the world, lived in Panama for three years where he learned the language, found his dog, and earned his nickname. Ten years prior he hiked the entire Andes trail barefoot. His face was an ageless golden brown with wrinkles only around the eyes. His smile showed just the right amount of teeth.

With a beer, seemingly the national drink of Mexico, in one hand, and a wrench in the other, Panama told tales so numerous and wild, that Ben finally decided he could never do them justice. There must have been a hundred of them. After talking for a few hours, Ben excused himself and walked down to the beach to his camp. He crawled into his sleeping bag and dozed contentedly.

A family was camped nearby, and Ben noted, with some amazement at his feelings, the comfort and security he felt just knowing he was close to other people. Normally, sleeping by himself in an unknown land gave him cause for loneliness.

I'm growing accustomed to sleeping, eating, and surviving in total solitude.

Now, he fell asleep quickly, with all the companionship he needed. Ben's journal reveals a conflicted battle with loneliness that seems to be waning. His maturity is toughening. Maybe.

The one phone in Puertocitos had been out of service, and he'd decided to wait one more day to see if the phones would be operational. With little else to do in this tiny village of about two hundred souls, he went to pay Panama another visit. They ended up talking, with Ben mostly listening, for the rest of the day.

September 18, 1996

It was Ben's birthday, and he didn't really want to spend the day by himself. It was bad enough not being with family that day, and he certainly didn't want to celebrate it alone. So Ben trudged up the dusty road to Panama's place and walked into the garage. Jay Panama was sitting down on the concrete floor beneath the same rusty yellow school bus, changing one of the front tires. "Hey there, Jay, how's it goin' today?" Ben said. "Same old shit. How about yourself?" Jay Panama's usual response. "It's too bad you're working. It's my birthday today, and I wouldn't mind goin' out for a beer," Ben said, even though he knew full well that there was no restaurant in town that served beer. In fact, there were no restaurants that Ben had seen at all. Besides that, he'd watched Panama finish off a six pack the night before, so he knew there wasn't any beer in the refrigerator either. Ben was just teasing him. It seemed a good way to inform him what was so important about the day. "It's your birthday? Well, hell, boy. Hop in the car. We'll go down to Speedy's Camp. That's the only place in this damn town for a beer. Time for a party! Work's a bore, boy, and I always got time for a beer. Let's go," Panama whooped.

Ben sighed and shook his head.

Why am I always getting myself into these situations.

Too soon, Jay had washed his hands and, with a pat on Ben's back, they were off. On the way they picked up one of Jay's friends, who only needed to hear the words *beer* and *party* in the same sentence to join the entourage. A few minutes later, and a half mile down the dirt road, they turned into a driveway. An old wooden sign marked the entrance to Speedy's Camp.

Old Speedy himself served the trio out of a wheelchair. He was half blind and half deaf. There was only one selection, and no surprise to Ben, it was quarts of Tecáte. Word must have spread, because more of Panama's friends dropped in, and before he knew it there was a table of twenty souls, drinking beer, and celebrating Ben's birthday. They didn't even know who he was, but that didn't seem to matter.

It wasn't really his type of party, and when one of the guys stood up to drink half a pint of tequila in one gulp, Ben watched as his eyes glazed over, and he swayed once left, then right, then face-plant himself onto the table. Ben knew it was time to go. No one seemed to mind. Being the only one sober, he realized that everyone had long forgotten the reason for the celebration. The only thing they were all interested in now was how drunk they could get. He sat there for as long as he could, and finally excused himself, unnoticed amid the cries and shouts of the partiers.

Ben walked back up the road that led to the beach, and stopped again at the only store in town. He hoped that the phone would be working. It was. Ben made the three phone calls that were on his agenda. The first to his parents, the second to his friend, Christian, and the last, and sweetest, to Heather. Heather surprised him by saying that she wanted to come down and meet him somewhere along the way. All he had to do was just name the city.

His spirits soared as he walked the rest of the way down to the shore. Now he was thinking about the weeks to come. He also was thankful that he'd not been forgotten back home. There was no reason that he should have been, but his lingering insecurities were still very evident.

This one settled for the moment, Ben was now ready to get on with the rest of the expedition.

Chapter 6

T hat night, Ben's sleep was fitful. The soft voice of Heather on the telephone lingered just below his conscious thought. Now it slowly seeped into his dreams, gaining clarity that defied being denied as reality. Ben tossed in his sleeping bag as that fateful night re-emerged.

One of the highlights of the party had been the shaving of my head bald. They'd used a disposable razor to bring it right to the scalp. Every- one stood around and watched as the true shape of my head emerged. The bumps and scars stood out in various places, almost like tattoos on an old pirate, telling of previous injuries, and adding to the oddity of this man that sat before them. Me. Naked. If anyone had questioned my sanity before, now there were certainly no doubts. I remember telling Heather to draw a design with permanent ink onto the back of my newly shaven head. Did I really tell her that? I did.

As she drew she said in the softest voice, "I'm marking my territory, Ben. Don't you forget it." I looked at my watch. Why did I look at my watch? Oh, yes. "I wonder if the newspapers are out yet," I said. "Let's go down to the store and see. I'd really like to read that story." It was nearly dawn. This is crazy. Guess not. We hopped in the car and drove to find an Orange County Register. We bought two copies and took them back home, sat down on the couch, and read the article arm in arm.

We were caught in the moment, snared by our own passions for life

and adventure, and for each other.
It was only the start of an unexpected relationship.

Ben tossed in his sleep. He didn't want to lose this dream. Renewed relaxation swept over him like a warm blanket.

The following week we went out three more times. At the end of the third date, Heather suggested that she should be the one to drive me down to San Felipe. I yearned for my last contact with civilization to be from this gentle and compassionate new friend. I eagerly agreed. The night before I left, we went down to the beach one last time. I looked out on the ocean that I would soon embrace. The moon had not yet risen, and the water looked as black as night. I looked at Heather, and then back at the ocean. My stomach tightened in fear. I turned to look her in the eyes. "I have no idea what I'm getting into, do I?" She shook her head, unable to answer the question. I was right.
The very next day she stood there, away from the group on the beach. The vision of her there gave me one more reason not to go. I remember. I turned around and raised my hand in a farewell salute. Or did I?
But it was too late.

The dream began to fade as Ben fought waking.

Why was it too late? The distance? Too soon? Already my quick stroke had carried me far out to sea. Heather. She's just a speck on the horizon. Heather. The sands of the beach meshed with her figure, and then faded away altogether. With heavy heart, I turn and continue to paddle.

The next morning Benjamin Wade awoke before dawn with that nagging pain in his bladder that told him it was time to take care of business. He stumbled out of the little tent, eyes still half closed from sleep, and jogged down to the water's edge. There were some sharp rocks that had to be jumped to reach the water. A carefree, and careless, jump – and a searing pain shot through his foot and up his leg. Ben staggered and nearly fell. His face grimaced as he looked down at his foot, and he saw blood already pooling on the rocks. Bellowing in pain, he staggered forward on one foot until he found a place to sit in the sand. The rock had nearly sheared off the top quarter of his big toe, leaving a painful, gaping wound. Ben crawled back to where the kayak lay. He momentarily forgot the need to pee. He poured saltwater over the cut to wash the sand and dirt that had already begun to clot with the blood. Gritting his teeth, he cut away the extra flap of skin that hung loosely to one side. Behind the seat of the kayak, securely strapped, was an emergency kit. With gauze, a sterile pad, and some surgical tape, the toe was wrapped like an Egyptian mummy. The wound really required stitches, but there was nothing he could do in this town. The hope was that it would not get infected.

About mid morning, Jay Panama and his friends came down to the beach to see him off. They looked bleary eyed, and well hung over. Ben sat gingerly in the kayak, avoiding anything that might cause pain to the throbbing toe. He'd discovered, after the initial shock, that he'd also bruised his hip, and scraped up a few more injuries.

To raucous shouts of encouragement from the shore, Ben cast off into the little bay. It was difficult to use the injured foot on the rudder, but he had no choice. He winced as the pain shot up the leg, but he pressed on.

The stop at Puertocitos was initially to find a telephone. The seemingly simple act of finding a working telephone became a major obstacle as Ben continued along the coast of Baja. Early in the voyage, he was having real trouble letting go of the need to stay in contact with home. It was loneliness, plain and simple.

One evening Ben tuned his little portable radio to an Arizona station. A grandmotherly type lady was being interviewed on a call-in show. Ben listened to the crackly, static voiced, conversation, and dreamed of being able to call in himself. All he could think of was how good English without accent sounded to his ears.

I am truly by myself. I have no means to communicate with another soul – interaction with the outside world is non-existent. I want to talk to someone, anyone. I dream all day of such a conversation, and, at night, of watching the beautiful sunset with someone to share its magic.
I am alone!

But real communication had another dimension. On board the kayak, Ben had no VHF radio, no GPS, nor an emergency locating beacon.

In this remote area of Mexico where the villages stretch out weeks apart from each other, finding a telephone is difficult.

To somewhat insure Ben's rescue in case of an accident, he and his friend, Christian, had devised a plan. While not a foolproof plan, it gave Ben hope that someone would be looking for him in an emergency. Nearly every week Ben called Christian to give him his exact location on the map. Ben and Christian had identical maps, and Ben would tell him where he expected to be within a week's time. If he hadn't heard from Ben within the week, Christian would know the approximate location to send the Mexican Coast Guard to look for wreckage, or any signs of life. There were a lot of holes in this plan. But it was the best they could come up with, given their inexperience and lack of real money for fancy electronic equipment.

Because Ben had stopped gainful employment too soon before leaving, and because he and Christian had not thought of everything he would need, money had dried up. Ben's cohort of friends declared this as a sign to cancel or postpone the trip. But he listened to none of their deterring excuses for turning away from his quest.

Ben seldom listened to anything but his own soul.

One problem with their safety rescue plan was the Mexican Coast Guard. They had only one ship deployed on this coast, a desolate desert of rugged cliffs and rock strewn sand that stretched over a thousand miles. The obvious consequence was that if an emergency did arise, it would be a week or two of delay, and probably too late for a rescue. Although Ben found all this out after the journey began, it did give him consolation to know that if he did get into any trouble, there would be at least some type of search and rescue attempt – or recovery of his remains.

That first day out of Puertocitos passed without incident. The weather was calm, and Ben relaxed as the time rolled by, lulled by the rhythm of the ocean around him. Early that evening, he spotted a school of dolphins in a small bay about two hundreds yards off to his right. Ben continued to paddle, but veered slightly in their direction and took out his camera. He put the camera on his lap, and readied himself for a closer look, hoping they would be curious about him. Indeed they were curious, and, after spotting Ben's clumsy attempts to maneuver, the dolphins changed course to see what strange creature swam in their territory.

Ben had been in contact with dolphins a few times before, both from a boat and from the shore, but never closer than twenty yards away. Each time he'd thought it an awesome experience. Tonight Ben was emboldened by the wonders and mysteries of the ocean that he was experiencing. It was nearly spiritual for him. He pushed perspective, and good judgment, further back in his consciousness. Ready to seek the sea's hidden riches with no thought of consequence, Ben hoped that on this pleasant evening he would experience more than he ever had before.

He did.

At first the dolphins cautiously approached the kayak, but kept their distance. But when it was evident that he meant them no harm, they came dancing toward him. In unison, they slowed to align themselves with the pace of the kayak. Now, around him on all sides of the small craft, Ben couldn't believe how close they were swimming. It was an incredible feeling to be face to face, almost at eye level, with the dolphins, in their own wild and untamed environment. Chills rolled up and down Ben's spine.

There were about two dozen dolphins in the pod. Two swam directly at Ben's side, so close at times that he had to watch where his paddle was hitting the water. He could have easily reached out and touched their glossy backs. They would surface briefly, and the sound and spray of their tiny blowholes reverberated across the water. The rush of water grew louder all around as they continued to follow Ben's course. He watched their eyes, intelligent and observant, stare intently into his own. The dolphins' powerful bodies, some over eight feet long, effortlessly parted the waves as they surfaced, breathed, and dove again. His heart racing, Ben continued to match their pace.

After a while the dolphins decided it was time to play. They showed off their speed and agility by performing different acrobatic feats. First they began to swim faster, racing out in front of him and spiraling up out of the water. Ben hoped that they were purposefully doing this for him, sensing that he would be an appreciative audience.

I definitely had the best seat in the entire ocean. Some rolled over on their sides, lifted their flippers out of the water, and slapped the surface with a resounding whack. Others swam out in front of the rest to be sure they were noticed, and then leapt out of the water and spun back to where I was paddling. At the last second, before their dorsal fin would hit the kayak, and a collision seemed unavoidable, they dove beneath the surface, leaving only a little ripple to break across my bow.

Ben felt an occasional bump on the underside of the kayak as a dolphin nudged the craft's slick surface. He continued to stare in awe at these magnificent animals and their every move. Looking into their eyes, Ben saw expressions that seemed to match his own. He marveled at their bodies, glistening in the last rays of the sun.

It was as if time had stopped, and the only things left on earth were these creatures, the ocean, and Ben Wade. Indeed, they were the only things that mattered at that moment. A form of communication emerged, and Ben found himself talking out loud to the dolphins that played around his kayak on that wonderful evening. He sensed that they might react to his soothing, coaxing, words. A connection blossomed that evening that most people on earth would never know. A gift from the sea, and from her Creator.

Eventually, the dolphins appeared to grow tired of Ben's slow, ungraceful movements, and his inability to take part in their festivities. They dove off toward the horizon in search of better company, and food. After they were gone, Ben stopped paddling, and sat back in his seat to revel in the beautiful experience that he'd just been a part of.

A gift from God, he thoughtfully sighed.

The water around grew silent, and the air seemed to hold its breath. All I could hear, as I resume a cadenced stroke, is the quiet whispering of the paddle slipping into the waves. The sun has now slipped beneath the barren, chocolate colored mountains, and the sky is turning from a soft pink to a vibrant crimson red. The whole ocean seems to freeze in time, and hold its breath for what I was about to experience.

Suddenly, the stillness was shattered in a watery explosion from the sea. Directly in front of Ben, the waters parted and a dolphin leapt clear of the surface, soaring high across the kayak's bow, and diving beneath the sea on the other side. Ben started with a jolt, having no expectation of their return. He stopped paddling, his body literally tingling with delight.

I knew that in their own way the school of dolphins had just given me their final gesture of grace, as if to say good-bye. I saw them no more that night, but the memory of that intimate experience will live within my soul forever.

Today was another marvelous page in the growing book of Ben's experiences.

Amazing what can happen when one lets go of his own world and dances with the raw beauty created by our Lord.

". . . Marginal drawings were crude. But they obviously were an attempt by Ben to add an explanation point to a particularly unique experience. A kind of ghost of the day."

Chapter 7

I know God will not give me anything I can't handle. I just wish that He didn't trust me so much.

Mother Teresa (1910-1997

A storm was boiling in the darkening skies to the east, and heading Ben's way. He could see the blue-grey clouds on the horizon piling up on each other, tinged pink by the last rays of the setting sun. He could feel the change in humidity as the rain got ready to pour. The ethereal pleasure of his experience with the pod of dolphins still lingered in his mind like the aroma of a fine wine. He watched the dark shadows creep about beneath the clouds, foreshadowing the heavy downpour he knew was to come.

Ben was still tucked into the small bay where he'd waved good-bye to the last of the dolphins. The water there was calm, and he knew better than to head out into the main channel at night with a storm on the rise. It was dark by the time he set up his tent and laid out his sleeping bag. The moon had not yet risen, and he took a moment to watch the night sky. Ben marveled once again at the beauty of nature, as uncountable sweeps of stars winked down at him. Miles away from the nearest civilization, the solitude was complete. Like so many other nights to come, the salt air and the desert sand, the ocean and the twinkling sky, were his only companions that night. But, as on other occasions, he was beginning to feel the incipient effects of loneliness.

His transformation was far from complete.

Ben looked to the stars, lifted his hands, and began to sing to *The*

Great Comforter. Ben knew his Lord God of the heavens and wrote of Him often. It was a precious moment. As he lifted his voice to the Lord to fill the night air with his solo song, he felt His hands on his shoulders, and heard His breath in the wind, joining his own.

I sense His angels around me, protecting me from the dangers, and watching out for my safety. He is good to me. No matter what I do, or how often I displease Him, He is there, faithful to the end - protecting, guiding and comforting me.

Ben's eyes brimmed with salty tears at his perceived unworthiness. His voice trembled. Alone in that quiet bay, miles from anywhere, he was filled with the Spirit of his God. Through the wind, the waves, and the sky, suddenly he did not feel so alone. His body seemed to be wrapped in that parental blanket of love.

What a sensation being truly alone with my God.

The Indian looked out across his bay. He squatted in the sand, 200 feet from the water's edge, and watched the dolphins play. It was comforting to see them forage for food in his bay. They usually came once a week to give their greeting. He smelled the air, saw the clouds, and welcomed the rain to come. He hadn't had a drink for a while - only the juice from nearby cactus, and the occasional dew he licked from his lips in the morning.

The sun caught something reflective in the water. It caused the Indian to look back at the pod of dolphins. There, amid his familiar beasts, was a small boat coming into the bay. The boat had one man sitting on top who obviously enjoyed the play of the dolphins. Both the man and the beasts seemed to communicate, and respond to the movements of one another. *This is odd*, thought the Indian, *the white man is usually immune to such hidden secrets of the sea.*

The boat looked familiar to the Indian. As it grew closer he realized, with a start, that it resembled the canoes his ancestors had used to migrate from the tip of Baja, north to where the great river flowed into the Sea of Cortez. But their life had changed many years ago. The great river, for some reason, had dried up. Only a trickle now remained. Boats that were bigger than any whale, now traveled up and down the coast. The boats were loud, with rumbles like thunder coming from within their hulls. He knew that the fish did not like this intrusion of sound in their sanctuary of silence and peace.

Long ago, when his father was still alive, he remembered paddling a canoe that had been in his family for many generations. They had come into this same bay, then past the rocks, and out into the wide open sea. His father had shown him how to catch fish by throwing a handmade net which spread out over the water and sank down beneath the surface. Then, after a minute of waiting, they would pull in the net together. In it were always dozens of fish of different sizes and colors. Once in awhile, a shark would find its way into the trap. They would eat it along with the rest of their catch. In those days, no matter where they would cast their net, the fish were in abundance. The ocean teemed with life.

When the first of the large boats had come by, they took little notice. But then there were more and more entering their haven, molesting their waters, and intruding in their bay. The ocean's life began to dry up. The tribe began to run out of food and space. The land and sea which they had loved was now being taken away, and they were forced to seek refuge in the hills. The tribe had scattered across the peninsula of Baja, finding shelter where they could. They feared the people who now swarmed the beaches that had once been theirs alone.

This Indian had stayed. Partly due to his pride, and also because he still believed that the land in the bay belonged to his family. At least the boats had diminished in size, he thought, and left this bay alone. It was dark by now, and the little boat that played with the dolphins had beached on the shore. The man that rode it was walking about, making shelter for the upcoming storm.

The Indian felt intruded upon in his quiet little cove. "Why can't they just leave me alone?" Anger crept across his furrowed continence. He scowled menacingly at the newcomer's unwelcome appearance.

Then, a strange thing happened.

The wind was blowing softly from the ocean, and across the sandy beach, and over the hill to where he, the Indian, was sitting. Mixed with the wind was a voice, a spirit, singing into the night. He looked down at the man who was barely visible as darkness set in. He could just make out the outline of the man where he stood, hands raised to the heavens, singing out loud.

The Indian felt a chill in his spine. "What medicine is this?"

Maybe it was the song, or maybe it was the man's boat, that reminded him of his ancestors, and memories of long ago. Whatever it was, the Indian felt a bond between himself and the strange white man in his bay. He realized that they both loved the sea, the life therein, and the spirits of the wind and sky. He was suddenly filled with wonder and curiosity at the structure of the boat, and decided to go for a closer look. Hopefully, if the man was awake he would talk to him. But if he slept, he would let him rest. Either way, the Indian decided to investigate.

Ben woke up with a start. His watch read 10:10 p.m., and everything outside was shrouded in darkness. He lay still and listened, knowing that something had caused his sudden alertness. Forcing himself to breathe slowly and deeply, Ben heard a sound outside the tent, not five feet away from his head. Footsteps. Someone was walking toward the kayak. But who? Who would be out here in the middle of nowhere without roads or villages? Ben's heart beat faster. His palms began to sweat. Quietly he un-zipped the sleeping bag, and as slowly as possible reached over and un-sheathed the 12 inch bowie knife at his side. He sat up and looked out of the tent. Whoever was out there had to have evil intentions. Ben could be in danger. Slowly his eyes grew accustomed to the dark.

Beside the kayak crouched an old man, half naked, and with very dark skin. Ben gripped the knife tighter, waiting for something to happen. But the old man just crouched there, looking at the boat and gently moving his hand over its surface. Finally, slowly, it dawned on Ben that the old man was just curious. When the small dark figure turned around, Ben saw with surprise, that he was an Indian - probably one of the migrating tribes who roamed the mountains of Baja California. He wore a heavy cloth around his waist. His body was lean and bronzed, accustomed to traveling long dis-tances, and hunting for his food. Ben relaxed a bit. Now it was his turn to watch in curiosity as the Indian walked around the kayak talking quietly to himself.

The Indian looked out across the water, and then up at the sky. As he turned around, he glanced over to where Ben's head was peeking out of the tent.

It was hard to tell in the soft moonlight, and maybe it was something Ben imagined, but it seemed as though he looked at him, and smiled know-ingly at an unspoken brotherhood between them. He bowed slightly toward Ben, and then slowly walked away. Ben waited for a few moments, and then climbed out of the opening. He walked to where the Indian had just stood, making sure everything was still intact. All was well.

Ben went back to sleep. But his sleep was filled with the restlessness of one not fully accustomed to his surroundings. When deep sleep finally came, it was filled with many dreams. Dreams of forgotten pasts, of legends, and of the people, some his own ancestors, who used to populate the earth and hillsides behind where he slept.

In the morning as he awoke, Ben wondered if his dreams had meshed together with reality. Had he imagined the Indian's curiosity toward his kayak. He walked outside and saw several small footprints in the sand. They led from his camp back into the hills. Ben looked over to the mountains and waved farewell.

He knew that the Indian was out there watching him.

Watching and protecting his bay.

Chapter 8

I have always depended on the kindness of strangers.
Tennessee Williams (1911-1983)

I t did rain that night, and all through the next morning. Everything around him, and inside the cockpit of the kayak, was soaked. But the air and water temperature were warm, so he didn't feel chilled. There was a silver lining to the storm. After it released its fury and moved on, the ocean became still, like a giant lake.

I take advantage of this break in our relentless dance. The ocean has performed beautifully, but now she stops, and waits patiently to see what I will do. I recognize this lull between us, and I feel it's my turn to take the lead.

Anxiously throwing his damp gear into the storage compartments, his heart beating a little faster than normal, Ben leapt into the calm water, and tore vigorously into the small waves with his paddle.

The kayak made good progress that day. It was getting late in the afternoon when Ben spotted several small islands ahead. He realized that he'd traveled over thirty-two miles that day. By now he was getting used to sleeping on the beach, and it didn't take much time now to chose a spot, set up camp for the night, and then tear it back down in the morning.

Ben smiled broadly at his change of heart, now caring less and less about the time it took to find shelter on land at night. His skills had increased, and now sleeping on the firm sand was a welcome break that

51

greatly outweighed the hassle. It was good to sleep on stable ground.

By the time he decided to pull in for the night, Ben had paddled past the five islands. Now they were clustered about on his left, providing good shelter from the open Sea. Shipping the paddle, he scanned around him and spotted a beautiful little cove. He checked the map and found that he was in a bay just north of Punta Bufeo. As he neared the shore he marveled at how crystal clear the water was. He peered down to the sandy bottom, some fifty feet below, and watched fish swim around in all directions, sometimes looking up curiously as the kayak's long shadow glided by. The sand rose up steadily to meet the shore. About fifty yards out, it gave way to the intrusions of rocks. Several trigger fish darted about searching for smaller prey. Ben wondered if there were stonefish hidden among the darker reaches of the rocks, waiting for their next victim. He'd heard many terrible stories about this deadly fish, and wished to stay as far away from them as possible.

The bay stretched around in a wide arc with both points marking the entrance as they turned parallel like pointers to the sea. On the south side of the bay, a mountain cast its shadow on the water. Above and among the rocks, about twenty houses stretched out in the same radius as the shore. The houses appeared deserted, except for one that stood in the middle of the arc that formed the bay. Bright and welcoming lights shone toward him, beckoning him to join their company. There were several palapas on the beach (umbrellas made from dried palm fronds). It was easy to tie up the kayak for the night. Ben was not going to be alone this night. He wasted no time, as he promptly strode up to the obviously occupied house, and found its owners.

Without pause, he introduced himself. It had been a couple of days since he'd talked to anyone, and he sought the company. But, seeing their startled and grim reaction, he wasn't so sure that his ersatz hosts shared the feeling. Not to be dissuaded, and maybe a little too bold, Ben nonetheless sat down and told the vacationing couple, an older man and his younger girlfriend, about his adventure. Fortunately for Ben, social tensions eased almost as fast as they had risen. The man ("call me Doc.") told Ben a little about himself and how he'd come to own the house.

Thirty years ago, he and his wife regularly participated in a motorcycle rally that started in San Felipe, and ended in La Paz. It was a two day, non-stop event, and those who made it unscathed were the lucky ones. There were no winners, it seemed, only survivors. After several consecutive years, Doc decided he'd grown too old to race, but he couldn't bear to give up this beautifully rugged section of Mexico. Several of his racing partners felt the same, so they built the community, now called Punta

Bufeo. It became their winter haven for peace and quiet.

The couple, somewhat reluctantly, invited Ben to stay for dinner. Ben writes that *I readily accepted.* He could tell that his presence was an interruption, but for some reason he didn't really give a damn. Ben was hungry, and tired, and couldn't wait to eat another hot meal. They ate giant sea bass, which Doc had caught earlier that day, and some salad and white wine. Doc and the girl seemed to warm to Ben as they sat on the front porch and looked out over the ocean. For a few minutes of silence, they watched the sunset illuminate the five islands on the horizon. The food settled well on Ben's stomach, as he sat back satisfied and content, and talked with his new friends until it was completely dark. Now, doubting his earlier boldness, he didn't wish to intrude further. He knew they longed for privacy. In the morning he would leave without further interruption.

Having received a good meal, and interesting company, Ben finally said goodnight, and walked back to the beach. Laying out his tent, Ben said his prayers and went contentedly to sleep.

September 21, 1996
Punta Bufeo Bay
Dawn

Ben went through his normal routine of warming up sore muscles, and then headed out into the bay. The water was so shockingly clear that he felt as if he was floating above it with no physical connection to the earth. He peered down at hoards of curious fish who studied his progress in the crystalline void above them. The variety challenged his mind. Fish jumped out of the water around the small craft. Flying fish cavorted with austere, sleek barracuda, to their peril. Color-flashing triggerfish challenged all to a fashion duel that was answered by the proud Beaubrummels. Barberfish, King Angelfish, and Hawkfish, twisted and turned in their unending search for food. He'd experienced this before. He also knew what would happen to them, as some of the wiser, and earlier rising, pelicans began to dive in and enjoy a good breakfast of salted fish.

The wind kept still until near midday, after Ben had rounded the Point of Bufeo. He was beginning to fall into a groove, a sort of rhythm. His muscles were adjusting to the grueling daily workouts, and Ben was learning to discipline himself in a way that maximized both time and effort.

Wake up with the sun at 5:30 a.m. Pack the tent and all my other belongings in the dry compartments. Eat one PowerBar and drink a cup of water. On the ocean by 6:00. Passing 8:00 a.m., although sometimes I'm hungry and thirsty, I don't stop - in spite of the pain. By 10:00 a.m., I stop for two minutes and take a few sips of water. Be careful of dehydration. More paddling until noon. Then I will usually jump out of the cockpit and swim around to cool off. Then back in the kayak and have lunch. At 12:15 p.m., I pick up my paddle, stretch out my muscles, and paddle again until 2:00 p.m. Then another swim to keep cool. The temperature in mid-September reaches above 90 degrees, and the cool water is most refreshing. For the rest of the day, I continue until I find a suitable place to spend the night, usually around 6:00 pm.

In the beginning, the pain in Ben's muscles pushed him past any sane or normal state, but he continually set new limits and standards daily. It would have been too easy for him to stop and rest each time he felt a twinge in his muscles, or a pain in his neck. Judging from his lack of progress on certain days, had he done so, the trip could have ended up taking him several years.

So each day, when his muscles would scream in agony after only a few hours of paddling, he would have to push through it, and drive on past any normal tolerance. It took some getting used to, but, by the end of the first week, having completed six successful days on the water, the pain subsided.

His body had partially adjusted to this new way of life.

His mind is another story.

Every day he prayed that the wind would change from the south to the north, or any variation in between. The wind was just as much of a determining factor as the tides. He was searching for at least one of the two to go in his favor. Now the tide seemed to go out only at night, while he slept. Unfortunately, that meant that when he woke early in the morning, an ideal time to push off, the tide was already coming in, and impeding progress even more.

Ben had also been paddling against a headwind since day one, and was wondering if it would ever change. He'd read somewhere that the wind would start to blow from the north in November. So, for now, he had to set his jaw and put up with it. Sometimes, though, the frustration would mount as the wind and tide allied their forces. That made it more difficult to take even the smallest break for lunch, because, when he stopped, if only for a minute, the two would visibly push him northward, and away from his eventual destiny. He continued to wait for wind and tide to help, not hinder. His patience was being sorely tested.

Ben reached Gonzaga Bay in the early afternoon in time to stop for lunch. The night before, Doc had told him of a little cantina on the northern end of the bay that served lunch. There were several more houses here that all faced the water. A few boats sailed about on the far side of the bay. The afternoon wind began to pick up again, and the water was frenzied with whitecaps. Ben was glad to be out of its way and on the shore.

It was easy to spot the cantina with its large bay windows trimmed with whitewash paint. It was the first building since he had crossed the border that looked American. It was a welcome sight. The white wooden boards and glass windows made the restaurant look like a New England lighthouse.

Naturally, Ben was the only customer. That didn't bother him today. He ordered three burritos from the cook, and went to sit down in front of one of the large windows that looked out over the bay. He'd hoped to make it to Punta Finál by nightfall, but was beginning to have doubts. Outside, the water continued to grow restless, and the wind continued to howl. Inside the cantina, however, the air was quite peaceful. If he had just sat back, closed his eyes, and listened to the radio playing the forgotten music of The Steve Miller Band, he could have almost imagined himself a tourist in the cays of Florida.

Ben brought his hand to his face, and felt the rough stubble of a beard unshaven for four days. It reminded him of the less than fine points of traveling on the ocean. The salt from the sea clung to his skin like a parasite, and the numerous swims in salt water seemed to have opened his pores further. It was almost like a second skin made of salt, sand, sweat, and lathered Aloe Verde. The abrasive nature of the water so irritated his face when he shaved, that he struggled through the process only twice a week, if then. At least the decision to shave his head would let him avoid the bother of a haircut for another week or so. He let his goatee continue to grow.

Ben finished the meal and moved to the bar to order another ice cold, and quite luxurious, Coca-Cola. His throat had long since forgotten the feel of a cool beverage, and this one seemed to refresh his taste buds all the more. Suddenly the door opened with a rattle that broke his reverie. Two men walked in and sat down next to Ben at the bar. One of them leaned over and said, "Was that you coming into the bay awhile ago in that kayak?"

"Sure was," Ben replied.

"You want a beer or something?"

"No thanks." This time Ben was not being persuaded.

"Where you headed? Don't see many kayakers in these parts," the other guy commented. They both looked like they had been in the sun too long. Ben would have mistaken them for Mexicans if they hadn't spoken first.

"Headed to Colombia or Ecuador," he said shortly, trying to avoid conversation. Ben had just made up his mind to leave the bay, despite the windy conditions, and he didn't want to sit around chatting with these two strangers.

"Ecuador?" the younger man said. "You crazy or what? Where'd you start?"

"Wait a minute," his buddy broke in. "You're the guy that was in all the newspapers a couple of weeks ago up in L.A. On the radio too, weren't you?"

"Yep, that's me. Started in San Felipe," Ben replied. It was kind of interesting to find out that somebody recognized him in the middle of Mexico.

Maybe it wouldn't hurt to talk for a little bit.

"Wow! You got major guts, man. Just how long you been out?"

"Only a week," Ben answered. "I won't be done for another six months though. Got a long haul ahead of me."

"Where are you from, man, L.A.?"

"Fullerton. Did my training in Newport Beach."

"No kidding. I think I seen you out there in the bay. I have a house out on the peninsula," the man said. And sure enough, that's where Ben had done all of his training.

After a bit of talking, he excused himself to leave. The men wondered why he was going out with the wind so strong, but he just smiled and said he couldn't let any moss grow under his feet. It was a lame comment, but the only thing that came to mind.

As he walked toward the kayak, he could feel how strong the wind was.

Now he wondered, as well, if this was such a good idea.

Chapter 9

Generosity is giving more than you can;
pride is taking less than you need.
Kahlil Gibran

T he waves pounded toward the shore, and the wind blew away from it, as Ben tried to keep the kayak parallel to the coast. Needless to say, not very successfully. The waves tossed about in all directions and, once again, Ben made the mistake of not putting on the spray skirt before the cockpit was half full of water. There was a point up ahead, just north of Punta Finál that looked safe enough to camp for the night. But it was obvious after a couple of hours that he would have to head for shore sooner. He was tired anyway, and the burritos he'd eaten for lunch were starting to give him indigestion. Living the life of luxury did not mix well with the intensity of his task.

As Ben moved closer to land, he spotted two men sitting on top of an old Jeep, watching his progress. Realizing that he was being watched, he dug in a little harder on the paddles. Ben wanted to look like he knew a little something about what he was doing.

Pride before the fall?

One of the men sported a bright pink baseball cap.

Maybe they're here to tell me that I can't camp overnight on their beach. Too damn bad.

Ben was too tired, and too frustrated, to deal with any hassles at this time of the day. Just as he touched the beach, the man with the pink cap jumped off the Jeep and walked down to the shore. He wore a big grin on his face. "Bet you're good and ready for an ice cold beer!" he shouted as he extended his hand forward, waiting for Ben to grasp it.

Boy, here we go again with this beer thing. Doesn't anyone drink water down here?

"Sure I'd love one," Ben responded, contrary to his thoughts. By this time, the other fellow had made his way over to them and shook Ben's hand. "Where in the hell did you come from in this thing?" The guy in the pink cap asked. "Man, this is heavy," the other muttered under his breath, as they all three grabbed a hold of the kayak and lifted it up onto the beach. "Tell me about it," Ben said to the guy who had mentioned its weight. "I have to haul this thing up above the high tide line every night."

"Where did you say you came from?" Pink cap asked.

"San Felipe," Ben said proudly.

"Man alive! That's a hell of a long way."

"Where you goin'?" The other asked.

"Never mind about that, Gary," said pink cap. "Let's get this old boy a beer. I'm sure he'll tell us all about it over supper. You hungry ain't you?" Ben nodded. Pink cap continued, "We got us a place up here behind this first row of mobile homes, and we got plenty of food. By the way, I'm Carl and this is my brother Gary." He took off his pink hat and wiped his brow. Now they had names. "I'm Ben." They all shook hands again. "You got a safety line?" Carl asked.

"Sure do."

"Good. Then let's tie it on to the back of the Jeep, and we'll tow it up on the beach twenty yards or so. Get you well above the tide."

They walked to the Jeep. Ben could see that it was a real beauty. A white 1940 Willies military edition. Original engine, he was told. Gary had welded a metal luggage rack on top, similar to the ones you see in the African safari tours. Carl turned the key in the ignition and seemed pleased to hear the engine rumble. They pulled the kayak up the beach and unhitched the rope, then drove on, and slowly crested the nearest sand dune. Two minutes later their 'home' came into view. It was actually two trailers sitting side by side. They looked like they'd been hauled to that spot many years ago. The base of the trailers had long since been covered over, almost cemented, by the blowing sand.

Under an awning that connected the two structures, sat three chairs, one table, a stove, and an antique refrigerator – circa 1950. Fishing gear, tackle, poles, and nets, were strewn everywhere. "Have a seat there, friend. I'll bet you're beat. We saw you come in. Been watchin' you for about an hour. Seemed to be makin' good progress at the end. Wind's a bitch today, don't need to tell you that, and the water seems awful tore up. I myself wouldn't be out there even in my fishing boat. Too damn dangerous. Freak wave come up, knock you smack out of the water. You must be crazy."

"A little," Ben admitted.

"Where'd you say you was goin' again?" Carl asked, obviously the more gregarious of the two. Gary seemed content to just sit across from Ben and listen. "Colombia, or maybe Ecuador," Ben said proudly. He was beginning to enjoy the reactions of people who heard his story. Or maybe it was the beer on an empty stomach. Carl handed him another beer. He really didn't want it, but he took it anyway. Carl continued, "I been comin' down here since 1965. Hauled these two trailers here myself. That was a trip in itself, comin' down these roads that ain't worth a tinker's dam. Every road that leads to this place is filled with holes and washouts. One time the rains were so bad that I had to wait three days before I could cross the river that had washed out the road. Gary, here, didn't want to have anything to do with it. Thank goodness we don't have to drive here anymore. Built an air strip out back ten years ago, and we been flying down ever since. I been flyin' planes for as long as I can remember. That's my Cessna 172 out back. Flew in a couple of days ago."

"Where did you fly in from?" Ben managed to interject.

"Up in Snelling, California. Kinda southeast of Modesto." Carl went on, seemingly without a breath. "I've got a landing strip at my house. Got two hundred acres of ranch land. Beautiful country, in the foothills. Pretty convenient to fly straight down. Don't have to deal with customs, or any of the airport bull. Gary, here, flies too, but I do most of the flyin' when we come down here. Only when the weathers calm, though. Don't like takin' off when there's a storm headed in. I've flown all the way down this coast and over to the mainland. By the way, where you gonna cross over to Mexico?"

"I don't know," Ben said. He hadn't thought about that question since he left. "Maybe from La Paz, maybe from Cabo. Depends on how the weather is and such."

"Damn, son. You tryin' to kill yourself? Have you ever been down there? The water is so churned up and choppy at the point that some of the big boats avoid it. And you're in a goddam tiny kayak. It'll take you what, four, five days to cross?"

"More like eight," Ben said, wanting to be an intelligent part of this

59

lopsided conversation.

"You're right crazy, you know that. You'll never make it. Storm comes up and you'll never be heard from again."

Thanks for the encouragement, Ben thought. Then he said, "Well, then, what do you suggest? I've got to make it over to the mainland, some-how."

"Well now, let me see. Mind you, I'm not tryin' to scare you or any-thing. I just don't want you to get killed. I've flown all over this peninsula so many times I can't count. Know it pretty damn good. One thing you're doin' wrong is goin' down the Baja side. It's good and all for us 'cause we like to get away, and it's easy to fly down here. But for you, it's all desert. No water. You could go for weeks without seein' anybody, a town, or even a boat. What do you do for water anyhow?"

Ben stirred in his chair. "I usually carry five gallons on board. De-pends on where the closest town is. The weight is the only problem or I'd carry more."

"My point exactly, Ben. You can't carry enough water to go for more than a week. That ain't much. Not out here. Baja is too desolate. It's a good thing you happened along our beach, I'll tell you that. We're goin' to set you straight, give you some good advice, and all the help we can. I'll give you anything you want. What've you got for maps?"

"Well," Ben said kind of sheepish like. "From Acapulco on south, I've got some really good navigational charts. But I figured the Sea of Cortez would be flat. You know, calm - like a pancake and all that. So, I've only got a AAA road map for these waters."

"A goddam road map?" roared Carl. Gary joined in the laughter. Ben felt like crawling under the table. "Flat as a pancake? Whoever told you that should be shot. Damn, boy, we're goin' to give you some help here, see? Look here, I don't want to see you get killed, or anything like that. It can be pretty dangerous out there, like you've probably already found out. Thank goodness you came to Punta Finál tonight."

Carl opened another beer and took a long pull.

Ben was becoming unnerved by all the carrying on that was taking place. Carl was rambling on, and maybe he'd already had a few beers be-fore Ben came along. But Ben looked up as Carl was talking, and could see genuine concern in his eyes. Ben was actually shocked. He didn't even know these people, and yet they were genuinely concerned about his well being. It touched him.

Most people he'd known, especially in Los Angeles, cared only about themselves. Ben's pastor used to put it eloquently, "People these days get all they can, can all they get, and sit on their cans." But these guys were different. They wanted to help. Not just with words of advice, but later on with any supplies that Ben requested. He felt instant admiration for the generosity of these two brothers. He imagined himself and his own brother, Peter, sometime living the same kind of adventure as these two.

Ben looked to each one in turn and said, "Thanks. Really, I mean it, thanks. I don't usually run across guys that want to go out of their way to help. In fact, last night I ran into a couple that could barely tolerate my presence. I appreciate the concern. I'm glad that I met you guys today. It wasn't just luck that brought me to this particular beach."

"Its nothin', man," Gary said, looking down at his beer. He got up to get another. "You want another while I'm up, Ben?"

"No thanks, Gary, but have you got any cold water? I'm dyin' for a good old drink of cold water."

"Sure, no problem."

"He said its nothin' all right," Carl said as he went over to the refrigerator to see what food was going to be prepared that night. "We're going to help you all right. Down here it's different from the States. Gotta stick together, look out for each other, and all that. Like I said, Ben, it's desolate out here. We got things, and you don't. Simple as that. We'd be either selfish, or crazy, not to share it with you." Carl handed Ben a glass of water, and continued his philosophy lesson, "Don't take it personal, but I don't think you're quite prepared for this trip. A road map? Gary, you know where my son's extra aviation chart is?" Gary sat up with a start, surprised to be allowed into the fun. "It's in the front trailer, I think. I'll go get it."

"We'll set you up, Ben. I'll bet that water tastes pretty good, eh? I give you a lot of credit for takin' this trip. It takes a lot of guts to do something like this. I don't even know if I would have tried it when I was younger."

"I just like to go for the gusto I guess," Ben said, trying for an entertaining answer. "By the way, Carl, how do you get this water so cold?" The water was even colder than the Coke Ben had enjoyed that afternoon. "Propane. That's the key down here. Everything we got runs on propane. Stove, refrigerator. Keeps everything cold, and it's not expensive either. You got that map yet, Gary?"

"Here it is," Gary said, coming out of the trailer. He walked over to where they sat and spread it out on the table. "Lemme see," Carl said, opening up another beer. "We're here, Punta Finál. You know why they call it that? Because its the last point of habitation of any kind until Bahia de Los Angeles. Well, except for Calamahue fish camp around the corner. But I mean that's it. Nothin' but rocks along the coast. Not one beach. Mountains fall into the sea like they've been sheared off with some great big knife. After that, it doesn't get much better. The tides finally start lettin' up past the Bay of Conceptión. I know. We've flown over it a hundred times. Haven't we, Gary?"

"Yep, sure have. And you've said that already, about a hundred times," Gary pointed out. Carl rolled his eyes and gave Ben a sidelong glance, just tolerating his little brother. "Well, don't get snappy," Carl said. "And remember, Ben, no water. That's the key. Look here." He pointed to a couple of tiny islands on the chart that stood out in the middle of the Gulf. "I think it would be best if you cross right here. That way, if things get bad, or a storm comes up or somethin', you can head for the shelter of these islands. You know what a Chubásco is?"

"Nope. What's that, a shark?" Ben said, laughing nervously. "Yeah, right. No sir, its a gale. a Chubásco is a gale," Gary said. "It's a hell of a wind that comes up out of nowhere, without no warning, 60 knot winds and more. Blow your kayak right out of the water, anywhere it wants. The wind comes up any time, but usually in the summer and fall. In other words, right now. You don't want to get caught anywhere, especially in the middle of the Sea of Cortez, when that sucker comes up. When it does, though, get to shore as quick as you can. It gets scary out there, even for some of the bigger boats." Carl was nodding with vigor to confirm the point. "So, you think I should cross here?" Ben pointed, getting his focus back on the chart. He was pointing to the islands. "Yep, positive. We even go across that way when we're flyin' down to Puerto Vallarta, in case somethin' happens. We bring plenty of water, too. Here, you study this chart for awhile. I'm gonna go make dinner. You hungry? I bet you are." Ben nodded in agreement and looked down at the chart.

It really wasn't much better than his road map, he thought, but he appreciated the gesture. It didn't have one topographical feature, and it only listed the cities with airports. Fine for a pilot that was soaring over it all, but the kind of chart Ben needed was the types he had for the southern part of the route. Nautical. The kind that listed depths in fathoms, currents, beaches, harbors etc. He carefully studied the aeronautical chart anyway.

Occasionally Ben looked over at Gary, definitely the quieter of the two brothers. Gary sat there, silently sipping his beer, and looking over at the chart once in a while. Their eyes met once or twice. Each time a smile slowly spread across his gentle face. Carl was busy clanging pots and pans together and making supper, so Ben decided to talk to Gary for a while. "You like it down here?" he asked. "Oh, sure," Gary replied. "It's the place to go to get away from everything."

"Are you married, Gary?"

"Yep. Same wife all these years. Got two kids as well."

"You live near your brother, Carl?"

"Close. A little place called Linden, California. I own a hardware store there. My house is not too far away. About twenty minutes or so."

"Do you live on a ranch like Carl? You got an airstrip too?" Ben probed. "Nope, to both questions. But I've got two acres of land with cherry trees and a walnut groove. It's beautiful country, just like Carl said."

"Sounds like it. I love the countryside. Growin' up in Tennessee, I had to. I'm going to have to come up there after I finish my trip and visit you two."

"You damn well better, boy," Carl shouted from the stove where he was cooking. "If you make it through this trip in one piece, I'll come pick you up personally in my airplane. You can count on that."

Dinner was served, and Ben thought that it was the most delicious meal he'd ever had. Chicken with lemon and other spices grilled on the open flame, beans, corn and bread. Carl was definitely a good cook. Ben asked him if he had ever worked in a restaurant. He said no, but he always did the cooking. Ben ate everything in front of him and more. It was amazing how good the food tasted, and how much he could eat after a week and a half of dried fruits and nuts.

The plates were cleared, and they continued to talk about the best place to cross to the mainland, and where to get water, and so on. Carl, again, reminded him that the mainland of Mexico had a lot more cities, and pumped water. In the end, he was beginning to convince Ben. After awhile, Carl got up and brought out a large block of ice. "Where's a knife when you need one? I need some ice cubes for my after dinner drink," he said. "I've got one," Ben said. He pulled out the knife that was clipped to his faded blue shorts.

He'd been given a couple of knives by a hunting buddy before he left. They were terribly sharp, probably the best knives he had ever seen. He was very proud to be their owner. They were as sharp as razors. Ben opened the knife, displaying its gleaming edge in the candle light. "Looks sharp. Here, cut this piece," Carl said. Ben brought the knife down quickly. It cut through the hard surface of the ice like butter. Carl held the chunk steady with both hands and said, "Here, give me a couple more chunks." Ben brought the knife down again.

But this time it slipped, and he cut more than just the ice.

"Ow! Shit! Son of a . . .," Carl yelled. "You about cut my goddam finger off!" He jerked his hand back, and covered it quickly with a towel. Ben hadn't felt anything, and, at first, he wondered if Carl was joking. Ben had underestimated the sharpness of the knife. Carl held up his finger to the light, and a large stream of blood spurted sideways. The knife had cut through the skin and severed a main vein. He was bleeding pretty badly, and all Ben could do was just stand there, helpless. He felt like a real jerk. *After all of his help, this was my way of repaying his kindness*, he thought. "Oh man," Ben said. "I'm so sorry. Are you all right, Carl? I'm sorry, man. I didn't mean to . . . it just kind of slipped." Ben didn't know that was going to happen. "Is there anything I can do?"

"Yeah, take off in that kayak of yours before I take that goddam knife away from you," Carl growled. "No, Ben, just kidding. I just need to put a bandage on this. It looks like it really needs stitches, but that'll have to wait until I get back to the States." Carl hurried into the trailer and back to the bathroom, still holding his finger. He soon had it wrapped and taped, but the wound was deep, and continued to bleed throughout the night. Ben felt terrible and could not offer enough apologies. "No real harm done," Carl said. "But if you don't shut up and quit apologizing I'm really gonna get mad. Here, join me with a drink, and cut off a few more ice cubes. Preferably without takin' my other hand off." Ben put his knife away guiltily, and sat down to have that after dinner drink.

Which now he needed.

By the time they got ready for bed, the two brothers had piled up several articles that they said Ben would need as supplies. They gave him thirty feet of floating line, two gallons of fresh water, maps, good luck trinkets, an anchor, some twenty-pound test fishing line, and different kinds of sinkers and lures.

Carl asked about the bandage on Ben's toe. Ben told him about how he had stumbled around looking to take a morning pee, and cut it pretty badly on a jagged rock. At Carl's insistence, he took off the gauze around the big toe. Carl had insisted that he take it off to look for any signs of infection. There was none, but because the wound was not getting enough air, it hadn't healed much. The skin was a ghastly white, and the wound continued to gape in an unsightly manner. They cut some of the dead skin away, and poured alcohol on the rest of the cut. Then, Gary gave Ben one of his own pairs of socks so that the sand wouldn't get in and cause any infection.

That night they slept under the stars, Carl, Gary, and Ben, on some old army cots. Ben slept well. He felt satisfied from eating such a good meal, and at having made two new friends.

Ben had a thought before slipping into slumber.

What a difference it makes to be among friends, to have a full stomach, and a bed to sleep on. Much better than being out on some deserted beach on the hard sand, alone, and hungry.

Chapter 10

All that really belongs to us is time; even he who has nothing else has that.
Baltasar Gracian y Morales (1601 – 1658)

B en and Gary stirred to the sounds of Carl's kitchen, as he once again prepared a fine meal. After the previous night's feast, Ben was surprised that he could put away such a big breakfast. After cleaning up their plates, and packing the new supplies into the kayak, Carl turned to Ben and asked, "Hey, Ben, are you in a big hurry to get out of here?"

"No, not really," he responded without hesitation. He truly hoped that they wanted him to stay for another day. He would welcome the rest. "Okay, then, let's go out to the desert. What do you say, Gary? We haven't been up to Los Palmas for a while. Let's take Ben out there, and show him all the palm trees and everything. Should be a good time of year to go, now that it's cooling off a bit."

"Sounds good to me," brother Gary said cheerily. "I'll make some sandwiches, and pack the cooler full of ice and drinks." It sounded good to Ben too. He readily accepted the offer of a free tour. In an hour they had everything packed and ready to go. They hopped into the old Jeep and took off, taking a dirt road that was just as bad as Carl had said it would be and, at times, almost invisible. They bumped and rattled straight across the desert floor, dodging bushes and cactus that appeared in their path. Thirty miles out, they neared the end of the barren plain of sand and sparsely populated Joshua tree forests, and began to wind up through a canyon. The rock walls on either side shadowed the road, as the Jeep continued to find its footing in the loose gravel and sand. Ben was glad to have a couple of 'natives' as guides. Eventually, Gary pointed ahead at a hundred palm trees that stuck out above the other vegetation. Clustered together, they were in stark contrast to the canyon walls that suddenly spread out to make way for the uncommon oasis. The meadow that spread out beneath the palm trees converged at the end on a well that was still used by the Indians. It was also water for the hard scrabble ranchers and the wild animals.

The clear water stood in the middle of the great trees, some of which were over a hundred feet tall. A rudimentary barbed wire fence surrounded the well, discouraging larger animals from getting too close, and eliminating the possibility of a fall, and a drowning that would poison the water source for others that depended on it. An irrigation trench had been dug from the upper reaches of the well to another trough, fifteen yards away. This allowed for another puddle of water to form for the animals.

Carl pointed past the well to the rugged mountains that rose sharply to a summit that reached above the clouds. This mountain, keeping watch over the oasis as it did, was the source of the spring. "There used to be a mission up there," Carl said. "The Spaniards came and tried to convert the heathens. Ruins still remain I hear, but it's an eight hour hike straight up the mountain's face. There's supposed to be another spring up there too, with birds and all that. Sometimes even from here in the valley we can see the big horn sheep climbing across the rocks. Wish I had the stamina to make it up there. Supposed to be quite a place, and hardly anyone knows about it cause it's so remote. It's also too hot most of the year to even think about tryin'."

Ben looked up, imagining the missionaries of long ago.

What a hardship that must have been, to live in the middle of the desert so isolated from civilization. Much like this journey of mine, the spiritual strengthening must have been immense.

They stayed for a couple of hours, ate lunch, and headed back.

It was late in the afternoon when Ben launched the kayak with the brothers' help. He didn't mind the delay at all. Ben took off with a different attitude than when he had landed, less than twenty-four hours prior. Until that point, his thoughts had been focused only on himself - how many miles he had to make each day, the books he was going to write after it was all over, his safety, his supplies, his time, his strength, and his courage. He came into Punta Final worried about the intensity and duration of the expedition, and how quickly he could get it over with, instead of considering his own personal fulfillment, enjoyment, and the satisfaction of undertaking such a trip.

He was losing sight of the original vision, but beginning to see a new one.

Yes, it was mandatory to a degree to think about his own safety, maintaining good speed, and keeping to a routine. It was too easy to become distracted, and to quit short of his goal. But it had become an obsession to cover as much ground as possible, with no more regard for the little pleasures and relationships along the way than if he was commuting to a job in Los Angeles. He'd begun to pursue this challenge with the same mundane enthusiasm as a daily chore. Looking back, he could see the likelihood of falling into that trap. The days were long and tedious, and the end was nowhere in sight. He was lonely, and longed for the loving arms of the people he knew well. Every thought and action up to this point had pointed its selfishly erect finger at him.

In the small colony at Punta Final all that had changed for Ben.

After being embraced by two strangers like a spring flower blossoming amid the desert scrub, I am beginning to sense a change in myself. Meeting someone whose actions defy the stubborn selfish pride that the human race has accepted as its modern standard has broken the mold of my own spirit of selfishness.

By giving their time, their efforts, their energy, food and shelter, without expecting anything in return, the brothers had slapped Ben where it hurt – in his sense of self. He was suddenly filled with guilt for wanting only to receive. He realized it was time to look beyond his pride and self-focus, and seek out the needs of others. He truly wanted to do more.

I wanted to be able to enrich people's lives knowingly, and substantially, by putting forth the effort and sacrifice that could enable others to benefit from my gains. I made a mental note then and there, to ease the focus of my own accomplishments, and to be aware of other's needs, desires, and dreams.

Ben turned around, pausing for a moment in his paddling rhythm, and looked back upon the two brothers who stood on the shore waving good-bye. They had done everything in their power to assist him in his quest, and he would be grateful to them forever. What they didn't know, however, was that they had helped Ben in a way far more beneficial to his mental health than anything physically listed among his supplies. Ben smiled and waved back, realizing that these two would be the first among a string of many that would mesh with his own personal goals, and increase the satisfaction of this expedition. Ben had come away from this encounter with a broader focus on life, and the memory of an untainted, untouchable experience.

Like it or not, Ben Wade was truly maturing.

Later that night, after leaving Carl and Gary, Ben reached a small village known by locals as Callamahue fish camp. As he paddled into the small bay he saw, with an initial start, several sharks swimming in the shallow waters near the beach. He saw their small black fins knifing the water's surface, and heard the water boil from their movements. But there wasn't any fear in him. The disturbed water seemed like a whisper to Ben, and was eerily soothing to his ear. The inhabitants of the village, Mexican fisherman, came out in time to see Ben step out of his kayak and onto the rocky shore. The beach had only a little bit of sand, and consisted mostly of pebbles and seashells. The surface was jagged and painful to walk on with bare feet. The smell of rotting seaweed and fish remains hung in the air.

The beach rose steeply from the water at an angle of almost forty five degrees, making it impossible for Ben to haul the kayak above the high tide mark. Indeed, he could not even move the entire kayak clear of the water. The lower half still rested in the bay among the lazily circling sharks. He looked for a rock or tree to tie the safety line. There was none in sight.

Among the variety of supplies that Carl and Gary had given to Ben was an anchor. Actually, it was an idea for an anchor. An ingenious idea that fit the circumstance well. They had given Ben an empty bucket which they told him to fill with rocks to give it enough weight to keep the boat from drifting away. A normal steel anchor would have been too heavy to carry on board. The bucket was perfect. Figuring it was a good time to use this new idea, Ben tied his safety line to the handle, filled the bucket to the rim with rocks from the beach, then dropped it into the gentle surf. Ben maneuvered around to the other end of the kayak and tied on another rope. He looked up at the steep slope rising higher than his head and began to climb. All he could find was a small rock no larger than a melon. He secured the length of rope, regretting that he didn't have enough to reach his tent so that he could wrap it around his ankle. Now looking at the two anchors, the bucket and the rock, Ben figured that it wouldn't be a problem. He went to bed without much worry.

Fortunately for Ben, the small sharp rocks beneath his tent provided only a restless sleep. He awoke several times during the night, each time hearing the sound of the Kevlar hull of the kayak gently scraping against the rocks. About 1 a.m. he shifted his body, searching for a softer spot. He paused and listened. With a start he sat up. Ben heard only silence. Awkward with sleep, he fumbled for the zipper that secured the flap. Finding its tab he opened the flap and looked out. It took awhile for his eyes to adjust to the dim, moonlit scene. When he could finally make out details around him, what he saw shocked him full awake. As he had feared from the loud silence, the beach where the kayak had rested just two hours earlier was empty.

Real fear gripped his throat, his heart skipped a beat, and his stomach sent knotted pains around his middle. Throwing back the flap, Ben stumbled out of the opening and onto the beach. He cursed quietly as the rocks dug into the soft and tender skin along his arches, as he both slid and ran down the steep slope of the shore to the water's edge. His eyes were still having difficulty adjusting to the night's darkness, and the shadows cast by the moon's pale illuminating light.

It's gone. The kayak is gone! Where is it?

Ben's mind raced.

What happens if I can't find my kayak?

Jumbled thoughts fought for his attention.

There's no road into this camp. No electricity. That means no radios, no telephones. How far to the last town with phones? I can't get another kayak. My trip's over! How could I be so stupid? I knew the damn high tide would come! Why didn't I think it would take the kayak?

Ben stood shifting from one foot to the other. He gritted his teeth as he shivered in the night's damp cold. He'd assumed that the anchors would hold. He was wrong. As he stood there he could not even begin to imagine how he would make it back to the States.

Even if I did, how humiliating it will be to explain to everyone how I missed my final destination by a mere 5,000 miles.

Panic rose in his throat, and swept through him like the incoming tide against the shore. He frantically searched from shore to the horizon, and then farther out to sea, in hopes that the glint of fiberglass in the moonlight would show him its location.

Then, when all Ben's hope seemed futile, he caught the faint silhouette of an elongated shadow about fifty yards from shore in the middle of the little bay. As Ben peered through the moonlight, he was flooded with relief as the shape of the kayak loomed distinct. He started forward, stepping into the cold black water, then stopped and retreated, stumbling to the shell strewn shore.

The sharks!

The sharks that were swimming in the bay when he'd paddled ashore the night before. They were still there. He could hear them. Ben knew why they were there; when the fishermen brought their day's catch home they cleaned the fish on the shore, throwing the guts and other remains into the water. Naturally the scavengers of the sea would attack the food in these great numbers. The sharks, sea gulls, and even a few crabs, would wait all day in anticipation of this free meal. Ben stood shivering on the shore, and listened to the commotion of the sharks thrashing about in the black waters. He knew it would spell disaster if he jumped in after the kayak, and was mistaken for something else, like food.

Ben looked out at the kayak, hoping that by some odd chance it would come back closer with the incoming tide.

The tide hasn't worked in my favor yet. In fact it seems as if when she sees I'm in trouble, she'll purposefully continue to push the boat further out.

Ben shook the cynical thoughts away. He knew he had to act fast, but the sharks in the water below were stalling his actions, and giving him real cause for hesitation. He stared into the night. His fists were balled up, and his chest grew tense, as he screwed up growing courage. Finally, he let out a yell, hoping against irrational hope that his predatory scream might frighten away some of the closer sharks, and dove head first into the dark water.

Swimming faster then he ever had in his life, Ben headed for the life-saving silhouette of the kayak. He thrashed about as loud as he could, hoping the movement would turn away any predator. Ben was ignorant of the fact that his actions actually attracted the predator sharks.

He was acting like food.

Something brushed his leg.

Something as rough as sandpaper.

He kicked hard, and felt the shark recoil and move away.

Then another brush, and a bump.

When will they bite?

Ben could hear his heart beating in his ears.

His breath came in ragged gasps and coughs as he strained forward.

After long minutes of intense swimming he reached the kayak, miraculously unscathed. He pulled himself onto the narrow deck, swinging his legs out of the water, and gasping rapidly to catch his breath. Things still bumped into the hull of the boat, just inches away.

Sitting on top of his tiny craft in the middle of the moonlit bay, Ben slowly let the fright drain away. He could still hear movement close to the shore. His fear, though was giving way to self anger for assuming that the tide had little strength. Ben reached down and pulled up the bucket that was still filled with rocks. In a fit of misplaced disgust he cut the line with his belt knife.

So much for that bright idea.

Now he realized that in his haste to retrieve the kayak, he'd forgotten to bring the paddle. He laid down flat on the bow, his face only an inch or two above the shark infested water, and paddled with his arms back to shore.

Sure that most of the fishermen, alarmed by his first war cry whoop, were enjoying the show from the safety of their tiny shacks, Ben imagined dozens of eyes peering out to the bay to watch his foolishness. He looked up to the top of the ridge and thought,

so they're having a good laugh ... at least my kayak is safe.

As he reached the shore Ben realized that his impulsive discarding of the anchor bucket now left him with a dilemma. How to secure the kayak. Glancing up longingly at his empty tent, he sat down on the waters edge, and tied what was left of the rope to his ankle. Hoping that dawn was not too far away, with its promise of a warming sun, he drew his knees up tight to his chest and closed his eyes. Before going fully to sleep he thanked God for waking him. An hour or so later, and it would have been too late. The tide was going out, and Ben knew it wouldn't come back for another six hours.

He fell asleep.

But woke every ten minutes to see if the tide had, in its hatred, secretly returned in the night to carry away the rest of his meager belongings.

Chapter 11

I know how men in exile feed on dreams of hope.
Aeschylus (525 BC-456 BC)

Baja California, Mexico, is a vast expanse of unspoiled and unprotected rock, desert, mountains, and beaches. It is unlike the mainland of Mexico, especially in the southern region which boasts of lush tropical rain forests, vast coconut groves, and sugarcane plantations. For the most part uninhabited, the peninsula of Baja is without a constant supply of fresh water.

The Sea of Cortez separates the Baja peninsula from mainland Mexico. Few boats venture north past the town of Bahia de Los Angeles. This is partly because of the large variance of tides and the lack of good harbors, but also because there are few towns or ports where one can stock up on fresh water and other supplies.

Desolate stretches of coast are the norm. Where the mountains meet the sea there is no room for gentle sloping hills. Indeed, it looks like the mountains have been parted by some great force that stopped them just short of the sea. There is only room for the narrow finger of water that creeps its way north toward the deserts of California and Arizona. Uninhabited, sparsely vegetated mountains of rock tumble down to the water from a thousand vertical feet. Boats find these stretches particularly hostile. There's no room to cast an anchor, and no small coves to seek shelter from a storm. The area of coast between Callamahue fish camp and Bahia de Los Angeles is no exception. The desert that stretches beyond the houses of Punta Finál gives way in the south to the rugged stone mountains that vault

73

toward the sky. The sight of these mountains is intimidating, calling forth only the brave - and the foolish.

Ben would not find one beach between the two points - only an endless rock wall, some seventy-five miles long.

Ben studied the AAA road map. Despite the lack of topographic detail he knew this was going to be a tedious part of the journey. He launched earlier in the morning than usual, hoping to get a head start on the day. It was 5:30 a.m., and his plan was to cover the seventy-five miles in three days. There would be little time for sleep as he drifted about in the open sea. It meant staying awake to take note of the currents, and the possibility of drifting into the rocks. He'd tried to prepare himself mentally for parts of the trip like this, but there was really nothing he could have done to be truly ready.

By nightfall exhaustion ruled as Ben put in fourteen hours of paddling. His neck was so stiff that he could barely turn around to retrieve the parachute sea-anchor that helped deter dangerous currents at night. The currents here were still too strong for the sea-anchor to fully do its job, and he forced himself to stay awake for another two hours. The longest two hours of his journey so far. His body cooled down rapidly in the night air, and he could feel idle muscles cramping. Several times he had to paddle just to increase the blood flow and relieve the pain.

The moon had not yet risen, and the blackness seemed to swallow the sea and the kayak. Ben imagined the tall figures of the mountains above looking like giants that stared down on him with contempt and disgust.

I saw their eyes boring into my soul, wanting to crush me whole, and discard me from this place of eternal solitude.

Every sound was magnified. The smallest noise, like the break of a wave, made him jump in anticipation of some unknown intrusion. Fatigue drained any clarity of thought. Several times he knew he saw sharks larger than the kayak glide by.

Were they released from the giant guardians above to prevent further violation of this unblemished region?

At 11:00 p.m. the moon finally rose, and dispersed the shadows and dreams, urging them back to the world where they were born. Ben's eyelids were heavy now, and he drifted off into an uncomfortable sleep. Cramped in the tiny cockpit, and apprehensive of the dangers, he woke with a start, tired and cold, after only fifteen minutes. It would be a long night. He paddled for awhile, embracing the madness that seemed to come with the uncertainties of night. Eventually, too tired to even lift the paddle for one last stroke, he climbed out of the cockpit, and lay down on the flat, narrow stern deck of the kayak. After a slight struggle, and once falling into the black water, he wrapped a rope and two bungee cords around his shivering body, allowing him enough stability and security to close his eyes and sleep. Now the rolling sea held him, cradling his body as if he were a baby sleeping.

I thank her for her compassion.

After only an hour of sleep, he woke once again, unstrapped from the kayak, and focused his eyes on the shore. It looked small and more amicable from afar. He'd drifted a considerable distance away, so he paddled for another hour to move closer to shore. Finally, satisfied with his location, he strapped himself back to the kayak and fell asleep. But now he was even more restless. Hearing the crash of waves on the rocks, and sensing that the sound was drawing near, he woke again after only fifteen short and unrestful minutes. It was a miserable night. Eventually he lost track of the number of times he'd tried to sleep.

Ben's demons of solitude prowled the night.

The solitude is almost unbearable, and the blackness of night enshrouds my soul again. It threatens to bring to life the nightmares that prowl just beneath the protective walls of reason.

By morning, and the first glimmer of a blue and pink dawn above the eastern horizon, Ben's muscles were too tired to respond. He wondered if he would have the strength to eat. But, with the rising sun came the warmth and promise of a new day. Nightmares vanished, sanity returned, and Ben felt the rumblings in his stomach. He retrieved two PowerBars from the front storage compartment, and looked at them dolefully.

How nice it would be to have something else, anything else, to eat! Pancakes, waffles, sushi, anything!

He shrugged his shoulders in resignation, knowing that this was the diet for some time. He took out a bag of dried oatmeal and washed it down with water. Stowing all of the trash, he resumed the paddling rhythm that spoke of progress.

Endless cliffs and faceless mountains passed by all day. The world was so melded in brown chaos that he gave up trying to look at the map. Anonymous mountains stretched as far as he could see. There was nothing to identify. He tried not to think about another sleepless night on the sea. The sun beat down on his back as it continued its relentless arc through the sky. Finally, he watched it set on the horizon, and the air grew cold, and chilled limbs began to stiffen. Already Ben found himself waiting expectantly for the sun to rise again. The night passed in the same way as the night before.

The nightmares and visions – more of Ben's demons - gleefully returned to haunt his mind and slow his progress. At times it was hard to determine whether he was awake or asleep. His eyes were half opened as he paddled blindly, drifting to some far off land and time**.**

My new job took me away from the green hills of East Tennessee, and out to the coast of California. It was there that I learned to quiet my soul. There where I found solace from my every day life by escaping from the crowded cities to walk along the beaches, talking softly to myself, and to God. It was there, near the ocean, among the rocks and sand, that I began to think clearly. Think of my problems, my past, and my path not yet taken. At times I could feel the breath of God in the wind, and see His powerful hands in the waves. The ocean rolled lazily about, and I felt the reassuring rhythm of the surf calming my thoughts, and paving the way for a more intimate relationship with its Creator; the Creator that would give me a personal peace that passed all understanding in times to come.

The concrete reality of sea, moon, and sky, seemed to slip into something just out of his grasp. Darker shapes crossed his mind, and Ben couldn't tell if he was awake or dreaming. The darker shapes melded into deep reflection. Dreams.

It's ironic that my vision to prepare for this impossible journey came when I was nowhere near that familiar ocean shore.

I was alone in the middle of the Mojave Desert, a hundred miles north of Los Angeles, getting ready to meet some customers for my new boss. The barren nakedness of the windswept desert might have been the catalyst that began to expose my discontentment with life. I remember mulling over the last few years of my life, sifting through my decisions step by step, like the sands that parted beneath my boots as I climbed the steep slope that crawled its way up the rocky mountainside. I knew that something was missing. I was restless, and in a spiritual rut. Simple solutions seemed out of reach. The money that I'd so desperately sought before coming to

California seemed pointless. A means to an end. My goals have changed. I'm not the hard driving graduate with a degree in business that sought fortune and fame more than halfway across the country just a few years back. No, my soul has taken on a freer spirit. I've shed the stuffy old shirt of corporate determination and success. Life's not as simple as it had been in college. I've been dealt a different hand. My mind is struggling to make something of it.

The date was March 13, 1996. It hit me then and there in the middle of the desert. Frighteningly clear and concise. It was as if the mountains had opened up to reveal the secret, and the answer was written in stone.

A goal.

A goal so far out of reach, that my mind reeled with both the dangers, and the anticipation of success.

My hands began to sweat, and my brow furrowed with intensity. I remember. I ran back to my truck and tore through the pages of an atlas that sat on the seat. The blue indication of water stood out on the page. It stood in stark contrast to the brown rock walls that surrounded me. It seemed to leap out before my eyes, and dance in the bright midday sunlight. Never mind the lack of pictures, or clarity of detail, that the map displayed. My mind already began to conjure up the challenges that lay ahead. Dangerous surf, rocky coastlines, and miles and miles of endless ocean. Yes, indeed, it was as if the message had been written in stone. I remember. The hand of nature that I loved and respected so much, was beckoning and calling me into its grasp. There was no doubt about it.

As I stood in the desert alone, afraid, and uncertain of what future my career was going to take, I knew what I was going to do.

Not rational.

But as real as anything has ever been to me.

I am going to South America.

By sea.

That morning it was harder for Ben to awaken from his trance. But, slowly, by mid morning the sun burned away even the darkest shadows. He felt a little foolish for entertaining the ghosts of the night. But were they ghosts? He wasn't clear about the dream.

That day was harder than the last, as exhaustion and fatigue set in. Ben knew that his muscles couldn't take much more abuse without resting. The lack of real sleep seemed to slow down his mind. The hours, minutes, and seconds, crept by. Twice that day he fell asleep sitting in the cockpit. But it didn't matter much now, because he could see, by the subtle changes in the topography that he would arrive in the next town by nightfall.

With the sun setting again, he could hardly bear to face another night alone. He now realized with a start, that he had no idea where he was, or how far he'd come. During the day his progress had been substantial. This he knew. It was as if the sea was finally blessing his journey, and having mercy on his toils. The tide had slackened considerably, and at times he could feel it aiding his progress.

Numerous coves, points, and cliffs, discouraged his calculations as he looked at the map that evening. Trying to locate his whereabouts in the maze of camouflaged wilderness was a challenge his weary mind was rejecting. The sun was still casting its last bit of light over the mountains when he looked ahead and saw a break in the coast line. His heart leaped with hope. Ignoring the pain, he intensified his efforts. An hour later Ben passed by the lighthouse that stood guard over the entrance to the Baia de Los Angeles – the Bay of the Angels.

It welcomed him into its quiet haven.

Chapter 12

Men are born to succeed, not fail.
                    Henry David Thoreau (1817-1862)

With relief, Ben spied the lights of houses emerging one by one, like a string of Christmas lights. He could hardly believe that he had actually made it in three days. A few sailboats anchored on the far side of the bay, and it was there that he made his way to beach his craft, and his weary body. His eyes were so tired that he could hardly see the waves in front of him. But the lure of solid ground beckoned him forth. The thought of a warm meal, some company, and a good night's rest, spurred Ben past the sailboats and onto the beach.

A lone fisherman sat on a stone wall. He rose and came over to help Ben pull the heavy kayak onto the shore. Directly in front of them sat three cottages. The one to the left was vacant. The one to the right had two men on the front porch drinking. On the porch of the middle house an older man sat in a chair, reading a book and drinking a cup of coffee. Like Goldilocks and the Three Bears, Ben found this last one to be just right. He thanked the fisherman for his help, and the man went back to the wall and his fishing rods.

Ben walked up to the older man and, fighting off the urge to sleep, said hello. Quickly, Ben told him about his adventure, and asked where he could get a good meal. "Well, we're from San Diego," the man said, as Ben's mind drifted elsewhere to a nice, thick, juicy, steak - medium rare, with a big baked potato on the side. "Down here fishing every day." Three other men of about the same age came walking out of the front door, curious about the conversation. "By the way, I'm Roger," the first man said, shaking Ben's hand, and then turning toward the others. "And this is Don, my brother Carl, and Phil." More hands were extended, along with curious looks. Ben shook all the hands, and promptly forgot the names. "We were going to have some dinner in awhile. Care to join us? It would beat looking for a restaurant," Phil said.

Ben grinned broadly. He knew he liked the looks of Phil from the beginning, and, besides, Phil had just said the one word that was music to Ben's ears - dinner. "Thank you so much, I'd love to. Do you happen to have a glass of water? I am dying of thirst."

"We got plenty of that," Phil said, as he grabbed a cup off the shelf nailed to the front wall, and poured water out of a twenty gallon container that stood on the stone porch railing. "I've got a good map in the trunk of the van," Phil went on, "and I want to see just exactly where you've come from."

As Ben was busy showing Phil and Roger the places he'd been, Don was busy filleting the fish they'd caught earlier and frying them in a skillet. The smell passed through Ben's senses like a laser, and filled his growling stomach with anticipation.

The steak can wait, Ben thought, *that fish smells good!*

When Phil closed up the map, he said, "Wow, boy! That's some task you've taken on. Now I'm really happy we asked you to stay for dinner. We're honored to have you here."

"I'm honored, as well," said Ben with a smile.

Once again, people willing to share what they had. This time Ben would not be so blind to their needs in return.

God is continuing to bless me, providing points along the way for people to greet me and welcome me into their company.

Ben pondered the thought. He liked Phil, and saw him as a kind and gentle man. That night and the next day they spent talking about the ocean, God, and their families. Phil had a son Ben's age. Ben could sense that what Phil wanted to talk about most was the differing values and outlooks of a younger generation. Ben was happy to oblige, steering away from the details of his expedition to give Phil what little he knew about growing up in the 80's. Phil had also spent some time on sailboats, and he offered to rig a better sail than what Ben had on board.

Even though their time together was short, Ben could feel another bond forming. His respect for his new friend grew with the passing hours. Ben noticed that when Phil talked about himself it was with extreme modesty, and without a hint of arrogance. He was hard working, seemed to make few enemies, and reminded Ben of his grandfather.

Ben's grandfather . . . The memory of him seemed to take Ben back to a better place in time. A time when life seemed to be going well, and had purpose and focus. But since his grandfather had passed away, everything had fallen apart. He never thought he could be so close to someone as he had been with his grandfather.

The stinging sorrow of his death, although a year and a half past, still brings forth a void so intense that my heart aches.

After graduating from the University of Tennessee, Ben had moved to California with the intention of taking over the business that his uncle owned. At least that was the excuse he gave. As he looked back on that move, however, it became clear to him that it was his grandfather, not the job, that he was moving closer to. The two summers prior to his move, Ben had spent in Whittier, California working as an intern in the company that his grandfather started in 1957. It was during that first summer that they'd formed an inseparable bond.

On Friday nights, regardless of other pressing engagements, Ben's grandfather would take him out 'on the town'; which meant they would visit one of the many malls that graced those suburban hills, and then share a meal at a nearby restaurant.

Those were memorable times for Ben, and some of his happiest in California. Every day after work, they would sit on the porch swing by the side of the house and talk for hours. Ben's grandmother would lovingly bring them sodas and snacks, so that the two wouldn't have to interrupt their conversations with meal preparations. One summer they spent every night studying blueprints of the machines that the company owned. Ben hadn't known the first thing about all the funny lines and scribbles that the strange smelling paper brought to life, but the patience and kindness that his grandfather displayed quickly motivated him to learn how to read the prints without error.

The summer of 1993 seemed to hold the promise of a new life, moving close to the two things Ben cherished most, the ocean, and his grandfather. By then grandpa was getting older. To Ben he seemed so frail, as he was nearing the age of eighty. But Ben thought those times would last forever, and over the next two years, he continued to nurture the flower that bloomed within their relationship.

He became my best friend in this new environment of financial responsibilities and hassles. I confided everything to him. Sometimes we'd go out in his backyard where his tool shed stood and work on various projects. Even at his age he could still work harder and longer than I could. I loved him more for that.

Then, one day in December, Ben's grandfather began to weaken. His strength left him, and in his mind he knew he didn't have much time. The fateful evening came as Ben was leaving to go out for the night. He heard the phone ring, picked it up, and with disbelief, heard the voice on the other end telling him that grandpa was in the hospital. He had suffered another heart attack. Racing to the hospital, Ben ran into the emergency room, and into the arms of his grandmother. His aunt was there also, and Ben could tell by the look of anguish on their faces that all was not well.

Grandpa died later that night. Ben was holding his hand. It was all just a bad dream for Ben. He waited for the reality of it to hit like a wall of glass, shattering his peaceful world. But nothing like 'reality' ever happened. Not that night, or many others to come, and not about the death of his dear grandfather.

There is only numbness, and a draining of emotions that seems to flow from my body into a pool on the floor. I feel myself drifting away. Far enough away to build a wall of protection where I can hide in emotional obscurity.

Ben truly waited for emotions to return, but they did not. After the funeral he cried until no more tears came.

I feel used up. Stripped of both sorrow and happiness.

Ben had not shed a tear since then, until that first humbling experience on the ocean when he thought he would have to quit. Then, frustration seemed to close all around with cries of failure.

Failure.

A stinging word to Ben Wade.

A humiliating wreath around his neck.

Maybe that's why it hurts so bad to look back and think about my past. Was I a failure? I can still remember my grandmother's words, so close after my grandfather's death. "The only thing he wanted was to see you take over that company, Ben," she said to me, tearfully.

The memory of those words now filled his mind, and stung what little emotions he had left. A year after his grandfather's death, Ben was still struggling to get out from under his self-inflicted sense of unworthiness; his perception that he didn't have the fortitude to 'stick it out' when things went wrong. He decided that he wouldn't go back to that company, no matter what happened.

But where have my goals drifted? What am I doing to solidify my happiness?

Thoughts that haunted Ben Wade. He knew that he had to crawl out from under the pressure, and do something to gain back his trust in himself. To do something that would require the challenges and dangers that only the ocean – his personal ocean - could provide. Looking back now, he saw that all roads, no matter where he turned or what he did, would lead to that fateful day.

A single juncture in the crossroads of his life.

One direction.

One plan.

One result.

SOUTH AMERICA.

A journey to fame or to oblivion, to life or to death, for young Benjamin Wade.

Chapter 13

None but a coward dares to boast that he has never known fear.
Ferdinand Foch (1851-1929)

Baia de Los Angeles
Baja California, Mexico
September 25, 1996.

B en mused over thoughts of his grandfather as he sat in the shade of the palm-crowned cabaña. The wind, laden with the smells of salt and sea, blew steadily toward the shore, bringing his attention back to the present. He was enjoying this day off, and the scenery was impeccable. Baia de Los Angeles, the bay of the angels, gleamed seductively beautiful in the bright afternoon sun. To the northeast loomed the towering mountains, whose ominous shadows he had passed beneath the previous week.

The mountain chain swung around girding the bay, then meandering along the coast to the south. It jutted out to form a monstrous point that protected the bay from the southern storms. Adjacent to that point, almost connected to the mainland, were several tiny islands that played randomly across the bay. Today they blocked Ben's view to the open waters of the Sea of Cortez. Farther away to the northeastern tip, another large island stood, covered in white from the sea gulls and seals that shared its beaches. This guano-white island stood out in stark contrast to the other brown landscapes, and the blue water beneath its furrowed brow. To the north of this island, and directly in front of the mountain chain, a long arm of sand jutted out from the mainland, adorned with a lighthouse at its tip. Nowhere in a viewer's gaze, sitting in the belly of the bay, could one see open water -

only the islands, one in front of the other.

It was a day of rest, and Ben took the opportunity to stock up on water and other supplies. He had made good time coming into the bay. Ahead of schedule, he could afford to take the rest. That night he made some phone calls, once again assuring everyone of his safety and whereabouts. Most importantly, he told his friend, Christian, of the changes in route so that he could send out the coast guard if needed. He now planned to make his Baja-to-mainland cross from San Fransiquito, a point forty miles south of the bay where he would sleep this night.

The cantina behind where he sat, wafted an enticing diffusion of smells. He thought of the meal from the night before, the one that Phil and the others had prepared and shared with him. The fish tacos had been delicious, and they'd sat past midnight, eating more than four pounds of sea bass among them. Phil had offered Ben a cot to sleep on. It was made of two wooden stands with a burlap bag strung between them. He slept comfortably under the stars, among new friends. The tent that he had pitched earlier stood alone. During the night, he'd heard it flapping noisily in the wind. By morning the tent had doubled over on itself, and had broken one of the fiberglass rods that held it in place. Roger mended the rod with electrical tape, and Ben hoped it would hold in the ensuing months.

It was sad to see the four older men leave early the next day. It was hard enough to leave family and friends back in the States. Now it was becoming a weekly ritual. Make new friends, and then, shortly thereafter, say good-bye. Sometimes he wondered if it would be better not to come ashore.

It always seemed lonelier after being around other people.

Of late, his insecurities had questioned the loyalty of his friends back home.

Have they forgotten about me?

As Ben's time alone progressed, he concluded that they would probably think of him less and less, until he was only a distant, passing memory. He knew that these thoughts were damaging to his mental health, but he found it hard not to get caught up in the depressing loneliness of his solitude.

Daily, he was forced to think of safety, survival, and security. Just once he would have liked to share a beautiful sunset, or an isolated pristine bay, with another person. The tacit support of a companion when things went wrong would have given him needed hope and strength to press on.

But he was all alone in a sea of emptiness.

Ben had only been gone for twelve days, but to him it seemed like twelve months. He studied the map in front of him, and took some comfort in seeing the ground that had been gained. The thought of the miles ahead, though, was overwhelming. He wondered how he could possibly survive the months ahead. These feelings of incompetence stemmed, no doubt, from his loneliness. The expedition had certainly turned out to be an adventure. But the overweighing burden of danger, monotony, boredom, and loneliness crushed down on Ben's soul like the great weight of the sea itself, always present, and unrelenting. Although, in his mind there was now no question of giving up. He wondered what the cost might be. There were so many things to consider: food, water, shelter, safety, number of miles, weather, wind, tides, death, and the elements that conspired to sap the strength from his bones. Certainly it had to get easier as time progressed.

Even the occasional thought that flitted through his mind like a shadow across a darkened room, the thought that he might one day be forced to quit, hung another weight round his neck. There was no stopping this insanity. It was getting dangerously close to overruling everything he knew to be possible, and attainable. Everything said that he was going beyond reason. Ben knew that he must complete the impossible, the unreasonable, the unattainable. There was a part of him that still reached out strongly toward the challenge. Maybe it wasn't just pride that kept him striving for the next town. There was a sense of purpose, knowing that the goal was closer at hand, and the completion of the task could be obtained. A light shined faintly for him, a glimmer of faith. Ben knew that he would not have to wait ten years for the results it illuminated. There would be only one thing that would stand in his way.

The unthinkable. The inevitable. His death.

Nothing else, he concluded, would keep him from his goal. He would make sure of that.

September 26, 1996

The day, and the trials, started early. About a mile from the shore, a ferocious wind came up and drove Ben back into the bay. Helpless in the churning seas, he remembered Carl saying that he'd better get to shore as soon as possible if a Chubásco – the devil wind - hit. Ben was thankful that now he wasn't along the rocky coast he'd traveled the previous week. The wind howled, sucking the sea into the air, often obliterating the point where sky met sea. The kayak took on several gallons of water in the cockpit before Ben made it back to the beach, landing several hundred yards south of where he'd slept the night before. Half blinded by the maelstrom, he quickly dove behind the kayak, cowering in the smallest fetal ball he could manage. He covered his arms and legs to shelter them from the pelting wind-driven sand.

Eventually the wind died down. But the day was already spent, and Ben had wasted so much precious energy that he couldn't hope to leave before the next morning. He quelled the frustrations that rose as he was forced to take another day of rest.

But he looked at the positive side for a change. He was still a day ahead of his schedule; a schedule that he was beginning to care less about as the days progressed. Maybe the time had come when Ben could make the change from an attitude of reckless, mindless, insanity, to a more reasoning calm and enjoyable outlook.

Yes, this is the ticket. Slow down and enjoy this trip.

Taking a deep breath, he let it out slowly to release the tension, and sat down to enjoy the improving view.

The sun was about to set when Ben spied a sailboat cruising in leeward of the islands. She was at least forty feet in length, and sliced gracefully through the blue water under her weather jib and a reefed mainsail. With obvious skill the crew jibed up into the wind, set her bow anchor, dropped the luffing sails, and secured a stern anchor. The beautiful vessel settled into her moorings in the bay close off the beach to where Ben sat.

He had never been in contact with any of these luxury cruisers, and felt slightly intimidated by this first sight of one. He watched intently as the crew, a man, his wife, and their baby, stepped from the sleek sailboat into a motor powered dingy, and headed for shore. They looked friendly enough, and despite his initial reluctance, Ben walked to the quay and struck up a conversation when they landed.

Stuart, Dee, and their six-month-old baby girl, Coral, were making their way down the same coast as Ben. They were planning to go by Costa Rica, and on through the Panama Canal, ending up in the Bahamas next year. Although only thirty years old, the couple had spent several years saving their money to buy a boat and sail around the world. They had set sail from Vancouver, British Columbia, early the previous year, in search of warmer waters and weather. Unexpectedly, the day before their departure, Dee had been told she was pregnant. Without hesitation, they continued their plans, and began their adventure right on schedule the following day. They set sail and left everything behind. Much like Ben, they'd gone out on a limb to pursue excitement, all sure that they were chasing after extraordinary, heartfelt dreams. Along the way, though, they had begun a family.

Nice touch, he concluded.

They were only in the bay for one night to pick up food and water. Ben joined their walk around the town helping them carry the groceries, and enjoying the time to talk. Ben found that it felt good to be able to help someone for a change. He tried to imagine the added difficulty of doing the simplest chores, with the needed attention of a six-month-old baby. They talked along the way about plans and progress. It turned out that they were planning to cross the Sea of Cortez to the very islands that Carl and Gary had insisted that Ben head for.

Coincidence, he thought.

Maybe not.

Over dinner, he asked, "What would you guys think about us leaving together? We could go over to the islands at the same time. I'd planned the same route as you, and I could use your help if things got rough."

"That's an idea," Dee said. But Stuart scowled and added, "I don't think you'll have much of a problem. The weather is supposed to be smooth for the next couple of days. Should be no problem to cross now." He could tell that Stuart didn't want the added responsibilities of his tagging along. But Ben pressed on, "Yes, you're probably right, but I'd feel much better if I had an escort along the way. At least for a little bit."

"I think it would be lovely," Dee said, before her husband could say anything else. "You seem like an interesting man. We'd love to have you on board, right Stuart?" He nodded hesitantly in consent. An uncomfortable silence followed, until Ben assured them that he would not be an intrusion. He would eat his own food, and sleep on the kayak. They would hardly know he was there. Ben didn't think Stuart believed him, but it sounded like the right thing to say.

It seems incongruous that Ben had, until now, thrown caution to the wind, and yet here he was insisting on having help to cross the sea. But he had heard something the night he'd spent with Carl and Gary which chilled his heart, and cast an uneasy shadow on his confidence.

"Good night Carl, Gary," I said when lying down to sleep. After a while, Carl began to talk in his sleep. At first, I thought it was funny, and tried to make out the barely audible words. Soon, the tone of his voice became louder and more commanding. When I finally understood what he was saying, I could barely breathe.

"Ben, don't go," Carl said loudly. "Danger, danger is waiting for you ahead. Stop now. Don't cross over to Mexico. Don't go. Be careful. It makes me so sad. On the second island, Ben. The second island, you're

going to die. Death is waiting for you there." He muttered something else that was incoherent.

But I'd heard enough to strike fear into my heart.

Ben didn't consider himself a superstitious person, but he couldn't forget those words. Now, sitting here in the tiny restaurant on the Baia de Los Angeles, he felt an urgency to accept Dee's offer of safety.

Ben needed their help to cross the Gulf. He was sure of that. In the end, they both consented. All went to their own boats to sleep. Ben headed for the kayak, and Stuart, Dee, and the baby, for their dingy. But before everyone departed, Dee insisted that Ben come aboard the sailboat to sleep. Hesitantly, and with no apparent reluctance from Stuart, he agreed. Lying down on the cushions nearest the steering wheel, Ben wondered if Stuart and he were going to get along. He hated to impose, but his pride was gently fading away. His last thoughts before sleep were comforting. He told himself that if things got too rough between them, he'd just leave and go it alone.

Chapter 14

Without friends no one would choose to live, though he had all other goods.

Aristotle (384 BC – 322 BC)

The *Running Shoe*, the sailboat that belonged to Dee and Stuart, was a forty foot long craft trimmed in blue and white. It was a pretty boat, not too big and not too small. The galley was comfortably small, with two stoves, an ice box, and a sink. Undoubtedly the crew felt like they were roughing it when it came to amenities, but, to Ben it was paradise. The ladder leading down to the galley from the foredeck ran right across the sink, dividing it into two separate parts. Once down the ladder there was a storage area for food to the right, and to the left were two benches and a table. The captain's quarters, with a queen size bed, was the forward cabin. It was littered with books, charts, and pictures of friends and family, long since left behind. It was a well-lived-in boat, and Ben felt at home immediately. On deck, Stuart stored all kinds of fishing equipment and scuba gear. There was even a wind surfer. All the toys, he explained, were for relaxation and fun once the coves and bays had been found.

The next two days were spent in preparation for the crossing, and it wasn't a bad place or time for Ben to be. That morning, they made their way to a hurricane hole, Puerto Don Juan, to stay out of the wind-tossed seas. In Puerto Don Juan they joined an entourage of other cruisers. The crews on the different boats were buzzing with the news that *Running Shoe* was escorting a kayaker making his way to South America. As soon as Stuart let down the anchor, people made their way in dinghies to his boat.

Soon there were a dozen on board, all curious about the tale of the new-comer. Dee made herself busy in the galley, fixing drinks and appetizers for the guests. Ben felt welcomed with open arms. The mood was so relaxing that he decided to break out one of his hand-rolled Honduran cigars that he had stashed for, he thought, the end of trip celebration. But now it seemed right to indulge. Even after everyone had left, Ben was still enjoying the cigar's mild aroma. He noticed that Stuart was glancing at the smoke. Turning to him, Ben asked, "Do you smoke cigars?"

"No," Stuart answered, "well, once, when Coral was born, but it was terrible."

"You ought to try this one. Good taste and very mild."

"Well, it smells awfully good, mate, so I don't mind if I do." Ben handed it over to Stuart and watched as his eyes lit up after an especially big draw.

From then on it became a ritual every night to light up one of Ben's Honduran cigars. He and Stuart would sit on the deck and enjoy the crisp night air, the brilliant stars above, and good conversation. They talked about a civilization long since forgotten, and of each other's hopes and dreams. There were no other sailors in the area close to Stuart's age, and being on board with two females, Ben could see where his – male – company, could be a welcome change. It seemed like this small cigar was bridging the gap. There were no more feelings of hostility, perceived or real, between the two men. Over the next several days that friendship broadened.

Ben was once again keenly aware that it would pain them both to part company.

Stuart was born in Australia, and had met Dee while she was working on a science project there. After dating for six months, Dee had to return to Canada, and it was not long before Stuart followed. Shortly thereafter, they were married and began saving their money to sail the world. Stuart was an outgoing guy. He had a good heart, and always a joke on his lips and a smile on his face. He was fun-loving and ready for adventure, not surprised in the least at Ben's plans to head farther south.

Almost immediately, he began to show Ben where things went, and how the sailboat worked. Soon, Ben felt like part of the crew, which made the awkwardness of his intrusion all the more bearable. Stuart showed him how to tie different knots, which he would have learned in Boy Scouts if he'd ever been to one of their meetings. He asked Ben to tie a bowline, which he promptly botched miserably. Stuart only laughed and said, "Look at this, mate, a granny slip knot, eh?" He had Ben laughing from then on. Eventually, he did learn how to tie all of the required knots for sailing. Ben happily adjusted to life on the sailboat.

Stuart and Ben finished their cigar and, after the guests left, Dee showed him how to dig for clams. The cove where they were anchored provided a good sheltered area, and a good variance between tides. That afternoon the tide was going out. This, Ben was told, was the best time to go clam digging, so they dug their toes into the soft sand where the water stood a couple of inches deep, and Ben followed Dee's lead and found the clams to be easily accessible.

No wonder the Indians loved this coast.

He asked Dee if there were many places like this left. Places so untainted and pure. Her response was no, as she shook her head sadly. Ben took an even greater pleasure then, enjoying what little natural habitat was left. They took only what they could eat, and left the others in the sand for the next visitors. Some of the clams were larger than his hand, and Ben's mouth was watering as they took the bucket back to the boat. Stuart boiled and sautéed the clams until the creatures inside were ready to be eaten. Ben ate almost forty of the tasty morsels, until he began to feel slightly ill.

The canopy was up over the deck, shading them from the hot midday sun. Ben propped his feet over the edge of the railing and let the sun warm his body. This was a life of relaxation he had not experienced over the last several weeks, and he knew it would not last long. Ben truly relished every minute he was on board this small, peaceful, sailboat.

The night of September 26, 1996 was a big event. A lunar eclipse was about to happen, and all the sailors in the area were going onshore to get a better view. They all climbed a couple of hundred feet up the hill, through cactus and thorny brush, to the top of the ridge. From there they could get a good look at the sunset as well as the eclipse. Each boat crew had brought over a plate of food that added up to a fine potluck. Ben helped Dee make a dish of twice-cooked mashed potatoes in clam shells. Blankets were spread out and the food was eaten. Cameras were set on their respective tripods, and everyone sat back and watched the sunset.

Finally, the moon rose, and all could see the sun's shadow quietly and majestically engulf the entire orb. As the shadow crept along the surface of the moon, leaving only blackness behind, the remaining 'lighted' portion turned blood red. Ben couldn't help but think of the Biblical passage in Joel.

"And the moon shall be turned to blood." A sign of the second coming of Christ. When the Savior returns, I wonder if I'll be ready. It will be an

awesome sight to see Him coming out of the sky, making this eclipse, and anything else I've ever seen, small and inconsequential.

The moon crept out from under the sun's shadow, as Saturn stood guard above and to the right of the grey-blue orb. The revelers made their way back down the hill to the harbor. Stuart, Dee, Coral, and Ben, climbed back into the dingy and set out for the *Running Shoe*. Back on board, after putting Coral down to sleep, Dee, Stuart, and Ben, sat out under the stars, drank some rum, and smoked another cigar.

A wave of absolute serenity washed over my soul, engulfing my senses with pure pleasure.

He couldn't help the smile that slipped across his face. Stuart noticed his contentment and nodded knowingly. He shared the same emotions as Ben.

That night in his journal Ben wrote:

My sojourn from needless worry, and the stress of the expedition, has changed this night to an attitude of peacefulness and serenity. I have ceased to worry about tomorrow, the time of day, or the mileage I can make. Even my final destination seems to be far away into the future. So far away that I need not concentrate on it. Now is the time to develop friendships with the people I have met here, and to add enrichment for both parties.

The ocean is such a wonderful creature, and I enjoy it when she and I are not fighting. Her peace steals into my heart, giving me a serenity that few have experienced, and I love her for bringing together and strengthening all who fall within her grasp.

On Friday, September 27, the day that *Running Shoe* and Ben's kayak were to cross toward the mainland, VHF radio alerted the boaters to two tropical storms approaching the area from the south. It was feared they could turn into tropical hurricanes at any moment. Although the water outside was choppy, and the wind whistled across the hills above, inside their cove the water remained calm, and the mood optimistic. They decided to stay put and wait for calmer weather. Ben thanked God once again that he had not tried to be a hero and cross over the day before without the protection of an escort.

Another boat had expressed interest in joining *Running Shoe* to set sail for the island in the middle of the Sea of Cortez. Its skipper was intrigued by the stories of Ben's journey. His boldness (they weren't aware of his fears) had opened a door to the sailing world for Ben.

Several of the captains remarked that they had heard news of his story. Sometimes, Ben felt odd being among the older generation of the cruising world, but they made him feel like a celebrity. Stuart urged Ben to flag down every sailboat that he paddled close to, and ask for any supplies he might be lacking. Stuart even made sure that the news bulletin for the southern latitudes informed other boaters to keep an eye out for Ben's small kayak. Ben was grateful to the couple who introduced him to this new world, and to those who accepted him with welcoming generosity and approval.

The next morning the radio reported that both storms had changed course and were on their way to the open waters of the Pacific Ocean. Relieved, all said their goodbyes and headed out. At first they ran into some rough seas around the point, rolling up and down on waves over ten feet tall. It was a hard day, but the island continued to loom near, and they were rewarded by actually seeing the results of their progress. At 5:00 p.m., Stuart called out to Ben and said that they were going to go past the Isle of Partita, which had been in their sight for most of the afternoon. The next island was six miles away, and, at their present rate, they should be landing in just over an hour.

But they didn't figure on the currents between the two islands, and their ignorance turned out to be somewhat of a mistake.

Stuart hailed the kayak following in his wake, "Ahoy, Ben. We're making three knots now, so it'll only take us two hours to reach the next island. Can you make it, mate?"

Ben waved, and shouted that he could.

Currents between the islands, though, would see to it that those two hours would turn into five. Were it not for the patience of Stuart, who slowed the engines down to further control the sailboat, Ben might have gotten discouraged, and headed back to the previous island. At 10:00 p.m., after darkness had long since set in, the island's ghostly form slowly emerged from the black horizon. At first they couldn't tell it from the rest of the sky. As it solidified its place in the distance, they could feel the current flowing at them pick up in intensity. It felt like they were standing still. "We're not even going one bloody knot," Stuart yelled, his engines at full throttle. To make matters worse, *Sunward*, the other boat they were traveling with, was nowhere in sight. It was a bigger and far heavier boat than *Running Shoe,* and they were struggling harder against the strong current. Now and then Ben could turn around and make out the *Sunward's* mast light, peeking out above the fog. Finally, though, it disappeared for good.

Shortly after 10:30 p.m., Ben and the *Running Shoe* pulled into the small harbor of the island. It took another hour for the *Sunward* to find it, and that whole time was spent on the VHF radio questioning quite loudly the decision to continue.

"*Running Shoe, Running Shoe*, this is *Sunward*."

"*Sunward*, this is *Running Shoe*. Over. Channel thirteen. Over."

"We can't see anything out here right now, Dee," said Ron, the captain of the other ship. "I think it was a bad idea to come to the next island to-night. We should have camped for the night at Partita when we had the chance. The sea sure is rough right now, and I don't know if it's a fog or what, but the visibility is down. I wish we wouldn't have pushed it this far tonight."

Ron had wanted to seek shelter near the previous island, but Stuart had urged all to press on, thus the resentment in Ron's voice. "Sorry about that, Ron," Dee said into the microphone, trying to soothe the angry captain. "Nothing we can do now, eh? Just keep coming toward our mast light. It's pretty rocky around the harbor where we are right now, so we'll wait for you here at the entrance. Once you catch up, you can follow us in. We've been here before and know the way." Dee was cool about the situation, and slow to react to Ron's agitated comments. Stuart and Ben were listening to the VHF conversation, slightly amused at the exasperation so evident in Ron's voice. "Okay, Dee, but I still say that we should've stayed on the other island tonight."

Drop it, they all thought.

"I'll talk to you in a bit. *Sunward* out."

The harbor, such as it was, was on the south side of the island, and, from the looks of the chart, surrounded by treacherous submerged rocks. It was now pitch black, and the moon was just starting to rise. Eventually, *Sunward* caught up. But now he had a new complaint. "*Running Shoe, Running Shoe*. We lost our damn dingy back there. The waves were too big," Ron shouted, not waiting to switch over to another private channel. "We're going to have to go look for it right now."

It was a fruitless effort to go sailing back and forth in the middle of the night looking for a six-foot piece of wood, especially with the currents the way they were. Their dingy, Ron said, was worth a pretty penny, so no one argued as *Sunward* turned back around. All aboard *Running Shoe* could hear them arguing about who tied the dinghy on last, just before they switched off the radio. They watched the mast light slowly disappear as *Sunward* headed back into the night.

Stuart was getting tired, and not a little irritable. He said he was not going to wait for their return. "The sea and the currents are too bloody rough tonight," he said. "I'm going to anchor the boat, and I'll just have to talk them in when they get back." Dee went up to the bow to look for exposed rocks with a flashlight. Stuart told Ben to keep an eye on the depth meter. "If that meter reads twenty five feet, you'd better let me know, mate," he said. "Read out the numbers every ten feet, okay?"

"Aye, aye, captain," Ben said, enthused to be a part of the crew. The meter currently read sixty-seven feet, and they headed straight for the cove, and into the shadow of the rock wall beyond. Dee and Ben shouted encouraging advice to the captain. The ocean was still pretty rough, and all the members of the boat were holding on to the railing. "One hand for the boat, and the other for yourself," Stuart had said earlier. Coral was asleep below, oblivious to, and no doubt used to, the commotion above. The depth meter was now holding at a steady forty feet, and Ben knew they were getting close. Usually, Stuart told Ben, he anchored the boat in thirty feet of water. Only a little further to go. The keel of the sailboat, Ben had been told, went down into the water six feet. So, if the meter ever showed that number they were in trouble.

The water grew calmer as they entered the protective stretches of the cove. All of a sudden the numbers on the depth meter flashed rapidly, as if in agitation. They jumped from forty to thirty and to twenty-two in a matter of seconds.

Ben shouted out the changes, and he could hear Dee shouting her own warnings from the bow.

The bottom was shoaling up fast.

Stuart reacted to the strain in their voices, turning the wheel quickly in the opposite direction.

Dee yelled for him to back up.

Quickly jamming the gear into reverse, Stuart pulled down the throttle for maximum power.

The *Running Shoe* still drifted forward from the momentum she had.

Ben called out the numbers as they continued to get smaller.

The boat was slowing down, and would eventually move in reverse, but they didn't know if it would be in time.

"Ten, nine, eight, seven ...," he called out.

They all tensed and gripped the railing waiting for the rocks below to rip open the hull of the boat.

But the blow never came. They had caught it in time, and Ben yelled out the growing numbers triumphantly. Coral, still unaffected by the mayhem, slept on.

Sunward came dragging into the rocky harbor well past midnight.

Stuart, tired from the long day, was in no mood to listen to Ron's complaints. They had not found their dingy, and everyone could still hear him whine about the poor decision to continue. After a polite "good night", Dee switched off the VHF. Everyone was exhausted from the long day, and hearing Ron vent was the last thing they needed to hear. "Why did they lose the dingy, Stuart? Were the waves really that rough," Ben asked, as they got ready for bed. "No, they weren't that bad. It was probably because Ron tied the old granny slip knot, and the boat just slipped away." They both chuckled over this one, trying to keep their laughter low because *Sunward,* and its scowling captain, were now anchored just a few feet away.

For now, everyone was safe and sound. They switched off the lights and went to bed – after, of course, a few smokes of the cigar.

Chapter 15

A baby is God's opinion that the world should go on.
Carl Sandburg (1878 – 1967)

T he next day they all agreed to stay in the harbor, and Ben didn't object. His muscles were again sore from the previous day's paddling, and he was getting used to a little relaxation. While *Sunward* insisted on going out again to look for the lost boat, the crew of *Running Shoe* decided to put ashore on the tiny uninhabited island and go for a hike. Dee wrapped Coral in a light cotton shawl so that her soft, delicate, pink skin would not be exposed to the harsh rays of the sun. Then she was put into a jumper – the Australian term for a sweater - that hung around Stuart's shoulders. Soon they were exploring the island.

There was no running water on the island, but they still saw signs of rabbits and other smaller critters. The path wound its way up and around the point, giving them an excellent view of the sailboat and the cove. It was easy to tell from this viewpoint why Stuart had been so cautious when entering the cove the night before. Scattered all around the boat lay the dark shadows of treacherous submerged rocks, lying just a few feet below the water's surface. "Stuart, you are the man for getting us in safely last night," Ben said. "Well, the harder it is to get into an anchorage, the more shelter it tends to give. But I wouldn't have tried to get in there at night if I hadn't been here once before during the day, mate," Stuart responded.

It took another hour before they stood at the top of the hill that rose five hundred feet above the bay. The last few turns of the trail had been very rocky and perilous. Ben watched several times, as rocks and dirt on the path tumbled silently over the edge. He was an experienced mountain climber, and was carefully picking his way along the edge, looking at the sea that frothed below. It was a straight drop to the water, and they were all being very cautious. Ben was amazed at Stuart's agility, making the same maneuvers as he, but with a fifteen pound baby clutching his chest. Ben followed his footsteps as he continued without the use of his hands which gently held and protected his child.

Ben envied Coral for the life she would lead. Starting out at such a young age, she would have no choice but to pursue the adventurous lifestyle of her parents.

No doubt she will one day be more adventurous than me! Mr. Adventure, himself, Benjamin Wade! Ha!

From the peak, they could see not only the boat in the harbor, but the island, and most of the sea that surrounded her. Stuart pointed to the distant peak of an island on the eastern horizon, and said that it was their next destination. The ocean spread out before them like a great carpet, and they sat atop it, enjoying the ride. The different and blended hues of blue and green in the sea sparkled in the late morning sun. The air was fresh and flavored with the smell of the sea and the mix of life along the water's edge.

After resting awhile, Stuart pointed. "Look, there's *Sunward*. The poor bastard doesn't look like he found his dingy, eh?" Ben took the binoculars out, and confirmed what Stuart had just said. The glint of light from the sailboat showed no small craft in tow. "We better get down to our boat so that we can be there when he starts complaining again," Dee chuckled. They set off down the hill.

Though they were giving Ron a hard time about losing the boat, they really knew he wasn't that bad of a guy. Normally he was a soft-spoken Canadian. On a budget like the rest of them, he was rightfully frustrated.

Ron suggested, after he reset his anchor, that Stuart take them diving for lobster. Ron asked Ben if he wanted to go. There was no question about that, of course he wanted to go. They all suited up and dove overboard. There were only two spears, one for Stuart and the other for Ron. They did have an extra set of fins and a mask, so after they dove in Ben followed shortly. Besides, he had a diving knife he could use.

It was a beautiful spot to dive, and an even better one for lobster. The rocks that lay below were a haven for all sorts of beautiful fish. As he dove beneath the surface, Ben's eyes were opened to a whole new world. Blue fish, yellow fish, and many other different colors, flitted in and out among the rocks. There were sea anemones with fingers extended, waiting for smaller fish to swim by. Ben touched the nearest one, and watched as the tentacles withdrew from his touch.

After Stuart caught several lobsters, he stood on top of one of the submerged rocks. He and Ron were busy talking about building a campfire on the beach that night. Ben was paddling toward them when some giant crabs caught his eye. They were milling about on the rocks to his right, and he was determined to have a closer look. He turned and swam toward the rocks. The sea bottom took a sudden sharp turn upward and Ben scraped his knee on the hard coral. He adjusted his mask and took a look at the configuration below him. He now realized that he'd have to crawl on hands and knees through the shallow water in order to reach the other side. Halfway across the shelf of rocks, Ben decided to explore the beauty of the marine life that lay hidden in some of the smaller niches.

The first thing he saw made his heart stop.

Inches from his outstretched hand, the beady eyes of a stonefish, hidden and camouflaged among the rocks, looked up at Ben. Its deadly barbs, already fanned out along its back, waited for his hand to descend on the lethal body. Ben froze in mid stroke and waited, hoping that it would not swim toward him. One prick from those three-inch spines would inflict enough poison to paralyze him. Three days from the nearest town, he wouldn't survive long enough to get to medical treatment. Ben slowly moved his hand to his side, and saw with relief that the fish was not going to attack. It seemed content to lie still, waiting for its next victim.

The stonefish, or scorpion fish, as some of the residents of Mexico call it, is one of the deadliest species of fish in the ocean. It's armed with three inch long barbs on its back and belly. The skin is brown and gray, blending and changing to the colors of its surroundings. If a predator of any type comes too near, the stonefish's spines spring out. The hunter becomes the hunted. Once the poisonous barbs pierce the flesh of another animal, the victim is quickly paralyzed. If not treated immediately the poison will work its way to the heart. The ending is a painful death, as the heart palpitates furiously before collapsing. The stonefish was only two to three feet in length, but from the stories he had heard from different sailors and fisherman, this was a creature to be feared and respected.

Ben was cautious at first, and a little nervous, as he waited for his heart to resume a normal beat. As he got accustomed to this deadly creature, he was enthralled at being so near to a creature that some said was as old as the sea itself. Returning the icy glare of the stonefish, Ben motioned for Ron and Stuart to come have a look.

Stuart had earlier been telling them a story on the dos and don'ts of swimming around the rocks. They stood waist deep in the water with their masks held tightly against their faces. From several respectful feet away, they anxiously looked down at the brown and gray tiger stripes on the back of the fish. It lay quietly watching them, confident that its reputation had proceeded it, and confident that it was feared by all. Ben looked at its coloring, and elegantly curved spines, and found it quite beautiful, in a rugged sort of way. Excitement buzzed through his head, and he tasted the makings of a kill.

Perhaps this creature had inflicted pain and death to unsuspecting swimmers, Ben thought.

I was suddenly filled with an unquenchable desire to kill.

He told Stuart of his intentions. With a look of warning in his eyes, Stuart handed Ben his spear. "You'd better hit that sucker dead between the eyes, mate," Stuart said with a rueful grin. "Or the bloody thing will swim out and barb us all." Ben certainly didn't want that to happen. He put his head under the water and lifted the spear, aiming with one eye closed. His hand shook a little as he tightly gripped the handle. It was the first time he had ever used such a weapon, and he wondered if his accuracy would be good enough to kill with one shot. He took a deep breath through the mouthpiece of the snorkel to calm his nerves. He could hear his heart pounding in his ears, as he breathed deeply again, this time holding the breath.

The stonefish sat motionless, waiting for Ben to make a move. *"Hey you! I'm going to enjoy splitting your cocky brain in two. So just stay there and continue to think you're too good to move."* Ben waited another second, then let go of the spear.

He can't say that he saw the moment the three-pronged barbs entered his prey's head.

My eyes blinked the moment I released the weapon. The quickness and fluidity of the spear as it sped through the water must have taken only a second to hit its target. when I opened my eyes, I saw that it was a direct hit.

As it attempted to violently wrench itself free from the spear, the stonefish jumped. This immediately caused a similar reaction in the three men watching. The movement sent shock waves along the length of the shaft that lay clasped in Ben's right hand.

It was surprising to feel such strength from a relatively small fish. So much so that I almost let go of the rod. But I gripped the shaft tighter, and brought the fish above the surface of the clear water.

Ben could hear Stuart yelling and clapping behind him, proud of his student's success. He brought his capture to the rocks where he had earlier seen the crabs, who must have sensed the bloodthirstiness of these hunters, and scurried off to safer locations. The stonefish was still trying to free itself, even after several minutes without air. On the rocks where they could see more closely, it was evident that it had, indeed, been a great shot. Beginner's luck, no doubt. One barb went through its left eye, the other through the middle of the brain, and the third had caught the right side of it's gills. Taking out his bowie knife and careful to avoid the barbs on top, he plunged the blade deep into its brain, splitting the skull with a sharp crack. With a final flop, the dreaded stonefish gave up its valiant struggle, and settled down on top of its rocky grave to die.

Ben looked at the other two men and grinned. Stuart reached over and patted him on the back. "Good job, mate! Don't get too close to it, there. Careful. Those barbs will kill you even after its dead." That was definitely true. Later, Ben took out one of the three inch spines for a reminder. Carefully, he put it into a protective glass jar. Unattached, the deadly poisons could still kill years after the rest of its body had deteriorated.

That night they all converged on the tiny beach ringing the harbor. A bonfire was built for warmth, and a smaller fire was lit to cook the food.

Later, Ben would record, and look back at, these carefree times with great joy. They were unrivaled through the rest of the trip, and enhanced by the delightful new friends he'd made. These were some of Ben's most relaxing times in a perilous, soon-to-be dangerous journey. They ate lobster, scallops, grouper, and the stonefish. Dee suggested after dinner that they pile all of the rocks around the campsite into the fire. They spread out a tarp over an enclosed area between two large boulders, and Stuart and Ben, using an empty cooking pot, gathered the heated rocks from the fire and put them in a pile under the awning. As they all gathered around the intense heat of the rocks, Dee took out some eucalyptus oil from her bag and poured it over the rocks. Steam burst forth, and the air was filled with the scent of the oil, its moisture rising, and stinging nostrils with its strong, sweet vapors.

The warmth inside the makeshift sauna eventually grew too hot for all but Stuart and Ben. They continued to urge the others to bring more rocks, and they sat there for another thirty minutes, squatting in the sand and sweating from every pore until the oil was used up. Ben's nose was numb from the constant sting of the eucalyptus oil. The rising steam filled the air in those close quarters, and his eyes were stinging with moisture of their own. Sweat beaded up along his brow. Both Stuart and he were drenched with a mixture of oil and sweat from head to toe.

Dee brought in an old wooden flute. Ben put it to his lips and filled the night air with its low, booming sound. After awhile, they climbed out of the tent. It was refreshingly cool outside the sauna and, ignoring the others, Ben walked down to the water's edge a few yards away. The sea was perfectly still as he sank down, letting her cool arms encircle his sweating form.

Ben allowed himself to float out a few yards from shore. After washing off the excess oil from his arms and legs, he looked back at the warm glow from the fire. Stuart was standing there beside his wife. Ben's thoughts were clear as he looked up at the heavens that shone brightly on the cloudless night.

They were in the middle of the Sea of Cortez, basking in its beauty and serenity.

I lay on my back and floated on the dark sea. The water was cool after the hot sting of the sauna. The stars shone with the brightness one only sees deep in a wilderness, and I felt a strange calmness wash over me as I floated there among my many thoughts. This is the best day of my life that I can recall. Here I am on this tiny barren island in the middle of the vast Sea of Cortez, and yet I want for nothing. I have dined like a king on the noblest of foods, and relaxed in the comfort of an old world spa, all while surrounded by friends, the hands of nature, and the majesty of the ocean.

Just how far has 'civilization' truly progressed?

He didn't try to answer. But he had more questions.

We considered this glorious coast as waiting to be 'discovered' by the 'civilized' conquistador. But it already was enjoyed years ago by the Indians that we 'moderns' fought persistently to drive off. Why couldn't the manipulative powers of the modern day government stop to think, if only for a moment, of the thousands of lives they trample by barging into other's cultures, and destroying the most natural and simplest of pleasures?

This is paradise the way God meant it to be. The Indians knew that secret. The secret of God. They only wanted to preserve what was theirs. Given to them by God. But the 'civilized world' had insisted that the land of those enduring nations be wiped out. And the economic pollution of the earth's wonderful resources is continually choked by the bone of greed and power.

Chapter 16

Courage is resistance to fear, mastery of fear – not absence of fear.
Samuel Clemens (1835 – 1910)

The next night the sailors camped in Dog Bay on the eastern tip of Isla Tiburon. They had hoped to see a trace of the Indians that once claimed this island as their own, but the only thing that was left on the shore were a few old rusted cans and several pieces of wood. Stuart informed Ben that the *Running Shoe* would be leaving the next day to go back over to Baja, and continue down its coast to La Paz.

It was time to part company again, and Ben thanked them all with heartfelt gratitude. The past several days had been an uplifting experience for his soul. Once again he couldn't find words appropriate for his emotions, and he didn't like long goodbyes. After sailing out from the bay for a few miles, Stuart lowered the kayak into the water and held the line firmly in his hand. Ben looked around the deck. "I really feel like I made some good friends here," Ben said to Dee and Stuart. He stood at the edge of the deck just beneath the blue awning, ready to climb into his kayak and set off. "Likewise, mate," Stuart said clasping his hand firmly. "Don't forget all of those knots I taught you."

"I won't," Ben said laughing.

"You take care," Dee exclaimed, giving Ben a warm hug. "Remember what we said. We're going to be in Mazatlan for Thanksgiving, and there's going to be a great big feast. I want you to be there and feel welcomed as our guest." Ben kissed little Coral goodbye and said, "I will definitely see you both for Thanksgiving turkey. You can count on that." He turned around and settled into the kayak. With another wave of sorrow, and ensuing loneliness, he pushed off through the waves and headed east for the mainland of Mexico.

October 1, 1996
East of Isla Tiburon
Adrift on the Sea of Cortez

I float aimlessly for the remainder of the day, lost in obscure thoughts and visions. I feel a loneliness that is more difficult to cope with than before. It is the first time in five days that I have slept without company. As the sun sets I can barely make out the Mexican coastline in the distance. I seem as unattached and separated from it as I do from the human race. I had not anticipated this sorrow, and I feel a wave of anger roll over me. Uncomfortable with the departure of my new friends, I am not confident that I will allow myself to bond quickly with the next people I meet.

Ben climbed out on the flat stern deck of the replenished kayak and strapped several bungee cords around his waist and legs. Stretching out just inches above the swells, he felt the rhythm of the sea beneath him as he settled in for another restless night adrift. The kayak was far enough away from land that there would not be a problem of running into any rocks. The waves were choppy that night, and the wind picked up. By now he was again getting used to the five foot swells that crested a foot above his head. The strength of the current worried him as he swayed with the rhythm of the waves, but the shore did not get any closer, and the night passed the celestial baton to an orange and baby blue sunrise.

Studying the charts with Stuart two days before, Ben had learned about the Canal de Infernillo – the *Straits of Little Hell*. It lay between Isla Tiburon and Bahio Kino, the closest port city in Mexico. He was told that the currents in that area were so strong that a visible wall of water, sometimes four feet high, could be seen at the changing of the tides. The warnings on the charts of this area were clear and concise, "Boaters, avoid this channel at all costs!"

Some people have called him "crazy", while others use the word "adventurous". But one thing Ben Wade is not is stupid. He wanted nothing to do with those currents. He set his compass and headed well south of the treacherous waters. A stiff wind blew from the south and headway was difficult. It was obvious to Ben that he wasn't going to reach the mainland by nightfall. Reluctantly he went about preparing the kayak for the night.

Drifting at night was just one cause for concern. Another was getting run down by larger boats that wouldn't be looking out for a craft as small as Ben's. His only defense was to switch on a light he'd strapped to his forehead to warn anyone who was out that night. Off in the distance, near the entrance to the Bay of Kino, Ben could see lights from the shrimp boats. Fortunately, none of them came his way.

The lights twinkled in the dark night. The moon had not yet risen, and the water was very dark. The slightest noise was magnified by the silence, and the lack of visibility once again played on Ben's mind. The gentle slap of the waves against the hull was no longer a peaceful sound. It was one filled with sharks and other creatures that would conspire to disturb his rest, or worse. At times the waves seemed to grow still. But then, after a few minutes of rest, they would rise up forcefully, and hungrily attack the kayak. Once or twice Ben felt the movement of something beneath the boat, possibly a shark, but nothing surfaced. Each time for that long moment he held his breath and waited, knowing that the beasts that lurked below could hear the pounding of his heart and sense his fear.

Ben's imagination conjured black images.

I feel their eyes staring out like lifeless souls from the dark.
I feel small and helpless in the middle of the ocean, a mere speck on the massive surface of an enormous, moving mass of energy.

The waters where the kayak bobbed were known for shark attacks, and Ben wondered just how long his luck would hold out. This night he stayed in the cockpit longer than normal. If a shark did attack he didn't want to be in a vulnerable position.

Easy to see. Easy to eat!

Twice during the night Ben switched off his headlight to recheck his bearings by the glow of the city lights of Kino. Twice, to his dismay, he found that he was drifting too far north and into the mouth of the Canal de *Little Hell*. Both times he sat up and paddled due south, swinging the kayak around until the compass mounted on the top of the bow pointed to the correct setting. Ben was attempting to compensate for, and battle, the powerful eddies, whirlpools, and currents, that he couldn't see and couldn't hear. But he knew their deadly pull was near, and vigilance was the only defense. The night was long, sleep was short, and without rest.

Ben had paddled nonstop the day before. The twelve hours of continuous activity compounded with the lack of sleep almost proved to be fatal.

107

Now he couldn't sleep for fear of being attacked or driven off course by the currents.

I can not remember the early morning hours.

Just before the sun came up, and a quiet calm settled across the ocean's surface, he finally dozed off for about half an hour. That was the only sleep Ben got in a twenty-four-hours. When the sun did peak over the horizon, he was so weak from lack of sleep, food, and rest, that his hands shook uncontrollably. His body felt fragile and exhausted. His mind felt detached and lightheaded. He was truly suffering from the abuse and torture he'd put his body through over the seventy-two hours since he left the sailboats.

October 3, 1996
Nearing Bahia Kino

The city was near, only about five miles away. Ben had drifted in close during the night. He shook his head vigorously to quell the disorientation. Once again, ignoring the pain that wracked every limb of his body, he dug into the ocean's surface like a madman, pushing the kayak through the water with fury. Ben strained to reach the shore where he knew he would find rest.

From the position of the morning sun, he could see that he could probably reach one of the northern beaches by noon. The water around the kayak was a light brown, a clue that it was fairly shallow. Ben guessed it to be about forty feet. The waves had settled down, and he was making good progress, even though his body was still under incredible stress. His breathing came ragged and shallow. Paddling mechanically, Ben's thoughts drifted to the lunch he would buy in a pretty little cantina. There had to be one.

Suddenly, the kayak gave a jolt.

He looked around startled, figuring he'd hit a sandbar.

But the kayak was still moving steadily forward.

He continued on, his senses now alert.

He scanned the water in every direction.

What is it?

A noise to his right . . . a noise like the suction of water down a drain.

Ben swung to look in that direction.

At first everything remained calm.

Nothing seemed extraordinary.

Then the waves parted, and a fearsome fin slowly emerged.

Another pod of dolphins? A wishful, naïve, thought.

But even as the thought arose, he knew that it was a false hope. This creature was not moving in a playful manner.

It was much too deliberate, its path aimed straight at Ben's tiny, defenseless, boat.

The fin continued above the surface, sharp edged and ominous.

It closed the distance between them, faster than Ben thought possible.

It sluiced side to side, a few inches at a time.

It taunted its victim, dancing one final dance.

My breath caught in my throat. I couldn't even scream. Everything slowed down. I stopped paddling and watched. The shark's fin slowly sank back into the water only a few feet from my outrigger. I could see the elongated snout. I reflexively reared back as it swam powerfully underneath the kayak. The water rippled eerily around me, propelled by the motion just below the surface. It slapped the outrigger sharply. I gripped the paddle tightly with both hands, and waited, white-knuckled and rigid with terror.

Ben sat wide eyed and braced himself for a second attack.

He felt the impact as the beast became more aggressive.

The shark seemed to sense a kill and the fear in its prey.

This second time, as it passed beneath the kayak, Ben could see the brown streaks along its back.

It was a sand shark.

These sharks were known to attack anything.

He estimated this one to be over nine feet long.

Again the fin emerged and circled to his left.

Ben fumbled for one of his knives, but in his haste he dropped it over the side, and almost lost hold of the paddle.

He became keenly aware of just how close he sat to the water. Ben was only inches above its surface, and he felt as helpless as a web-trapped bee, watching the stealthy approach of the spider.

Sometimes it was on top of the water, then just a few inches below.

Wherever it went, the water moved and swirled to make room for this perfect predator of the sea.

When the shark emerged a few yards away, Ben sensed that this time it would attack.

He grasped the paddle, squeezing until his knuckles ached.

He watched the monster approach in seeming slow motion, gills flared, and jaw flexed, for his final coup.

When the shark was only a few feet away Ben raised the paddle in anticipation.

The shark lurched forward in a terrifying explosion of sea spray.

Its gaping, jagged-tooth filled mouth reared out of the water inches from Ben's exposed waist.

Ben peered into the eyes of the beast that flexed its muscles against his boat.

With all his might he thrust the oar forward, and into the open jaws of the shark.

There was a sharp cracking noise. A noise like a tree being splintered in two by an axe.

Then came the moment of deadly struggle.

The shark's tail whipped around and slammed into the side of the boat.

Ben lost his balance, and water sloshed into the cockpit.

He let go of the paddle with one hand, and flailed wildly for the edge of the kayak.

He would not be thrown out.

The shark grasped the paddle in a death grip.

Ben held the other end in white knuckled fear of losing his only weapon.

With a final vicious jerk, the shark loosened itself from the paddle, and with a quick flick of its tail, turned around and slipped back into the murky water from whence it came.

Ben feared that the paddle had been broken.

With eyes hard to focus and trembling hands, he saw that only the tip had been split in two.

Slowly turning the paddle for a closer look, he froze, staring.

One of the shark's flesh ripping teeth was lodged in the broken section of the paddle, wedged tightly in the fiberglass structure.

Ben pulled it free and looked at it, shuddering at the thought that it could have sliced through his stomach, had he been a second too slow. It was then that Ben noticed the gash in his left hand just above the middle knuckle.

Reality set in as adrenaline ebbed, and a crimson flow trickled, then ran, down over his wrist and into the water. He took out the medical kit stowed behind the seat and tried to wrap the cut in gauze. His hand shook so violently now that he could barely cut the tape that bound the gauze.

Ben saw the spreading stain on the brown water.

He jerked his hand back over the cockpit. He didn't want any blood to alert other sharks in the area. Blood began to pool in the tiny cockpit as Ben looked at the blood drip from the saturated gauze. He grabbed a tee shirt from where he'd stuffed it earlier and wrapped the wound. Blood soon seeped through the mass of cotton cloth.

It wouldn't stop.

Am I going to bleed to death right here?

He pressed as hard as he could on the wound and stared in disbelief and a touch of panic.

I don't think I could have moved from my trance-like state if my life depended on it.

It would have.

His nerves slowly calmed down and the blood flow diminished to a trickle. It would bleed this way for another day.

As he often did, Ben then gave thanks to God for his continued safety, even if this was a very close call. He paddled on, now looking out more closely for further disturbances.

There were no other mishaps that morning, and no more sharks.

He reached the shores of Bahia Kino a few minutes after noon, exhausted and shaken. Events of the last several days, coupled with a total lack of rest, had taken its toll. It took super human effort, as Ben spent his last ounce of strength to tie the safety line to a nearby palm tree.

He crawled beneath the outrigger of the kayak, and fell into the sleep of the dead, this time devoid of dreams.

Chapter 17

I show you doubt, to prove that faith exists.
Robert Browning (1812-1889)

Evening, October 3, 1996
Bahia Kino, Mexico

Ben awoke in the early evening feeling refreshed. He sat up and looked around as he brushed the sand off of his back, and tore into a PowerBar that begged for his attention. Ben stood, shaking off the stiffness, and walked to a road that was several yards up from the beach. He looked one way, then the other, twice before he saw it. A most welcome sight. About half a block down the street, half buried in the drifting sand, was a pay phone. A bright yellow pay telephone. It was the first Ben had seen since San Felipe. A big grin crossed his sunburned face as he thought of the people in Los Angeles who would get a collect call from Mexico that day.

Most were surprised that he'd made it across the Sea of Cortez alive. Ben felt on top of the world. His world. He had traveled over five hundred miles, and he was still alive and healthy. Except for the cut on his hand, now clotted and sore, Ben had suffered no lasting physical injuries so far. He felt a new wave of support from family and friends. They seemed to realize that he might just make it alive.

A man zoomed up on his moped, stopped, and stared at Ben. He was a white man named Frank, and he was shocked to see another white man in the city. With a laugh and a handshake, Ben and Frank settled into a relaxed chat. Frank invited Ben to his place to clean up and spend the night.

The ever-trusting Ben was elated.

God keeps putting people into my life every time I turn around.

Frank's place was a half mile down the beach. Ben recovered his kayak and pushed off into the shallows. In a few minutes of practiced paddling he pulled up on the beach in front of the house Frank had described. Frank sat out in front, sipping some type of frozen drink. Ben walked up from the shore, his deplorable appearance being painfully evident. Without saying a word, Frank pointed to an outdoor shower. It was Ben's first fresh water shower in almost a month. It felt great to wash away the sand, sweat, and Aloe Vera lotion, that stood in little white lumps all over his skin. Over the next two days he showered as often as he could, sometimes every hour.

Frank had recently moved to Mexico, and his nemeses, Ben soon found out, were women. Bald and with a tan that even the Mexicans envied, Frank was a mild-mannered middle-aged man, who drove around town daily on his little scooter looking for young, available Mexican ladies. Much to Ben's relief he didn't drink much, and the first thing offered to him was water.

Frank was plainly homesick, and he kept talking about his old life in California. Ben felt a little sorry for him at first. But as he continued to talk about the boat he used to have, and the business he used to run, by the end of the day Ben was weary of the mindless chatter. Ben figured that after they watched the news on his color TV, the first he'd seen in Mexico, he would get out of the house for some fresh air. At the right moment, he thanked Frank and excused himself.

Ben walked down the street to the bright yellow, half buried pay phone he'd used earlier. He picked it up and dialed. After a couple of rings a familiar voice answered. "Hello."

"Heather? Hey, it's me," Ben said, thrilled to hear her voice. "Oh, my goodness, Ben? Are you okay?" She squealed. The enthusiasm in her voice seemed to reach out through the phone and touch him. "Yeah, I'm fine. I made it across to the mainland in one piece. I'm in a town called Bahia Kino," Ben said, speaking too rapidly, and revealing his weariness. "Are you all right, Ben?" She asked with concern. "I'm okay, just tired. It took a little longer than I thought."

"I know. I've been worried about you. You said you'd call in six days. When you didn't, I thought something had gone wrong. I called Christian yesterday and he hadn't heard from you either. He was so worried, I think he even called the Coast Guard."

"That's what I heard," Ben replied quietly. He was sorry to have caused everyone so much worry. "What happened?" Heather asked, trying to keep the anxiety from cutting her words too short. "Oh, the usual," he answered, trying and failing, to be nonchalant. "Strong winds, high waves. I did get some help from two sailboats. Met some really great people. Anyway, I had to avoid this channel they call 'little hell'. I paddled south several miles to get away from the currents."

Ben purposely left out the shark attack.

No sense in causing her more worry.

"It's so good to hear your voice," she said. Ben could feel his face flush with her warmth. "I miss you, baby," he said. "Are you going to be able to come down and meet me somewhere?"

"That depends on whether or not you're going to be good."

"No problem with that," Ben replied emphatically, "I'll get a room with two double beds if I have to."

"That won't be necessary, Benjamin. Just get two rooms." They both laughed. "I can't wait to see you," Ben continued. "I'll be in San Carlos in a week and a half. Can you make it that soon?"

"I'll try," she said. "I'll talk to my travel agent tomorrow. How will I know if you've made it or not?"

"I'll call you when I get there. If I haven't called before you leave, postpone the ticket."

"I can't wait to see you," she purred, softly.

"You don't even know," he said.

When he hung up the yellow phone, Ben sensed a strange reaction in himself. Deep down inside, there was a part of him that regretted calling Heather and his other friends so often.

Or it seemed too often to Ben.

It was as if I was still clinging to the old world. But for my sanity, I just could not let go. Not yet.

The next week would be a good one for Ben. The thought of having her near made the days go by faster. Each new dawn brought with it a building excitement.

I long for her passion and her love. The warmth in Heather's touch will soon be near. If only for a few days, my loneliness will dissipate.

Before Ben left Frank's house the next day, they watched the TV news to see if any tropical storms were coming their way. The only one threatening had veered off to the west away from the mainland.

Ben knew it would be safe to continue.

He'd been wrong before.

Chapter 18

Great deeds are usually wrought at great risks.
Herodotus (484 BC - 430 BC)

Punta Baja, Mexico
October 6, 1996

Whenever Ben camped for the night on shore, he was faced the next morning with a fight through the breakers to regain the open sea. If the surf was small it wasn't a problem. But if the breaking waves were larger than five feet, he spent precious time and energy getting back to sea and on his way. Also, there was the very real chance that a wave would upset the kayak, and send it, and Ben, crashing back to the beach. So far it hadn't been a problem for him. He would simply run out through the waves, give a final push with his feet, and leap into the kayak. He counted on the momentum to carry him long enough to pick up the paddle, and hurl himself through the next few oncoming breakers. Although currents had been strong, the waves hadn't been as much of a problem.

At least not until now.

Today, the waves were strong, their height reaching over five feet. Just as Ben started his jump into the kayak, a wave slammed violently into it. His feet were lifted off the sand, and the hard Kevlar shell crashed into his right hip. After the initial shock, and the growing soreness, the blow didn't present a problem for Ben that day. But, the next day it was a major problem. His entire leg was engulfed in a creeping black bruise. Ugly streaks crept down the leg past his ankle. As the day progressed, the leg added

117

colors of yellow and green to the ugly ebony of a deep muscle bruise.

I feared that the wave's blow might have fractured some part of my hip.

At the very least there was internal bleeding, and a deep muscle bruise. For weeks after, the pain in the hip interrupted his sleep if he rolled to that side. This additional attack on his rest was dragging Ben down. It was serious.

Wincing with the pain, Ben finally got situated in his seat, and progressed past the surf line. Now he looked out across the ocean ahead. Today it had a different feel. It seemed to be flowing stronger, and with greater intensity. It was not the sudden, short bursts of violent energy as before. Now it showed a continuous surge of power. Sensing this change gave Ben pause. He knew that it would gradually become harder to come in and out of the shore. Perhaps one day he wouldn't be able to camp on the beach at all.

Today Ben caught himself tracking the negative, and consciously pulled up a more positive thought.

This change in the ocean is a reassurance that the waters of the Pacific Ocean are finally getting close. I will be sailing free of the confusions of the Sea of Cortez, and entering a body of water that I know so well from my training. The currents will even out, and the wind may even assist my progress.

But he was not there yet.

The strong headwind continued. Ben didn't know that further south Hurricane Hernan was churning the Pacific Ocean. It was already flexing its muscles in Acapulco, several hundred miles south of where he currently paddled.

Ben would soon find out.

The wind continued to pick up, and by 1:00 p.m. he was making little progress. In the distance, clouds were beginning to creep over the horizon. Ben smelled the threat of rain in the air. Dampness now clung to his skin.

Just as Ben had decided to head for shore and call it a day, a gale from the south rose suddenly and slammed into the kayak, throwing it back and nearly upsetting it. Ben had been sitting out on the back of the small craft, stretching his legs. The blast caught him off guard. With one hand on the paddle, and the other on the rim of the cockpit, he forced himself back into the seat. Clinging to the paddle with both hands, Ben struggled to maintain control as he squinted through the saltwater that whipped into his eyes. The wind gusted so strong that he could barely see ten yards ahead.

Despite every effort to paddle toward shore, the wind pushed him backwards at a frightful speed. The rain began to fall, joining the sea spray. It came lightly at first, and then increased to fat, heavy, pelting, bullets. Ben dug into the water blindly, as the churning waves swept over the bow, threatening once again to overturn the boat. The kayak tilted sideways, and Ben looked up to see a wall of water breaking overhead.

He quickly turned his face away as the monstrous wave engulfed the frail craft.

For a moment it was completely submerged.

The water swirled and rushed around the kayak like a freight train.

Ben closed his stinging eyes and held his breath.

He could only hope to resurface quickly, as water continued to hammer into his ears like thunder.

It pounded his head, and threatened to rip him from his seat. After an eternity, the kayak's bow broke above the waves. Gasping for breath, Ben shook his head to clear his vision. Blinking through the stinging salt, he saw a cluster of rocks jutting out of the foaming water just ahead. To him they looked like hungry teeth, eager to devour everything.

Somehow the kayak had been turned around by the last wave and was facing north, away from the wind. Another wave loomed from behind. Ben felt its sickening strength as it sucked him into the curl. He knew somehow that this wave was more dangerous than the last. There was but a split second to grab onto the rudder line that ran along the kayak's hull before it swept Ben entirely out and away.

No matter what else happened, he did not want to get separated from the kayak.

Taking a quick breath, he dove deep into the giant wave, the line grasped firmly in his left hand, and the paddle in his right.

Ben felt the wave's power catch his body and surge upward.

Now deep beneath the wave, he couldn't see, but he felt the rope cutting into his hand as the kayak sought its own survival. The rough unyielding surface of the rocks tore into his already injured right hip.

Ben fought the urge to open his mouth and scream.

He kicked forward and pressed toward the surface.

He must reach a breath of air!

A lifetime flashed by until Ben reached the surface and opened his eyes, despite the sting of salt and sand. It was just in time to see another towering wave roaring toward him. Instinctively, Ben let go of the rope at

119

the last second, and dove away from the kayak directly into the crashing wave. This time, swimming freely, he avoided the rocks. For the next ten minutes, which seemed to last for ten hours, he plunged into each new wave. He used his buoyancy to stay clear of the jagged, grasping rocks, swimming here and there, playing a cat and mouse game with the rocks and the angry ocean.

The wind never relented. The taste of salt water on Ben's lips added bitterly to his predicament. In the distance, and barely above the roar of the wind, he heard the sound of a hollow boom echoing from the Kevlar hull of the kayak as it smashed against the rocks. He wondered what would be left when he eventually found it.

But then, he may never know.

The next wave loomed.

He drew a breath and focused on survival.

Ben was swimming for his life.

His muscles were tiring from treading water.

He wondered if the storm would ever ease its grip on his life. Then, as suddenly as the gale had begun, it stopped. The wind slowed to a steady breeze. The waves, after a few minutes of final gesticulations, settled down. Every so often a small gust would rear up as if to demonstrate that nature had the last say about when the storm was finished.

Ben's right hip was throbbing. He looked down into the clear water to see a small trail of blood flowing out through his shorts and into the water.

I must have scraped it on another rock.

He could still feel the pain from the previous accident, and some of the blood coming out was black. It came from the bruise that had formed earlier in the trip when he might have fractured the bone.

At least it's the same side. Otherwise, I might not be able to sleep on either side at night.

Irony wasn't lost on Ben Wade. But now the humor faded, as Ben's thoughts turned to sharks being attracted to the blood. He scanned the water beneath his legs. No sharks in sight. But that could change in a second. He raised his gaze to the horizon and saw it. The kayak bobbed some fifty yards from where Ben slowly treaded water. He'd assumed that it was in a thousand pieces, smashed and strewn over the rocks. He began to swim in its direction. As he came closer it looked to be in one piece.

The kayak had fortunately lodged itself between two rocks, and was not drifting away. Ben prayed that it would be in suitable condition to stay afloat with his weight in the cockpit. By the time he reached his boat, some twenty minutes later, Ben was exhausted. He climbed aboard using sheer will. There were several scratches and dents along the sides of the hull. But for the most part, the kayak was in surprisingly good shape. The Kevlar structure held tough and lived up to its expectations.

But, the cargo and extremities of the kayak were not so fortunate. The leeboard, a wooden attachment used for additional steering in rough water, was split in two. The rudder had been completely torn off. Supplies were floating nearby. Ben didn't bother to pick them up because he knew they were ruined. Ben was just thankful to be alive. Wearily, he paddled toward the nearest beach, thankful that the rain had stopped. It was with his last bit of strength that he hauled the kayak on to the shore and tied it to a nearby palm tree. Ben laid down and closed his eyes. He shivered from exhaustion and relief and vowed to go no further that evening.

October 7, 1996

Frank, the man Ben had stayed with back in Bahia Kino, had come up with a great idea the night before he left. Frank had an extra cooler in his garage, and had offered to give it to Ben to carry the water supply. They had washed the inside with soap and water, then filled it with purified water, and a large block of ice that they had custom cut at the ice store. Frank had warned him that the ice was not necessarily purified, but that he'd been buying ice from there for several months and never had a problem.

Ben was not very reassured.

It looked too slimy for my taste.

Reluctantly, he had put the cooler, and its ten gallons of fresh water, on the space between the outrigger and the seat, and secured it with rope and a bungee. It survived the crash into the rocks.

But there was a growing problem.

I keep thinking about how slimy the ice looks. Even the color is wrong. Instead of being a frosted white, it's more like a mottled grey. I'm worried about that for sure, but what can I do? I'm headin' south and nothing's going to stop me.

By that night the ice had melted a little, and Ben could taste a strange

121

pungency in the water. He dismissed it as a slight residue of soap on the sides of the cooler. He took a big drink, ate some trail mix and dried fruit, and lay down to sleep. But, before he went to sleep, Ben noticed his gums had started to bleed.

Oh well, I hadn't really been flossing well lately. That must be the reason.

The next day Ben woke up feeling light headed. He prepared to drink his regular eight ounce morning ration of water. In disgust he spit it out. The water tasted and smelled like gasoline.

What kind of bacteria does the ice contain?

Fresh water in the middle of the ocean desert was a precious commodity. There were no towns or other boaters in sight. No one to supply him with fresh water. Ben tried to drink more of the tainted water with his breakfast. The taste was too strong, and he managed only a few fearful sips. At this point Ben was not showing good reasoning, as his journal attests:

I poured a five gallon can of concentrated Gatorade powder in the cooler, hoping that it would diffuse the taste. It did not. Next, I put some dried tea leaves in, but that only made it worse. It tasted like turpentine.

Slowly shaking his head in resignation, and wondering when he would have a chance to find some fresh water, Ben packed everything up and headed out to sea. By nightfall his gums were bleeding profusely and he felt more lightheaded. He put ashore in the protective lee of a protruding peninsula, and looked hopefully into the cooler. Then he turned away and spit out another mouthful of blood. Ben shook his head in disgust.
His water supply for the next week was ruined.

What a great idea. But my own method had been just fine. I wish I had left it the way it was.

Finally, Ben had to face his problem. The fresh water maker that he carried was only a back-up. It wasn't intended for regular use, only for emergencies. He pumped saltwater through the desalination kit. After an hour he gave up with only a few teaspoons in his cup. At this rate Ben would have to spend the whole day just to get enough water for one day, a life threateningly low return on invested energy. Ben decided not to waste any time, and hoped there would be a small town nearby. But none was listed on his map.

Surely, there's a fishing village that I'll come upon by tomorrow. Besides, I have a woman to meet in San Carlos. Can't keep her waiting now, can I?

Ben's clear headed thinking now suffered from the thirst.

The few ounces of contaminated water that he'd sipped that morning were making him violently ill. He could still taste the bitterness in his mouth. He felt a fever rising and his muscles weakening. Ben vomited everything he ate. There was a strong taste of metal, as blood continued to flood his mouth. He struggled ashore, and fell asleep on the deserted beach. He slept a restless sleep. Through the long night he dreamed dreams which were as poisoned as his water.

The ice towers above me a thousand feet, its vertical wall as blinding as the sun that reflects off its brilliant white surface. My eyes squint, and my neck begins to cramp from looking up at the glacier that looms before me. This 14,000 foot peak sticks out from the others in the mountain range. My breath is coming quickly in the thin air where I stand at a little over 12,000 feet.

Yesterday, my close friend, Darius, and I, hiked to this point, twenty miles from the start. It had been a grueling two day hike. We are deep within the Sierra Nevada Mountains. The Palisade Glacier, the monster that stands before us, is one of the largest of its kind in the contiguous forty-eight states. Every year we hiked a different mountain. This one with its glacier had promised to reward us more than the previous ones. We had both counted the days leading up to this small adventure, yearning to get away from civilization, and enjoy the majestic peaks that now surround us. We also love the bonding time with each other, with nature, and with God.

I look behind us at the bluish green stream that bursts forth from the base of the glacier ice. Spread out on either side of the stream is a lush meadow full of green grass as thick as any carpet. Otters splash in the ice cold water, frogs chirp in the nearby ponds, and an eagle soars overhead. This is yet another day in paradise. I feel like I can stay here forever.

As I turn and prepare to climb, Darius stays behind and films my progress. He is aware of the dangers and wisely keeps his distance. He had learned his lesson the last time we went climbing. While free forming a fifty-foot ledge, Darius had lost his footing. He sprained his ankle, and landed twenty feet below on a pile of snow. Now he lets me go on and cheers my progress, but takes no part in the activity. It is risky climbing the ice wall without an ice axe or crampons.

This time we had opted not to rent the equipment needed to safely reach the upper slopes of the glacier. All I have are a pair of hiking boots, and a walking stick I'd picked up along the way. It's too late to turn back now. The challenge lies ahead, and I will not be defeated. The best alpine climbing in the nation lies tantalizingly before me.

I begin by balancing my body with the stick in my right hand, and cutting small steps with my left boot. Making sure I am close enough to the ice, hugging its surface, I inch my way up the mountain. The only thing I focus on is the tiny patch of ice directly in front of my eyes. After thirty minutes, I stop and look down. The rocks at the bottom where the ice stops look distant, but are there, nonetheless. I can barely see Darius perched on a rock high above the stream. He's watching every move I make. I wave the stick above my head. He's too far away for me to tell his reaction. The slope is becoming steeper, and every step counts. One slip and my next resting place will be seven hundred feet down amidst the jagged rocks. I go as high as I can without the use of ropes, and then begin to make my way down.

The descent is a bit more difficult than the climb. I can't see the steps I had previously cut. I have to blindly grope with the toes of my boots to find sure footing. One look behind to see where my feet will go could cause disorientation.

I don't want to chance falling.

A third of the way down, I place my foot into one of the steps. Instead of holding my weight, the ice buckles. I begin to slip. Thrusting the stick into the ice, I brace myself against the slope. I try to throw my weight against the wall of ice, but it's too late. My other boot slips out of its hold, and I can feel, with paralyzing slowness, the weight of my body falling backwards.

I am suspended for a moment before I crash back against the ice. I'm falling rapidly. The ice wall is a blur. I shut my eyes to block out the pain the rocks will soon inflict.

Nothing to hold on to now.

Nobody to save me.

I am alone.

All alone and falling into darkness.

I cry out in fear, but my voice is caught in my throat.

No one around for miles to see my plight or hear my screams.

Ben woke with a start, perhaps hearing his own cries for help. He grasped for the ground beneath him, searching for a better hold. He found himself clutching the sleeping bag instead. Ben spent the rest of the night restlessly awake, and thinking of that day on the mountain. The glacier had stood before him like an ominous challenge. It had beckoned to him like the ocean had, to sip its cup of dangers. As the fear of falling receded further into the night, and the boldness from conquering the mountain returned, Ben looked back on that day with a growing sense of pride. The feeling of taking on whatever nature had to offer was as rewarding as it was dangerous.

The greater the risk, the greater the reward.

Or the greater the dreadful price to pay.

That fateful day he had made it to the top. He had survived, and reeled with the high that only life, really living, could give. No alcohol, no drugs, only the pure and natural adrenaline. Taking life to the limits and imagining the dangers only made the high greater. At that point, though, Ben had wanted more. He wanted to cheat death again, but this time for a longer period of time. He could remember sitting on top of that mountain and wanting all that life had to offer. Something that would make him a better person. Better mentally, physically and spiritually.

Was I testing God and His protection over me? I didn't think so. It only made me close to the One that gave me a strong heart and body. The God who allowed me to attempt such adventures.

That day as Ben climbed back down the glacier's slick white face, he slipped once but caught himself from falling. It reminded him of the dangers that surrounded every move. And he wanted more. But what? Where?

Ben's vision would one day come clear.

As it did that day in the Mojave Desert when he had first decided in a flash to make this grueling sea trip.

Then I knew what drew me. What unforgiving, and unrelenting, area of torment and fury; what powerful force of nature as vast and as desolate as anything in the universe.

The ocean.

125

Chapter 19

Do not fear death so much, but rather the inadequate life.

Bertolt Brecht (1898 - 1956)

October 8, 1996

The fouled drinking water was so strong now that he could only stomach a few drops, his mouth and throat so dry that he couldn't swallow. It had been three days since Ben had tasted good water. His fever was still high, and the blood was still coming from his gums. Spots of blood caked the outside of his lips, but he couldn't bring his tongue far enough out of his mouth to clean it off. The sun was blazing hot and the temperature soared to at least 95 degrees everyday. Ben normally averaged a gallon of water a day out in the sun, and lost most of that to sweat. Three days out from Bahia Kino, he had managed to swallow less than a third of that.

Ben was sick.

I put my hand to my face to rub the stubble and found a dozen small bumps, almost like pimples, amid the growth of hair. There was also a metallic taste in my mouth that seemed to be coming from my gums. When I leaned over and spit into the ocean, the color was a dark red. Was this an allergic reaction to the melted ice, or the film on top of the cooler? There is nothing much to do except paddle like hell, and hope to get as much ground as possible before dehydration really sets in.

The sun is hot, my skin is irritated, my mouth is dry, and my muscles are cramping.

All in all, a bitch of a day.

Dehydration causes more than a *bitch of a day.* It can and will kill. The effects of dehydration begin with thirst, and progress to more alarming symptoms as the need for water becomes more intense. The initial effects of mild dehydration appear when the body has lost about 2% of its total fluid. Some of these mild dehydration effects are thirst, dry skin, flushing, cotton mouth, fatigue, weakness, chills, and dizziness. When the body experiences fluid loss of 5%, more severe effects are experienced. There is increased heart rate and respiration, decreased sweating and urination, fever, extreme fatigue, and muscle cramps.

Ben Wade was getting deeper into trouble. His journal entries began with clarity, and steadily declined into scrawls of fantasy. His actions were placing his very life in danger, as he apparently neared severe dehydration – a body fluid loss of over 10%. He was experiencing muscle spasms, vomiting, confusion, and chest and abdominal pain. The last symptoms of breathing difficulty, seizures, and unconsciousness, could prove fatal.

Phoenix, Arizona
Earlier that day

Mr. and Mrs. Bill Ronstadt boarded the plane at Sky Harbor Field. They were ready for this long awaited vacation. Bill had recently finished playing all of his music gigs in town, and he'd arranged for a substitute to play in his band while he was away.

It had been years since he'd worked a regular nine-to-five job and he was enjoying the life of a famous local musician. Around the town of Scottsdale, his band played at all kinds of coffee shops and clubs. Several years earlier he'd played with his famous cousin, Linda Ronstadt. But life on the road wasn't the best place to be while trying to raise a family, so he'd given it up for another job. Now in his forties, his decision to semi-retire from the harsh world of musical politics was proving to be the right road.

He looked over at his wife, Liz, and smiled. Her long black hair falling wistfully on her shoulders gave her the timeless beauty some women can only dream of. Bill knew he was lucky to have her. Now his thoughts turned back to the sun-drenched shores of Mexico, and of the sailboat that lay anchored at the harbor in San Carlos.

At least once a year they would come down to sail on their boat, the

Sarafina. Bill loved to test the waters as far north as Bahia Kino. He knew he would never be one of the hard core cruisers that sailed around the world to who-knows-where. But that didn't seem to bother him. He was content to sail to nearby ports in his thirty foot sailboat, and take the adventure as it came.

In less than an hour they were preparing for landing in Guaymas, Mexico. Here they were only ten minutes from the harbor at nearby San Carlos. Bill frowned as he looked out over the wing of the plane. Out to the horizon the sun was hidden with dark rain clouds. The weather looked formidable. "One of those freak autumn storms," he muttered under his breath. As he sat back in his seat and tightened the lap belt, he hoped that the weather would clear up, and allow them to have some peaceful time on the water. The aircraft's wheels squealed their arrival.

Once they made it to the boat dock, Bill listened to the radio and learned it was only a passing storm. He had nothing to be concerned about since he wasn't going out until tomorrow. As he sat back and looked out over the bay to where his boat lay anchored, he could already see the clouds dissipating. The storm was moving further north. He wondered how many boaters had been caught out on the water when the storm hit. At least, he thought, their own timing had been good. He took Liz's hand and wrapped it around his elbow. With practiced élan that she found cute, he led her down to the dock and onto their boat. This was definitely going to be a good week, he thought.

The sun began to defeat the clouds and shine through with the promise of good sailing tomorrow.

The Next Morning

All the gear was stored and Bill Ronstadt set about rigging for the day's sail. He rigged a jib and hauled the mainsail up the mast, leaving the sheets loose and the sails luffing in the slight breeze. Liz emerged from the galley with a 'casting off' cocktail, as Bill released the last of the mooring lines and let the boat swing out away from the dock. The sails filled with a pleasant 'whump', and the graceful boat began to slice the blue waters.

Throughout the previous day, despite the growing numbness in his mouth and throat, Ben had forced himself to continue on. Stroke after stroke, one arm forward, the other arm back.

His gums were bleeding less, but the fever was still high.

I'm uncoordinated. It shocks me. The sores on my face turned into weeping boils, but now they've all dried up. No liquid left. I'm not sure how much progress I'm making today, or yesterday. My mind is focused only on putting the paddle in the water. I see neither ship nor town. The feeling of complete solitude has broken my subconscious thoughts. It threatens to crush my spirit and render me powerless to continue.

No one is here to help me!

No one to rescue me, to save me!

Ben crunched the kayak up onto the sand, and slept that night on the very edge of the ocean, lying on his belly in the sand, and letting the water wash over his tired body. The fever was now raging, and the cool sea water helped bring his body temperature down, giving him a modicum of relief. Occasionally, as the tide ebbed and flowed, the waves would either completely engulf him, and he'd wake up sputtering, or they would leave him high and dry without any comfort whatsoever. In the morning Ben stood on the shore and looked down at the poisoned blue cooler in disgust, and then looked out at the ocean, hoping for a ship to come.

Confusion.

I remember reaching down and, with all my remaining strength, grabbing the blue cooler - it looked so blue against the brown sand - and flinging it toward my kayak. The water emptied out, and I think at least my kayak will weigh less.

Ben dragged the kayak into the water, climbed aboard, and set off paddling. It was by muscle memory, not by conscious thought.

The compass that is mounted on the front hatch seems a mile away. The point seems blurry, surreal, and out of focus. I turn left, always left, to the south, always south and, although I can't read the letters SSW clearly, I see that the shore is to my left, and so I keep paddling.

Sitting in the seat of the kayak, Ben drifted in and out of consciousness. He woke up sporadically with a start, sometimes by a jerk of his head that had lolled forward in sleep, other times when a wave slapped against the hull, and occasionally by an actual wall of seawater that splashed into his lap. Ben would look around, disorientated, and try to determine if it was real, or another nightmare.

Looking over to the shore, I see with a rush of joy, a little village tucked into a cove. With renewed energy I turn left and head for shore. As I get closer I look to see where I can land, and who will come out to greet me.

It's gone!
Where?
Now I realize that it is only the rocks in the hills.
My mind has tricked me again into thinking that rescue is here at my grasp.
Foolish man, to think that I can escape that easy.

Ben continued on. Left paddle, right paddle, look up, try to swallow, left paddle, right paddle. He dipped his hand into the water and splashed his face. Then he'd dribble a little saltwater down a parched throat - making things worse.

Another town to my left!
More hope.
Another desperate attempt to paddle to shore.
Another mirage.
Darkness is closing in.
Pinpoints of light explode around my eyes.
Darkness is pinning me down, trapping me beneath....
Is the end near?

Ben is in trouble. Hallucinations are overtaking reality to a frightening extent. This journal entry is a 'ghost entry', written with shaking hand as Ben actually thought he was saved.

Another town, this one with people.
There's an old blue plastic oil drum, filled with black water.
I get out of the kayak to look.
I drink my fill.
I vomit, and drink some more.
It dribbles on my chest.
It's foul tasting, but I'm saved.

Ben presses on.

In and out, left paddle, right paddle, sleep, jolt awake.
Is that another town?
The heat and the thirst are unbearable.

131

The water all around me is sloshing, so inviting and so cool.
The seductiveness of the movement is calling to me.
If I could just roll over, outside the kayak.
Close my eyes and drift away . . .

A rogue wave crashed over the bow of the kayak. Ben was under water and totally disoriented. At first he thought he'd dived headlong into his fantasy and was letting himself drift away on the current. But instantly he realized that he was still sitting in the soaked cockpit of the kayak.

A chill ran down his spine, whether from adrenaline, or fear, or both. The fever was running high, but now he felt cold, freezing cold.

The reality of the hand of death closed in around me, and squeezed me
so tight that a warning went off in my head.
You are a few second away from dying.
This is it. This is it.
NO! Not like this.
Wake up, get up, come on!
You cannot give up.
This is not the end.
There has to be a way out.

With hands shaking so badly he could barely grasp it, Ben took out the only map he could find. He couldn't focus on it. He looked to the shore and saw that he'd just entered a huge bay.

He looked down at his watch to see that it was just after four.

And then things got out of focus and the watch blurred, the map
blurred, and the world began to spin.
This is not it. There is a way out.

With the dizziness and nausea washing over him and threatening *to overwhelm my very being*, Ben feebly scanned the bay, fruitlessly looking for any help.

Then he saw it.

At the other end of the bay, a pinprick of light, a spot of movement.

He looked again and it was gone.

He shook his head, squinted his burning eyes, and saw it again.

It was less than one quarter of an inch on the horizon, and disappeared with each little wave that pushed by.

Then it was gone again.

Ben reached up and clawed at his face, trying to slap himself into reality. He splashed water in his face, and stood up on shaking legs in the kayak. With the paddle planted between his legs for stability he looked out, ravenously hungry for hope, the last hope, in a ferocious nightmare.

And there it was, this time maybe a half an inch on the horizon, the unmistakable triangle of a sail, moving slowly into the bay at the far end, several miles away. Ben strained to see until his eyes blurred.

He sat down, his body shaking from exhaustion.

I am saved.
They have come to rescue me.
My nightmare is over.

But then Ben was hit with an unmistakably clear thought.

That sailboat is coming into the opposite side of the bay for the day.
Then they're going to leave the same way they came.

In a sudden panic, Ben picked up his paddle. Ignoring the pain that shot through his body, and the nausea that lurched in his stomach with every stroke, he paddled as he'd never paddled before. For almost an hour, he paddled with his sight fixed on the white triangle of a sail. At times it was in sight, at other times it disappeared behind a crest.

But closer on it came and, with its sight on the horizon, new hope shouted at me so desperately that I continued to move at a rapid pace.

The sailboat came closer, closing the distance to the tiny kayak. But Ben's energy was now completely drained. Suddenly, intense pain racked his gut, and cramped every muscle fiber in his tortured body. The dehydration was turning deadly. He dropped the paddle into his lap, and curled into a fetal position. He peered thru squinting eyes to the boat that lay only a hundred yards away.

He tried to stand but his body refused.

He tried to yell but no voice would come.

So close, so close to being rescued.

The blackness came with a vengeance, and his eyesight exploded with fiery stars. Ben grasped the paddle with new intensity and gave a few bold strokes, pushing the kayak through the water. But it was too much for his body to handle. Another surge of pain and cramping agony swept through his body. This time it was so great that a ragged cry, almost like a rustle and crackle of dry leaves, escaped his parched cracked lips.

Then the darkness won, blacking out everything and ripping Ben's consciousness into a senseless state.

The only thing that I could think of was this: no more pain.

And then there was nothing.

"Do you think he's in trouble?" Bill asked his wife, Liz. A moment before she had seen the flash of a white paddle's blade as the kayak came into view a half mile away. "Let me get the binoculars," she answered. Then, "My God, he *is* in trouble. He's slumped over, out of the boat." Bill Ronstadt pulled the tiller and brought the sailboat hard on the wind, aiming straight toward the bobbing kayak. Liz picked up a coiled line with an orange life ring attached, and carefully made her way along the safety rail to the bow. She stood ahead of the jib and braced herself against the forestay. She had a clear view of the distressed kayak and its unmoving occupant. "Heave to, Bill!" She yelled as they bore down on the tiny craft. He expertly swung hard over, lost the wind, and killed their forward motion.

Ben had fallen out of the cockpit, and lay draped over the outrigger boom. It was the only thing that kept him from drowning. The sailboat eased up to within inches of the kayak. Liz Ronstadt was already in the water and swimming with strong strokes to the stricken sailor. Bill reached down and secured a line between the boats. The breeze was light, the sails luffed, and both boats bobbed in place. Bill stepped down onto the kayak, holding on to his own life rail. With his free hand he grasped Ben's wrist as his wife pushed Ben back up into the cockpit. A gasping cough came from Ben's lips, much to the relief of his rescuers. The Ronstadts dragged Ben onto the sailboat's deck and checked him for injuries. It was evident from his pallor and swollen cracked lips that water was the first order of business.

Chapter 20

Whoever rescues a single life earns as much merit as though he had rescued the entire world.

The Talmud, Mishna. Sanhedrin

Fortunately the currents in the bay were slack, and Bill was able to anchor his sailboat and secure Ben's kayak. Ben's treatment was exactly right. Cold compresses, feet raised, and protection from the sun. He was given Gatorade as fast as he could keep it down. The manual in the sailboats first aid kit had all the instructions the Ronstadts needed. Ben was responding, and weakly began to talk a little. But it was a couple of hours before he was totally lucid. The Ronstadts were in no hurry. As the afternoon passed they decided to stay anchored for the night.

Later in the evening Ben sat up, finally clearheaded enough to at least wonder where he was, and who these people were that tended to him. "Welcome, back," the captain said to Ben as he noticed the blinking eyes. "Uh, ya, yes, sir. I'm, I'm, uh... have I been out long?" Ben said weakly, looking around. Bill answered, "Long enough. What's your name?" Ben had a blank look, but shook it off. "Ben, uh, Ben Wade," he mumbled, having to actually think about the answer for an instance.

"Nice to meet you Ben Wade," Bill said, offering his hand, "I'm Bill Ronstadt. Welcome aboard the *Sarafina*."

"Man, er, Bill, thank you. I think," Ben turned to look out over the bay, "I think I was a gonner." His voice trailed off.

"Yes you were, Ben, yes you were."

Just then, Bill's wife, Liz, came up on deck. Her long black hair, streaked with gray, and her long white summer dress flowing about her ankles, *made her look just like a captain's wife should look,* Ben thought. Her presence sharpened his consciousness. "Well, do we have a guest for dinner?" She said with a lilt in her voice.

"Maybe a little, ma'am," Ben offered, finding a smile. "I'm hungry, but I'm still a little queasy."

"Then some hot soup's in order …. "

"Ben, Ben's his name, Liz," Bill added, coming to the social rescue. "And, Ben, this is my wife, Liz."

"Okay, Ben. Nice to meet you. Soup's on its way."

Bill turned to Ben, now slouched in a deck chair. "Where are you coming from, San Carlos?" He asked. "No," Ben replied, "I came from San Felipe. Do you know where that is?"

"Wow!" Bill exclaimed, "That's a long way."

"Yah," Ben said slowly, "and I'm going all the way to South America." He waited for that to sink in, then added, "I've been out for three weeks. Long time, I know."

"Long time, indeed. How long you been out of drinking water?"

"A few days I guess. Got some bad stuff in Bahia Kino. Made me sick. None since."

"Look, Ben, the deck's small but we've plenty of room for you. Looks like we met up just in time."

"Yes, sir. Lucky for me."

Benefactor or not, Ben liked this man. His smile was warm and friendly. Tall, with a full head of thick, wavy, gray hair, he looked just like the kind of man you would expect to see on a weekend outing with the local yacht club.

Ben found the soup to be exactly what he needed, and soon he was asleep on the deck of the gently bobbing sailboat. A blanket and pillow completed his comfort, and sleep, deep sleep, soon followed. The Ronstadts sat on deck for awhile, watching the stars twinkle on, and being sure their charge was settled in for the night. He was. They retired.

The next morning Ben awoke, stiff but happy with life. His youth, and the good care of the Ronstadts, had combined to produce a near complete recovery. Ben was hungry. Tea and an egg set well with him.

Bill Ronstadt was enthusiastic about Ben's trip and got out several maps to see where Ben had been, and where he would soon be going. Ben told him about the storm and the various mishaps that had happened along the way. After breakfast, they talked about their respective families, and, for a second time, Ben fell right in step with the relaxed way of life on a sailboat.

The Ronstadts were lovely people, kind and generous with their time and belongings. Bill was an amateur photographer and took pictures while Ben was on board their boat, and some with Ben in his kayak.

Ben was again touched by the sincerity of the people he was meeting.

I know that God has special ways of meeting the needs of his children; even saving their life for another day.

That afternoon the trio moved to a small bay about three miles north of where they'd rescued Ben. With the wind coming from the south, Ben was able to paddle the kayak on his own, and set up his camp on the beach long before Captain Ronstadt's boat was firmly anchored in the soft sand of the harbor.

Ben was invited to dinner. They ate fresh fish and a salad and enjoyed a good wine.

This seems to be the standard fare for people who partake of the ocean's bountiful feast.

Ben never gets tired of eating this kind of meal. It was different from the "fresh" fish fillets he'd eaten back in the States.

There is something intriguing and delicious about watching your meal swim under the boat just minutes before plopping it on the skillet and eating it with gusto.

After dinner, Bill played his guitar. On the candle-lit deck, Bill and Ben sang some songs that they both knew. The boat rocked gently in the small swells. It seemed to creak with delight, and add its voice to their music. The moon shone brightly down on the festivities, and Ben learned once again the intimacy that only the night air over a salty sea can bring.

He slept in his tent on the beach, careful not to lie on the twice-injured side. Inspecting the hip by candlelight revealed that the rocks had torn away a good piece of skin. He wiped it with a wet cloth from the medicine kit and bandaged it up. It stung, but Ben ignored the pain and tried to sleep as best he could. The good meal certainly helped.

The next morning, bright and early, Ben joined Bill and Liz for breakfast before setting out. As he prepared to cast off, Bill reached over the side and handed him a long, heavy orange tube. It was about a foot long and six inches in diameter. Ben looked at it, not knowing exactly what it was. Seeing his puzzled look, Bill said, "That's an Emergency Locating Beacon, an

ELB. Inside the waterproof compartment is our address. We want you to write when you get done with your trip. This will give us another excuse to see each other again."

"I can't take this from you," Ben said, bewildered at such an offer. This unit, he knew, cost several hundred dollars. He just couldn't take it from people he had just met. "No, I insist," Bill said firmly. "We definitely don't need it down here, because we don't go very far from San Carlos. You need the ELB much more than we do, and I'll be offended if you don't take it. Besides, like I said, you'll have to make a trip over to Arizona to give it back to us so we can enjoy your company again."

Without further resistance, Ben paddled off with probably the most important, and valuable, piece of equipment onboard the kayak that morning. A gift given to him by the memorable Ronstadts. Ben waved once more before turning his focus ahead.

Approaching San Carlos
Baja California, Mexico

Paddling without a rudder is difficult. At times, Ben had to stop altogether, and push the paddle in a reverse motion. It severely slowed his progress, but it was the only way he kept a straight course. San Carlos was not far off, and, normally, Ben would have made that distance by night fall. But having to almost double his stroke when the current pushed in a different direction, he knew it would take the whole day. He was in no condition to do more. Ben decided that when he did reach the city, he would call his friend, Christian, and ask him to send down a new rudder.

Ben's arrival was uneventful, and he took the next few days to relax. Heather wasn't coming until Tuesday so he had those few days to himself. He rented a room in the hotel. The clean sheets and, best of all, the warm showers made him feel like he was in another world. He took so many showers that he began to lose track of how many bars of hotel soap he went through in a day. Sometimes he let the clean, hot, water run for an hour. Residue from the dried saltwater was finally off his skin and newly growing hair. He took time to rinse all his clothes in the sink.

Ben was a new man.

A man that now appreciated the smallest of comforts in life.

A man that appreciated life.

Chapter 21

There is always some madness in love.
But there is also some reason in madness.
Friedrich Nietzsche (1844-1900)

October 15, 1996
San Carlos, Sonora, Mexico

B en Wade looked nervously out of the window of the cab that carried him from San Carlos to the small airport outside the nearby
town of Guaymas. Heather was arriving in Mexico. As Ben watched the
small twin engine plane bank onto its downwind leg, his mind churned with
thoughts torn between worry and anticipation.

> *"Am I ready for this?"*
> *"What if she doesn't find me attractive anymore?"*
> *"What if our chemistry has been lost?"*

The aircraft continued its turn onto its base leg, then onto final approach to landing.

Unseen by Ben Wade, a very anxious young lady peered through the
small, sand-crazed, aircraft window toward the airfield that rushed up to
meet her. Her feet tapped nervously on the carpeted deck, her thoughts mir-
roring Ben's, *what if. . .?* Heather mused over the butterflies that flitted in
her breast.

The pilot skillfully guided the plane through its steep descent, holding
a slight crab angle to adjust for the wind coming across the dirt runway.

Then, with its ten passengers and crew of two, the plane flared, straightened out to align with the runway, and touched down in a cloud of Sonoran desert dust.

Ben paced nervously as the small aircraft taxied back to where he waited. His mind was filled with the heightened tension of the moment, and his breathing and heart joined together in rapid ascension. One by one the passengers deplaned, and for a moment, when there was a gap in the line coming down the stairs, Ben thought that she had not made the trip. But those thoughts quickly faded as he saw Heather step out of the plane and down onto the tarmac.

Looking every bit the model she was, Heather's golden hair blew around her face as she squinted slightly thru the glare of the sun. Wearing a mid-length skirt and denim blouse, she would certainly catch the eye of everyone at the airport that day.

She looks terrific. I must be the luckiest guy in the world!

All the doubts and worries Ben had a moment ago suddenly vanished. He was filled with wonder and anticipation of what might happen later that night. In fact the raw edge of fear and near fatal disasters that had permeated his life for the past few weeks were also gone, washed away by this new challenge that had just stepped off the plane.

The ocean, the kayak, and the entire traumatic voyage, faded to gauzy memory, replaced by the crystal clarity of this moment, this perfect moment, when everything seemed right with the world. Ben edged over to watch Heather clear customs. Then a few quick strides and they stood face to face. He swept her into his arms, oblivious to the other people that fussed and bustled past the couple. Ben held her close for a moment, letting the sensation of love and relief wash over his emotions. He pulled away, still holding her hands, and looked into her eyes. "It's great to see you babe," he said, barely finding his voice. "You too," she replied, squeezing his hands, and looking lovingly into his eyes. "You look incredible, Heather," Ben said. He couldn't take his eyes off her. "I'm so glad I could come down," she said, pulling him close with another hug. "I couldn't think of anything else these past two weeks! Work, school, modeling. Every time I tried to concentrate I just thought about you. I've been so worried that something would happen to you that I haven't been able to think straight."

"Me too," Ben responded gently, making sure that he kept his body in contact with hers in as many places as possible. Still holding her hands he continued, "I paddled harder than ever the last several days. Nothin' would have kept me from seein' you. It gave me the extra push I needed to get through what I had to get through to see you."

There were more moments of just standing there, staring into each other's eyes. Finally, they turned and walked slowly to the waiting luggage, a hailed taxi, and the ride back over the little hills that separated Guaymas from San Carlos. The ride took only a few minutes, but Ben didn't see the scenery. His eyes were locked on Heather, this beautiful girl that had come to be with him.

It took only a moment to check into the little hotel. They took the flight of stairs to the room and opened the door. Ben hefted the bags onto the bed, and Heather opened her suitcase and proudly displayed the "gifts" inside. She'd brought an extra suitcase just for Ben, and he was like a kid on Christmas. He stood there fidgeting and moving from side to side, looking at more than he had imagined or asked for. Laid out on the faded chenille bedspread were new clothes, a new rudder for the kayak, dried fruit, fresh bread, trail mix, pictures, and a camera.

Ben handled everything as he examined each item before setting it all aside. He knew that Heather's suitcase would be full again on her return. The extra weight of things that he'd frivolously packed initially had been more than a burden. With currents and storms getting worse, he needed to make judgments of value versus weight in order to travel as light as possible. Heather's suitcase was repacked with the boombox, 24 D cell batteries, a cooking pan, the extra flashlight, and various reading material. All would return home before Ben. He did not, however, rid himself of the AAA road map!

The hardened kayaker turned to look at the beautiful young woman. He crossed the room and grabbed her hand, trying to draw her close to him. This time Ben wanted more than just a light kiss. But as he sought to pull Heather close, she pulled back quickly. Looking at him and frowning, a new hint of fire in her eyes, she said simply and brutally, "I want you to come home. I can't make it another month without you ... just sitting around and worrying and thinking that you might never come back. I want you to come home to me. Please baby."

The beauty and tenderness of the moment had evaporated.

Ben's arms were still outstretched toward her.

He let them fall to his sides in exasperation.

"You know I can't do that," he said with a tinge of anger ruffling the edges of his voice. "You know I have to finish this thing. I told everyone I was gonna do it. No matter what happens, I have to be true to my word. I know everyone thinks I'm crazy, and everyone thinks I'm gonna get killed. But, you're not everyone, Heather. You and Christian were all who supported me in the beginning. Are you saying you're bailing on me now?"

That angry retort stung its victim. Heather's composure crumbled rapidly. Throwing herself on the bed, she let the frustration, pent up anger, unrequited love, and sheer worry, explode. "What the fuck do you want me to do?" She yelled, pounding the bed with a clenched fist. Loud and course for such a small girl. "Sit on my hands and wait for you to come home? I worry about you every day, every night. I knew I shouldn't have gone out with you in the first place. It was doomed from the beginning. Yet I trusted you, and wanted you. This is what I get for starting to fall in love with you!"

There, she had said it.

Ben walked over and sat beside her, gently stroking her hair with his hands. He snuggled close, and tried to reassure her. Gently he laid his head on her shoulder and whispered in her ear, "I'm gonna make it. I promise I will. Nothing is going to stop me, but I have to do this. I have to follow through with this. Please tell me you understand." But the moment of tenderness had passed, at least on Heather's part. She stood stiffly and walked to the balcony. She looked out at the setting sun, out over the water and toward the streaks of light that were filtering their way thru the clouds. *Why does it always have to end up like this,* Heather wondered.

They spent the night in the same bed, but on opposite sides. Both tossed and turned, and didn't sleep much. The monumental decision to try to attempt a relationship under these circumstances was finally eroding the confidence both of them had felt earlier that week. On the phone, it was much easier to distance themselves from reality, and to pretend that nothing would stand in their way. Face to face, however, was a different story.

Sometime that night Ben got up and went to the balcony, his journal in hand. He penned a few paragraphs to help assuage the guilt and agony he felt inside.

Why is it that when I finally find someone I want to fall in love with, something gets in the way?

I have this beautiful woman lying here in my bed and yet, I'm impotently removed with my emotions for a trip that I don't want to continue, for reasons that I obviously don't understand.

What would happen if I just packed up and left everything behind?

What if I just went back home with Heather?

Would people still love me?

Would they see me as a quitter?

Would people still respect me?

Would I still respect myself?

What do we truly have in life but the past, the present, or the future? That's what I have to think about. That's what I have to communicate to Heather.

The next morning, sleepy-eyed and groggy, Ben woke to find Heather no longer in bed. Tired from the restless night, she had dressed early, and walked down to the beach. Finding solace there in the quiet patter of waves, she thought about what kind of man would do this to himself voluntarily. *Is he a coward? Is he crazy? Is he brave and noble? What does he have to prove, and why am I not enough for him?* The thoughts raged through her mind, overlapping and swirling, like the water at her feet.

When Heather returned to the hotel room, the bed was empty and the shower was running. She poked her head inside the bathroom, watching the steam lazily swirl past her and into the room. "Isn't this like the third shower you've taken since I got here?" Heather asked. "More like the sixth or seventh," Ben responded. "I just can't seem to get clean, my skin is still crawling from all that salt and sweat and sand ... by the way, you wanna come in?" he asked jokingly. "Yeah right! Not until we finish what we started last night."

Ben emerged from the shower a few minutes later, eager to resolve the argument, and the strain of the previous evening. He looked quickly in the mirror, wiping away the steam that fogged its edges. His eyes swept down to his chest, and then his arms, and finally his stomach. The muscles looked strong, deceptively so. They appeared powerful and capable of anything.

But Ben knew better. He might look tough on the outside, but on the inside he was facing a challenge he'd never faced before. He might be stronger than most in a kayak, but what he was now up against was much more than just the wind and the waves. It was his character, even his own soul, that he was up against.

The demons that haunted his mind were getting stronger, now that Heather had arrived.

They sat on the balcony patio together. Steaming mugs of coffee sat on the small table between them. For a moment they said nothing, just stared out on the horizon. For Ben, looking at the blue sky, the white clouds, and the dark sea, was a calming reassurance of the elements, and the consistency that belonged to them. Those things that surrounded him daily at sea. He tried to compartmentalize everything, putting Heather and his feelings on one side, and the monumental voyage that he was undertaking on the other.

Finally Heather broke the silence and penetrated his thoughts. "Are you going to say anything, or are we just going to sit here and stare at the water?"

"Well, it is a mighty fine view isn't it?" Ben responded trying to ease the tension.

It wasn't working.

"Okay, so you know I couldn't sleep last night," he continued after a pause. "And that's because I was thinkin' a lot about you and me, and everything that's happening right now. I don't pretend to know everything that's going on - with you, with me, with life. I spent a lot of time by myself the past month. Being alone with yourself for so long changes you, it changes me. You get to thinkin' out there, and prayin', and wonderin' just who you are, what you're meant to do, what your destiny is . . . at least for the time being." He looked over to see if she was paying attention.

It was warm in the morning sun, but there was still a slight chill in the air and Heather was wrapped in a blanket with her feet tucked underneath her. She was not only paying attention, but she stared intently back at him, apparently locked on every word. More importantly to Ben, there was a slight thaw in her demeanor, a look in her eyes that he immediately noticed to be one of softening. "I know that I was called to take this trip," he continued with more confidence. "You remember when I told you that I had a vision of doing something great, something that no one else had ever done? Out there in the desert, I saw it clearly. To get in a kayak, and go as far as I could. To do the impossible, to get out on the ocean, by myself, and do something that would go down in history."

Ben stood and walked to the railing. Gripping it with both of his large, calloused hands, he continued to make his case. "I know that most people don't follow their dreams. They work, they get stuck in traffic, they obey all the rules, and what happens? They lose sight of their dreams, and a part of them dies inside. The hope that everyone has when they're growing up - to be someone great, to slay the dragon, to win the damsel, to marry the prince - that all goes away when people get older. Some call it reality, but I can't except that, not now, not ever. Things have changed inside me. Now I think I know where I am - and where I'm going."

"But what about me?" Heather interjected. "I hear what you're saying. It's dangerous, and brave, and outside the box. But you still haven't talked about us. What do you want from me, from this relationship?" Ben stepped back to the table and grasped her hand. He leaned over, bringing the tiny graceful hand to his mouth for a gentle kiss. With his eyes closed, he put all the feeling and passion he could muster into that kiss, hoping that she could feel his love, and sense that she could trust him, and that she would be safe. "I was getting to that," Ben said gently as he sat down, "I know this much to be true. I'm falling in love with you - and the conflicting emotions that I have are sometimes more than I can bear. The thought of losing you, or losing my sense of self, is overwhelming at times. But I know that you're an amazing woman. I know that you've given me hope in the darkest hours and in the strongest storms. When the waves are crashing all around me, and I feel that I can't go on, you're there. I want you, I need you, and I love you. No matter how crazy that seems, and how short a time I've known you, I know all of this is true."

The tears in Heather's eyes matched the shimmering water below. She unwrapped herself from the blanket and came around to where Ben sat. She looked down on him with a smile, and the expression that came across her face was one of intensity, love, and admiration. She reached down and enclosed his hand in hers, gently pulling Ben toward her. Ben rose and wrapped his arms around Heather's lithe body. They stood there on the balcony melding body and breath. Finally Ben cupped her face between his hands and looked into her eyes … and smiled. "What I want from you now is your heart," he whispered, his lips brushing her forehead. "Right here, right now. The present is all that matters. The past is behind us, the future is too far away to grasp. All we're left with is the present, and I want to drink everything right now, and never let go. That's what I want from you."

"I love you Ben. More than anything right now," she said as she nuzzled his cheek. With that, she worked around to his mouth and kissed him. As Ben opened his mouth to drink in her passion, all of his thoughts and worries slipped away completely. Their athletic bodies entwined, passion burst forth, and the love that both felt in their hearts released in a violent torrent.

The ocean continued to move and swell in the morning current. The sun beamed down and smiled. The wind tickled and caressed everything it touched.

All was now in perfect harmony.

The next few days with Heather went by quicker than Ben wanted. They played tennis, swam in the pool, walked around the town, and ate at all the best restaurants that San Carlos had to offer. To Ben, this mini vacation, and the lavishness with which he allowed himself to be treated, was indeed a stark contrast to the previous month's challenges. Deep inside his mind he knew that leaving Heather and San Carlos behind would be tougher than his first stroke away from the beach at San Felipe in September.

The night before she left, they had another long talk. They had just finished a dinner brought by room service, and were quietly enjoying their last few moments together. "Are you glad you took on this expedition?"

Heather asked, raising her eyebrows slightly as she sat across the table from Ben. He felt a flush of anger at the hint of sarcasm in her voice. *Not another fight!* Instead of responding, he grasped her hand and looked at her in the candlelight. After a moment of silence he replied, "Yes I am. Without a doubt. But the last few days were something I wanted, and something I desperately needed."

"Are you happy?" Heather said, drawing out the words. "I know you're lonely. You said so yourself. But you must find the peace and quiet refreshing." She thought now of going home to LA, and the hustle and bustle that awaited her there.

"I've found some beautiful places out here," Ben said smiling in recollection. "But more importantly I've found freedom." He shifted in his seat and looked away. "Freedom to chase my dreams, freedom to do what I want, when I want, and a peace about what I'm doing, and who I will become when I come out the other side."

"Last night I looked out over the water," Heather began. "I felt scared to think of you out there all alone in the middle of that dark expanse. Tell me what that part is like."

"The loneliness is devastating," Ben said, nodding his head and continuing to look away. "Sometimes I think that's the biggest obstacle. Every night I look out at the sunset and feel an ache inside me because I'm alone." He turned back and fixed his gaze on Heather. "I know I've told you this before, over the phone and all, but I think it's hard for you to comprehend. I don't talk to anyone for days, even weeks at a time. If I could only share some of the beauty with someone ... I think it would be better. If I did have someone there, you know, like you babe, I don't think I would want to stop. Maybe just keep going on around South America until I reached the Atlantic or the Caribbean."

"Really?" she asked, looking as if she really did think he was crazy. Her eyebrows lifted and her mouth turned downwards. "Don't worry," Ben chuckled and patted her hand. "I'm not going to talk you into this! But with all the loneliness, I will tell you one thing. The ocean, and everything else I'm experiencing, can be painfully beautiful at times. And I feel myself changing. Every day I'm out on the water, I grow. Not only physically, but mentally as well. I think I like that the most. Plus, I don't have to worry about a job, finances, traffic, or any of that stuff. It can be very peaceful at times. Just the sea, God, and me. I like that part the best."

Heather looked as if she was relieved that there was some compensation for all the torture Ben was experiencing. "I wish you'd hurry up and finish and come home. I miss you and I worry about you. You don't know how many nights I sit in bed, awake, wondering if you're okay. It drives me crazy." As Heather spoke, she reached over and took hold of Ben's hand. He looked down at their clasped hands. "I know, baby," he said. "I'll be home soon. You know it's hard for me to go on, but I have to. In my heart I know that if I don't finish this trip I'll never be able to live with my-self again."

"Don't say that, Ben." Heather exclaimed, pulling her hand away from his. "Why do you have to continue if you don't want to? Can't you just stop?" She was pouting now. Sitting back in her chair and refusing to look at Ben. Her eyes glistened, arms folded across her chest and her mouth turned down in a frown. Ben smiled. Heather looked up. "What are you smiling at?" She asked, trying not to grin herself. "Nothing," he said. "You just look cute when you're mad. Anyway, this is something I have to do. I'm not going to quit now. Too many people, including me, are counting on my making it to South America."

"You've gone a long way already, though," she pleaded. "Most people didn't think you'd make it this far."

"I know. But you know, as well as I do, that there's only one thing that can stop me from continuing."

"What's that?" Heather asked looking up with wide eyes. "You?" Ben paused, the question exaggerated. He waiting for it to sink in. "No, just kidding," he said trying to ease the tension that he'd ignited. The mood re-fused to lighten, so Ben added, "Death." He was serious. "Or something close to it."

"That's so damn stupid, Ben" Heather said, standing abruptly and moving to the window. She looked out over the darkened water, as if to search for answers - answers that predictability were not there. "Nothing is worth getting killed over," she continued. "Especially if you don't like what you're doing. I think that that's what it is that *will kill* you."

"Listen, Heather," Ben said, walking over to where she stood with her arms still hugging her sides. He put his arms around her and held her close, trying helplessly to comfort her anguish. "When I hiked all over the Sier-ras, I spent days trying to make it to the highest peak. I didn't necessarily enjoy the intense hiking, or the sixty pound backpack that cut into my shoulders at every step. But, I did it. The rewards at the end are greater than the pain. The view from the top, and the beauty of the wilderness, is worth it all. Same thing here. If it wasn't so difficult, I wouldn't enjoy the end re-sults as much. When this is all over, I know that I will look back and be proud of myself. It'll be worth the risk, and I know that now. That's why I keep going. Besides, the ocean is beautiful. Even if she is moody, I don't think I could have picked a better location. I've seen the worst part. The coast is just going to get better."

"That doesn't tell me anything. Just hurry up and finish so that I can see you again soon. And in one piece, please. Do you hear me, Benjamin?"

"I will," he said, still holding her in his arms. "Nothing is going to happen to me." Ben slowly and gently turned her around to face him. He kissed her ardently, but gently, on the lips.

It would be hard to leave her behind, but he knew what he had to do. It felt good being with her, but he wondered how long it would last. They were both so independent. And there were still several months left in the trip. There was an unspoken agreement in those few days. Ben and Heather never spoke of *our* future, just *the* future in general. No strings attached. No false promises made. They felt it was better that way.

One step at a time.

The next day Ben watched with an all engulfing sadness as Heather turned and walked toward the airplane. The time together was gone. The emptiness that he felt at being alone again filled his gut. It stealthily encouraged him to follow her and get on a plane for home. But Ben steeled himself, knowing it was time to move on. The plane taxied out, revved up its two engines in a whirlwind of dust, and rolled with increasing speed down the dirt runway. Nearing the end it turned a sleek nose skyward and climbed into the blue sky. Ben was sure he saw Heather's face at the tiny window, saying one last goodbye.

All his speeches, his lectures … all the rationalizations … were they for Heather?

Or for Ben Wade?

He turned and walked away, confused and conflicted.

Chapter 22

That night Ben sat at the hotel room window and stared out at the sea. Storm clouds and lightning played on the horizon. The sunset's shadows blended in with the storm's own darkness, and seemed to reach toward his heart. Ben Wade made a poetic note on a piece of hotel paper that ended up folded and stuffed into a corner of his journal. It reflected his melancholy.

It's as if my soul's been laid bare, and is blending its sorrows into the picture painted before me. The fire of romance, like the blood-red sunset, is gradually being extinguished by the growing darkness.

In the darkness of the night, and the darkness of his growing despair, Ben didn't know if he would ever be close to Heather again. A few small flashes of lightning pronounced a faint sign of hope for him, but quickly faded into the night. Then there was only darkness. An ache came over him so deep and overwhelming that he had to sit down. His eyes stayed riveted on the powerful images of the thunderstorm outside his window.

As the celestial lightshow moved on, darkness reclaimed the night. Ben hated that he was alone. Again. The longing for love and companionship lingered. As he inhaled the last traces of Heather's perfume in the sultry air, doubts swirled in his head.

Do I really know why I'm continuing this expedition? Is it my pride?

My determination? Or, damn it, is it just that I have nowhere else to turn. Is this my destiny? Or am I running away from my past and the emotions that come with it?

Desperate for answers to the racing questions he felt helpless, small, alone, and afraid. Tears began to stream down his face. He put a hand to his head and let it all pour out, punishing himself for his self-centered stubbornness.

Ben Wade wished desperately that he had never heard of the continent of South America.

Sunrise came all too soon. Ben took his last shower, lingering under the hot spray, and knowing that the comforts of San Carlos would not be repeated for some time. He left the hotel looking both forward and back - sad to leave the good memories behind, but anxious to get on with his journey. Reality was slapping at Ben once more. No more romance, just prepare to survive.

One of the most important items Ben had requested, and Heather had brought with her, was his new rudder. It had been brutal trying to keep the kayak straight after the old rudder was damaged. The new rudder was in place, and the kayak was once more poised to launch into the unknown.

Drifting clouds drizzled a cool mist, and the sea seemed to welcome Ben's return with a flourish of activity. As he left the protection of the bay, and ventured again into the open sea, a severe headwind slapped the tiny craft. The water was extremely choppy. Only a few boats were out, and all of them tossed about wildly in the pounding fury.

Ben Wade was once again immersing himself in both the fact, and the deep spirit, of his adventure.

The ocean has definitely been upset by my absence. Now she demonstrates her power and might by embracing me with her arms. I look at the sea's waves sloshing over the sides of the kayak, and imagine hands caressing my body.

But Ben didn't seem to fully share her erotic enthusiasm for his return, and he begged her to be calm.

Be still, oh wind and sea. I have neither the strength nor the will for your wild dances. Calm thyself and give me the gift of thy tranquility.

Despite the imploring commands, the wind continued to howl, and the sea continued to churn. By mid afternoon he found shelter in a large bay just north of Guaymas. His muscles had quickly tightened and were sore. It would take time again to get used to the rigorous schedule. How to get re-focused? Ben's mind still lingered on Heather and the time they spent together. He wasn't making good progress, so he paddled to shore for the night. He made camp, ate a meal, and slept without pitching his tent. Sleeping that night without the comforts of a mattress beneath him, he was reminded of the simple pleasures he'd left behind. The nights, for now, were not too cold. The sleeping bag provided ample warmth. He curled up tightly, wondering where Heather was, what she was doing, and if her thoughts were also of him.

What a miserable man I am.

The only solace he could find were the reassuring sounds of the wind and the sea. They were the only two companions he had for now.

As the sun rose to reveal details beyond his camp, Ben found that he was in a shallow bay outside the town of Guasissimas. The water was not as clear as it had been north of San Carlos. The scenery was beginning to change. The barren slopes of the windswept mountains, and the vast deserts that covered the land to the north, now gradually gave way to more vegetation. Half-dried swamps and lagoons began to show, and the few palm trees that grew close to the shore provided sturdy anchorage for tying his line at night. Ben paddled all day, still with the waves choppy and rough. Every hour or so he would stop and pull out the pump, trying to rid the cockpit of extra water. With muscles still cramping, he took more breaks than usual. The PowerBars and dried oatmeal tasted like sand. It was hard to muster up an appetite.

That night the camp was in a clump of mangroves. Their sand-banked roots came down to just shy of the water. There were few waves in the cove, and it wasn't a problem to surf to shore and find a tree to tie the safety line. For once, he didn't have to endure the nuisance of the rope cutting into his ankle. Ben sat on the spit of sand, and used the solitude and peacefulness of the evening to refocus his mind on the reasons behind his journey.

All day long the thoughts had pestered him. Ben could come to only one conclusion.

He was certifiably crazy!

How on earth had I thought of this insane idea to travel for many months on the ocean alone? Why? Have I gone completely beyond reason? I'm certain to feel lonely for the rest of the trip, so I must find ways to cope.

At times like these, Ben always turned to his God. He found comfort in His open and consistent grace. He prayed fervently that night.

I could feel His hand on my shoulders as I went to sleep.

Ben's journals were to reflect on God often.

October 21, 1996

Ben set out early, the wind at his back for the first time. Sea swells increased to seven feet, and the power of the ocean rose with the sun. He considered this his daily greeting, and welcomed and accepted her power.

Sometimes I wonder if one day she will grow too strong.

More thunderclouds appeared to the west and the wind picked up in intensity. Something was wrong. Ben couldn't quite put his finger on it, but he sensed the weather changing for the worse. Paddling for as long as he could that day, he struggled to keep up his previous pace. All day the ominous signs of another storm were evident. He saw no boats. Periodically the wind would blow in what seemed like several different directions at once. The ocean dipped and bobbed. At times, as he paddled down the swells swirling well over his head, the shore would disappear from sight.

The coast was long and flat now, and he angled toward the shore until he was close enough to surf the waves onto the sand. By 6:00 p.m., the wind gusts were so strong that Ben could barely stand. He prayed that a hurricane was not in the making. At one point he tried to pitch the tent on the shore, but the wind caught it like a parachute and pulled him all over the beach. Finally, Ben tied the bottom straps of the tent to the outrigger poles of the kayak and was able to climb inside.

The wind was now incredibly strong. The line of black clouds that fully surrounded him said that there would be no relief for awhile. He huddled in the tent, and listened to the sounds of the ocean pounding against the shore. The tent flapped wildly about him, adding to the noise and the insanity that belonged to the elements swirling outside. Waves pounded with such force that he felt like they would consume him where he lay. Ben opened the flap and peered out into the inky black maelstrom. He saw nothing. He yelled at the ocean to be calm. Nothing happened. He lay back down as his thoughts swirled about on what tomorrow would bring – if he was here to see it.

He also wondered, once again, about his own sanity.

Near midnight the wind still howled like a pack of hungry wolves. Without warning, the rods that supported the tent snapped in half. Ben crawled out of the tent and fought to wrap strips of duct tape around the broken metal. But, as soon as he set the tent down, the wind caught the sides and shook it until the poles broke again.

Ben looked out at the ocean and its turmoil, and once again bestowed human foibles on the scene before him.

Is it because of my absence that the ocean is reacting this way? Have I displeased the forces of nature in some way?

Surely not, but he couldn't help thinking it. The wind put a chill in the air. Ben wrapped his arms around his sides to keep warm. Breakers pounded their way toward the shore in sets of ten, and the tiny strip of sand where he stood was a pitiful hiding place. As far out as he could see in the semi-darkness of the ghostly filtered moonlight, the water foamed and curled in angry snarls. The air was heavy with the briny spume as the wind picked up the water and swirled it in all directions. White streaks snaked toward shore and flung their salt foam contents in his face. Ben choked down real terror at the power of the howling, haunting, dance between the wind and sea that swirled deafeningly before him. He could not have heard his own words had he shouted at the top of his lungs.

Ben turned and climbed back inside the disheveled tent, which still lay halfway on its side. He leaned hard against the kayak, seeking some reassurance from the firm hull that he would not be blown away. The tent fabric flapped wildly, slapping him about the face. Outside, the gale wind howled, and the sea crashed and roared just inches from his feet. Over the next hour he listened in terror to the storm.

That night I lay huddled in my tent, buffeted by the storm that raged outside. Deep inside me was a feeling that was raw and unyielding. There was no hiding from it, no escaping it. Everywhere in the darkness that I turned to find some comfort, the feeling confronted me. I couldn't push it back, I couldn't run away. For the first time in my life I felt the gripping, paralyzing, and deadly emotion of the raw and naked fear of imminent death.

Then the tent poles broke once more, and the structure enveloped him in a maelstrom of fabric. Ben pawed through the mess, found and opened the tent flap, and was met by the metal zipper that careened back in the wind and cut his face. A crimson trail of blood oozed above his eyebrow, as the wind brought him to his knees.

Ben could barely see with the sand blowing in all directions. Feeling around for the broken poles, he threw them aside. Now turning his attention to the tent, he tied a piece of rope to the top and wrapped it around the outrigger. There was only a foot of space left inside the tent, but it was enough to cover him. He huddled as close to the kayak as possible for the rest of the night, as the howling wind, and the rumbling ocean, filled his ears. Sleep was as restless as the storm itself.

Ben would take on any challenge without fear. But when he granted the elements the twin human traits of anger and berserk behavior, he instilled dread within himself.

I knew then, with full understanding, the personality of the ocean, and the anger she possessed. Indeed, she is coming to take me home, and that is the last thing I want.

Ben didn't know it at that time but the eye of Hurricane Hernan was only two hundred miles south, rapidly heading north and directly into his path.

Chapter 23

The journals of Benjamin Wade contain his fears and his elations, his guilt and his innocence, his prose and his poetry.

I am the sea.
I am powerful and mighty.
Nothing can compare to my strength.

My arms stretch out to distant shores.
When my will is strong
Nothing dares defy me.

With one hand outstretched
I can wipe out entire cities.
Those who dishonor me
Will cry out for mercy.

I warn you, who so carelessly tread
Upon my brow.
With but one flick of my wrist
I send you crawling
Back to your hovels
Upon the dry land, thinking

That safety has come upon you at last.

Fool, pitiful man.
Know not thou my force,
Or hath thou forgotten thy foe?
Doth thy own feeble mind forget
The whipping I gave thee last,
When thou came upon the mighty sea?

It cannot be true
That thy life will continue.
For I know all
And control thy destiny.
Tempt me not.
Treat me well.
For I am the sea,
Almighty and powerful.

But now I turn to one
Thou tread upon my shores,
And look to me for challenge.
Thou pillage not my treasures
Nor rape me of my contents.

Yet, thou art there
For many a day,
Looking to conquer my power.
Can I have that here?
Certainly thou thinkest wrong.

Little man
Come into my death chambers,
And welcome to thoughts of despair.
Thou will not pass these waters unmolested,
Nor will thou see another day.
At first I could not reach you,
For my finger along that coast wanes thin.
But now you enter
Where my strength returns
And must know thou cannot win.
You feel my power growing each day
And see my strength prevail.

Come close, now, I beckon thee.
Today will be your last-
You cannot hope to escape me.
I come to bring full wrath.

You sit on top thy little boat,
Across my mighty chest,
And think you can challenge my might
Then sleep safely at night on land.

But thou know not of my powers
Or of the old law to which I belong.
I live by the rules of nature
And answer to only one.

Here, now is my right hand
Lifting high above the sea.
Do you like the height I have put you to?
For miles around you can see.
Now plunge downward into my trough
And feel the rush of death.

I can sense your fear now, little man.
I can feel thy feeble heart
Pounding with the rhythm of my own.

This wave will surely be thy death.
My finger stretches toward the sky.
Twenty fathoms have I tossed you now,
And still you ride above.

Like a mad man on the midnight wind,
You give me more than I bargained for.
But so much more the pleasure then
Of destroying what you think is your soul.

Aye, now comes the point of time
I will bring thy spirit to thy knees
And see what ere thou art made of.
One hand hither and the other yon
Converging together in one great feat

And crashing upon thy soul at once.

I feel thy little heart beat
And taste your boat beneath.
Submerged within my breast,
You cannot hope to ride this out.
I now have gained control.
You are on my shoulder for one last ride-
Approaching my maws of death.

See how black they are.
Sense me.
Smell my power.
Feel thy fear.

Hark! What distant rumbling heareth me
Yet louder than my own.
Tell me, no, it is the man
Who formed me from the bone.
'Tis true, the voice of my creator.
The lord, the God above,
Who tells me now to stop thy plight
And calms me like a dove.

Thou, oh mighty seas
Which I created with my hands.
Quell thy spirit of destruction now,
And quicken not my child's death.
But take back
Thy harmful thoughts and pride.

I will make you still and mild.
You know I have the power to do
So require me not to ask thee twice.
You will not try again this year
To take this young man's life.
I hear the words of God himself.
I dare not disobey.

I now am growing calm again
Though not by my own will.

T'was the God above
Who made me now-
To quiet my heart and set me still.

I am the sea.
Hear me roar.

Chapter 24

Tuesday, October 22, 1996

Ben was sure that he would never live to see the next day. During the night the ocean's level rose fifteen feet. It was a full blown hurricane storm surge. Breakers, some over twelve feet high, crashed in maddening sequence onto the shore. They licked hungrily at the edges of his tent, and soaked the sleeping bag where he slept.

Ben woke with a start, disoriented and confused, as a surge of water pushed him and the disheveled tent into the side of the kayak. Before he could move, the kayak and the tent, with Ben trapped helpless inside it, were pushed floating up onto the beach. Still in the twilight between sleep and wakefulness, Ben momentarily imagined that he'd spent the night on the sea in his craft. But he was outside the kayak, being dragged to where he didn't know.

In near panic he clawed his way free of the tent and stood in the howling wind. What he saw in the filtered dawn light drew a scream from his lungs that he could not hear over the raging din.

The water was everywhere, clawing, swirling, reaching, and washing over all I had as it tried to suck me, to drag me, into its maw.

Ben stood his ground. With a death grip on the safety line of the kayak, he kept it guiding back and forth in the waning storm surge. As his vision and thinking cleared, he could see that the water was now mere inches deep, and just playing at the edge of the surf. Finally there was more sand than sea, and the craft came to rest.

As the wind and chaos eased, Ben took stock of his possessions, then carefully wrung out the salt water, and placed his soaked gear into the kayak's compartments. The powerful waves a few yards away posed a threat for him, possibly even deterring him from getting out into the Sea of Cortez.

As far as he could see from his vantage point on the little sand dune, there were walls of white foam from the waves. Fear once more crept into Ben's thoughts. Mist from the morning's drizzling rain filled the air with an unusual chill, and added to his sense of doom. Ben's new found instincts warned of danger. His senses told him to wait, and he found one ray of good hope. The wind was blowing from the north, and Ben thought that if he could just force the kayak out past the dangerous surf, the wind would be at his back. If he made it out there, he might be able to make substantial progress.

Progress was not his only thought that morning, as he dragged the heavy kayak to the ocean's edge. He thought of the alternative of sitting on the shore all day, just watching the clouds pass overhead, and counting the number of crabs who tried to steal his food. This thought was rejected with a loud laugh. Despite the treacherous waters of the Sea of Cortez, Ben knew he couldn't sit idly by for another day. No matter what the conditions, he was prepared to face them.

Regardless of her fury, he thought.

Foolish man.

Ben took a few deep breaths, and set the paddle firmly in place beside his seat. He lowered the new rudder into the sand and pushed off. He leapt into the cockpit and braced himself, as the first wave smacked against the side of the boat.

He turned to meet the next wave, and shuddered.

It was huge.

Closing his eyes and taking a quick gulp of air, he braced for the impact.

The wave was over ten feet tall, and all too quickly engulfed him.

His neck jerked violently back as the rush of water hit with full force.

The kayak stayed upright, but the rush of blue water nearly pulled Ben from the tiny cockpit.

His lungs burned for air that was out of reach. Only reflex and training could save him.

He dug deep with the paddle, using it as a lever to keep the kayak upright until his head broke the foaming surface.

Air, sweet air.

But for how long?

Now on top of the spume and water again, Ben watched the waves crash around and in front of him.

All around the ocean rose up in rage, trying to rid herself of this hapless invader. The cockpit was half full of water. Ben had been waiting for an opportunity to put on his spray skirt, and it had come too late. He kept trying, waiting for a lull in the bouncing, spinning dance. He looked over his shoulder toward the shore, and saw that he was already about fifty yards out. No turning back now. The intensity and power of the water increased with every moment. The next wave formed in front of him. As it built, Ben could tell its size would be awesome. Craning his neck, he could barely see the wavetop's white fingers curling over twenty feet above his head.

I felt my heart leap in fear, as I held the paddle in a death grip that whitened my cramping fingers.

If the wave sucked the kayak into its curling vacuum, Ben would not have a chance to keep the boat from turning over and throwing him out into the sea. He couldn't survive being separated from the boat. The force of the kayak landing on his head could knock him out or break his neck, and he would drown in the boiling water.

There would be not a ripple to mark my passage.

For a split second the wave seemed to hesitate. The kayak raced up its monstrous face. Ben reached the top in a rush of motion just before it broke. Aided by his furious paddling, momentum carried him over the top in a blur of foam and white water. Once on the other side Ben careened rapidly down its back. The kayak's bow sliced through the water, and he paddled frantically to keep up with the pace. Now he was taking deep breaths, intensely aware of his fear. The fear seemed to prick his senses, telling him he was alive, if just for the moment. Mixed with the raw sensation of fear was a rush of excitement.

This is it.
Man against nature.
No time for panic or irrational thinking.

He knew if he lived through this ordeal, it would be an unforgettable day.

If he lived.

A wave broke quickly, crashing against the bow. Saltwater and seaweed slapped his face. Eyes tightly shut, Ben winced as they began to burn. Temporarily blinded, he instinctively struck out into the water with his paddle. He forced stinging eyelids open despite the pain. The cockpit was full to the rim with water. Ben could feel the increased weight beginning to sink the small craft. He was not yet halfway across the field of white froth. The surf still thundered all around. For just a moment, Ben wondered,

What kind of idiot would go out in the teeth of such a storm?

He knew.

The eye of Hurricane Hernan was a scant two hundred miles to the South, and her fingers of energy were stretching out toward him. He was in her shadow, oblivious to her power and direction, paddling like a madman possessed by demons. These demons swirled around his head, blending with the mad waters that encircled him. He reached out, grasping for some hint of what he was doing, or where he was going.

For a brief second Ben floundered beneath the surface of madness.

What has become of my desperate journey?
More deep breaths.

Keep calm! Ben cried out to God to calm the winds.
The howling did not cease.
He peered ahead through salt stung eyes.

Where is a smoother way? No answer.
Only white snarling teeth, and a wind that tore at his skin, responded.
He was fighting for survival.

I strain with all my strength, bracing against each new wave. One hit so hard that the kayak vaults backward toward the shore. For a moment I wonder if it will be thrown all the way to the beach. But slowly, painfully, I gain ground on the wind and waves. Paddle, paddle, easy now.

Then in an instant he loosed himself from the breakers' grip and continued out to sea. Ben now battled with raw fatigue. The dark waters were once again producing frustration and despair. It was all too obvious that today the ocean's fury had taught him another lesson. A critical, life changing lesson. It was time to pay the piper. Ben had gained a few small victories from these waters, but now the mighty harvester was plowing her fields.

His excitement was gone. Now consumed by dark reality.

*Alone on the ocean I know that this is no longer an ego-born chal-
lenge. This is a fight for my very survival. "God please give me strength
now," I plead.*

*At that very moment two smaller waves broke ahead. The momentary
lull in the ocean's fury that I've been looking for appears. I take advantage
of her inactivity to bail a few gallons of water from my cockpit. I have just
enough time to mount and make the difficult adjustments in the spray skirt
before the waves increase once again.*

His strength was drained. Ben thought for a moment about turning
around and heading for shore. Then he thought better about re-engaging
with the surf. He turned and looked over his shoulder. His choice was not
the surf. The shore was nowhere in sight. Now, unable to see land, Ben realized that he must be at least five miles out to sea. Not wanting to be swept
further out by the storm, he focused on paddling toward the rising sun that
now gave off a faint pink glow behind the high clouds. But only a few
miles away, darker, and more foreboding clouds were moving forward. The
haze beneath them told of worse weather to come.

The waves were finally giving way to the larger swells of the open
ocean. Ben didn't feel safe traveling parallel to the coast, but at this point
he had no choice. He could only paddle in the same direction as the massive rolling waves. At the moment, it meant heading directly into the storm.
He turned to face southeast, and slowly settled into a decisive rhythm.

Ben's grim face was set hard against the wind.

He was not willing to give up.

Not yet at least.

Chapter 25

The ocean carried Ben forward. Within the hour he saw, to his immense relief, the outline of the distant shore. The sight lasted only a second as he plunged down the face of another ocean swell. Staying in the direction of the waves, which now rose and fell over twenty feet, Ben had a truce with their violence and was even able to bail more water from the boat. This gave the kayak better maneuverability and his spirits rose in hopes that he'd seen the worst.

For now, despite the walls of water that rise sharply and thunder on all sides, I might be safe.

He could not have been more wrong.

Rain began to fall. Falling softly at first, then thundering down. Already soaked and miserable, Ben set his jaw and continued forward. Despite the heavy rain and strong gusts of wind, he could see for miles around. In the few seconds that he rode atop each wave, Ben could see the entire ocean spread below. He spied the shore line now, and the mountains that rose behind it.

The rain continued to fall in sheets.

Suddenly the wind rose to a howl. The ocean reacted. Menacing wave-tops foamed, boiled, and crashed. The wind gusted forcefully, and the rain now poured down like the flood gates of heaven had opened. Visibility dropped and Ben lost sight of the shore.

He giveth and he taketh away.

"Oh, my God, wha . . .

With a suddenness that didn't allow for a breath, the floor of the ocean gave way.

The kayak plummeted into the abyss.

Now weightless, Ben held a death grip on his seat.

Down, down, into inky, impenetrable darkness.

There was no bottom.

And then there was a spine jolting bottom, and he bounced back up again, racing up the other side of the rogue wave.

All the time he paddled furiously, but Ben had no real control of what was happening.

From his new perch he saw the next wave flex its muscle.

In an instant he was sucked up on its mountainous back.

There he perched unsteadily.

Time seemed to stop.

He looked down into the cavernous mouth of the trough that was about to swallow him up.

The water was darker there, waiting for him.

Ben knew that he was looking at the last few seconds of life.

Thirty feet below, rumbling with discontent, was his final destiny.

Terrified, he tried to let out a yell.

No sound would come from his throat.

Ben yearned to turn back time, to avoid the whole disastrous situation.

It was too late.

He didn't have time to put on his life vest, or even to throw out the safety line.

After the wave collapses, I'll be thrown from the kayak. How long I live after that is anybody's guess. I wonder what it feels like to die. Will I just drown, or will the force of the kayak landing on top of my head knock my senses from me? No doubt my skull will split in two from the weight of my boat. I hope it'll be sudden and not full of torture.

As Ben floated there, on top of this huge mountain of water, he braced himself to begin flying down the wave's face, end over end, and into its jaws of death. He closed his eyes, and waited for the moment of impact.

It was then that he heard the voice.

He knew he heard the voice.

"My son, what have you done for me lately?" the voice questioned. *"Lord,"* Ben said. *"This is really a bad time."*

"There is always time. What have you done for me lately?" It repeated. Ben looked around.

The trough of the wave still yawned thirty feet below.

But the wave hesitated, as if unsure of what to do.

"I will protect you," God continued. Ben in his reverie was now sure of the voice. It was his God. *"I will protect you, and as a result, the name of my Son, Jesus Christ, will be on your lips for the rest of the journey. Everyone you meet will hear his name."*

Ben bowed his head, awed by what had just happened. He looked up to the heavens and a smile broke across his face. He began to pray.

The sudden rush, the feeling of lightness, and the sensation of falling, overwhelmed his senses as he crashed down the face of the wave.

The water rushed by in a blurring motion.

The speed was terrifying, the wind sucking life from his chest.

Ben watched in rising horror, as the front of the kayak began to sink beneath the wave.

The speed at which he was traveling down the arching wall of water, drove the bow deep into the bottom of the wave.

Ben knew that at any second, the boat could end up flipping over, or spinning sideways.

He grabbed the safety line for balance and leaned back to reapportion some of the weight.

As he leaned halfway out of the cockpit, the front end of the kayak began to emerge from the swirling dark water. It bottomed out several feet in front of the crashing white water.

As the foaming water thrust the kayak toward the bay, Ben paddled with renewed energy. After the wave's power was spent, Ben sat still for a moment in the dead wake. Then, with wrenching power, the next wave picked him up, and pitched him forward with ease. His head snapped back from the force, and he watched the water all around him flying by in a single motion.

Ben's water stained journal had an entry here:

My life stops. Everything around me hesitates as if the ocean is unsure of its next move. Distant memories float by. Better times, better places. With pain and sorrow, I think of my family and other loved ones. My pain is not for me, but for the ones I will leave behind. They will be disappointed when they hear of my failure to complete the trip in one piece, or, of my death.

After Ben's thoughts about his past life, and maybe the end of life, he jerked back to the present. Somehow, the kayak managed to avoid upending.

Ben felt another drop in the pit of his stomach as he sped up the back of the next wave.

He quickly slipped back into the center of the cockpit and dug his paddle into the water.

There was no pain now. It was just plain and simple fear that drove him beyond any human limits.

Beyond his own capability.

Early the night before, as he sat in his tent listening to the violent storm building outside, he had spent a good hour poring over the charts. He had noticed a lighthouse a few miles ahead that marked the entrance to a small bay. There was an island to the west side of that bay, and he knew that if he got into trouble that would be the place to head for. Now, as Ben began to gather his senses, and realize that he was still alive, he looked around to get his bearings. The next wave was huge, but not as large and threatening as the one before. He looked ashore, and saw the lighthouse he'd noted the previous night. He knew that if he could make it to the bay he would survive.

The question remained; *can I make it that far?*

Figuring that the bay was about three miles away, with an audible cry of relief and joy, Ben turned the bow and headed for safety. Again, enduring the pain, he urged himself on, ignoring the ocean's call to death. Ben gritted his teeth and paddled for his life. Three hours later Ben had reached a point of fatigue that was almost unbearable.

I could not recall the seconds, or minutes, or anything else for that matter, about the time gone by that day.

Then he saw the welcoming beacon of the lighthouse. This time it was much closer. Although his mind had slowed, blocking out the waves of pain, a hope arose within. Most of the waves were now headed in the direction of the lighthouse. The wind, however, was blowing the other way. As a result, smaller waves were beginning to form. They came in the opposite direction from the existing breakers. This created a pocket of compressed air between them that, when the waves collided, broke through the surface and sounded like a shotgun blast.

On one such occasion, Ben watched in amazement as he too became a part of this phenomenon. A ten foot wave came from the front and rose up to meet its adversary behind. He felt himself sink down as the two waves came together and met with stunning force. The ringing in his ears began as soon as he felt the cold water slap his face, and completely submerge the kayak. He saw nothing but darkness, and had to achingly jamb his knees inside the cockpit to keep from being pulled out of the boat.

The ocean swirled about, pulling him one way and then another.

Ben could feel the icy fingers of water reaching in, desperate to squeeze out his last breath.

Unsuccessful with his body, the icy fingers reached for his paddle and wrenched it from his hands.

Involuntarily, Ben let go and lost his grip to the much stronger force of the water.

The weight of the ocean then ripped the spray skirt from around his waist and swallowed it down.

Ben felt like a small rabbit being hunted by a fox.

Now he is hunted by the ocean. Chased down and pounced upon by her unrelenting jaws.

Ben began to wonder where reality and fantasy drew a line.

Finally the front of the kayak surged upward toward the light, and the life he so desperately sought. Ben's free hand struck out for the poles of the outrigger. He threw his full weight onto the rails and refused to be thrown off. With a rush of sound like a hundred freight trains, he broke through the surface. The buoyancy of the kayak lifted the craft several feet into the air above the ocean. Then it came crashing down upon its surface with a loud whack. Ben felt the cool air and breathed in deeply.

His lungs ached from having held his breath for so long.

The sharp pain only served to remind him that he was alive.

Somehow, Ben was still alive.

The light from the sky was in sharp contrast to the darkened waters from which Ben had just emerged.

He was blinded.

It took a moment to clear his head and look around at the new conditions.

He could no longer feel the reassuring foam rubber of the cockpit seat.

It seemed as though he was floating in the water.

Sure enough, as his senses and sight returned, he could see that his lower half was dangling in the ocean, his arms still clutched the outrigger's poles with the grip of death.

But not his death.

Not this time.

To Ben's dismay, he saw that his supplies were everywhere. They were bobbing up and down, just out of reach in all directions. Three gallons of water passed rapidly by his outstretched fingers. He knew it would be a hopeless effort to try and retrieve them. Ben climbed back into the cockpit. The percussive effect from the convergent, colliding waves had so deafened him, that now he could hear a high pitched ringing that mixed with the muffled sound of the ocean. Without the spray skirt, the kayak was sinking, and Ben had just enough energy to pump out some of the excess water. There were several cuts on his arms and fingers and the blood was trickling over into the water. The rain continued its downpour.

Ben thanked himself for being such an idiot.

Why on earth had I been so foolish as to think I could navigate through a squall?

Now he wondered if he could make it to the safety of the bay.

How long will it be until my body involuntarily stops itself?

Without his paddle, Ben was like a sitting duck. He looked in front of his seat where the Emergency Locator Beacon was strapped down. If he could pull it out, he might have enough time to transmit a satellite signal to Washington. The SOS would probably not be answered for 48 hours. By that time he had no idea where he'd be. With a start Ben realized that the E.L.B. was not where it should be. It had been swept overboard, along with his radio and other things too numerous to count.

A white object in the water caught Ben's attention. He saw that it was the blade of his paddle. He prepared to jump overboard and retrieve it when he noticed it was floating his way. Ben reached out and grasped the handle just as it went by. Several feet away he saw the orange head of the E. L. Beacon floating in the water. He quickly paddled over and retrieved it, placing it firmly between his legs.

The waves had died down somewhat for a moment. Now they began to grow restless again. Ben watched helplessly as the rest of his supplies scattered about and were swept away by the breakers. Reluctantly, he turned again for the backside of the island.

Almost two hours later the lighthouse reappeared. It was only a hundred yards to his right. The waves were breaking directly toward the island and Ben stopped paddling to let their momentum carry him for awhile. He was almost too weak to lift the paddle. His hands hung limply at his sides.

I know not how I survived.

Hour after hour I'd paddled, committing every fiber of my being to the task of surviving. Raw fear had succumbed to a strange mix of looming dread and surging adrenaline. Like never before, I feel the welling up of superhuman strength that both frightens me and spurs me onward. Though totally spent, my pace increases. There is something else. I have the feeling that I have looked death in the face and defeated it! I feel a euphoria now that has me laughing, crying, and yelling aloud at the water around me!

It was with a mixture of awe and fear that he stared down the face of those last few waves. At times he felt detached from what was going on around him. The pain in his shoulders stiffened. He could barely keep his head up. The fatigue was complete.

As I near the bay behind the island, the sea has become unusually shallow. I'm a few hundred yards from shore, and have a mile to go. A wave now catches me in its sucking draw and I ride to the top of it.

I lean back in surprise and fear as I see only sandy bottom below me! If I crash through, it will be the end!

My kayak slides down the back of the wave and is immediately lifted onto the next.

Once again there is no water in front of me, only the hard sand of the sea floor.

The waves are large, and the water so shallow.

God help me through before they smash me to pieces!

Twice more Ben takes the frightening ride, then settles himself on the face of a gentle wave that slipped, with water beneath his keel, toward the shore. With one last futile push the ocean calmed herself as Ben floated into the shallow bay. Once behind the island, Ben only wanted one thing. To stand again on solid ground.

Thoroughly exhausted, his mind shut down for a few minutes. The current slowly pushed him through the now serene waters. Ben prayed for the next several moments, thanking God for his protection. He would never forget what He had told Ben on top of that wave. During the frightful events of the morning, which lasted over four hours, Ben had postponed any show of outward emotions.

Now, as he felt the kayak nudge the soft sand of the island, tears rushed up to his eyes. He rolled out of the cockpit and onto the soft beach. Shaking, he pushed up on his hands and knees, and vomited what little was left in him. When he closed his eyes, he could still feel the terrifying power of those waves grabbing at him, still trying to rip out his soul.

Chapter 26

For the next several weeks, nightmares of that morning continued to haunt Ben. Even during the calmer days on the ocean following the storm, Ben would have flashbacks. Perched on top of the wave, he could still see himself looking down into its mouth. He felt the fall, and the rush of death.

That day Ben had survived what turned out to be the tail end of a hurricane, the last of the season. It was truly a miracle that he was able to survive a few minutes, let alone four hours, in the dangerous, pounding sea. In the months that followed, Ben never again encountered a storm with half the intensity of that day. He was fortunate to have been saved.

He would also not forget the promise he'd made to his Lord.

Ben had found refuge from the storm on Isla Lobos, Spanish for wolfs' Island. The island is divided into three regions. To the south is desert. Giant sand dunes stretch out and roll in waves like the ocean beyond. No vegetation grows in this area, and it was over these hot dunes that Ben walked to get to the second region.

In the middle of the island, blending into the desert, is the beginning of a forest. Ben's exhaustion from the vigorous morning waned as he found himself surrounded by trees. The shade was welcoming. It was the first time Ben had seen vegetation so dense since he began his journey. Palm trees towered high above the trail, and tall gray-green grass grew on either side. He looked down at the small dirt path he was walking on, and thought about how it had been carved out by the animals' constant movement across the tiny island. At one point he stepped across a tiny stream. Animal tracks in the mud were a telltale sign of their dependence on the water that flowed there. No humans inhabited the island, and that was okay with Ben Wade. He felt comfortable among the trees and blended well with the nature around him. He breathed in deeply and reveled in the musty aromas of life.

Ben let his mind wander as he walked across the island. He had almost forgotten his bout with the ocean. Almost. But he was beginning to feel rested and revitalized, and his sanity, which he truly believed had been nearly lost in the storm, was returning. His hands had long since stopped shaking, and he was ready to cautiously venture out onto the ocean again.

The clouds overhead broke and the warming rays of the sun filled the skyline with hope. Once out of the forest, the trail led to a swamp, the third region. The partially dry lake bed was covered with gracefully drooping pussy willows. In some places water stood in tiny patches. More tracks in the mud, larger than the prints in the forest, told Ben that they could possibly come from the animal for which the island had been named. Wolves.

Indeed, after Ben returned to the kayak, he heard rustling in nearby bushes. Looking up, he was surprised to see the wild and fearless eyes of a wolf looking back. The wolf's body was covered with a fur far thicker than any dog Ben had ever seen. She crouched there, content to watch him while she remained hidden among the thickets. When Ben took a step toward her, she retreated deliberately and majestically into the forest. Rounding up what was left of his gear he set off again. The island, three miles long and several hundred yards wide, had taken a few hours to explore. A distraction that soothed his fragile nerves.

After kayaking around the island, Ben set a course south, past the tip of the mainland. The storm was completely spent, and the ocean's fury had quieted. But he was taking no more chances that day. He promised himself that if any other signs of formidable weather or waves reappeared, he was heading straight for the shore.

A few hours later Ben saw two shrimp boats. They had been grounded by the high waves and rested several feet up on the beach. Apparently Ben had not been the only victim of the morning's storm. Hoping for some friendly company, he put into shore and set up camp nearby. Curious about the unexpected visitor, a diver from one of the boats came over to Ben's camp. After talking to Ben for a while, he motioned for one of the captains to come over. The other man brought some of the catch he had on board. Crabs. Some freshly boiled crabs. Delighted, Ben eagerly listened to a quick lesson on how to tear back the carapace to reveal the pea green 'stew' inside. His cringing look of revulsion when he first looked at the green soupy mass inside, elicited guffaws of laughter from the fishermen.

But he joined the laughter and, using the bright red carapace as a ladle, he dug in and found it quite acceptable. But he found the meat extracted from the ecto-skeleton more to his taste, and quickly ate five of the succulent crustaceans. Wiping away the feast's debris with the back of his hand, Ben told the men his story.

It was nice to have a different meal. Something other than dried food. The company of men was a good diversion from the monotony and grief of the perilous sea.

That night the wind picked up again. It battered Ben's tent, but his weary mind and exhausted and bruised body gave way to sleep despite the noise.

Wednesday, October 23, 1996

The day went by without any problems. Ben was prepared to head for the shelter of the next Island, Huivuilay, if the water grew turbulent, but the sea remained calm. It seemed to Ben that the water was offering an apology to him for the abuse of the day before. Frightening memories returned sometimes, but Ben continued to move forward.

That night, noting that the water remained tranquil, Ben decided to continue paddling and not to head for shore. There were several lighthouses on the map that marked various inlets and towns. Navigation was not a problem. He slept several hours and the night quickly turned into day. More than once, unfortunately, he woke up screaming. He remained fearful that the ocean would rise again and claim its prey.

As the sun rose, Ben could see the village of Yvaros, Sonora State, Mexico. The salt and shrimp boats were working busily in the harbor. He stayed clear of the bay and cut straight across to Agiabampo, another small fishing village. He was beginning to make good progress, almost thirty five miles this day. His muscles were recuperating from the storm, and he could paddle six hours straight most days without stopping for a break. He pulled into the village after passing by the estuary that marked the boundary between the Mexican states of Sinaloa and Sonora.

As Ben pulled the kayak onto the shore, he could sense trouble coming. Police were everywhere, seemingly hassling the locals. He'd heard rumors about the policemen in Mexico being corrupt. Several of the officers looked his way, as he pitched his tent on the beach. Ben didn't like the look of the cruel smiles on their faces, or the tone of the comments they whispered to one another. Ben figured his best policy was no policy. So he ignored the uniformed men, and set about fixing dinner.

Another delicious gourmet meal of beef jerky, trail mix and water. *A meal fit for a king. Ha*!

After dutifully cleaning up the food wrappers, Ben looked again at the dreary village. Usually, the town's people would come up to have a closer look at the gringo and his kayak. That night, however, an eerie silence settled over Agiabampo. No one came to talk to him, and the lights all went out shortly after dark. With a twinge in his stomach, Ben sensed that something was not right. First thing in the morning he would leave. This place was starting to give him the creeps. He curled into his sleeping bag, escaping the chill of the night air, and went to sleep.

Thursday, October 24, 1996
Agiabampo, Sonora, Mexico

Ben packed his gear back into the kayak and untied the safety line. He was nosing the bow toward the waves when he heard voices behind, yelling for him to stop. He looked around, and, to his shocked surprise, saw one of the policemen approaching on the run. His rifle flopped up and down, making him look a little silly as he tried to tuck it to one side. His uniform was a dark blue with long sleeved shirt and pants. Ben waited patiently for him to approach. When they were face to face the panting officer asked Ben for his papers. Ben opened the front compartment and pulled out his passport, unwrapping it from the plastic bag that kept it dry. Opening it to his picture, Ben handed it to the officer. Then Ben looked for the photocopy of one of the newspaper articles which would explain his unusual mode of transportation. The officer waved them aside after just a brief look, handed them back to Ben, and then pointed to the kayak's storage area. Ben could tell by the gleam in his eye that the various items in the kayak had piqued his curiosity. By this time, two more police officers had come up behind Ben, their rifles grasped firmly in both hands. They waved the weapons menacingly in his face as he stooped over the kayak. Ben got the impression that they wanted him to stay put. He straightened back up and stood aside.

Guns were still pointed at him.

As if I was going anywhere with half of the Mexican police force breathing down my neck.

Ben once more pointed at the newspaper article, then at the ocean. But the first man, obviously in charge, seemed uninterested. He motioned for one of the other men to come over and, without another word, began to take everything out of the kayak. Outraged, but helpless, Ben stood with his arms folded.

They have no right to search me.
But I have to remember I'm in a foreign country.
What could they possibly be looking for?
Drugs?

When the men had finished, Ben's clothes, food, and rope were strewn across the nearby sand. They didn't bother putting the supplies back where they'd found them. The first man, intent on carrying out his little operation, motioned for Ben to open the other compartment. Ben threw his hands in the air, disgusted. While Ben was busy putting his supplies back into the front of the kayak, he heard one of officers curse. All three began to talk rapidly in Spanish. In low voices, they talked excitedly, like they'd just stumbled upon a sunken treasure.

In a way, they had.

Ben glanced over and saw them holding his ten pound box of vanilla weight-gain powder. It had been donated to him for the voyage. He used it to make sure he was taking in enough vitamins and minerals.

No problem here.
There's nothing incriminating about that.
Just white powder. What a hassle!
Unless.
Hold on.
White powder substance.
Oh no!

Drugs were what they were looking for, and drugs they were going to get. Regardless of the truth, Ben knew he was in trouble. He began to explain as best he could.

The powder is used for my strength while I paddle on the ocean.

Ben pointed again at the article but his efforts were in vain. One of the men made an about-face, a little awkwardly in the sand, and walked off, the box of weight gainer tucked under his arm, duly confiscated for evidence.

These guys obviously did not have a clue. Trying to make light of the situation in his mind, Ben tried to imagine the officers later that night. They would probably be making fun of the gringo who was unlucky enough to run into such smart policio officiales. No doubt the evidence would be spread out on the table, and they would be sampling the goods through their own nostrils. What a shock that would be. Ben smiled at the thought, and the officer that guarded him wanted to know what was so funny.

Obviously, not sharing Ben's sense of humor, he lowered his rifle toward him. It was only inches away from Ben's body pointed directly at his stomach. "*Dinero ahora*," the man said. The other one brought out hand cuffs, and took a few menacing steps in Ben's direction. In disgust, Ben spit on the ground and went over to the kayak. Seeing that the only way out of this stupid predicament was to give them the money they'd asked for, he agreed.

This government is so corrupt, Ben thought bitterly as he pulled out his wallet.

Why doesn't somebody do something about this?
This would never happen in America.

Ben had really begun to like the people of Mexico. It was a shame that a few corrupt police could ruin the reputation of an entire country. Until now, Ben had kept his money in separate places just for situations like this. Heather's arrival in San Carlos had prompted a bit of spending, and he only had about $300 dollars left. Unfortunately, it was all in one place. His wallet. Ben pulled the money out, trying to conceal the amount, and hoping to get out of the situation with a couple of twenties. He was not so lucky. The officer who had taken a few steps in his direction was suddenly beside him. Lowering his gun, he wrenched Ben's free arm behind his back. Ben winced in pain and dropped to his knees, afraid that his elbow might give way. The other man, his gun still pointed at Ben's belly, grabbed the entire roll of money from his hand. Ben stared at him, and, as he caught Ben's glare, his gun went up to Ben's face, scraping his nose. Ben dropped his eyes to the sand, just as the first man released his arm. Now sitting back on his ankles and rubbing his sore elbow, Ben couldn't believe it was all happening.

Where are my rights? These bastards are the law?

Ben moved his hands a little, forcing the blood back to that area. The pain still lingered in his mind as well as his arm. The man folded the money, tucked it into his shirt pocket, and slung the gun back over his

180

shoulder. That, at least, was a good thing. He smiled at the other man and, without another word they turned and walked away.

Ben wanted to yell out, to run after them, but there was nothing he could do but hold his tongue against their injustice. A few people had gathered at a safe distance. They watched what had happened to the gringo. Now that the show was over, they averted their eyes and slowly began to walk away.

Ben felt empty and violated. Left alone to lick his wounds.

Never had he been so humiliated in his life.

He looked in his wallet and counted the bills that remained.

Seven dollars.

What am I supposed to do with that?

Seven dollars would not go far, even in Mexico. One week's supply of water would exhaust that. Ben shook the sand off each of his prized possessions and placed them in the kayak.

That day Ben paddled without much energy. He felt sapped of motivation, and his mind was elsewhere. That night he pulled in and camped on a remote and uninhabited stretch of beach. He sat alone on the sand and contemplated his next move. He wondered what other difficulties he would encounter in the coming months. He always hated to worry about finances but now he had no choice. One thing was for sure, if he didn't get his hands on more money somehow, he could not go any further. The trip was over. His feelings turned dark and lonely.

A voice inside him screamed in frustration.

Ben's emotions were raw that lonely night.

Journal, Thursday, October 24^{*th*}

I have no money now, thanks to the Mexican government. I was ripped off blind today, because the police thought I was carrying cocaine. I tried to tell them that it was vanilla powder, but they were too stupid to listen. I have hardly any money left, only seven dollars. Seven worthless dollars! That will not go far. I have never felt so wronged in my whole life. What did I do to deserve that? What am I going to do now?

I feel so lost. So lonely. So helpless.

No direction of where to go from here.

Why should I continue such a miserable journey?

Why did I take on such a challenge in the first place?

181

Pride, yes pride.

They couldn't take that away from me today, could they?

I have been humbled, humiliated, and reduced to tears by this ocean and this country, but I will not quit!

I have too much pride to give up now, and I don't want to go home to my friends and family. I feel so lonely now. But I know that I can't go home. Everyone will say, "Its okay, we know you did your best."

I would think differently, though. Inside, I would know I was a quitter. Sometimes I hate this trip. A challenge? You better believe it. The next time I want to do something extreme, I'll think twice about it. One thing is for sure, I'll never again do this alone. If I had a companion, at least right now, we could sit here and talk about it. Draw strength from each other. Now I can only talk to myself. My only solace is to get these words out as quick as I can, on paper, and then move on.

Being alone really stinks. I feel so down, like everything has gone wrong and everyone has deserted me. I feel out on a limb, and the branch is being cut. Falling now, in this dark, forsaken area. The solitude has crept into my mind. Nowhere to turn, no one to help. Except God. I know He will deliver me from these perils. Is that enough? It should be. I know it is enough, but then why do I still feel so empty?

Ben lay back down to sleep after writing the journal entry. He held back the lonely tears and pain as best he could. The loneliness had abated somewhat when he awoke the next morning. The cheerful rays of the morning sun always seemed to put Ben in a better mood. It was the one constant source of strength in an ever changing environment. He knew everyday that the sun would rise and with it, the expectations of a new day.

Hopefully a better day than the last one.

Ben was still thinking about the good old U.S. of A. when he paddled out that morning. He missed a roof over his head, a home to sleep in, and the companionship of friends. His need for stability was increasing.

Stability.

Maybe that's another reason why most people never do anything out of their own comfort zone. The comfort zone that provides stability and familiar surroundings. They are too afraid to lose what they already have.

Ben certainly didn't have anything to lose. Knowing that, he stepped out of his comfort zone, and stepped out onto the ocean to chase his dreams. Thinking about his goal and the promise of strength that went along with it gave him hope that morning as he continued to paddle south.

The wind was blowing slightly from the north with new vigor and a will that Ben knew could only come from God.

The coast flew by.

He would not be defeated by this expedition.

Not yet.

Chapter 27

One area south of Topolobampo, and near the Isla de San Ignatión, was particularly smooth. The gentle ocean swells parted gracefully as the bow of Ben's kayak sliced through their backs. Sets of large breakers formed at the entrance to the each bay that hid behind the many islands he passed by. The breaking sea was probably caused by rapid changes in the depth of the water. Ben chose to stay away from these areas and out to where the deeper water remained calm. He knew better than to get too near the rumbling white froth, and foam speckled waves.

There were so many islands scattered about that sometimes Ben wondered whether the horizon was an island or the mainland. Once in a while he would see a break in the string of islands and the land borne mountains that swung down all the way to Mexico City. He marveled how they reared their majestic heads to thrust mighty peaks against an azure sky.

Near a protected stretch of beach on the outskirts of Topolobampo, Ben surfed his trusty craft onto shore. The tiny store he walked to was like all the rest of the places where he'd bought water along the way - small, dusty, and full of little children and dogs, all playing in timeless harmony. He picked up five gallons of purified water that cost him twenty five pesos, around three dollars in American money.

Topolobampo, Sinaloa, Mexico is an ugly-beautiful, dusty little town that used to support shrimp fishermen, but now succumbed to Pemex plants and tourists. With its hills and offshore islands, some call it a Cinderella without a fairy godmother. Ben enjoyed talking to the people he met when he came into a town like this, telling them of his journey.

185

Now, he added comments about the protection God had given him.

Ben was back on the water late on Saturday night, the 26th of October, as it began to rain. Ben put on a waterproof wind breaker. But, with the torrents of rain that fell, it was impossible to stay completely dry. Rain continued to pour long into the night, soaking the kayak and all his belongings. The cool night air along with the rain chilled him to the bone. He didn't want to ruin the sleeping bag or anything else in the dry compartments by opening the air tight lids, so he continued on his way with a shiver.

At least it was fresh water.

Even with the cold, Ben found it becoming easier to travel at night. The demons that had so haunted him earlier in the trip faded into the mist as his familiarity with the ocean, and his own inner peace, increased. The water was calmer at night than in the day, and Ben was surprised at the distance he gained by the additional hours of rhythmic paddling in the dark. There were plenty of lighthouses marking the entrances to the various bays, so he was able to maintain a fairly straight heading. Occasionally, he looked down at the compass that hung around his neck to be sure he was going in the right direction. On clear nights, the stars that he had become so familiar with were a welcome addition to the ebony velvet sky.

Sleeping for only fifteen minutes at a time was, at first, incredibly exhausting. Now, it almost seemed natural. Like a short afternoon nap, he awoke refreshed and alert. The night air worked as an alarm clock. When he stopped paddling to sleep, his body temperature would slowly drop. After twenty minutes or so, he would be cold enough to involuntarily awake. He welcomed the warming sensation of his exercise-circulated blood, and was always eager to resume his rhythm.

It continued to rain for the next three days, and Ben presumed it was the monsoon season just finishing up in the southern latitudes. He didn't complain. It was to him a sign of his southerly progress. The tailwind continued, and Ben saw the outlines of a few towns as he passed by. To prevent his entire supply of food from getting wet, he placed just a few days' rations at a time in the cockpit behind his seat. He was also careful to protect his journals. He didn't want any of his previous writings to get ruined by the rain.

The surf on the shore was noticeably larger than before. Ben could see the tops of breakers off in the distance. They were electric blue, turning to white as they curled over and broke against the sand. He knew by looking at the charts, now kept in see-through plastic bags, that the Pacific Ocean was beginning to push around the tip of the Baja Peninsula.

Ben was finally in the open ocean, and he welcomed the great rolling power of the long, sweeping, Pacific swells beneath him. He was happy and relieved that the chop of the smaller breakers in the Sea of Cortez was being left behind.

Though he was traveling a good distance from shore, he could still hear the waves' low and continuous rumble blending together with the spatter of rain on the water.

Ben was now in the full grasp of the wide open Pacific Ocean.

October 28, 1996
Nearing Mazatlan, Mexico

The rain stopped late in the evening, and Ben saw the distant lights of Mazatlan reflecting off the roiling base of the dark, cloud laden sky. The light play was a glow of yellow that warmed his eyes and thoughts. Tomorrow he would be able to rest, dry off, and concentrate on raising enough money to continue.

Tonight though, he was rapidly tiring. The night air, the rain, and lack of real sleep, were taking their toll.

How long has it been since I rested a full night? Three days? I can't remember.

If Mazatlan had not been so close, with the human contact and real rest it promised, Ben would have pulled over to the shore and slept where he was. He paddled on.

The money situation continued to intrude on Ben's thoughts that night, as he paddled closer to the beckoning lights. Now down to three dollars and some change, he knew he had a problem that maybe, hopefully, he could solve in a city. At first, he'd thought about calling his mom and dad. They could easily wire down a couple of hundred dollars. But the more he remembered the disapproval they had of his expedition, the more he knew it would hurt them to send the money. Anyway, it would be too hard to beg family for money. He was raised with the principal that whatever money you got, you earned. Handouts were just not allowed.

Maybe I can get a job, work for a month, save some money, and then move on? Or maybe Christian could raise some cash back home from my sponsors? Maybe take up a 'Ben Wade collection fund'? Lots of maybes. Nothing absolute.

Still, he hated to ask for money. Ben came up with no conclusions that night, and decided he would just have to play it by ear.

October 30th, 1996
Mazatlan, Mexico

The kayak glided silently into the city's fine harbor. The long stretch of hotels lining the main street seemed to welcome Ben back to polite society. He passed two forest covered islands on his right, and spied the guano-whitened island in mid harbor that provided the cruise ships with a landmark. With renewed vigor, Ben headed for shore through the wide mouth of the bay. The surf rose eight feet high to crash on the shore. But there was only one set of breakers curling at a time. He rode expertly between the swells, timing their surge just right, and landed on the shore with ease.

Ben knew, like it or not, he would be in Mazatlan for a while, so his first order of business was to find storage for the kayak. He needed to raise some money soon. So far, along the way, he'd been careful not to leave his belongings alone for too long. In the big city, a few moments unattended could bring disaster. It was just past 6:00 a.m. when Ben stepped out of the kayak and onto the beach. His legs felt a bit shaky, and he realized that it had been three days since he had set foot on land. He leaned back and stretched tired, cramped muscles.

The city was asleep, but Ben could see a road just past the edge of the sand, and a few cars already whizzed past. He climbed the stairs from the sand and looked up at the hotels that towered above. He felt a little awkward and out of place, surrounded by the modern structures. The smell of exhaust made his nose twitch, and the pavement under his feet felt hard, cold, and unmoving. It wasn't the soft, giving, sand he was used to.

After Ben got over his initial culture shock, he looked down the street as a cab was slowly approaching. Ben beckoned to the driver to stop. With a friendly honk he pulled over to the side. The driver didn't seem to be in a hurry, so they talked for a while. They even walked down to Ben's kayak and looked at a few newspaper articles about his trip. Ben explained to him that he needed a place to store the boat for a few weeks. The driver smiled and said he had a brother who worked in a warehouse next to the train station only a few blocks away. "No tengo mucho dinero," Ben said in his best Spanish. "No problema," the man responded, smiling again. "Tu eres famosa."

So, I am famous, Ben thought with a smile.

They hauled the kayak up the beach, took off the outrigger, and secured it all to the top of the taxi. The kayak was now considerably lighter than when Ben had first started. There had been a lot of rearranging in the last several weeks. Everything that was more of a luxury than a necessity, he'd thrown away. The ocean too had done its part to lighten the load, claiming some supplies for herself.

Ben remembered back to when they had first loaded the kayak onto Heather's truck in Fullerton in September. It had taken three men to heave it on top. Now, the taxi driver and Ben handled it with ease. After a few moments of rope tying, with a properly tied bowline knot, they were driving through the central part of Mazatlan. After a few stoplights, the warehouse loomed into sight.

The taxi driver's brother, for some reason awake at such an early hour, shook Ben's hand warmly. He was proud to be of help to this *famoso* guy. They placed the kayak in the warehouse, the storage area actually a part of the train station. Ben wondered about the legality of the situation, but he was too tired to ask any questions. After chaining the kayak to a steel pole, Ben closed the lock and shook hands with both men. He gave his last three dollars to the cab driver for fare, and told the men that he'd be back tomorrow to recover some of the supplies.

Ben walked away, relieved that his first dilemma had been taken care of.

He was oblivious to the new problem he had just created.

Chapter 28

Know how to ask. There is nothing more difficult for some people, nor for others, easier.

Baltasar Gracián Y Morales (1601 – 1658)

B en Wade immediately fell in love with the city of Mazatlan. The tourist season had yet to start and the population of over 300,000 relaxed in the foreigners' absence. While many people lived in the inner city, urban clusters spread out over an area of ten miles. Some parts of the city felt like isolated villages, as they sat apart from the shopping malls and traffic laden boulevards, as if deep in some mountains.

With the kayak stored in the warehouse, Ben found himself walking through a section of the city called El Centro. This was the old part of town where the city first began. He smelled fresh baked bread on the corner, and watched two señoras patting homemade tortillas from soft dough. Ben reveled in the sights and sounds of this old world civilization. He strolled past narrow streets, and meandering alleys with shops, small restaurants, and kiosks. Most shops had apartments above them that towered over the tiny streets. The sun seemed to have little chance to reach the ground, but the closeness only added to the quaint setting.

Concrete urns filled with fragrant blooming flowers were carefully mothered by proud owners. A man sold fruit from his little wooden cart. He had papayas, coconuts, pineapples, watermelon, and cantaloupes displayed in a colorful semi-circle, as he cut and peeled them with his sharp knife. On another street a smiling, gold toothed mother made tortillas by hand, as her three children frolicked playfully around her colorful skirts. Ben watched as she rolled the dough, and flattened the tortillas on a wooden board, moving with practiced haste as she prepared the delicious flat bread for her customers who would arrive each day at noon. Local people walked on every street, some strolling, but most moving with a purpose. While some gave Ben a sideward glance, he didn't feel rushed or crowded. Fresh, fragrant air blew lazily through the avenues, reminding one of the gentle and easy pace that Mexico is so famous for.

Once out of the downtown area, Ben followed the curve of the ocean, strolling along the avenue that ran parallel to the beach. He could see out to the entire bay, and beyond to the islands that dotted the horizon. The bay waters winked and sparkled brilliantly in the late morning sun, framed like a Mexican velvet painting by the winding boulevard.

Beyond El Centro, the city changes rapidly. Nearby was a section that was newer than oldtown, but still weathered with age. Later Ben learned that this was a popular area for Hollywood vacationers during the fifties and sixties. The buildings reached skyward, still hoping to show off their now faded glamour, but their era had passed, and their days of dominating the city's night life were long over. The once sparkling white towers were now yellowed and worn, like the tattered lace curtains that flowed sensuously from some of the upper windows.

Eventually, these golden age buildings gave way to the new buildings of the gold zone. *La Zona Dorada*. In a sudden sweep before Ben's eyes, the city changed into a glittering array of newly built hotels, restaurants, and shops. He strolled around a circular street that was reminiscent of the great Trafalgar Square in London, and stopped, blinking in astonishment, as the tourist section of the city unfolded before him. Nightclubs, resorts, and fancy restaurants, beckoned the new generation forth. The skinny, sleek, modern architecture, and the ever present bustle of the visiting *gringos*, spoke of this as the next great resort city along the Pacific. But Ben saw it as different from some of the older popular resort cities, like Acapulco or Cabo San Lucas. To Ben's eyes, Mazatlan's center of excitement was neither oppressive nor hectic.

Everywhere he looked there were hidden jewels. On one corner a private restaurant with a balcony gave diners a view of the lush greenery that flowed down the mountain. On other narrow lanes there were tiny shops tucked behind larger buildings. Waterfalls poured into stone basins that were gracefully shaded by miniature palm trees. No space was wasted. The streets were clean, and everyone walked around excited at what this city had to offer. Ben had found a new haven in this busy tropical port.

At least for the moment.

As deepening shadows announced the arrival of evening, Ben realized that he had no place to sleep, and nothing to eat. During the last few months, his tent had provided adequate shelter. The food in his kayak, although at times a bit dry, had satisfied his hunger. Now he realized that he had neither.

This was the first time he'd been separated from his kayak, and its meager, but life-sustaining, bounty of provisions and supplies.

Ben felt naked.

Now the happiness and energy of the people passing by only served to heighten his feelings of alienation. With his tent and sleeping bag, Ben could sleep anywhere. Now, with the kayak in storage some five miles away, he felt isolated and alone.

The ocean had been his home for almost two months.

This day the reality of his homeless state sharply emerged.

He had only the clothes on his back.

No food, no shelter, no money.   *Nice planning, dummy!*

As I walked the streets of Mazatlan, I noticed the tourists purposely avoiding me. Once, as I passed a bread maker, my stomach growled with hunger. I drew a breath, deliciously fragrant with the aroma of fresh baked bread that I could not buy. Coming toward me a tourist couple turned their heads away, and crossed the narrow street to avoid meeting me.

Ben had not eaten in over twenty four hours. His mental and physical states were catching up to him. He became keenly aware of people avoiding him, and of his grumbling, empty stomach.

By mid-afternoon it begins to rain, and I duck under the awning of a restaurant where some sidewalk tables stand. A couple, I presume to be American, sit eating. I step over and humbly tell them my story. They look me up and down, wrinkle their noses, and refuse to help, or even to speak to me. Embarrassed, I glance the other way and peer at the mirrored door that faces me. Wearing a pair of faded blue soccer shorts, a tattered t-shirt, and a week old salt crusted beard, a wild-eyed stranger stares back at me. I stand there, crushed, then turn away from the disturbing reflection, and sit at the table next to the Americans. A waiter rushes up and asks me to leave. Desperate, I indicate that I am with that other couple. Fortunately, they don't see my ruse. As soon as the couple leaves, I grab their plates and wolf down what remains of their meals.

An hour later, still roaming the streets, I am once again hungry.

Ben now regretted his folly and lack of foresight. Civilization provided him comforts. Its citizens helped him to forget his loneliness. But with this promise of security comes responsibilities that Ben had woefully failed to remember.

I'm cold, miserable, and alone. As the night comes on, another feeling grips me. Fear. I yearn for the nights on my kayak, or on the beach. Here I cannot sleep. I have nothing for anyone to steal, so robbing me would probably end badly. I cannot sleep. But I must. I see an alcove near a closed shop in the far corner of an alley. I huddle here, and peer out with what must be feral eyes, darting here and there, looking for danger, real or imagined, and for people or animals that might discover my hiding place.
I'm totally alone. I'm totally despondent,
I am totally afraid.
I don't know what to do, but I'm drifting away to sleep.
The quarters are cramped, but I must sleep. Sleep

Morning light roused Ben, and he shook himself back to his present, pitiful reality. As he stood and stretched, he spied a brightly lit sign announcing the local marina, *La Marina del Cid*. A large blue plastic sailfish perched atop a kiosk near the sign, and Ben looked down at the small sales booth beneath it where a man stood, readying his business for the day. Ben wondered if the man standing at the table spoke English.

As Ben started in that direction, he stopped by a trash can, and faced one more degradation imposed by his aching hunger. On top of the can were the discarded ends of some hotdogs, complete with remnant buns, and smears of mustard. He glanced around, retrieved them, and savored what could well be his only sustenance of this day. Wiping his fingers on the edge of his tattered blue shorts, Ben refocused on the kiosk.

The man was trying to sell tours and timeshares for a resort to the Americans that walked by. Ben could hear the English being spoken, and wanted to cross over and talk with the man. But he decided to explore a little more first, and maybe find some more food to fill the ache of too little. He would not be successful.

Later in the afternoon Ben arrived back in front of the marina. He stopped short of the kiosk, and watched as the man he'd seen that morning failed to attract a rather corpulent couple, who were more intent on eating their ice cream than hearing his offer.

After the man finished his spiel, Ben walked up, smiled, and said hello. The man nodded politely, but without eye contact. Ben asked, "Do you know if it's safe to camp on the beach around here?" He tried not to sound too desperate. Now the man looked quizzically at Ben, and replied, "I'm not sure. Maybe down past the marina." Ben, with his usual youthful exuberance and lack of guile, decided that he'd broken the ice, so he told the man his story.

The man did warm up, and even smiled. "My name is Juan," he said. Ben eagerly offered his hand. "I'm Ben. My kayak is up in the old city. Left my tent in there and everything!"

"Actually," Juan said. "It might not be a good idea to camp on the beach. Usually the city is safe, but you never know."

"What do you suggest I do?" Ben replied, hoping the man had a better alternative. "Well, you could always sleep here. The floor is hard, but you'll be out of the weather, and no one will bother you." Ben readily accepted, and thanked Juan for his help, knowing that God again was providing for his needs. Later, Juan's wife came by, and Juan closed the steel gate, locked it, and said goodnight.

The small kiosk had a fan, two stools, and a wooden counter. Ben chose the wooden counter as his bed. He took off his shirt to use as a pillow, and curled up on the polished wood. He was accustomed to the soft sand on the beach, sand that molded to his sore hip, and accommodated slow moves. The counter was hard and cold. The rumble of cars that passed by the busy intersection reverberated in his ears. Ben was glad to be around people again, especially those who spoke his native tongue, but now he yearned for a quiet, peaceful, camp on a deserted shore. Once or twice that night, Ben thought he could hear the whisper of the waves. In his dreams they called him back to their world. Once he woke from this fitful sleep to listen.

It was only the warm scented wind in the potted trees.

Chapter 29

Eyes forward, never backward. Once you look behind, you lose sight of your goal.

Ben Wade Journal

Mazatlan
October 1996

B en woke before dawn to the sounds of rain spattering on the tin roof. Juan came to work early and opened the metal door. They talked, and Ben again thanked him for a place to sleep. He spent the morning dodging rain showers and looking for work. The best job he could find paid thirty pesos a day, the equivalent of three U.S. dollars. That wouldn't work. He had to find something better.

Ben's next goal, having failed at the first, was to find a room for rent. He badly needed a shower and a bed. His obvious problem was that he had no money.

Who will rent me a room in Mazatlan on credit?

If all else failed, Ben could stay a few more nights in the marina sales booth. But that would work for only so long. Even if Juan agreed, Ben was in no hurry to go through another restless night on the hard countertop. After he gave up on finding work that morning, Ben walked back by the shop and asked Juan if he knew of a place to stay that didn't cost a lot of money. He took Ben to a nearby hotel away from the main strip. Its name was La Misión.

The rooms were old but clean. The lady at the front desk told Ben he could stay there for three weeks for sixty U.S. dollars. The price made him smile, but Ben had no money and he told her so. He also quickly told her that he would have it in a week. Which, of course, he didn't know for sure. But it sounded good at the time. To his surprise, the lady smiled coquettishly at Ben, and, after listening to Juan explain that Ben had nowhere else to go, she agreed to let him stay. He had to promise that he would have the money by the following week. Of course he promised. Once they settled on the price, Ben picked out a room that he liked. It was upstairs in the back of the hotel. His window looked out on a small courtyard filled with blooming flowers. Ben set his few belongings on the bed, then stepped into the dimly lit hall, latched the old wooden door behind him, and walked back out onto the street.

He took a bus down to the train station warehouse to retrieve some food from his kayak. He'd not eaten anything substantial for over thirty six hours, and Ben's rumbling stomach made sure that everyone knew it. Juan had gone with him to the warehouse, covering the bus fare, and interpreting Ben's valiant attempts at Spanish. Once at the storage area, Ben packed as many PowerBars and oatmeal bags as he could into a plastic bag. Now he had a place to stay and food to eat. Life was good. With things beginning to look up, Ben hoped that, next, his financial woes would be resolved.

Juan spoke fluent English, so Ben figured that, while he was there, they could ask how much money it was going to cost to keep the kayak in the warehouse. There was a different manager on the day shift, and Ben told him he would need at least three weeks of rental space. "Cuánto para el alquiler?" Juan asked. (How much for the rent?) "Dos mil pesos," the man said without smiling. "What?" Ben asked incredulously, thinking he had not heard him correctly. The manager said it again, "2,000 pesos." Ben felt the pit of his stomach tighten. Now he would have to raise an additional three hundred dollars on top of what he'd already calculated the rest of the trip would cost.

They must have seen me coming.

Ben vowed that as soon as he could, he'd move the kayak to another place. Waiting tables for three dollars a day just wasn't going to cut it. Ben's decision was simple - find a decent paying job, or call home and ask his parents for a loan. The latter was his *last* option. He hated borrowing money from family. But the way things looked at that moment it might just be his *only* option.

Juan and Ben went back to the booth. They'd been chatting for a few minutes when Juan asked, "Do you want to sell tours?" Juan never stopped watching the people pass by, ready to make a quick sale. "I don't know," Ben said. "Doesn't seem like anybody is buying anything." Juan just laughed. "It's a little slow right now, Ben, but you can make a lot of money here," he said. "Commission only. But if you push the tourists you can really rake in the bucks." *Sure*, Ben thought. He sat back and watched. Needless to say, Juan didn't make one sale in the next three hours. Ben figured it was a waste of time. He shook his head slowly, wondering if he was going to have to beg for money. Ben sat at the desk and contemplated his deplorable state.

The few tourists that walked by were all dressed in fancy tropical garb. There were bright flowered shirts and neatly pressed khaki shorts. Most of the people were well groomed. Ben definitely felt out of place. He looked down at his clothes, and realized that he'd been wearing the same pair of shorts and shirt for the last three weeks. The once white T-shirt was now caked with mud, sand, and sweat. It had been a while since he'd considered his appearance.

My God, Ben. Has your absence from the world changed the way you see yourself? This is not the old Ben Wade of sartorial splendor!

Now, with more than a few people staring at his shoddy appearance, he felt incredibly self conscious. Ben desperately wanted a change of clothes.

Another fellow came into the booth to work, taking Ben's focus away from his appearance for a brief instant. The fellow seemed friendly, with a broad smile on his face. Ben tried to talk to him, just small talk. But he didn't seem very interested. His English was as good as Juan's, so Ben persisted. Finally, as he usually did, Ben started to talk about his trip. He could see the man's eyes riveted on his own as he told his tale. "You're kayaking the entire coast?" The man asked eagerly.

"I sure am," Ben replied.

"That's like rowing, right?"

"Yep. With a double ended paddle. You know, it's like having two oars," Ben said, demonstrating the forward motion with his hands.

"Have you ever done any crew, like with a team?"

"No, not really," Ben said. "Why?"

"Well, I used to coach a National team. It was a long time ago. We competed in Mexico City," he said. "And won!" His head dropped to his chest. "I wanted to coach at a university."

"What happened?" Ben asked, curious.

199

"Not enough jobs to go around," was the quiet response.

"So now you work here?" Ben asked.

The man looked up, obviously discouraged. But, when Ben asked him if he wanted to talk more about rowing after work, his eyes lighted up. "By the way, I'm Ben. What's your name?"

"Alonso Gutierrez," he said. They shook hands eagerly.

That night over dinner, Ben listened to Alonso tell about his coaching days. He was disappointed with how his life turned out, and his future seemed to be without hopes or dreams. To hear Alonso abandon something that he so obviously enjoyed was discouraging to Ben. "Alonso," he said. "It's not the politics that keep you from doing what you want in life." Alonso looked surprised. "It's not?"

"No. It's not your government's fault either. The only thing that's standing in your way is you. If you want something bad enough, put your mind to it. No matter what the cost is, you can achieve it if you really want to."

"Well, maybe that's true for you," Alonso replied in a tone tinged with subdued pique. "But I think it's different here in Mexico. There are no coaching jobs anywhere right now. I've looked!"

Alonzo picked up the dinner's small tab, and they walked out into the evening. After strolling in silence for a while, they found some plastic chairs just outside a small taco stand and plopped down. Now deep within the alleys of the old town area, they were the only two speaking English. Several people stared as they passed by. It might have bothered Ben a couple of months before, but now he hardly noticed. Ben was about to tell Alonso something he couldn't deny. He felt drawn to Alonso's problems, most likely because he'd been faced with the same ones at the beginning of the year. This was a subject close to his heart, and one of the fundamental reasons he had taken off on such a crazy journey.

"Alonzo, don't give me any excuses," Ben said, now intent on swaying Alonso's beliefs and outlook on the future. "*Everyone* who tries to do something great in life runs into obstacles. Take my trip, for instance. My kayak is locked up like a prisoner down there at the train station. And, I don't have a dime, not a peso to my name to bail it out. What would be the easiest thing for me to do right now? Quit? Do you hear me?" Ben had his full attention. "But that word," Ben said, continuing, "has ceased to be part of my vocabulary. You, on the other hand, are doing just the opposite. You've *already* quit. What's the matter? Are you *satisfied* to stay here in Mazatlan? To sell timeshares to the tourists?"

"Well no," Alonso said, somewhat taken aback by Ben's attack. "But what other options do I have?"

"Options?" Ben continued, "Man, the world is at your finger tips! Let's start with this. My dad told me before I even started college that I should focus on something I could do for free. Something I truly loved. Well, at the time, I thought it was just talk, so I majored in Business. Look where it got me. In the middle of the Pacific Ocean. That's not what I went to college for. Is it? It didn't take me long to know that I was miserable at work. I hated getting up in the morning. Finally, I decided that was *not* the way I was going to live my life. *I decided* to make a *change*. Hear me, *I decided*! There was a moment of silence as Alonso looked absently at the ground beside his feet. "So," Ben continued, without mercy. "What job would you do for free?"

"I want to coach rowing!" Alonso said emphatically. "I have done it for no money in the past, and would not hesitate to do it again if I had the opportunity."

"Then, that's what you're going to do!" Ben said, not allowing him any room to argue. "Get to Cabo, if that's where you think the money is. Save it up and then go to the United States. What's stopping you from doing that tomorrow?"

"I guess nothing," Alonso said sheepishly after a moment of thought.

"Well, then, I guess it's settled. Do it."

They continued to talk. Eventually the conversation turned back to Ben's financial difficulties. When Alonso heard that Ben had no other clothes with him, he said he could fix that. They walked a couple of blocks to Alonso's house where he lived with his mother, father, and two sisters. Ben saw that it was a small place, made of stone, and without carpets. He knew that the Gutierrez's did not have much. But when he left, they had given him two pairs of pants, a belt, and a couple of shirts. Ben was incredibly grateful to Alonso for letting him feel like a new man. "Listen," Alonso said before Ben left. "I've been thinking about your situation. The newspaper stays open late. Why don't we go down there and tell them your story. I know they would love to write an article about your trip. Maybe they could even help you raise some money."

"That sounds great," Ben said. "But it's almost 9:00 o'clock. Maybe we'll try tomorrow morning."

"No, Ben," Alonso insisted. "We'll go right now. I'm telling you, they're open until midnight."

Most businesses in Mexico, Ben learned, were the same way. They open at 8:00 in the morning, and close at noon for lunch and some time with their family. In the afternoon they reopen at 4:00, and work until they think it's time to close. Ben and Alonso went down to the newspaper that night and, with Alonso as the interpreter, talked for two hours. The editor of the newspaper, J. Roberto Rivers, was extremely helpful and receptive to Ben's story. He promised that the article, accompanied by three photographs, would appear in the morning newspaper.

Good to his word, it did.

Chapter 30

In prosperity, our friends know us; in adversity, we know our friends.
John Churton Collins (1848-1908)

Ben climbed out of bed hoping that the phone in the hotel lobby would not stop ringing with a barrage of phone calls from Mexican business's that wanted to sponsor his trip. But Ben was disappointed. Not one company called that morning.

Discouraged, he went back down to the kiosk to find Alonso. Ben asked him to call the newspaper and thank Roberto for the article. Alonso did, and also asked Roberto to keep his ears open for further news and assistance. Next, they telephoned the train station to set up a meeting on Monday.

The Monday meeting also led to a dead end. Although they agreed to reduce the fee to a flat rate of $200 dollars for the duration of his stay, Ben could still not get the kayak out until he'd paid in full. The manager insisted that it was the best he could do. He apologized for the discrepancy, and said that whoever made the initial transaction was not authorized to do so. With a heavy heart, Ben left the warehouse and returned to the hotel. He wasn't going to give up yet.

He sat on the tiny bed in his room that night and stared up at the ceiling fan as it slowly mixed the air. Over on the stone wall a few lizards crawled along the smooth surface, waiting for an errant bug to pass by. Despite the vegetation and lush forests around the city and on the hills behind Ben's hotel, there was virtually no humidity. It was changing into a tropical winter, and the refreshing night breeze through the open window over his bed was cool. Ben relaxed and began to come up with other options. They were few.

A couple of days later, Ben took the job as host at the restaurant outside the hotel. He had no other offers. He agreed to work for three meals a day instead of the thirty pesos. At least he wouldn't go hungry any time soon.

I have a roof over my head and friends on my side. Now, all I need is some money, and my kayak.

Sooner or later, something had to turn up. Ben continued to make contacts throughout the city. Instead of becoming more discouraged, as each day passed he felt a growing confidence that all would soon be resolved. During those two weeks his relationship with Alonso grew stronger, as Ben found him to be trustworthy, reliable, and fun to be with. Almost everyday after work, they met on the corner near the kiosk and traveled to town. Sometimes Alonso would pay for the movies, or a bite to eat. Mostly, though, they talked of the future.

Ben called home every week - collect of course. He wanted to keep his parents from worrying. Ben laughed to himself, *"They're always glad to hear I'm still alive!"* Finally, early in the second week Ben broke down and told his father that he might need him to wire down some money. Ben had used his last resort. "Well," Mr. Wade said sternly. "I'll send you a plane ticket instead. Maybe it's time to come home."

So much for help from home. I guess that idea's out.

Ben also talked to Heather a few times. They spoke fondly of her visit to San Carlos, and of future times. Ben wondered if the next few months would change their attitudes.

Surely we can have a normal relationship when I get home.

After expressing regrets for spending so much time apart, they hung up. At the same time, his old friend, Christian, was rallying support back home. He'd already gone to several people to ask for donations. From those who couldn't send money, he asked for cards and gifts. "Christian," Ben said on one call, "I need some money pretty bad. I'm working on some sponsors down here but haven't had any real luck. The land lady at the hotel keeps asking when I'll pay the rent."

"I'll see what I can do." That was all he said. Two days later Ben got a call back from Christian. "Is there a Western Union office near you?" he asked. "I think so."

"Well, you need to get to it by two o'clock this afternoon. Can you do it?"

"Okay, I guess I'd better." Ben said. He called Alonso, and the two of them went down to collect eighty dollars from the local Cambio teller. Ben was ecstatic. Finally, he had some money. Although it wasn't enough to solve all his problems, it was definitely a start. The first thing he did was go back to the hotel and pay half of the rent. After taking Alonso out to eat for all the help he'd given him, Ben stashed the rest of his fortune in his room. Ben found out later that his friend Dave, the person who had given him his knives before the start of the trip, had been the one responsible for the wire. A good friend.

If there's one thing Ben learned in his short life so far, it's that true friendship is not based on good times and hanging out.

The metal of character is tested not when times are smooth, but when everything seems to have fallen to pieces. If a friend is then willing to sacrifice his own personal wealth, emotions, and time, to benefit a person in turmoil, that's a bond worth keeping.

All other relationships are meaningless to me.

October 14, 1996
Mazatlan, Mexico

Ben picked up a copy of the *Oceanic Reporter*, a monthly publication for American residents and tourists. On the back page, where the classifieds are listed, he saw a small column written by the editor. It asked for articles. Ben flipped to the front page, and found that the editor's name was Matt Vesnick. An address appeared below his name. Ben certainly had a story to tell. He decided it would be worthwhile to pay the editor a visit.

On the day of Ben's visit, the editor was in the process of moving to a different office. When Ben approached, Mrs. Vesnick was standing outside and greeted him. Ben showed her some of the articles about the expedition, and planned to ask if he could write a few pages about his trip for the *Oceanic Reporter*. "Is Matt going to be back any time soon?" Ben asked. "Yes, he's at the other office right now," She said. "He should be back any minute." It wasn't more than a minute and came walking through the door. He took a look at Ben and said in a booming voice, "Who the hell are you?" Ben looked up, a little intimidated by the huge man standing before him.

I had no idea at the time, that this man would be the one who really got things moving in Mazatlan.

It was not by chance that Ben walked into his world that afternoon, and, as he had suspected, things began to get better in a hurry.

Chapter 31

Matt Vesnick was a big man, six foot three, and about 240 pounds. He was 46 years old, and had played a lot of football in college. After graduation he'd tried out for the Green Bay Packers. Fortunately for Ben, he didn't make the team. After many years of work in the United States he'd married a Mexican lady, moved to Mazatlan, and started an English language newspaper.

Ben was more than a little intimidated when Matt first walked through the door, but he soon realized he had nothing to worry about. Matt was a very fun loving and down to earth farm boy. Everyone in town knew Matt. He liked to have a good time, and it seemed that everywhere he went people surrounded him. He owned the *Oceanic Reporter* with his wife, and had two beautiful daughters, four and eight years old.

As Matt listened to his story, Ben could see the wheels turning in his head. "You know, Ben," Matt said with a chuckle, as he remembered some of his own wild experiences. "A couple of buddies and I went on a canoe trip for seven days about thirty years ago. It was the best time I ever had. Problem was, we'd go down the rapids too fast and tip over. Most of our supplies ended up in the river. Of course, when that happened, I'd always go for the beer first."

Ben liked him already. Matt had a great sense of humor, and Ben felt like he was a big brother. Ben warmed up to him immediately, telling him of all the problems that he'd seen. Matt agreed to publish Ben's article. He also said he'd talk to some local businessmen. He knew several of them personally, and thought it would be a place to start looking for sponsors to raise the extra money. "Hey, Ben. I know a good way to start you off with a little cash," Matt said that day. "What are you doin' right now?"

"Nothing really," Ben said, "I'm workin' for food!"

"Well, come on and help me take my furniture to the other office," Matt roared, slapping Ben on the back. "I'll pay you to help me move." Ben did, and Matt paid him $20 dollars for an hour's work. It was a fortune compared to working for food. That night, Matt took Ben to a local sports grill where they watched NFL football and talked about their adventures.

The next four days Matt and Ben visited several local companies, asking for $50 donations from each. In return, they told them, they would give them publicity that took the form of mentioning the company name on the local television, or having a space on Ben's kayak for their logo. It worked like magic. Every company they talked to agreed to the terms. Casa Country (a restaurant), Iguanamo's (a bar), Anglers Inn (a fish and game specialist), Boyas de Mexicana (a buoy manufacturer), Ray Demeral (author of *Mazatlan, Inside Out*), and BV Marine were all contributors. Matt also gave Ben, via the *Oceanic Reporter*, fifty dollars, as well as a lot of his time and effort. On his own, Ben set up an interview with *Señor Frog's* clothing store and succeeded with another sponsorship. All told, it was a great week.

They collected more than $350 dollars.

Ben was on cloud nine when Matt drove him down to the warehouse, and they took the kayak and placed it on top of his station wagon. Ben felt like a missing part of his body had just been reattached. He was a new man again. "I couldn't have done this without your help. You know that Matt?" Ben told him after they finished loading the kayak. "You know, Ben," he said with a big grin on his face. "I only ask one thing from you in return for all my help."

"You got it, Matt. Just name the price." Ben said.

"When you get done with this thing," Matt continued, "you're going to be famous. You'll be the biggest thing to happen in America since sliced bread."

"Well, I don't think that's going to happen."

"Trust me, Ben, you are. The press is gonna jump on this story like a duck on a June bug. Hell, they already have. Look at me! Anyway, when you get big and famous and they offer you a big contract in some movie, don't forget old Matt."

"I won't, Matt, don't worry."

"That's not all, Ben. When you get that movie deal I want to be in it."

"No problem, Matt. What part you want to play?"

Matt stood up to his full height, planted his feet wide apart, and spread his massive arms, palms forward. "Okay, here it is," he said. "I wanna walk through a swinging door, just like in the old Westerns, with a big chaw of tobacco. I'm gonna walk through that door, all tough like, and spit that wad of tobacco on the floor. Or maybe on a dead man, or even a dog. In that order. You got that?"

"You bet, Matt. I got that!" Ben said laughing, as Matt took three giant steps forward, opening an imagined tavern door. "Remember, boy. Spittin' tobacco. If I can't do it on the floor, then I'll walk over to a dead man, and then a dog!"

"Whatever you say, Matt. We do it your way."

Over the next few weeks, everyone in Mazatlan heard about the film that Matt would be in one day. Ben must have listened to him tell that story a dozen times, and laughed every time he did. Matt was quite a character, and Ben owed a lot to him. He just hoped he hadn't promised him something he couldn't do.

Only time will tell, Ben Wade thought. *Only time will tell.*

The hotel where Ben was staying was a human zoo. The population included messed up ex–Vietnam vets, drug dealers, and bums of all descriptions. It made for interesting times for a naïve twenty-something man/boy - day and night.

The wonders for Ben never ceased in the city of Mazatlan, where residents and visitors alike embraced him with love. Even a few families who came to the city for vacation took him under their wing.

There was one in particular that he remembers fondly.

I was sitting in the restaurant where I worked, relaxing after the day's work was done. Like many afternoons, I had joined Matt and Alonso for dinner. We were eating and talking when three people walked in and sat down next to our table. It was a man, his wife, and another lady, whom I presumed was their daughter.

The husband looked like a pretty rough character. The kind of guy you wouldn't want on the opposite side in a brawl. He had tattoos up one arm and down the other. When he looked at me, I made sure I looked away because I didn't want to spark a confrontation. His jaw was set in a way that led me to believe he'd had his share of fights, and possibly a few nights in the city jail. I turned out to be right on the money. His wife was just the opposite - dark skin, bleached blonde hair, and a big wide grin she seemed to wear most of the time. As she sat down, she began to laugh at something. She looked at her husband playfully as they both ordered Margaritas, obviously enjoying their vacation.

Best of all was their daughter. She looked about the same age as me with long blonde hair. Her body was slim and attractive, and she walked like she knew it. I love a person who is self confident. I looked over several times, trying to make eye contact. Sometimes I succeeded, but didn't think much about it.

Watching the three of them leave an hour later, I shrugged my shoulders. Matt laughed. "Well, Ben, there went your chance!" He said loud enough so that everyone in the restaurant, including the girl and her family, heard him. "Whatever," I said, a little embarrassed. I smiled anyway to show him it didn't matter one way or the other.

The next day Ben was working in the restaurant, and was surprised to see the tattooed man come in for lunch. The place was a small, open air cantina, and Ben watched intently as he made his way over to the bar and sat by himself. Ben was just getting off work, so he went over and sat on the stool next to him. Ben found out he was from Seattle and was in Mazatlan for a short vacation with his wife and step daughter. "You can call me DW," he said. Ben shook his hand. He had a grip like a steel vice.

After he heard parts of Ben's story, he was interested in the possibility of Ben writing a book, and said so several times. After a while, his wife came in and they continued talking. She introduced herself as Sharon, and invited Ben to go to the Mexican Fiesta that night with the rest of the family. He readily accepted. But, when Ben found out that the price for the fiesta was twenty dollars apiece, he hesitated. DW insisted that Ben go, claiming that it was well worth the money. It was.

There was all the Mexican food you could eat, and any drink you could imagine from Pina Coladas to milk shakes. Ben piled his plate high with chicken tacos, enchiladas, tamales, and other treats too numerous to name. After dinner, the hotel put on a stage show to display the native culture. By the end of the night, Ben felt like he'd been adopted into the family.

Mazatlan was becoming too comfortable.

Chapter 32

Over the next week, DW would come by after Ben finished work and they would sit and talk. His wife and daughter would be off either shopping or catching some rays on the beach. Ben imagined that DW appreciated the time away from 'girl stuff'. Sometimes they would talk for an hour or so before the girls would meander over to where they sat. Since Ben knew the city pretty well by now, he offered to take them on a trip to the open air market downtown. There, they looked at everything imaginable - From an unborn calf carcass to hammerhead sharks, and from pyramids of colorful peppers to Mazatlan T–shirts. They also visited the cool confines of the old cathedral that had been built a century before. The ancient, stately, stone walls seemed a stark contrast to the gaudy tourists that thronged inside. Ben sensed that DW didn't concern himself with the spiritual aspect of the detour, but he didn't complain about anything.

DW was heavily tattooed, and Ben, himself, had a tattoo of a crown of thorns banded around his right arm, a representation, he said, of his Lord, Jesus Christ. Lately, he'd been thinking of getting another tattoo, one that portrayed his perils on the expedition. Ben wanted to put something graphic, depicting his experiences, on his left shoulder. Coincidence or not, one day DW told Ben that he was going to get a tattoo in town. "I got one there a couple of days ago," he said. "Real clean and real cheap." He rolled up his shirt and showed Ben the new, and still healing, tattoo. "Why don't you get another one too?"

Ben chuckled at the apparent mind meld. "I'd like to," he said. "But I don't know exactly what I want to get. Something about the expedition and all that, I guess. But I might not have enough money."

"Don't worry about that," DW replied. "I'll slip you a couple of bucks when my wife's not looking. We'll come up with an idea too. Shouldn't be that difficult."

"Okay," was Ben's simple reply. He got a pen from the bar and began to scribble on the paper place mat. "I want to put something about my expedition and how God has helped me through. Maybe a shark, or my kayak, and a cross."

"Let me see that paper," DW said, grabbing the pen from Ben's hand. It only took a minute, and he produced a crude drawing that Ben liked immediately.

After some rearranging with the tattoo artist's help, they decided on the picture Ben would have carved into his flesh. He was happy and satisfied with the end results. Curled around his kayak was a shark. Waves roiled up on either side of the kayak, threatening to engulf the tiny craft. Above the cockpit, where Ben normally sat, was a cross made up of the two oars. "Just think," DW exclaimed excitedly after he saw the new art work. "Every time you look at that tattoo, you'll think of me!"

That was how DW was. Bold and brash, and never afraid to speak his mind.

Saying goodbye to DW, Sharon, and their beautiful blonde daughter, Rainee, as they returned home from Mazatlan, left Ben feeling lonely for the first time in three weeks. He thought about giving Rainee a serious kiss goodbye, but the thought of Heather waiting for him back in California made him think twice. Ben gave both women a hug and DW another firm hand shake. After promising to call them when he finished, they waved goodbye, and closed yet another chapter in the expedition.

Ben's list of new and interesting friends in Mazatlan was growing. The last week before Ben left Mazatlan he found it hard to cope with his emotions.

I'm having difficulties leaving my new home. I've made many new friends in Mazatlan. I'll keep in contact with some of them, but for now, I'm going to begin to distance myself from the town and its people.

I'm keeping more to myself these last few days.

I'm reminded of the last few weeks I spent in Fullerton, California. Before this trip.

Ben avoided going out in public everyday. As the sun came up he would take the kayak out into the bay. His muscles were incredibly lazy, and out of shape, as he began the slow, painful torture of preparing them for the rest of his journey. But Ben was not in as bad shape as he thought he would be, and he felt the old form returning after only a few workouts. The kayak was conveniently locked up in front of a beach house across the street from his hotel. Two guards, one at night and one during the day, kept watch over the grounds.

Although there was a part of Ben that was reluctant to leave the city, the rest of him was ready to go. More than once, while enjoying the luxury of this piece of civilization with his new friends, he had felt his mission pulling him. It tugged gently and told him it was high time to continue on. Ben had been dormant long enough. It was time to push on further toward the goal.

With almost an entire city behind him, Ben felt an overwhelming wave of pride and support urging him on to complete his mission. Even the people back home, seeing that he was somehow still alive, had reluctantly changed their positions. They were beginning to see things from his point of view. Instead of trying to dissuade him, they were encouraging him to persevere. The outpouring of positive support proved motivating at a time when motivation was important.

It was late November, and time to celebrate American Thanksgiving. As he had promised, Ben walked down to the Marina to visit his friends, Stuart and Dee, and baby daughter Coral. He looked forward to taking them up on their invitation to meet in Mazatlan for Turkey Day Dinner. He hadn't been in contact with them since the crossing to the mainland.

Ben searched the registries, but couldn't find their boat registered in any of the slips. He did find another sailboat that had traveled with the *Running Shoe* for a few days. In fact Ben had met them while they all ate clams in the hurricane hole, Puerto Don Juan. Ben found the sloop's mooring. After exchanging some pleasantries, and mutual surprise at seeing each other again, the crew members informed Ben of what he had already suspected. *Running Shoe* and his friends had gotten tied up on the other side of the coast and had decided to stay in La Paz on the Baja peninsula for Thanksgiving. Ben thanked the captain for his information and told him to give his regards to Stuart and Dee when they ran into them again.

On a positive note, the Mazatlan newspaper, *Noreste*, ran another article about Ben on the day before he set sail. It seemed that everyone in town wanted to say goodbye to him. Some asked if Ben wanted to have one big send off party. Wisely, he decided it would not be such a good idea. Ben was ready to leave, and the last thing he wanted was to watch his friends waving sad goodbyes while he turned his back and rowed away. Ben was never much for long farewells, not after his first departure. He preferred to slip into the water, and just carry the good memories out to sea.

Reluctantly, however, he did agree to one small get together on the eve of his departure. One of his sponsors suggested they hold the festivities at his restaurant and said that he would pick up the tab. Matt Vesnick smiled when he heard the news of Ben's slight concession, and was happy to see him off this way. That was Matt. Always positive and reassuring. Ben clung to his enthusiasm that last night, knowing that soon he would be on his own, uncertain of the future. He was pleased to see all his friends one last time.

Ben offered a toast, promising to return in early March. Matt and Alonso sat at Ben's table and chorused 'here, here', clinking their glasses together. Before leaving, Alonso motioned Ben to the side of the table. "You're leaving tomorrow, early, aren't you?" he asked. Ben hadn't told anyone the exact date yet. The lines in his face told Ben of the pain he was going through. They'd had some really good times together. "I don't know, Alonso," Ben said honestly, placing his hand on his shoulder. "I don't like good-byes. That's why I haven't told anyone when I'm leaving. You've been a great friend these last few weeks. I will never forget all of your help. Remember, I can help you when you make it to the United States."

"Thanks," Alonso said looking at the ground. "You know, I've decided to save up the money, either here or in Cabo, and then go to America to coach. I just might take you up on that offer."

"Good for you, Alonso. You're on the right track. Remember, follow your heart."

"You have really opened my eyes, Ben," Alonso said. After a few minutes of silence, each of us trying to guess what the other was thinking, he added, "I would really like to see you leave."

"I know you would," Ben said. "Everyone would, but that's not the kind of person I am now. The ocean is calling for me, and I can't ignore her any longer. I hear her at night, whispering through the window, and I feel like going right then. I might even leave tonight. I just don't know."

"All right. Make sure you call me when you get done. I know you'll come back to Mazatlan for a few days, so give me a call before you do."

"I will, Alonso." We hugged and parted sadly.

The next morning Ben went to see Matt Vesnick one last time. He was in the newspaper office. Ben knocked lightly on the door. Matt looked up, saw Ben and waved him inside. "Well," he said standing up and smiling. "Guess this is it, eh."

"Yeah, I guess so."

"You're one crazy guy, you know that?"

"You better believe it!" Ben said chuckling.

"Seriously, though, Matt, I can't thank you enough for all of the help and support you've given me. I couldn't have done it without you."

"Don't mention it," Matt said. "Just remember me in that movie. Guy with the tobacco, right?"

"I know, I know. I won't forget."

"One more thing," he continued. "Call me collect any time. I want to hear how you're doin'. When you get done and come back up to Mazatlan, we're gonna throw you a big party, so you better make it back in one piece. I'm countin' on you to do it."

"Don't worry," Ben replied. "I'll make it."

"I wish I could go with you. By the way, when are you leavin'? I can see something in your eyes telling me it's gettin' time."

"I don't know, but you're right. I'm leaving soon. I can feel the call."

"I'll bet you can. Let's check the weather out." Matt walked over to his computer screen and got on line. He pulled up the National Weather Channel. "Weather feels good out there to me," Ben said while he looked over Matt's shoulder and waited for the screen to print the images. "Cloud cover and all, but I think the weather will hold."

"Uh oh. Look here," Matt said as he pointed at the blue and red streaks dotting the screen. "Big storm there. You can tell by the big swirling clouds," he continued. "By the looks of the air currents it's comin' our way."

"Oh, well." Ben said. A bleak thought crossed his mind about how the ocean was getting ready to welcome him back. He had hoped she would forgive him for his absence. But that didn't look to be the case. "You gonna hang out here and see what she does?" Matt asked.

"No, probably not. Time to go."

"Yeah, I don't blame you." They shook hands and patted each other on the back the way two tough men do in Mexico. With the 'brazo'- this manly hug - one can be affectionate, and still prove his machismo at the same time.

An hour later, 11:00 a.m. local time, Monday, December 2nd, 1996, Ben Wade set sail from Mazatlan, Mexico.

Destination?

Destiny itself.

Mississauga, Ontario, Canada
The Gauthier Residence
June 20, 1998

Marlene set the manuscript on the table. Her hand, palm down, rested on top of it. She sat for a moment before speaking. "Wow, honey," she said, looking up at me. "This kid, Ben, is growing up before our eyes. Early on he seems to regress to an infant. You know, his lonely spells and all.

Now he's the man-about-town who's strong enough to throw it away again, and head out to sea. Is he really different now? And what about Heather? What happens to her?"

I filled my coffee mug and joined Marlene at the table. "We'll have to see, honey. I'm trying to let Ben tell the story. I purposely don't read too far ahead in his journal. It's funny. If I listen closely he really does speak to me. I mean, I think I can feel his presence sometimes."

"What do you think about his state of mind?" Marlene asks. "He bounces all over the place."

"He does that, for sure," I answer, "but I don't read anything clinical into it – you know, like manic-depressive or such. He's just a confused kid."

"Confused?"

"Yah, confused about relationships. Confused about his feelings. But I'll tell you one thing. This kid is the most task focused human being I've ever known. He brings himself relentlessly back into focus on his mission after every deviation or distraction, whether it's a good experience – like Heather's visit – or nearly killing himself from thirst."

"And he does write flowery, kind of poetic, stuff, huh," Marlene reflected. "Do you have any clue yet if he made it? I mean, survived this thing?"

Two hands on the warm mug, I blow across its dark surface. "No, is the simple answer. I've made a few inquiries, but nothing yet. It's a mystery to me. Where I found this stuff? No other signs of him. No. I don't know if he survived."

"We're going to find out," Marlene whispered.

"Yes we are. As God is my witness, we're going to find out what happened to Ben Wade."

Part Two

The Pacific Ocean

Chapter 33

Go confidently in the direction of your dreams! Live the life you imagined. As you simplify your life, the laws of the universe will be simpler.

Henry David Thoreau (1817-1862)

Ben was thankful to leave the crowded shipping lanes of Mazatlan behind. Once beyond the busy port, the coastline stretched out in a long, unremarkable, straight line. As he paddled to avoid the late morning traffic in and out of the harbor, Ben turned and waved one final farewell to his new second home.

There were not many coves to sneak into that first night, so Ben decided to spend it out on the water.

Might as well get used to the rigors of surviving on the ocean again as soon as possible.

The coast was open, and exposed to the power of the mighty Pacific. Ben could feel a distinct increase in the pull of the currents and the size of the swells. The waves that thundered against the shore with eternal regularity were huge, and he wondered what would happen if he got caught in their powerful jaws.

He remembered, and he knew the answer.

By nightfall, Ben was tired, so it was an easy decision to stop, eat some dinner, and set up 'camp' on the ocean for the night. With a lighthouse blinking its mariners' message a mile or so away to the south, Ben knew he would not have any problems keeping his bearings through the night.

It had been a long time since he'd been out on the ocean for a full day, and, once again confined to the cramped quarters of the cockpit, his muscles twitched, and his back ached. The memory of the soft bed at the Hotel La Misión lingered in his mind, and made it harder to drift into sleep. That old familiar loneliness settled softly across his shoulders. Already it threatened to sink him into a state of depression. This time, though, he shook it off.

This time he accepted the solitude.. . . . *shrugging off those personal demons that sought to ensnare my soul.*

Ben knew that, now, with more than half of the trip ahead, he would have to face it with a new attitude.

He retrieved a fresh page and began a new journal.

I force myself to welcome the time alone. I'm once again free of the worries and hassles of civilization.

The ocean charges little for her quarters, and the beaches never ask for rent.

Tonight, I can take courage in the miles I've conquered, and I can take hope in the ones yet to come.

Still, it was a troubled sleep that night. Ben tossed and turned through the dark hours until dawn. The constant and persistent sound of the surf breaking against the shore had made its best attempt to lull his weary eyes to sleep. The rhythm was indeed soothing, but the reality of his discomfort outweighed the rhythmic chant of the siren, and Ben was awake as the sun began to rise.

Immediately, he noticed that sometime during the night he had passed the lighthouse. He was now two or three miles south of the marker, and could still feel the gentle pull of the current urging him on. The difference of having the tide help him, instead of hinder him, was a phenomenal mental boost. As Ben watched the shore pass slowly by without his making any real effort, he felt that he could stay out on the sea for the rest of the trip.

The storm that Matt had seen on his computer screen was now moving farther north. Cloudless, azure skies gave Ben little cause for worry.

It looked as if the ocean had welcomed him back to her bosom on good terms.

She provided me with gentle breezes and relatively calm waters that day. I thank her and the Creator for their mercy.

Ben was still stiff from the previous day's work. It reminded him of the first few days of the trip. After leaving San Felipe, it had taken him more than two weeks to settle into the demanding routine. Paddling ten to twelve hours a day was not something one was able to just pick up and do. He hoped that this time his body would not take so long to adjust. Those memories seemed distant now, but he realized that he'd only been away from home a little under three months.

Life back home was a different time, and a different place, now almost like a dream. Sometimes, memories from that other world drifted by, and he would sense a longing for a return to his former life. But for now, his whole focus and experience revolved around the water that passed beneath the keel of his tiny craft.

The shoreline continued to run without a break to the south. The sun stood high in the sky, and the air was hot and thick with humidity. Ben wondered how soon mosquitoes would be swarming his nightly campsite. He had some repellent, but he didn't think he had enough to last very long. Supposedly, the rainy season was over, and Ben hoped the chance of getting malaria was slim. The coast was a pleasing sight with its backdrop of deep green mountains and lush tropical forest that flowed right down to the beach. Soon the landscape would host a variety of wildlife. From his research, Ben knew that jaguars, monkeys, pythons, and other sub-tropical animals, lived just a few yards from the surf.

Ben had four gallons of drinking water left. To be on the safe side, he stopped just north of the entrance to a lagoon that spread out across the swamps. The lagoon near where Ben had come ashore was the mouth of the Agua Bravo, one of the largest estuaries in Mexico. Sitting on the border of Sinaloa and Nayorit states, its mangrove wetlands spread far inland and sheltered all the wildlife Ben knew about.

The small, rustic village of Teacapan, Sinaloa, Mexico, lay north of the shore where he beached. He secured the kayak and walked down the stretch of sand. A Pemex gas station stood just beyond the beach, and Ben bought three more gallons of purified water. After walking around the beach for half an hour to stretch his cramped legs, he climbed back into the kayak.

At this time of day, it was a little more dangerous getting out past the surf. Mornings were calmer. In the early hours, swells died down to less than two feet. Now, in the afternoon, the breakers crested above five feet. Ben waited for over twenty minutes until there was a calm break in the waves' frenetic activity, then shoved off and paddled away from the beach.

Once again, Ben was thankful to be away from the Sea of Cortez, and out on the mighty Pacific Ocean. The waves here came to shore one at a time, and from the same direction, and Ben managed to get through them with only a few gallons of salt water sluicing inside the cockpit. Once beyond the surf, he unhooked the pump from behind the seat and bailed out the water that randomly swirled around his legs. He desperately wished his spray skirt had not been lost in the last storm, but there was nothing he could do about that now.

Out past the estuary's entrance, the shore ran as straight as an arrow for as far as Ben could see. In the afternoon he passed another lighthouse. These lighthouses that appear so frequently are not like those in the States. They are merely a few iron stakes placed together with a small light on top. Nonetheless, they're much appreciated.

Ben checked the chart and decided he was nearing the town of Agua Brava. But first Isla Isabelle appeared on the horizon, rising like an ancient serpent. There were a couple of beaches to camp on with no rocks in sight, and, in the distance, Ben saw a cluster of buildings, but he decided to press on a bit farther, hoping to find a better spot to land, a spot away from where people might be. On closer inspection, Ben saw that what he had thought were small houses, were actually some type of thatched huts. Three of them. He meandered closer to the shore, staying about a hundred yards out, and paddled by the cluster of tiny structures. Whether they were inhabited or not, Ben couldn't tell. A mile or so past the huts, he pulled in. There was a small inlet, possibly a river or stream. He looked again at the chart and saw he was almost to the village of Los Corchos.

Ben set up his dilapidated tent, with its duct taped poles and torn bottom, in the dark. There was only a slight breeze coming down from the hills behind. The wobbly frame would hold for the night. Ben wondered how much more abuse the tent would take before it entirely collapsed. Once again he was in the middle of nowhere, but now, unlike before, he felt an almost eerie calm within himself.

It's still too hot to use the sleeping bag, so I sleep on top of it. This is where I belong. Out here, miles from the nearest person, at one with nature. I close my eyes, and listen to the sound of the waves. Their music floats up the beach, filling my thoughts with comfort, and easing the pain in my soul. The mysterious sound of the sea wraps its arms around me, cradling me like a baby until I sleep. I smile, and let my mind become lost in the wonder of it all. Indeed, I am where I belong. I feel so different now from when I first began my expedition. Somehow I realize that times like these will not last forever. I should enjoy them while I can, but a part of me wants to go on and on, and never return.

December 4, 1996
Near Playa Los Corchos, Mexico

As the dawn broke, Ben felt more refreshed and alive than he had in a long time. He sucked the warm morning air heavily into his lungs and stretched luxuriously. Rested by sleeping on land, and less cramped than two days before, Ben's outlook had changed.

Journal entries proliferate with the change in his fortunes:

I can't quite pinpoint when or where. Maybe I stayed in Mazatlan too long. The whole time I was there I could feel the chains of civilization weighing me down with more hassles than I am accustomed to. Money, food, obligations, they're all part of the package. You couldn't have one without the other? I don't know, and I don't care. All I know is that I feel like a weight has been lifted from my soul. It's definitely a change for the better. I am beginning to look at everything in a new light. I feel like a new person. No longer am I alone and afraid, chased about by the ocean, and by those nightmares of death. No, I'm a man, free from the burdens of the world. I am free to do, to think, to act, and to say, what I want. Out here on the open sea, I answer to only one Being, God.

Ben realized, finally, that he was living a life that few people dared to dream of. He was filled with awe at the reality of it all. One person, alone, in pursuit of a dream. The ocean's wild and boundless majesty beckoned him forth. It was real to him. Almost in a trance-like state he would slip back into her clutches.

She parts her waves gently on either side this day, and embraces me at my return. As the swells roll along I can feel her breath rise and fall like one in a deep slumber. I sense her rhythm, and join in again with the dance. My mind has lost itself in the simplicity of it all. My body slips away, now free from the daily routine and monotony of living in a closed and structured world. My senses take in the new surroundings. The bitter taste of salt on my lips, the smell of fish and kelp, the wind that blows over my skin and dries the saltwater that has splashed in, the roar of the waves in the distance, and the gentle slap of swells parting before my bow, prick my senses.
They show me I'm more alive than I have ever been.

The tiny river that flows near Playa Los Corchos passed by almost un-noticed. The only thing that alerted Ben to its presence was the change in color of the water around the kayak. For a moment the dark blue ocean water gave way to the murky brown tones of a river. Ben was reminded that the ocean is a great collector. Everything seems to flow into these mighty waters. From the rain high in the mountains that seeks its own level, to civilization itself, breaching these vast expanses to conquer worlds not yet known, all is collected by the sea. Ben was proud to be a part of one of the greatest mysteries on the planet.

From the mouth of the river, he crossed the seaward opening of a small bay spanning from Punta Cameron to Punta Los Custodios, and avoided the town of San Blas, known for its famous surfing waves. His water supply was still good so he continued to paddle, lost in the reverie of his good fortune.

As the sunset evolved into a blaze of gold, pink, and baby blue, Ben landed on Punta de Mitta, just north of Puerto Vallarta. He thought about the next day, and decided against going into the giant bay that cradles the famous resort city. It would take one day to paddle into the monstrous bay, and another to come out. He also had no desire to jeopardize the tranquility and peace of mind he had developed over the past few days by going ashore in a large city. Being around a group of gawking, loud, tourists was just not something Ben thought he could stomach.

The air was heavy with humidity, and the earthy smells of a moldering jungle floor. The lush trees on the point above the beach where he camped housed a number of exotic birds - and large swarms of mosquitoes. He heard their whining in his ears just before the sun dropped into the sea. He quickly zipped up his tent and was not bothered by the insects this night.

Thursday, December 5, 1996, 6:01am
Near Puerto Vallarta, Mexico

Ben left the point and headed to the other side of the bay before the sun rose. He wanted to leave early enough to beat the regular boat traffic coming in and out of Puerto Vallarta. He didn't need any dangerous encounters with shrimp boats, and for the most part he succeeded, seeing only three other vessels besides himself. Setting eyes on the lighthouse at Cabo Corrientes, it guided him across the bay without any problems in about three hours.

The farther south Ben got the more he saw an increase in maritime activity. This day, he patted himself on the back for thinking ahead. Often, and at odd hours of the day, a ship would pass in the distance. Ben knew that he was not in such a remote area as he had been farther north in the Sea of Cortez. The possibility of a ship running him over always lingered in the back of his mind.

The ocean was as smooth as opaline glass the next day as Ben sailed away from his camp beside the small river Tomatha. Dark clouds formed farther out at sea, but the wind seemed to be pushing the storm to the north. Later in the afternoon, the lazy swells gradually increased in size. Ben figured this was related to the dark clouds out on the western horizon. Their dark and ominous forms stretched to great length. Ben smiled, glad to be a safe distance away, as the wind was not strong and no whitecaps reared out of the rolling water to challenge his passing.

It was a good day.

So far.

The swells began to grow.

Too soon, Ben was riding up and down on giant mounds of indigo blue Pacific water, ten to fifteen feet high. Easily gliding down the backs of these mighty creatures, he felt the true proportion of his insignificance on the sea.

I am but a speck of dust beside a giant force of nature.

By evening, Ben had tired and decided to go ashore. His water supply was dwindling, and he wanted to eat some real food. He'd guessed that the lights ahead belonged to the town of Tenacatita, and, after coming ashore, he realized he was right. Ben set up his camp and walked into the small town.

He could only imagine what he looked like to the owner of the small market who stood behind the wood plank counter tabulating his bill. Ben's head was newly shaved, his skin blistered and burnt, and he wore a big, sombrero-like hat and tattered clothes. *Come to think of it*, Ben thought as he chuckled to himself, *I'm probably not too different from all the other crazy gringos that come this way.*

Ben bought five gallons of water, a loaf of bread, ten bananas, and some chocolate candy bars. As he walked back down to the water, he stopped by a small taco stand and ordered four *carne asada tacos*. They cost the equivalent of about one Yankee dollar. In Mazatlan, Ben had exchanged the rest of his American dollars for *pesos*. The conversion rate was seven *pesos* to one dollar, so it was not hard to figure out the cost of each item he bought. As to the *carne asada tacos,* Ben made sure that he put four or five whole jalapeno peppers on each one. He wanted his stomach and tongue to feel the rapturous fire that they were now growing accustom to.

The town was unimpressive, and Ben was thankful that it was devoid of tourists. Two small children stood looking at his kayak on the beach. It stuck out on the sand like a beached whale. Ben smiled as he walked up to them, and they went running away back up the beach to the town. After storing the groceries he'd just bought, Ben sat down on the bow of the sleek kayak, his feet nestled in the rapidly cooling sand, and enjoyed the last few rays of the sun setting through rose fringed clouds.

For some people, a moment like this, surrounded by the beauty of nature, would be forever etched in their memory. The sunsets, the beaches, the mountain heights, were all exquisitely beautiful. For Ben, however, it was just another day to be in touch with the beauty of the handiwork of God. Those people, though, would see this scene from a safe distance, sheltered in their cozy hotel rooms.

Ben made sure he was now *a part* of the glorious environment.

I have successfully slipped away from the harsh exterior of a man-made world, and enclosed my soul in the simplicity of the natural world.

But was it simple?

Chapter 34

T he sleek gray kayak with the blue stripe glided into the marina at Manzanillo in the late afternoon. Ben snuggled the small craft among the much larger boats moored there, and made sure it was securely tied and nicely hidden from curious eyes and hands. He stood on the dock and stretched sore muscles. It was still light enough that Ben saw the opportunity to play tourist for awhile.

As he made his way from the docks, the smell of tar, decayed seagull droppings, and old wood, followed him up to the street. The city was considerably busier than he'd expected, and Ben noted the stale air that hung over it, figuring that the various lagoons surrounding the downtown area were to blame. He stood a moment looking, then crinkled his nose in disgust at the smell of stagnant water, and hurried back toward the fresh ocean breeze of the harbor.

The waterfront streets ending at the harbor looked less than welcoming – even dangerous, especially once the sun had set. Ben had a little extra money in his pocket, so he decided to rent a hotel room for the night. He walked down a narrow road that was boastfully marked Highway 200, and, after a few short blocks down a street called Tiniente Azueta, he saw a hotel. The faded sign in front was the only clue. His room cost sixty pesos for the night, about eight dollars. The room was bare, but relatively clean. Ben headed straight to the shower. The fresh water flowed luxuriously and he stood there for half an hour. Ben felt a twinge of guilt for enjoying these

227

luxuries. But only a fleeting twinge. The ocean would just have to wait until morning. For now, Ben couldn't help but sit back on the clean bed and relax. *Luxury.*

He left the hotel the next morning, but not before explaining to a few stray inquisitive tourists about his expedition.

They always seem enthralled at meeting someone as stupid and crazy as me.

He bid them farewell with a flourish and returned to his kayak.

A simple release of the securing line, and he was on his way once more. Inside the harbor the water was as still as a giant lake, and Ben crossed the bay to Punta Compos with ease. The coast south of Manzanillo was bare and without much greenery. The gray sand banks gave little room to camp, as the cliffs behind rose sharply, and the surf along this stretch was extremely dangerous and rough. From his vantage point, riding the gentle swells a mile out, he could see the white water furiously thrusting itself onto the shore. Spray from the waves flew off the crests, and Ben was glad to be far enough away. Ahead he could see the massive bluff that rose above the jutting peninsula like a beacon.

The late afternoon sun still beat down unmercifully, and Ben would welcome the cooler night air. He decided to camp behind Punta Compos for the night, hoping that the stretch of land would shelter him from the heavier surf. He was right, and a few small sailboats had already anchored in the cove. Ben put in, dodging the boats as he rode the quieter surf to shore.

The bluff rose five hundred feet above Ben's small camp. The cliffs were covered with dense trees. All around, the landscape was covered with forests. It was an impressive sight as the sunlight waned and sharpened the shadows in the cliff face. It was still hot and muggy, and, to Ben's chagrin, he was bitten by more than one mosquito before crawling into his tent. Once safely ensconced in what protection the tent provided, he brought out a navigational chart. Ben was amazed at his progress. He'd paddled close to forty miles that day, and identified where he'd landed as Punta Cabeza Negra – Point of the Black Head. *Aptly named*, Ben thought as he glanced out through the flap to the dark cliffs and trees.

The lull of the wave's rhythm, and the long day's exertion, took its toll. Ben slowly lay back on the sleeping bag as his eyes became heavy, and the chart slipped from his loosened grasp. Tomorrow would take care of itself. For now, sleep, only sleep.

As he often recorded, Ben's dreams were vivid. This night it was about the world's record he had set out to earn.

Ben hadn't thought about it in a long while.

Why do people ask me these questions? I came up with the idea to kayak to South America long before I knew there was a previous record! How will I tabulate and verify the longest solo kayak trip as a world's record? Is it true that the current record for an ocean solo kayak trip is 3,600 miles? Will the record count if you stay in a hotel one night? What if you take a week off and go inland? What if someone else goes with you for part of the way? I don't know, I don't know! I don't know the answer to any of your silly questions!

Ben tossed for only a little while before the dream faded.

Silly questions! I said I'll make it to South America and, regardless of who likes it or not, I will!

Ben had thought about some of this before. When he left San Felipe, going for the record seemed important. Now, two thousand miles later, it didn't matter one bit to Ben if he set it or not.

Technicalities are rules for a society governed by ifs and buts.

Ben would have none of that on his trip. It was clear to him now. All that mattered was his personal safety, his happiness, and his growing relationship with his God.

More importantly, though, Ben was guarding his very sanity.

I feel the change that has come over me these past months. In the beginning, I obsessed on my loneliness that was, at time, nearly unbearable. I craved the company of people. I wanted to shop, eat out, see things, do things . . . but then something changed.

At the time, I didn't realize it, but looking back now, that night on the island in the Sea of Cortez was the beginning. Any need for the blanket of civilization to stimulate me, and surround me with comfort, has seeped away.

A lot of changes had taken place in his mind over the last several months. He had truly found peace within himself, even though these were the tough times for him. Ben had spent his birthday and Thanksgiving alone, and now he realized that he would be spending Christmas by himself also.

A test?

As I wean myself from society, I feel stronger. My will to survive, and to thrive, has replaced the former confusion. I can be alone. I can forge my own character. I can be free.

In the end, even Ben's dreams validated his conclusions. This trip was not about some silly piece of paper, or Ben Wade's name in a book. This trip was about his goals, dreams, and desires.

Sunday, December 8, 1996
Progressing Toward the Bay of Maruata.

Ben broke camp and pushed off from the beach early that morning, as a few clouds formed overhead and dropped a spatter of rain. It only lasted about a half hour, and served to keep him cool as the sun jousted with the dark clouds. The sun finally prevailed, and Ben traveled all day without any problems. He continued to make good progress, so good in fact that he decided to go on shore again that night.

There were plenty of sheltered spots now with easy access in and out of their harbors. The waves were gentler in the areas protected by an outlying bluff or a jutting peninsula. Today, Ben had time to spare, aided by the powerful current that continued to flow south. By evening he rounded a small point named Punta San Telmo. But here the rocky bluffs behind the beach gave little room for an easy landing. He pressed on in the gathering twilight. Soon he saw another protruding stretch of land, Punta Piedras Blancas. Its one hundred foot high white rock face jutted out of the water close to shore. Earlier in the day Ben had noted on the chart that this would be a good indicator for the entrance to the Bay of Maruata, his goal for this night.

It was tropical darkness by the time Ben maneuvered through the narrow entrance and into the tranquil bay waters. The rocks on either side seemed to watch him as they guarded the passageway. The narrow channel gave little room, even for his small kayak, and Ben was thankful that there were no other boats around as he passed through. He made his way in the gathering darkness, and, as a small stretch of sand loomed directly in front of him, he gave a last pull on the paddle and slipped up onto the shore. A quick meal, and Ben was soon asleep inside his tent.

No chanting, cajoling dreams this night.

At daybreak Ben walked around the bay to the village of Maruata. The white sands on the shore were different than the gray colored beaches he'd seen the last few days. The fishermen in the community were already awake, and, across from him on the northern end of the bay, they cast their nets from the waist deep water. The vegetation behind the curving beach was lush and green, with the ever present coconut trees and banana plants wagging softly in the gentle wind. There was an air of peace and easiness about this small town. Ben liked it.

Back on the beach, he watched a lady walk toward him carrying several loaves of freshly baked bread that she offered for sale. Ben bought one, and ate a small breakfast on the shore. Shortly thereafter, he left the Bay of Maruata astern, and reentered the ocean's realm.

Sometime around noon Ben stopped paddling and made a lunch of his leftover bread and a few bananas.

It's ironic. Banana sandwiches were my favorites at home when my mother made them for me.

He had paddled for seven days now, stopping only at night. His muscles were beginning to show signs of lingering fatigue. Once in a while a tendon in his arm would quiver. Ben had overworked that particular group of muscles, and they now began to have frequent spasms. The excitement of the open ocean, and the absence of any real problems over the past few days, had numbed his senses.

Now reality sank in.

As Ben ate, he found it hard to lift hands to mouth without shaking. He knew he must stop soon and rest a full day. He was concerned that if he continued paddling, he would do further damage to the muscles. So, after eating, he sat back, stretched, and let his body relax. After a few hours he felt stronger, and promised himself that in a day or so he would stop in Ixtapa and rest.

In the late afternoon Ben passed a large bluff named Bufadero. The reddish cliffs of the point were steep, and the surf broke wildly at its base. He pushed on, seeking better shelter for the night. His aching muscles told Ben that he was more than ready to quit for the day. He had to take more breaks than usual, and he knew he couldn't go much farther

The coast, however, had other plans.

Ben watched in dismay as the relentless surf pounded on the shore. The sun quickly dropped over the horizon and he could still find no place to pull in safely.

Ben was forced to spend another night on the black water.

Chapter 35

All day the temperature hovered at a grueling ninety degrees. The air was sticky, and sweat clung with the salt to Ben's skin. During the last week and a half, the temperature and humidity had too often forced him to stop paddling and jump in the ocean for a swim. Still wary of another shark attack, and afraid of being caught helpless outside of the kayak, Ben made the swims as brief as possible. At night, though, the higher temperatures proved to be helpful for sleep. His body cooled off less rapidly in the still hot air of the night. Now he slept longer. Sometimes, for almost an hour at a time.

That night Ben paddled for as long as sore muscles would allow, and then let the kayak drift away from shore. He didn't want any possibility of running into the dangerous surf that broke close to the coast. He climbed out of the seat and tied himself onto the deck with various ropes, looping each of the three strands once around his waist and once around the hull of the kayak. Ben made sure that he wouldn't fall the few inches into the water while he slept. If he became separated from the kayak at this point, it could prove fatal. Try as he might to get lost in the beauty of the ocean, Ben could not forget the unforgiving nature of his surroundings, and the punishment for those who chose to be careless. Safety ranked high on Ben's priority list.

He closed his eyes and slept for two hours.

When he woke it was inky dark, and it took his eyes several seconds to adjust. There were no lighthouses along this barren stretch of coast, so Ben didn't have any point from which to reference his progress. The moon was hidden behind a mass of thick clouds, and peeked around the edges only long enough to define their towering shapes. Ben couldn't see anything, not even his compass. For a moment he panicked, fearing the current might have taken him several miles out to sea. It was intimidating enough to be out on the ocean at night in a small boat, but now it was doubly so, because, virtually blind, Ben couldn't see the land.

After this brief moment of disorientation, Ben realized that he had been using only one of his senses, his eyes. Now he strained his ears and listened for night sounds. Sure enough, off in the distance he heard the ever accompanying rumble of the waves breaking on the beach. Ben untied the ropes that bound him to the kayak and, much relieved, paddled for awhile toward the sound. He found that if he listened carefully enough, he could tell the approximate distance from the shore. When the crashing grew just a little louder, Ben was satisfied that he was in a safe location. He crawled back out on the precariously narrow rear deck of the kayak, tied himself down, and tried valiantly to sleep.

Around 2:30 a.m. the moon broke through the clouds and illuminated the water with a cellophane sheen. The dark coastal mountains loomed as huge silhouettes in the distance. Ben drifted in a good location, far enough away from the beach to avoid the waves, but not too far out to get lost. He opened a compartment and took out the waterproof jacket. Wrapping it around his body to keep warm, he lay back down and finally drifted into sleep.

Morning light found the coast still void of substantial landmarks, and it was nearly noon before Ben could establish bearings and locate his position on the chart. The mountain chain that hugged the coast for over a hundred miles had finally receded to reveal a low-lying flat area ahead. It was marshy, and mangroves and all sorts of other vegetation thrived in this area. This change had given him his bearings. Ben was happy to see the tropical scenery again. For the last two days he had seen nothing but dark reddish mountains, some of whose peaks rose over 3,000 feet. Now, in the absence of the mountains' red hue, Ben could see changes in topographical features, and locate them more easily on the chart. He smiled, feeling confident once again.

Pinpointing a position was another skill that Stuart had taught him during those few days on the *Running Shoe*. Ben now recalled the conversation – and the lesson: "Take that point over there and look at the compass," Stuart said. "Got it," Ben replied. "Good, now write that number down on the chart, and take that other island's bearing there. You got it? Now write that number down too."

"Got it. Now what?" he'd asked. Ben actually felt puzzled and completely unable to read the various other numbers on the chart. He looked at Stuart. "Simple, mate," Stuart continued. "Just draw two lines at their given angles. Where they intersect, that's where you are."

It never ceased to amaze Ben, how much he had learned from all the people he met on this trip.

It taught him a permanent lesson that he recorded in the journal:

We should both learn from, and teach, everyone we meet. This intercourse among the human race saves our sanity and, on occasions, our lives.

Tuesday, December 10th
Nearing Ixtapa – Zihuatanejo
Mexico

Instead of the lethargic twenty to thirty miles a day Ben had been covering at the start of the journey, he was now flying at almost forty. Paddling the sleek kayak fourteen hours a day, and averaging about 3 nautical miles per hour, he was rapidly closing in on the beach resort area of Ixtapa - Zihuatanejo. His tired muscles and weary mind took their own personal encouragement from the change in progress. With grim, but relaxed, determination Ben was able to stay focused that day. He knew that relief would soon be in sight.

He rounded Punta Mangrove, and the lighthouse that stood at its end, and approached the mouth of another river as it met the sea. All too quickly, the ocean went wild as it contested the rushing waters of the river, which was much larger than previous ones he'd seen. Breakers foamed and crested in all directions, and Ben quickly paddled farther out to sea.

There was an instant when he thought he'd reacted too slowly. The long arms of the waves stretched out toward his kayak, attempting to draw him into their grasp. But, after a few minutes sailing up the face of several newly formed breakers, he emerged into calmer water. Ben sighed and glanced back toward the beach, as he was reminded again how quickly the ocean, in all of her enchanting beauty, could turn angry and treacherous.

It is without a moment's notice, if I stay unaware.

Once clear of the dangerous breakers, Ben bailed out the few pints of water that had collected around his legs. With renewed vigor he cut straight across the Bay of Petaculco. It was a large angled bay, five miles wide and fifteen miles long. He was thoroughly exhausted later that evening when he first saw the impressive hotels of Ixtapa.

There were three islands a few miles west of where Ben paddled, and he passed between the inner two. The breakers still looked impressive, and Ben waited until he saw a small break in the surf line to dig in the paddle and neatly surf onto the sand. The name of the beach was Playa San Juan.

After securing the kayak to a *palapa,* Ben looked around and found himself staring in awe at the glitter and glamour of the city. There were new hotels and shops everywhere. The whole city looked new, as if it had been built yesterday. The streets were swept clean and there was fresh paint on the buildings. The city began a few blocks north of where Ben had landed on the beach, and he quickened his pace as he neared civilization.

As usual, he immediately felt out of place. Yet it still drew him like a moth to a flame. There were too many people, and things seemed to be going at a faster pace than he remembered. He didn't feel like spending money for a hotel room. He knew that he couldn't afford it anyway. Out of curiosity he checked the prices of the nearest hotel for one night. A room in Ixtapa was almost three times more than the one he had stayed at in Mazatlan. Resigned to this reality, Ben simply shrugged his shoulders and walked back onto the sand to sleep on the beach once more.

The new day dawned tropically comfortable and calm. Ben allowed himself several hours to slowly browse the colorful shops around the town. He needed the extra rest. Ben found this little city to be a stark contrast to the more laid back cities he'd seen in Northern Mexico. To him it was commercial and 'plastic'. It seemed like a slap in the face to the old customs.

I hope this trend of nuevo ports with their fancy hotels and shops will not continue.

Ben knew how futile the wish was.

After the short morning stroll, Ben spent the rest of the day inside one of the hotels giving his muscles the rest he'd promised. Most of the time, he dozed on one of the overstuffed couches in the lobby, and between naps Ben watch the people walk by.

They're all in such a hurry, and dressed like they're going to a parade. My clothes are tattered, but I had the decency to put on a shirt before I walked inside. Guess I still looked like a beach bum.

The hotel receptionist challenged Ben's presence, and he deftly feigned waiting for a friend. Awhile later, she grew impatient and renewed her efforts to evict him. At his own leisure, he finally left the hotel, and stopped long enough to buy three gallons of fresh water on his way back to the beach. Ben left the city shortly after 5:00 p.m., feeling refreshed, full, and well rested. He decided not to spend another night on the beach because he wanted to arrive in Acapulco as soon as possible.

The sun set shortly after 6:00, and it was several hours before the moon rose, and was able to cast enough light to show Ben the way. During the short period of darkness, he set the compass on the bow to a steady one hundred and twenty degrees, south by east. He settled into a decisive rhythm and waited for the moon to rise. By midnight Ben's eyes were heavy. He stopped the stroke, strapped the paddle to the outrigger, and went to sleep. Again, though, it was restless sleep. The fear of drifting away from the coast was too close to his consciousness. By morning he felt more tired than he should have.

The rising sun chased away the flickering beam cast by the lighthouse at Punta Japuntica as Ben passed by, a mere spec on its horizon.

Friday, December 13, 1996
Nearing Acapulco, Mexico

Rounding the point of Lorenz, and passing between the mainland and Isla Roqueta, Ben could see a mass of skyscrapers reaching toward the sky. He had reached Acapulco.

It is an assault to my eyes to see such a throng of people concentrated in one area. It has been months since I have seen such a large city. I am intimidated by the size and mass of this city. I'm beginning to have second thoughts about this.

During a phone call with his parents some days earlier Ben had resisted their insistence that he delay his trip and come home to Tennessee for Christmas. It was a strong temptation for Ben, but in the end he settled for allowing his parents to wire enough money to him in Acapulco to provide for a needed rest over the Christmas holiday. For Ben it was a no-win compromise. He had to disappoint his parents, but still accept money from them for the stay.

The changes in my thinking are making these decisions difficult.

237

He pulled into shore on a beach he later found to be Playa Caleta. Once ashore, he walked up the sand to the nearest house. It had a great iron gate that protected the entrance, but no one was at home. Ben needed a place to store the kayak for the next couple of weeks, and he didn't want to waste time hunting any further. He took a closer look through the dense underbrush on the side of the house and saw that it was totally deserted. No cars were in the driveway, and the grass had not been mowed for several weeks.

Ben walked back down to the beach to find a couple of tourists looking at his kayak. One of the men spoke English. He was tall and thin and his face was red, probably from being out in the sun too long this vacation. Ben asked him if he'd seen anyone in the big two story house up the street. He said that he'd been coming to this beach for two weeks and hadn't seen anyone there. "I figured the place was deserted," the man said. "By the way, my name's Richard." He reached out to shake Ben's hand. "We're staying at a house on the corner and I haven't seen anyone in this place since we got here."

"Thanks, Richard. My name's Ben. Good to meet you. Look, Richard, I'm just needing a place to stow my kayak for a couple of weeks. Is there any chance I can put it up at your house?"

"Sorry," Richard said. "You can if you want to, but we're leaving day after tomorrow."

"Hey, no problem, man. Thanks anyway. I'll just put it up there by the fence out of the way. If anybody asks, just tell them I'll be back soon. I'll even write a little note." Richard looked skeptical with a raised eyebrow. Ben didn't really care. He asked Richard for a hand and, after a few minutes, they set the kayak down inside the fence on the lawn. It was incredibly light, as the over two hundred pounds of food it carried had been consumed since the beginning of the trip. Richard wished him good luck and walked back up the beach. Ben quickly wrote a note and attached it to the rudder.

To the owner of this house:

This kayak is only here for a short time. I am in the process of taking a long distance trip to South America and needed a place to store it during Christmas. I hope it is not an inconvenience. When I get back, I will compensate you with what I can. Thanks in advance."
Signed, *Benjamin Wade, Kayak Extremist.*

That signature seemed a little absurd at the time, but Ben thought some people might like that tongue-in-cheek type of thing. He placed the letter in a plastic bag and tied it to the chain with a small piece of rope, and prayed that it would be safe until his return.

Playa Caleta, the beach where Ben had landed, is situated in the *Peninsula de las Playas* section of Acapulco, one of the city's oldest neighborhoods. The beach is popular with budget tourists from Mexico City, and other visitors longing to spend time surrounded by Mexico's golden years. It was perfect for Ben Wade. He could balance occasional trips to the turista activities in new Acapulco with his love of the native culture.

There were scores of nice, small seafood restaurants and several large hotels nearby. Ben opted for a small local hotel, La Tropicana. It was clean and very basic. The manager was a friendly outgoing man. His name was Jose Vargas and his short stature and dark complexion, reflected his Indian blood.

The Playa Caleta is referred to as the "Morning Beach" because it receives the most sunlight early in the day. All very suitable to Ben. The beachfront was a principal terminal point for busses that ran back and forth along Costera Miguel Aleman, the coastal road that hugs Bahia Santa Lucia, and along which many hotels, restaurants, and attractions are located.

Perfecto, Ben thought.

We'll make it a good Christmas.

Chapter 36

The true meaning of religion is thus not simply mortality, but morality touched by emotion.

Matthew Arnold (1822-1888)

La Navidad en Acapulco
Ben's Christmas, 1996

On Ben's first bus ride into the heart of Acapulco he found the holiday festivities in full swing. Several weeks before Christmas, elaborately decorated market stalls, or puestos, are set up in the plazas. Natives travel for days from remote areas to visit these markets. The puestos offer crafts, food, and flowers of every conceivable kind. Ben gazed on piles of neatly arranged cheeses, bananas, nuts, and cookies, and rows of brightly painted clay pots displaying orchids, poinsettias, and many flowers that Ben did not recognize. Their perfume filled the air.

The sights, sounds, and smells, of the season swirled around him. He was doing his best to relax and learn. At one particularly large display of crimson poinsettias an old women carefully explained the flower to him. The poinsettia is native to Mexico and was first used in connection with Christmas in the 17th century when Mexican Franciscans included the flowers in their Christmas celebration.

Ben listened to the legend connected with the flower.

A little boy named Pablo was walking to the church in his village to visit the Nativity scene when he realized he had nothing to offer the Christ Child. He saw some green branches growing along the roadside and gathered them up. Other children scoffed, but when he laid them by the manger, a brilliant red star-shaped flower appeared on each branch.

This felt right to Ben.

But by the second full day he was finding a part of the activities that was quick to wear out its welcome.

Christmas in Acapulco feels like I'm living in a Dr. Seuss book. Thinking back, most days in Mazatlan had felt that way to me too. But it's especially true now. I'm beginning to believe that the Mexican government mandates that each citizen is required to make five times the normal amount of noise during the holidays. Music of all kinds is blasting from every house, club, and car stereo. Fireworks are going off on every street at all hours of the night. They are especially popular after 4:00 am, apparently after the tequila runs out. Noisemaking toys are in the clutches of every kid. I believe that making noise is a favorite pastime in Acapulco.

The noise isn't limited to humans. Mexican dogs are kept on the roofs of homes, and they love to bark at night. All through the night. I can't blame them. If someone stuck me on a roof all day and night, I'd try to make as many other people as miserable as I would be!

It was Sunday afternoon, and Ben was sitting outside La Tropicana lazing in the sun. Though the temperature hung around 90 degrees, the cool sea breeze wafting across Playa Caleta made it comfortable.

"Hola, Señor Ben," a voice broke his reverie. Ben looked up to find his friend, the hotel manager, surrounded by four colorfully dressed young girls standing demurely, hands clasped in front, and eyes cast down. "Hola, mi amigo," Ben replied. He stood and shook the man's hand. "Who are your beautiful friends?"

"Mis hijas, Señor Ben. My daughters." Dark sparkling eyes looked up to smile at Ben, then quickly looked down again. "Mi gusto, señoritas," Ben offered. "They are beautiful, Jose, you are a lucky man." The girls curtsied and exchanged glances and giggles. "Are you enjoying your holiday, Señor Ben?" Jose asked.

"Yes, but I needed a little quiet from the touristas."

"I understand, señor, it is a very busy time of year," Jose said. He hesitated, then asked, "Señor Ben, we, my daughters and I, are coming from preparing for the procession for San Jose y Madre Maria tomorrow night. You are a gentle man, señor, and from the questions you asked me when you came to the hotel, I think you are interested in our life and our customs. Es verdad?"

"Es verdad, Jose. I am interested."

"Entonces, Señor Ben, please join my family and me tomorrow night for the first of the Posadas."

Ben's journal records his response to Jose, and the experiences he had as a welcome guest of his new friends.

Christmas for Mexicans is a very religious holiday, a celebration of the Nativity - the birthday of Our Lord Jesus. To prepare for the day, enacting Las Posadas, literally translated as 'the inns', is a most delightful and unique Mexican tradition. Beginning December 16th, it commemorates the events in the journey of Mary and Joseph from Nazareth to Bethlehem. After dark, each night of the 'Posada', a procession is led by two children. The children carry a small pine-decorated platform bearing replicas of Joseph and Mary riding a burro. Other members of the group, all with lighted long slender candles, sing the 'Litany of the Virgin' as they approach the door of the house assigned as the first 'Posada' - or Inn. Together they chant an old traditional song and awaken the owner of the house to ask lodging for Mary. The people in the house mockingly threaten the group with beatings unless they move on. Again, the group pleads for admittance. When the owner of the house finally learns who his guests are, he jubilantly throws open the door and bids them welcome. All kneel around the manger scene – 'El Nacimiento' - and offer songs of welcome, Ave Marias, and a prayer.

On Christmas Eve another verse is added to the Ave Marias, telling the Virgin Mary that the desired night has come. Small children dressed as shepherds stand on either side of the nativity scene, while members of the family kneel and sing a litany. Then the Christ Child is lulled to sleep with the cradle song, 'El Rorro' (Babe in Arms).

The simple devotion of these good people warms my heart. I feel honored to be included in their celebration.

At midnight the birth of Christ is announced all over the city with fireworks, ringing bells, and blowing whistles. The people surge into churches to attend the famous 'Misa de Gallo' or 'Mass of the Rooster'. Following Mass, I joined Jose and his family for a tremendous dinner of traditional Mexican foods like tamales, rice, rellenos, 'atole' (a sweet traditional drink), and menudo.

One last note by Ben is telling.

The cool thing I noticed about Christmas in Mexico is that it feels

more genuine than in the States.
Hugs instead of presents rule the day.

Near the end of his stay, Ben strolled over to visit his kayak. As he walked back through the winding roads to the point of Bolsa Chica, he had a brief disturbing thought that the boat might not be there. He began to think he might have been foolhardy to leave it near the beach and trusting the locals. But once he saw the corner of the street where the house stood, all of his brief worries were put to rest. Nearing the gate, Ben saw the blue stripe along the gray fiberglass hull. He opened up the side gate and stepped beside his old friend. The note he'd written was missing, but everything else was in good shape.

The supplies that he had so carefully selected before the trip began, had finally dwindled down. Ben had begun with over two hundred pounds of dried food. It was supposed to last for the entire trip but was now thoroughly depleted. He checked the compartments and found only a dozen PowerBars, ten bags of oatmeal, and a few bags of dried mashed potatoes left. Ben retraced his steps to his hotel, and then grabbed a bus toward town and the Super *Mercado*. He stocked up on the same type of items he'd begun with.

No sense in changing a good thing. I've been in surprisingly great shape and good health during those first several months, and I'm not about to start manipulating my nutritional routine.

In all, he bought sixty eight bags of oatmeal, six boxes of *Zucharitas* - Mexican frosted flakes, ten pounds of beef jerky, and six loaves of bread. The memories and flavors of the meals he'd feasted on over Christmas with Jose and his family were fresh in his mind as he looked bleakly at his groceries. He knew it would take at least a week before he finally adjusted back to his life and diet on the water. A part of Ben was still annoyed at the confines of society and the hassles it brought. But another part would miss the comforts he'd enjoyed over the past two weeks. In addition to the food, Ben bought three more bottles of Aloe Vera gel. Being continually out in the sun and exposed to the abrasive nature of the saltwater, severely dries out his skin. During the first four months, he'd used four 24 oz. bottles of lotion. Ben took the four bags of groceries, plus six gallons of water, back to the hotel.

He was growing more anxious to complete the last leg of his journey. The comforts of hot water, a firm bed, and warm meals, were a plus. Sore muscles were rested, and tendons stretched to more normal positions. He felt confident that this experience was well worth the stop. But the freedom out on the sea was something he relished. He was more than ready to leave the confines of the city. Jose offered to help him with his gear and groceries, and Ben gratefully accepted. He'd grown to love the man and his family. As they crested the hill and walked down to the beach, Ben took one last look at the huge city of Acapulco. He smelled the smog that hung thick in the air, heard the traffic, saw the swarms of people, and rejoiced that he'd never have to set foot inside the city limits again. The gear was stowed and the kayak pulled to the water's edge. Ben and Jose shared a lingering brazo and hand shake. Jose bid him farewell and quickly retreated up the beach.

This past week, the ocean has called to me more and more every day, 'Come back to me, Ben. Come lie on my breast.' Although I have enjoyed the festivities through the eyes of some good people, there is a part of me that has remained detached. It is as if my soul is dormant, shrouded by a dark cloud that wafts between me and my lover. 'Feel my embrace, Ben. Let me caress you with my waves, and sing my lullaby to you at night,' she calls, over and over to me. I answer, I will come as soon as I am able. I will be with you soon, my love.

It was nearly 11:00 a.m. on the Playa Caleta. Ben ignored the few couples lounging in the sun along the water's edge who stared at him as he pushed the kayak's nose out into the water. He didn't bother to return their gaze. Ben was anxious to be off and had no time to waste. The new supplies were stowed in the storage compartments with care, arranged according to frequency of use. It was important that Ben knew where everything was in case he needed to reach something while floating across the larger swells of the Pacific. He couldn't waste time searching. Consequently, food and charts were always in the front area, the more accessible of the two compartments. Ben was continually reaching for another chart, or a bite to eat. In the back compartment, was the Aloe Vera gel, his wallet and passport, and the tent, sleeping bag and bed roll.

After a few long strokes of the paddle, Ben paused a moment in prayer. He thought back over the last four months.

Dear Lord, I have a lot to be thankful for. You have blessed me with life, of course. But, God, you have also blessed me with great health.

With the exception of drinking contaminated water, there had not been one time where weakness or illness had impeded his progress.

245

Also, dear Lord, the various people you allow me to encounter along the way have been welcoming, supportive and generous.

Although hard to look ahead and aware of the solitude again, Ben felt a wave of confidence sweep over his whole being.

With God on my side, I shall complete the rest of the expedition and return in one piece, mind and body.

Ben was sure of it.

Amen.

My pulse races as I guide the kayak through the water. The anticipation I feel is strong, my breathing full and deep, and my heart beating fully in my chest, as I move to mount the ocean's breast once more. Again, the ocean welcomes my return. As my paddle breaks the swirling water, I feel great peace of mind returning, and I smile. I am keenly aware of my surroundings, and my very soul breathes in deeply of the sea. Pelicans soar overhead, waves crash behind, and the breeze gently stirs across my face.
I'm home again.

All was exactly as he'd left it.

Chapter 37

B y midday the air was oppressive with stifling humidity. Ben's energy was sapped after only a couple of hours paddling. He'd anticipated tiring more easily this time and had taken several breaks. Now he was only good for about an hour of paddling before muscles begged for rest. He used the periodic pauses to take out charts and check on progress. It was obvious that he would not travel a great distance that day. But the lack of mileage didn't bother Ben. He knew from past experience that it would only be a few days before his old form returned.

By mid afternoon the beaches of Playa Culetilla came into view. From there Ben headed straight across the bay. Passing the lighthouse on the Island of La Yerba Buena he was tempted to stop for rest on the shore, but wave activity gave him second thoughts.

Once out in the deeper bay waters, Ben felt surprisingly vulnerable. There was a large amount of motorized boat traffic, and he felt once again the helplessness of being the slowest and smallest vessel on the water. Despite the muscle burn in tired arms, he forced himself to quicken the pace. He was just looking to avoid the other boats and reach the safety of the other side as soon as possible. Fortunately, all worked well, and after another tense hour Ben passed Punta Diamonte. Finally, the hotels, houses, crowded streets, and city stench of Acapulco, were a fading distant memory.

That evening Ben headed for shore. After the surge to get across the bay, he had only been able to paddle for thirty minutes at a time. He was now aware of a deep throbbing pain in his right shoulder, but he intended to keep focused and push through the pain that wracked his upper body. Getting back into the best possible shape by the end of the week was the goal.

No pain, no gain.

Most of the beaches had heavy breakers, and Ben waited patiently as he moved slowly and cautiously closer to the shore. Finally he found what he was looking for, an entrance to another lagoon. It was near San Marcos, and Ben decided he'd had enough for one day. Surfing the smaller waves to the sand, he leaned back in the cockpit and enjoyed the helping hand and power of nature as it pushed him to shore. He grinned and watched the water rush by as he steered the kayak safely to the beach. One look around told him that it was deserted. Ben was once again alone. He ate a small meal and set up his dilapidated tent.

Before going to bed Ben brought out his journal and wrote.

I'm surprised. Tonight I don't feel the depressing walls of solitude closing in like they'd done so frequently before. Sure, I miss my family and home. But even these memories are evaporating like distant vapors. I truly once again feel at peace with my surroundings. Thank God the agony and suffering of isolation that I endured earlier in this trip is long gone. It's a great feeling to be able to look ahead and focus on other problems.

This morning I woke to the familiar voice of the ocean crashing against the shore and calling my name. Breakfast was a small lot of oatmeal and cereal. It's early, about 5:30. I'm headed out to sea.

December 31, 1996
New Year's Eve
On the Sea, off Punta Maldonado (Guerro State, Mexico) Nearest town, San Juan Golbrado, 59km inland

It was near midday when it dawned on Ben, that it was the last day of the year. He began to think about what his friends would be doing back home.

Should I have waited another day? He asked himself as the sun sparkled across the water and dazzled his eyes.

I don't think so. This is where I belong, was his answer.

Ben's thoughts scattered like the popping of a cartoon balloon. The ocean ahead grew restless and demanded his immediate attention. Like a tiger's trainer or an elephant's mahout, Ben had to be alert at all times to her sudden changes of mood. Inattention, even for a moment, can easily lead to disaster.

The waves that rolled in to shore near the Point of Acamama were starting to form more than a mile out. On the horizon Ben saw the water lunge forward, directly in his path. White tops broke in perfect rhythm with his stroke, and the water around him grew increasingly restless. He steered the fully laden kayak out toward open ocean and, from a safer distance, watched the graceful, artistic wave movements like an audience enraptured by a stellar performance. Ben could ill afford to be drawn any closer to shore by the waves. Now he headed even farther away from the beach. After several hours of continual but unstrained work, his muscles gradually loosened and he didn't feel so tired.

I could not say that I feel like my old self, but I'm getting there.

Night was closing in fast and Ben looked for a place to camp. There was none. As he neared Punta Maldonado, the pewter tinged breakers were still forming far from the shore on the exposed reef, reaching seven to ten feet in height. He knew the kayak would probably upset in the heavy surf if he attempted to reach the beach. As tempting as the white sand looked from his vantage point, gleaming in the last rays of the sun, he dared not attempt it.

The night on the water passed uneventfully, but with little sleep. Ben thought more than once of his warm bed back in Acapulco. The night air was hot and humid so he was able to stay warm without having to wrap up in the sleeping bag. He settled back into the seat in the tiny cockpit and looked up at the stars.

His New Year passed without much flair or festivity. Ben thought about lighting a cigar to celebrate, but, when he looked, there were none left. He lay back again, cramped in the cockpit and a bit disgruntled, and waited for the night to pass.

A few shooting stars celebrated the night as they burst forth across the heavens. Ben didn't keep track of the time, so when midnight passed and the New Year was born, he was either asleep or too tired to notice.

New Year's Day passed without incident.

That evening Ben was able to find a safe place to put in, and he set the day to his journal.

My body feels stronger with each passing hour. I estimate I'm gaining ground on my per diem goal of fifty miles traveled. Now I'm doing about forty three. Happy New Year. What is it . . . 1997?

His camp, a lone sandbar near Rio Verde, provided Ben enough shelter so that he was able to sit outside his tent that night and marvel at yet another beauty of nature. The sky radiated above him with a fire unmatched in his memory. The few stray white clouds that hovered on the edge of the horizon flashed like crimson stained shadows across the water. Ben watched in rapt awe, as the sky slowly darkened, while traces of the sun's red glow lingered on the bluish gray heavens for more than a half hour. As he sat there on that small sand dune in the last of the heavenly light, Ben imagined himself as the only person in the world to see such beauty.

He felt blessed to be so acutely in tune with the simplicity of this natural world.

I feel my body shift restlessly, as if waiting to be lifted up by the winds that blow steadily by. I sit back against the cooling sand and look at the vibrant colors still splashed about. I let my eyes wander freely across the skies, half closed eyelids focus on the fading view. Clouds swirl down as their mist surrounds my mind. I reach out, and am lifted off the sand. I race upwards toward the now soft pink sky and dance together with the last rays of the sun on the clouds. Moving from one cloud to the next, I am lost in the illusion of my dreams. Detached from the rest of the world on a never ending sojourn, I soar higher and higher past the brink of reality.

I know not when I closed my eyes and drifted off to sleep, but the smile that graces my face in admiration must have carried my soul to peaceful dreams long into the night.

Once again, I feel close to heaven.

January 2, 1997
At Sea.

The weather continued hot and muggy in the afternoon, but the clouds offered snippets of welcome shade from the relentless sun. Ben imagined the heat would be almost unbearable in the months to come, and he gave thanks for starting when he did. There were brief showers all afternoon that cooled the air a little. Soon the small storm broke, and the sky pushed the clouds aside to let the sun take over its rightful place once more. After another hour of paddling it was almost four o'clock. The heat was beginning to slow Ben down again, and he set his paddle across the outrigger to rest. It was time to cool off, and he decided to take a brief swim around the kayak. Crawling out of the cockpit, he swung his legs lazily over the edge and into the cool water. He shifted his weight back onto his hands as he began to slide into the water. Then he saw it.

Ben froze, his muscles locking.

A shadow loomed. His heart pounded and his lungs felt crushed in his chest.

Just beneath the surface, and only inches from his dangling legs, the dark mass of a shark moved by.

Ben could tell by its odd shaped head, and its side to side movement, that it was a Bull shark.

Twelve to fourteen feet long, almost as long as the kayak, its powerful movements sent ripples to the surface, and a chill up Ben's spine.

Slowly, slowly, he drew his feet up out of the water, trying not to draw the beast's attention.

He held his breath, and with a white knuckled grip on the edges, eased back down into the cockpit and watched as the shark glided slowly by.

Perhaps I fooled it with my inactivity.

Ben gingerly picked up the paddle from the side of the outrigger, hoping to paddle away after the Bull shark was gone.

But, as he brought the paddle parallel to the water's surface, he caught sight of a second shadow just a few feet behind the first.

Ben instinctively jerked his arms back at this unexpected, and unwelcome, appearance.

The paddle clumsily hit the side of the kayak with a resounding thud that echoed across the still water.

Ben held his breath and froze.

He could see the head of the second shark jump in response to the sound, and look around sharply for the source.

Swimming in a wide arc, the second Bull shark came closer to investigate, followed closely by the first.

This time they came much closer, less that a foot away from Ben's stomach that was only six inches above the water –exposed and indefensible to any aggression.

I see their eyes, full of evil, stare into my own. The specter of their gaping jaws, filled with rows of misshapen, jagged, knife-like, teeth, sends shudders along the ridge of my spine.

After a few tense minutes, while he held his breath, fearful of another attack, they slowly turned ever widening circles and swam away, blending into the oblivion of the deep ocean's darkness.

Fortunately, this time, the sharks are just curious.

Ben breathed a sigh of relief, and immediately gave thanks to God for his safety. He was still shaking as he paddled away from the site. Now aware of the multitude of sharks in this area, Ben made up his mind that no matter how powerful the breakers were, this night he was going to sleep on dry land.

Although the coast was jagged and rocky, there were plenty of small coves in which to seek cover. Ben chose one that was protected by small cliffs to the north and south, and whose waves crested only a few feet before emptying their contents onto the beach. Before the sun had set, and while there was still light in the heavens, he rode the surf onto the protected sandy beach. The isolated shore was an ideal location, and Ben felt like he'd entered another paradise. On either side of his camp the hills rose over a hundred feet. Palm trees moved lazily in the breeze, transferring their idyllic rhythm first to the waves, and then to the soul of the lone young man on the pristine beach.

The water was extremely clear, and the most marvelous shades of blue. I found myself especially content that night in the solitude and still-ness of that place.

On the 3rd of January Ben paddled an easy ten miles to the northern tip of Puerto Escondido. He stood on the beach called Bacocho and looked out to the ocean. The sun sparkled off the indigo blue water like a million diamonds. The few rocks that stood alone at various distances from the soft sand, passively withstood the pounding breakers. Walls of white water crashed over their backs, thundering in conquest. They paid it no mind. Palm trees a hundred feet tall, and in groves a mile long, watched from the background, knowing that their roles were sufficient just guarding this sacred property.

On the beaches children ran and played, jumping in and out of the surf. A few fishermen waded out into deeper water to cast their nets and hooks, hoping for a good catch. They made sure they were well away from any people when they did their work so as not to disturb anyone's fun. In the middle of one of the beaches, older tourists lounged about under cabanas, sipping their soft drinks and soaking up the sun. A small restaurant sat beneath a thatched roof, serving fresh fish and shrimp to anyone who would partake of the ocean's bountiful feast. Ben welcomed this scene with hardened appreciation. It had been five days of exhausting travel on the sea, and he was ready for a break. He decided that in a day or two he would push further on in hopes of completing the expedition by early March.

Ben's gaze moved to the south, past the cabanas and fisherman and tourists, to a stretch of sand where the waves were less powerful. Protected now by the curving upper arm of land and rocks that thrust out into the sea, Ben guided the kayak through the tranquil waters and onto the beach. After a few minutes of needed stretching, he locked the kayak to a palm tree and began to walk up the beach. He learned that he was not yet in Puerto Escondido, but a mile north of it.

That night, instead of pressing forward, Ben walked to the outskirts of the small town and looked for a room for the night. There were a few hotels along the beach where he'd landed, but they were too expensive for his budget. He did, however, take advantage of their location, and protective boundaries, and left the kayak where he'd tied it. Meanwhile, in the town it was the peak season for vacationing tourists, and he could not find one room available. Ben walked for a good hour, checking every hotel in sight. He was told repeatedly that there would be nothing available for another two days after the weekend.

Ben was about to go back down to the beach when he saw a man waving for him to come over. The man asked if Ben needed a room for the night. He did. The man showed Ben his place which consisted of four very small wooden cabins. Ben immediately took the only one he had left.

The outside walls of the ramshackle cabin were made of wooden slats which barely met in some spots, with some gaps measuring several inches. A few cockroaches clung to the walls, waiting for the night to arrive. Damp and rank, the bathroom looked like a prime breeding ground for mosquitoes. Later he found bat droppings on the bed sheets from the rafters above. The shower was cold water only. But, to Ben, a roof over his head, a mattress to sleep on, and running fresh water, was a good change of pace. He took his first shower since leaving Acapulco, and put on a clean pair of shorts. The sun had set but there was enough light yet to see the ocean and the bay a hundred feet below.

The cabanas had a nice wide front porch, called a veranda, which looked out over the water, and several bamboo chairs spread out along it. He sat down to watch the sunset.

On the veranda next to his sat a man and woman, and, naturally, Ben struck up a conversation with them. They were from the Czech Republic, and very open and friendly. The man, Jakob, was about six feet, six inches tall, and towered over Ben. He and Ben had similar appearances with shaved heads and goatees. Jakob's wife, Lucia, was medium height and build with shoulder length blonde hair. Both were more tanned by the sun than Ben. They had stayed in the cabana next to his for over a month, but were soon headed north, up the coast. Jakob and Ben looked at the map of Mexico, and Ben told him of the best places to visit, and the ones he should avoid.

By the time he went to bed, Ben decided he would spend one more night in the little town of Puerto Escondido, Oaxaca, Mexico.

Puerto Escondido means hidden port in Spanish.

Funky and rustic, it was just right for Ben Wade.

Chapter 38

The morning broke clear and warm, and sunbeams streaked brightly through the cracks in the walls of Ben's hut. He ventured out onto the veranda, and was joined after a few minutes by Jakob, who was drinking hot tea from a gourd of some sort. Right behind him, Lucia brought a colorful, tea filled, gourd out for Ben. Ben nodded to Lucia as he took the exotic container, and they stood in silence for a few moments, sipping the tea and looking out over the dazzling blue water. After a while Jakob looked over to Ben and spoke, "You got any plans for today?"

"I'm not sure," Ben replied. "What are you guys doing?"

"I think, my friend, that we are going to a river nearby to fish. You are not going to continue on your kayak today?"

"No, I don't think so. Not today," Ben said. "I need a break from the action."

"Okay. Why don't you come with us, then?"

So with that they were off, Jakob driving a ramshackle bowered car that groaned in protest, but stayed true to its task. Ben didn't necessarily go with them in the interest of fishing. He just wanted to see another part of Mexico besides the coast.

Lucia and Jakob turned out to be a very down to earth couple. On the way to the river they talked about all kinds of stuff. They had been married for five years, but still displayed the affection and playfulness of newly-weds.

Ben felt comfortable being the third wheel.

After an hour of winding through the verdant foothills, they reached

255

their stop. A dirt road led down the hill and meandered off to the left side of the paved road. An old metal sign with the words *La Cieba* told them they were in the right place. On the way down the little track that led to the river, they passed by several small quaint farm houses whose facades reflected the hard scrabble life of their occupants. The air seemed drier here, and the surrounding wilderness reminded Ben of places he had visited in the Sierra Nevada Mountains of California.

The mountains that the little group approached, part of the Sierra Madre del Sur where the river began its course, loomed ahead. Birds chirped in the trees overhead, and a few cows grunted contentedly in the tall grass on the side of the road. They heard the lazy flow of the river around a bend in the road before actually coming upon it. The road ended on a long spit of gravel, and soon they stood by the water's edge. A cool, light breeze over the river smelled of the mosses and reeds that guarded its banks.

The smells of natural life.

Jakob had picked up a Mexican guide along the way, who now pointed further upstream. "Mas pescadores, more fish, there," he said. Ben didn't know exactly what the arrangement was, and he hoped the guide wouldn't ask for much money. He shrugged and followed the other three past the gravel to the grass beside the river. After a few minutes of walking upstream, they could tell by the encroaching vegetation that the banks of the river would soon disappear, and it was time to cross to the other side. The river was only about twenty feet wide, and clearly deep enough to have to swim. They all stripped down to swimsuits and, holding dry clothes above the water in one hand, swam across to the other side. They stopped at a place in the river where the water spread out to form a small pond. There was a little waterfall leading out of this area that marked the first surge of power to the river below. The water was only about five feet deep. Heading to some overhanging trees on the far shore, they set up a day camp.

The day was spent relaxing in various ways. Lucia collected rocks, and sunned herself on a spit of sand. Jakob and the guide first caught crayfish for bait, and then cast their lines. They saved some of the bigger crustaceans in a plastic bag to eat that evening. Each quickly caught a fish, and Ben smiled at the thought of the meal they would eat later on.

Ben was content to sit on the far shore and meditate. As he gazed up into the shadowed clefts of the mountains above, he imagined the life of the indigenous Mixtecos and Triquis Indians. Looking into the depth of the forest greenery, Ben could imagine the glorious contrast of a group of Triquis women, dressed in their bright red hand woven dresses, known as huipiles, coming down to the edge of the powder blue river. The sights, the colors, and the sounds of old Mexico.

The warm sun felt good to Ben, along with the dry air. It was nice to be around other people, but he needed his space as well.

About 2:00 in the afternoon, the group jumped laughing and squealing back into the river. With their clothes still held above their heads in triumph, they let the current carry them swiftly to the road. The flow of the river to the ocean reminded Ben again. .

. . . she is pulling me closer to her grasp.

The trio walked up the hill to the road, bid farewell to the guide, and guided their rusty ride back into town.

The next morning, after a shared breakfast of sweet bread and hot tea, Ben said goodbye to the young couple from the Czech Republic. Before paddling off toward the horizon, he wished them safe travels.

The sun was high in the sky and the ocean swells were large, but not threatening. Ben settled into a comfortable rhythm as he glided out to sea. The sun blazed hot and the water rolled by. Ben reflected on the memories he was accumulating with each new meeting of people.

These will not fade away completely into the past.
Not yet.

With head held high, and facing the southern horizon, Ben continued paddling on into the evening.

A few days after leaving Puerto Escondido, Ben passed by the beautiful towns of Huatulco and Puerto Angel. The beaches in the different bays along the coast of Oaxaca were some of the prettiest he had yet seen. The majestic Sierra Madre del Sur mountains, spilling from the Oaxaca Altiplano, rose from the sand some 2,000 feet. But he was no longer threatened by their presence.

Soon Ben neared the Port of Salina Cruz, and the landscape changed completely. The once green hills, lush with vegetation, now turned brown, as barren sand dunes ravaged the majority of the coast. Once beyond Punta Chipehua, Ben moved out past the breakers and set his sights on the horizon. There were several large boats moving in and out of the docks, and he stayed well out of the way. As he neared the harbor he spotted a residential section on the Bay of Conejo. The landscape here was ugly with sparse vegetation. There was, however, a good beach to land on. Only a foot tall, the breakers there just lapped onto shore, and Ben was soon standing on the warm, soft sand.

A road ran along the beach for a couple of miles. Ben walked across it to a row of houses. One of the smaller buildings, its back to a small lake, looked particularly inviting. Outside was an old man who was patiently scraping paint off of an equally old Whaler. Ben asked him if there was any place close by to store his boat for a couple of days. After hearing that it was only eighteen feet long, the old man said he would watch it himself. In further conversation, Ben learned that the old man worked on boats in his spare time, restoring them to their former seaworthiness.

The old man's grandson helped Ben drag the kayak across the rutted dirt road and into the lake, where Ben climbed into the cockpit and paddled over to where some other boats were anchored. He tied the kayak to one of the larger schooners and, satisfied with its safety, swam back to shore. Ben handed the old man a few pesos, and thanked him for his cooperation. He smiled when he saw the money and shook Ben's hand, pleased with the transaction. After talking to the grandson for a moment longer, Ben set off to Salina Cruz for a break.

Earlier, as he paddled along the coast, he'd noted the change in topography. This 200 kilometer stretch of coastline between Salina Cruz and Huatulco in the state of Oaxaca, Mexico, is one of the last frontiers in mainland Mexico. The arid badlands that border the Gulf of Tehuantepec are reminiscent of the desolate Central Baja. Ben could see that they were also no more hospitable. The coastline has one of the most consistent surf swells in the world, picking up the same powerful, southern hemisphere generated, swells as Puerto Escondido, but with no crowds. Ben had enjoyed the propelling power of this sea flow on his approach.

He quickly found that this town was for hardcore surfers who want to surf, eat, and sleep. It was not for people looking for a tourist vacation, which suited Ben just fine. The region has few tourist facilities and is virtually untouched by development. Ben learned that Salina Cruz is a blue collar Mexican industrial town with an oil based economy featuring a large Pemex plant, oil refinery, and commercial port.

Finding a hotel was easy as there were only two, Las Haciendas Salina Cruz and El Pescador, in downtown Salina Cruz. Both were simple but clean. Ben selected El Pescador and settled in for a couple of days rest. The days were taken up with conversations, and shared cervezas, with surfers from all over the world. Ben didn't quite get the rest he'd figured on, but the comradery was first class.

Bidding farewell to his new "buddies", Ben walked back down the road to where he'd left the kayak. It was as he left it, floating easy in the lake and still tied to the other boat. The old man and his grandson were nowhere in sight, as Ben quietly unlocked the chain and stowed it in the front storage compartment. It was harder to haul the kayak alone back down to the beach, but most of the way was down hill. After several minutes of huffing and puffing, the kayak slid into the ocean water and Ben set off.

The water along the shoreline of the bay was filthy, and he picked his way with care through the broken bottles and other floating garbage. Ben felt incensed that people could treat something so beautiful with such contempt. It was disgusting, and he felt violated looking at the trash that filled the bay. The stench of garbage overlaid the sweet salt smells of his precious ocean as   Ben paddled out of these waters as quickly as he could. Glancing over to Salina Cruz, he was thankful not to have tarried any longer than he did. It was an ugly, dirty city. The manmade harbor had giant barges cluttering its entrance, abandoned, and left to rust.

Since it was already 1:30 p.m., he knew that he wouldn't make a lot of progress that day.

At least, he wrote, *I wanted to get out of the city.*

The only relief in the scenery was the unusually sturdy stone lighthouse at Moro de Salinas. Ben could see the whitish-brown bluff towering some two hundred feet above him. The ocean lapped lightly at its base, sheltered by the point he'd just passed. The bright walls of whitewashed stone stood out on top, and the light shone brightly, even in the midday sun. Soon the kayak passed the jetty and entered the calm bay of Salina Cruz, Oaxaca, Mexico. Ben was thankful that this was a different place than its grimy namesake city.

Farther out on the horizon the ocean looked restless. Strong gusts of wind whipped sporadically across the bow of the slender craft, as Ben braced himself in the cockpit, gripped the paddle tighter, and set his jaw for the task ahead. The open ocean came up fast, and with it the power of the swells, as salt water spume lifted off the waves to smack his face. The trusty kayak bobbed up and down in the choppy waters, but continued on nonetheless.

Once past Cerro Morro, Ben fell into a steady rhythm, undeterred by the angry water that surrounded him. He now entered a stretch of water that could become one of the most dangerous in the world.

He had to be alert and ready at all times.

Rest was no longer an option.

By sunset, Ben had reached the entrance to Lago Inferiór, a small lagoon on the outskirts of the peninsula. The waves that broke toward the shore started their white frothy foam a good four miles out. Fortunately, they were still only a few feet high as they reached land, as their added thrust of motion sped the kayak to shore. Once on the beach, Ben set up camp and crawled into the tent. Before going to sleep, he lit a candle for light, and read a guide book on Central America that a friend had given him.

His reading confirmed what he'd suspected. Now, in addition to the ever present dangers of the sea, he would also have to worry about the different political situations. The last report Ben had received from his friend Jakob was that Guatemala had just ended some type of civil war a week prior, and that El Salvador and Nicaragua did not like Americans at all. On top of that, he read that malaria in Central America was on the rise over the last three years.

Every page he turned seemed to indicate some new danger - parasites, yellow fever, or malaria. Tired of these negative images of Central America, Ben snuffed out the candle and closed the book.

He mused as he drifted to sleep,

Most of the time, that stuff is mostly hype anyway. Relax. Look at all of the dangers people warned me about Mexico. I only had one problem in that country the whole time I traveled there. Besides, I have more urgent things to worry about at the present. The future would work itself out.

Hopefully.

Chapter 39

The only thing that makes life possible is permanent, intolerable uncertainty;
not knowing what comes next.

Ursula K. LeGuin, author

A *Tehuantepecer* is a peculiar northeasterly gale that strikes with little or no warning, even when skies are cloudless, and the barometric pressure has not dropped. It occurs year round, but most prevalent from October through April. In the worst month, January, the storms can occur once every four days. Wind speeds can reach over forty knots, with 18 to 25 foot waves. In a matter of minutes, such a gale can capsize a boat and push it twenty miles out to sea. The Gulf of Tehuantepec is so treacherous at times that few boats risk even entering. Most stay two or three hundred miles out to sea.

January 13, 1997
Daybreak
The Gulf of Tehuantepec

Early that morning Ben cautiously headed out into calm water. The breakers he'd ridden to shore the night before were now little more than ripples. An eerie calm had settled over the water and the air smelled stagnant. Ben was smack dab in the middle of the Gulf of Tehuantepec - at the worst time of year. He knew it was only a matter of time before he ran into one of the horrific gales. He was tense and nervous, feeling like hunted prey.

If I let my guard down the beast will pounce.

A knot in Ben's stomach seemed to press up hard against his diaphragm as he waited for the dreaded Tehuantepecer to appear. As he paddled, he remembered the advice Stuart and Dee, crew of the *Running Shoe*, had given him three months before.

"Stay twenty yards from shore, mate, just outside the pull of the breakers," Stuart had said. "If you feel the wind start to gust, get on shore as fast as you can."

"What happens if I can't make it to shore?" Ben had asked. Stuart had answered grimly, "I wouldn't give you much of a chance to survive it, that's for sure. The *Tehuantepecers* are nothing to fool around with. Dangerous buggars, they are."

With those haunting words still fresh in mind, Ben continued to paddle close to shore. By noon the waves were becoming restless. A stiff wind sprang up from the north and he struggled to maintain an accurate course. He sensed the wind building, and debated on whether or not to head for the shore. Looking over to the beach, some fifty yards to his left, Ben assured himself that there was enough to land on should a storm occur. The chart indicated a coastline of irregular cliffs coming up. He would reach them in a day or so. There looked to be only a few good beaches for cover.

He prayed that a storm would not hit while he was in one of those unsafe areas.

January 13, 1997
2:00 pm
The Gulf of Tehuantepec

Ben heard a noise that made his heart leap into his throat.

At first it was barely audible, but too soon the distant sound increased in intensity. After a few moments, he could distinctly hear a low groaning from far away. It sounded like the wailing of the dead.

For a few minutes, Ben sat motionless, just listening to the wind. Finally, he took a deep breath, began to pray and turned the rudder sharply to port and toward the shore. By the time he'd quickened his stroke and headed for the beach the moaning of the wind had risen to a violent shriek.

In a matter of seconds the wind swept viciously down the mountains and ripped into the ocean.

The *Tehuantepecer* was real, and here, and Ben hoped he could make it to shore before the full force struck him.

Across the bow of the kayak, he could visibly see the gale's force as it roared down the mountain, seeking to tear into the choppy water.

Clouds of dust, trees bent flat to the brown earth, even airborne debris, marked the frontal wave.

Only a few yards away from the shore, the full force of the *Tehuantepecer* hit Ben hard.

The sand on the beach kicked up violently, blinding him.

He lowered his head in a vain attempt to avoid the stinging amber grains raking him like broken glass.

He felt the water beneath him surge as the wind reached it.

The surface seemed to boil.

The unyielding wind swept across the kayak, and gave him fear that he was going to be ripped from the cockpit.

Even before the kayak's bow scraped into the beach, Ben made a desperate leap into the shallow water.

Still shielding his face from the incessant pelting sand, Ben grabbed the safety rope and half stumbled, half crawled onto the sandy shores.

Thankful to be on solid ground, he quickly hauled the kayak a few feet from the water's edge.

A seashell, thrust into the air by the wind, found its mark.

Ben felt the sharp edge cut into his skin.

Reflexively, he yelled out in pain, and looked down to see a small stream of blood trickling, its droplets launching away on the wind in a pink spray.

Ben cried out, and grunted with the strain. It gave him badly needed self encouragement to keep going, but his voice was lost in the shriek of the gale.

Ben found that he could no longer stand up to the force of the wind, so he turned the kayak over and crawled underneath. There was no opening in the hull to crawl into for safety, save for the tiny cockpit that was now upside down. So Ben hugged the outside as best he could, and tried to shelter as much of his body as possible.

Closing tearing eyes and gritting his teeth against the sting of sand on exposed legs, Ben prayed to God for safety.

I am thankful that I am not out on the water. I watch in amazement from beneath my boat as the ocean tosses and turns. It looks as if a giant being lay just beneath the surface of the sea, like in a huge bathtub, tossing the water as high in the air as possible. The waves seem to grow arms

263

themselves. They reach well over thirty feet in height. At times, two waves collide and the vacuum of air between their crests explodes. The sound is just barely audible over the vicious wind.

At one point the wind gusts so strong that my kayak begins to lift off the ground. I quickly grab the inside hooks of the cockpit and hold the kayak close to my body. I am lifted off the sand, and have to stand to keep hold of the kayak. It is like a kite as it goes skidding down the beach to the water. Then the craft slams back down to the ground. Again, I duck beneath it, trying in vain to hide from the winds.

After what seemed like an eternity, but was actually only an hour and a half, the winds subsided. Ben crawled out from under the sheltering kayak, and lifted his hands in supplication to the God who watched over him. He washed out the cut in his leg and bandaged it. It took fully an hour after the *Tehuantepecer* passed before Ben got up the nerve to place the kayak back into the water.

It was as if the great wind had rolled over the ocean and flattened its entire surface. I knew I had better act fast and, although I did not want to travel for the rest of the day, I knew I had better get out of the Gulf as soon as possible. Another gale could happen in a day or so, and I want to be as far away as possible.

My legs are raw and red from the pelting sand. I still shake as I recall the encounter with the evil wind. The sea still churns and the waves crash in my minds eye. That had been a spectacle indeed! Now, it is a memory.

Ben's fears were calmed for the rest of the day. He could not have asked for a calmer sea.

To this day I have never seen the Pacific Ocean with such peace.

But in the back of his mind he knew he'd better hurry. It would probably be another three days at most before another gale struck, so he had time to reach safety. He hoped. He put his head down and paddled like a madman, and by late afternoon he saw the lighthouse at Puerto Arista. He paddled into the small village's bay where several sailboats still lay about, anchored in its safe harbor.

Ben left the kayak on the sand and walked over to the nearest store. He bought some water and a loaf of bread and walked back down to the beach. The captain of one of the nearest sailboats had watched Ben's arrival. He lowered his dingy and headed Ben's way.

As the captain stepped onto the shore he waved. He was a skinny old man who looked barely fit for the harsh torments of the ocean. But on closer look, Ben saw a hardened look in his eyes, and thought twice about his initial impression. "What the hell are you doin', son? You get stuck out in that gale?" he asked in a gruff whisky voice.

"Thank goodness, no," Ben said. Then he asked, "Were you anchored here?"

"Yep. We heard the report on the radio just a few minutes a'fore it hit. Had time to throw out another anchor. Sea got awfully rough, eh? We were holdin' on for dear life. Almost went completely under one time. Where'd you hole up?"

"Up the coast on a stretch of sand," Ben shared. "Wasn't much room for me to hide under the kayak, but not much else I could do." They talked awhile longer, and, before leaving, the old man asked if Ben needed anything. Without hesitating Ben said, "I could sure use a bite to eat." Flashing a knowing smile, the old man raised a hand to signal 'wait here', and then rowed back over to his sailboat in the dingy, returning soon with a few ham sandwiches. "Wife just made 'em," he said. Ben thanked him, and then relished a mouthful of the succulent treat. The old man wished Ben luck and shoved off, waving goodbye.

The coast ahead was full of rocks and swamps. There was no time for dawdling. Ben reminded himself that he had just two more days before another gale would hit. His nerves were raw, and even the slightest gust of breeze caused him to jump and cower.

The next forty miles to Santa Cruz seemed to take forever, and it was past nightfall when he spotted the lighthouse on the small point. The ocean was relatively calm and the breakers were practically nonexistent, so Ben paddled his way cautiously toward the shore and found a good stretch of beach on which to camp.

The moon was hidden behind a dark mass of clouds. The wind came down from the mountains in a continuous moan. But it was not the shrieking of the gale. It was useless to put up the battered little tent, so Ben laid out the sleeping bag, crawled in, and promptly fell asleep in the open air. Despite the wind, the night air was hot. Most of the time, he slept with half of his body out of the sleeping bag. The mosquitoes were kept at bay by the strong winds, and he emerged in the morning with only a few bites.

But, for malaria, it takes only one.

Chapter 40

Every decent man is ashamed of the government he lives under.
H.L. Mencken (1880-1956)

The travel reference books Ben had on Central America continued to warn of malaria, especially in Guatemala and Panama. He promised himself that, upon reaching the next town with a pharmacy, he would make a purchase. Chloroquinine, the medicine used to prevent 75% of all types of Malaria, was sold throughout Mexico without prescription, so he knew he'd have no problem finding it.

Two days later, just before passing the lighthouse at Barra San Juan, Ben watched several exceptionally large waves crash onto the shore. He sighed in relief because he knew that the breakers officially signaled the exit point out of the Gulf of Tehuantepec. It was now back into the open ocean for Ben and his small craft. As usual, he felt the ocean surge beneath him in renewed power, and he moved out from the shore several more miles to avoid any contact with the currents.

The next day continued to be hot and humid, and the sky was clear and bright with no sign of rain. Ben hadn't experienced rain for several weeks, so temporary relief from the heat was a dip in the deep blue sea. As he jumped into the salt water to cool off late in the day, he yearned for a cooler climate. But before swimming around he peered out over the water, and directly underneath the kayak, for sharks.

There were none, but I kept a sharp lookout for any stragglers.

An hour later, now cool and refreshed, Ben resumed a comfortable stroke count. Ahead he spotted an opening in the land on the other side of a narrow peninsula. He headed for the calmer waters, and sought out a safe spot to rest for the night. It was this spot where the Huixtla River poured out into the ocean. Ben avoided the inter-tidal breakers forming where the river met the sea. But once behind the long finger of land that stretched as far down as the Guatemalan border, it was like gliding across a large lake.

At daybreak, he was out to sea. For a few miles on either side of Ben, the sand dunes rose up to meet the horizon. On the Mexican mainland side, now over his left shoulder, he could see the large rugged mountains above the beaches. It was still early in the morning, and he took a rare break from paddling to let the current between the mainland and the island carry him eastward.

Just before noon, Ben pulled ashore at the small city of Puerto Madero, and watched some fishermen taking the morning's catch out of their nets. Ben walked a few yards to the boats and pointed back at the kayak. He asked them if they could keep an eye on it, explaining that he'd only be gone for an hour or so. They smiled through tobacco brown, ugly teeth, and one of the older men extended his hand. Ben shelled out a few pesos and hiked up the small beach to the main road.

Much of the beach was separated from the road by a wall of boulders that effectively blocked the view of the ocean. Walking down the road, Ben passed between rows of small restaurants on his left and a cemetery on his right. The restaurants displayed faded names like Charly, Palapa Eddy, Palapa Paty, and Palapa Yasmin, and their proprietors vied for Ben's attention, to no avail. Ben noted that the cemetery was not like others he'd seen in Mexico with their walled mini-city structures. This one had above ground structures laid low to the earth, with tombs scattered here and there, facing this way and that. Some wires stretched between slender sticks stuck in the sand formed a boundary of sorts. Faded pink, blue, green, and purple paper streamers and cutouts now sulked in reminiscence of the last Dia de Muerto celebration. No one bothered to clean up the celebratory mess, or the regular trash that also piled against the tombs. Ben hurried on, focused on his mission.

Bienvenido a Guatemala!

Since the coast of Guatemala is about 200 miles long, he deemed it best to obtain a visa and any other required papers at the border before entering their national waters. Everyone Ben had met over the past few months had warned about the political situations in Guatemala, El Salvador and Nicaragua. He knew that these countries had distaste for Americans, and he didn't want any red tape tying up the expedition.

Ciudad Hidalgo, the closest border town to the ocean, and near the Guatemalan frontier, was only a forty five minute bus ride away. Ben soon found one that would take him there, and the fare was less than one American dollar. There were several little villages along the road sides and, as the bus jangled on its winding course down a long and dusty road, more and more people came on board. The narrow seats were now crowded and hot, and the tall Anglo sat like a monument among the diminutive Indians and Guatemalans.

Once at the border, Ben saw a large bridge that connected Mexico and Guatemala. There were hundreds of people milling around and looking for a handout. The stench of burning trash filled his nostrils, and he breathed in as little air as possible. Everything was filthy. The people, with their bare feet, matted hair, and dirty clothes, made Ben realize just how clean the ocean kept its surroundings.

He had seen poor people all along his way, but poor did not equate to the sheer lack of self respect he saw here. He shook his head in sorrow, simply amazed at what some people could tolerate. Only a few people were in line ahead of him, and he prayed it would not take long. While Ben shuffled along the line, a few children came up to him and tugged at his shirt. Their tiny palms were pointed up toward him in hopes he had something to give them. He shook his head sadly. These brown skinned urchins must have thought that surely the *gringo* had more money than they. Ben wanted to do more, but any gesture of giving would have brought hoards to his side.

For the next thirty minutes Ben moved slowly with his growing escort of children. He felt utterly trapped in this strange new world, so far away from the security and beauty of his ocean. More than once Ben looked around, hoping to catch a glimpse of the water, but, of course, there was nothing to be seen. After an eternity of only thirty minutes, the line moved and he found himself standing at the window of the immigration office. The passport was handed over, the visa was intact, the officer asked a few inane questions, and Ben told him as little as possible. With many other people to deal with, the officer shrugged and stamped a thirty day clearance into his country.

Ben quickly walked back to the bus, gently avoiding the children that now swarmed on all sides, some with bright smiles, but most with a leaden look in their eyes.

Of the several busses running, he took the one that went through Tapachula, and on the seventeen miles south to Puerto Madero.

I thought I would shout with immense relief when I saw the crystal blue waters of the Pacific Ocean again. It was just after the bus rounded a small bend in the road, and there it lay like a beautiful painting, sparkling and winking at me in the hot afternoon sun.

Ben hopped off the bus, waved to the driver, and walked along the boulder sea wall and down to the beach, taking deep breaths of the clean air. The salt and sand soon erased the filth and squalor of the border town, as Ben closed his eyes to relax for a few minutes.

The fishermen were still busy as he brought the kayak to the water's edge and shoved off. With a smile and a wave he paddled into the narrow inlet. Four hours later, helped by the surging current, Ben approached his first Guatemalan city, Champerico.

Long before he surfed the waves to shore, Ben could see the black sand beaches, and caught faint scents of civilization on the breeze.

There must have been active volcanoes here. It sure isn't much to look at. I timed the break of the waves, and paddled as quickly as I could before the next one could sweep me up, and jumped out of the kayak into the shallow waters.

It was late in the afternoon and the sun had sunk low on the horizon. Still, Ben could feel the heat coming off the black sand.

It hit me full in the face, like the back of a hand. I stood on what felt like a furnace. It was not long before my feet burned, and I quickly jumped back into the water to cool them off. I held the safety line of the kayak, and went over to the front compartment to take out my sandals. I definitely needed them here.

Ben immediately noted a difference from the Mexican coast and culture. The Guatemalan town was in poor shape, and he was uncomfortable with the sinister looks cast his way by some of the locals. Shacks and dilapidated old buildings were in various states of decay, well beyond restoration. Garbage littered the streets and was being enjoyed by pigs, chickens, and flies. The pungent smell and humidity in the air was stifling.

Before Ben reached the main street he was drenched in sweat.

The attitude of the locals seems to reflect the more hideous side of humanity, as if the black beach had darkened their souls. I try to speak to everyone I see, but am regarded with smug faces, rudeness, or just plain silence. After half an hour, I give up and walk back to my kayak.

Already, I can tell that the passage along the Pacific coast of Central America will hold few pleasurable moments.

Keen to avoid causing a disturbance with the villagers, Ben moved several hundred yards away along the beach, towing the kayak behind him in the shallow water.

I walked down the shore until I was out of sight of the townspeople, and hopefully out of mind. There was no telling what they would do when night fell.

The heat continued to radiate from the sand long after the sun had set. Lying outside of the tent, Ben caught glimpses of different constellations in the sky, a night sky brighter than he could ever remember seeing. Contrary to his fears, no one disturbed him, and Ben slept soundly that night. He awoke to the colorful dawn with new vigor.

I'm ready to overcome any obstacle this new continent decides to throw my way. I took out my chart and looked at the coast line. Within a few weeks I'll be entering the Gulf of Fonseca, the proud property of Honduras. There, hopefully, I will find friendlier shores. I will try to stop as little as possible until then, but that will mean several hundred miles of Guatemalan and El Salvadoran coastline. I'm ready.

The next town Ben landed at was Semillero. It was even worse than Champerico. Not only did the locals refuse to welcome his arrival, but he heard several whispered comments in the dark alleys running off the narrow main street. It was hard not to assume they were directed at him, and Ben was not at all comfortable.

After buying three new gallons of purified water, and heading back to his boat, Ben passed by three middle aged Guatemalan men.

"Hey, *gringo*," one of them shouted in a rough growl.

Ben froze, and turned to face them.

271

Chapter 41

B en watched with growing concern, as one of the men unsheathed a machete and ran his thumb over the blade. The man stared, his eyes mere slits, and his tongue playing on his upper lip that was barely visible under a black bushy moustache. Curbing a rush of adrenalin that cued up his 'fight or flight' reaction, Ben looked at the man with a steady gaze, then slowly turned and continued to walk, ignoring other comments meant to raise his temper. His heart beat faster as he nonchalantly glanced over his shoulder to see if he was being followed.

He was not.

Ben felt unnerved and a little cowardly, but his actions were a good choice. He continued to the beach without looking back.

The sun had already set, but Ben wanted nothing more to do with Semillero. He stowed the tent and sleeping bag in the storage compartments and shoved off, paddling out into the dark, heaving ocean and heading south.

As the blackness of the tropical night enshrouded him, Ben contemplated his next move.

Obviously, it is foolish to visit anymore towns in Guatemala. Maybe El Salvador will be a more hospitable place. Sadly, I sincerely doubt it. I wonder if I should just head straight for Honduras?

Ben made a quick calculation, and decided he didn't have enough drinking water to make it to Honduras.

The breakers now seemed to save their energy until the last few feet from shore, where they surged abruptly upward and fell crashing onto the beach. The sand rose sharply away from the ocean, leaving only a few feet of shore. This steep ascent caused a powerful undercurrent and discouraged Ben from any thought of landing. He decided to remain on the water for the night, the first time in a week.

The air was very warm, and Ben lay still in the cockpit and let the ocean rock him to sleep.

The swells bobbed me up and down several feet, cradling me first in their troughs, and then exposing me on their crests.

Friday, January 17, 1997
Approaching San Jose, Guatemala

The light streaks of the breaking dawn was a welcome sight, as Ben stretched cramped muscles, ate a small cold breakfast, and set his paddle to work. Near noon he could see the tall hotels of what he had heard to be one of the nicer coastal cities in Guatemala, San Jose. But he chose to continue past, now aiming at a village to the south of San Jose, called Montecito.

He was still hesitant to stop at another Guatemalan village.

He would decide when he got there.

Ignoring the ache in his arms, Ben dug in and propelled the kayak forward, but by three o'clock his muscles signaled *enough*. Ben could go no further. He had not yet reached Montecito, and that was fine with him. He turned toward the shore, and as he neared it, he was surprised that the rumblings of the waves grew silent.

Instead of finding a rugged, black sandy beach, the kayak, and its young commander, were now navigating through a small waterway that led into a quiet, mysterious and verdant lagoon. The water was crystal clear, and, as the little craft entered the channel, tropical vegetation rose up on both sides. Brightly plumed birds of all kinds moved about in the tall, tangled jungle, their cries filling the air with raucous chatter.

The air was extremely humid, now sheltered from the sea breeze, salt, and sand.

What is this place? Where did it come from? I had no warning. A stillness settles over the water here, and into my own soul. I feel at peace in this giant secret sanctuary. Is it real?

Once inside the lagoon, Ben gently paddled over to a long stretch of mossy shore. A few large turtles peeked their orange flecked heads above the water, startled by the human presence that entered their pristine environment.

After a few seconds they swim away, leaving only a few small ripples in the still water. Perhaps their curiosity is satisfied, or maybe they fear for their lives.

Ben pitched his tent against the tropical landscape on the damp mossy ground under a giant palm. Now he was able to get a better look at the variety of vegetation that thrived in this paradise. Water lilies floated near the bank. Multi-legged mangroves, covered with dozens of liana vines, crowded the sand. Other large-leafed tropical plants vied to complete their conquest of the coast.

Nature was alive all around him, breathing heavily, and watching.

Ben was lulled into a deep state of relaxation, and, for the first time in several days, he felt safe and peaceful. The sun was slipping behind the rim of trees that stood guard over the entrance to the lagoon, sending the last of its strobing rays over Ben's small camp. He was relieved to be off the water and sheltered in this haven. Sleep came easily this night.

Bird calls met the orange and baby blue dawn, gently rousing Ben from a dreamless sleep. After a quick breakfast he climbed aboard the kayak to explore the swamp. In some places he had to duck down in order to pass beneath the overhanging branches of the dense vegetation. Ben was sure that few boats had ever navigated these waters, where the channel was only a few feet wide, and the burgeoning trees and jungle plants tangled with each other in attempts to see who could reach the water first.

Overhead, there was only a tiny patch of morning sky peeking through the tall trunks and rustling leaves of the soaring trees. Vines cascaded in absurd abundance from every branch, hanging down and knotted together so complexly that Ben could not tell vine from tree. The tangled growth provided extra shade for the uncountable reptiles, birds, and amphibians, that chose to call this earthly paradise their home.

More than once, Ben started at the shriek of an unseen waterfowl. Usually it was some kind of heron that lifted its great wings and took off, disgruntled with the disturbance of its solitude. A tangle of fallen trees limited the view to a few feet beyond the water's edge. Flowers of infinite shapes, sizes, and colors draped themselves over trees and water alike. Brilliant red petals, fluttering down, and, looking like drops of blood, caressed the kayak's bow at every turn. The jungle seemed to pulse with life, and everywhere in the dense foliage could be heard the rustlings of unseen creatures monitoring his progress.

I am in another world this morning as I paddle as far as I can go. The little river, in most places only a few feet deep, ends in a tiny trickle. It's too shallow for me to continue. I can see the land in front of my kayak take a turn uphill, toward the source of the stream. I sit motionless in the cockpit for a minute. I'm almost afraid to breathe as I look across the swamp. I inhale the musky smell of life, and I feel drawn into the silence, a part of the wild, steamy jungle. As I sit still, there are only a few sounds - the water running down the hill, an occasional movement among the trees, and the constant beating of my heart.

It's a rhythm that joins with the powerful dance of nature, and with the unseen beasts.

Ben could have stayed all day in that magical sanctuary, but the mosquitoes had another agenda.

Despite the protective lotion that he smeared on arms, legs, and face, before leaving in the morning, their impatient whine was increasing by the minute. It was mealtime, and he was the only candidate for the menu. Ben swatted furiously at those that landed, but, despite his precautions and stealth-like movement, several were able to penetrate the defenses and attack with vigor. By nightfall, Ben was covered from head to toe with little red bumps that he tore into with his fingernails – if he could reach them. Reluctantly, the kayak was turned around and headed out the way it came.

No doubt this is what the Amazon looks like, Ben told himself, as he pretended for the moment to be one of the early explorers. He slowly looked side to side and wondered,

Are natives peering out of the brush? Are jaguars and other big game peering at me from their hideouts?
The minute I turn away, they will be at my throat.

Ben laughed aloud with the sheer joy of the moment.

As the kayak moved smoothly along, Ben reflected on an old memory. He thought of the degrading comments made by his peers before he left, and the sting he'd felt.

Bwana. Great hunter.

There was still the twinge of resentment.

Where would man be had it not been for the pioneers, ignoring the threat of death, and pressing on to higher limits? Had not everyone thought Christopher Columbus was sailing to his death in the 1400's? Yes, I know it's a little different from my circumstance today, but the thought of the similarities makes me smile none the less. This isn't such a crazy idea after all!

Ben laughed again. For a lot of reasons.
All his own.

Back by his old campsite he stopped for a few minutes to rest and eat. He looked again at the navigational charts and realized that there were no convenient cities to obtain a visa for the next country, El Salvador. The only cities along the border, showing on the chart, were too far inland for Ben to easily reach in a day. El Salvador was only twenty miles away so there was no turning back to another city for information. Since El Salvador's coastline was only a hundred and fifty miles long, he decided to press forward.

It was short enough to paddle through in a week.

Ben hoped he wouldn't get stopped.

Once past the channel and into the open ocean, the kayak was steered southeast again. Ben looked down at his water supply and grew nervous. There were three gallons left, and he didn't want to stop before reaching Honduras. Choices were to stop at a town along the way, or to spend a couple of nights on the ocean, always trying to paddle as many miles as possible. After the run-in with the Mexican police, Ben wanted no trouble with any other government – or officials. Since he did not have the correct papers for El Salvador, he knew it was even riskier to stop and raise questions.

The day continued without clouds or rain. Ben knew that in the summer months this area was unbearably hot. The temperature today was in the nineties.

Ben couldn't tell when he'd crossed the border from Guatemala into El Salvador. Near nightfall, he assumed he was paddling in the latter's waters. Waves were coming into the shore at a phenomenal velocity and size. Their backs arched high into the air, and Ben could hear them crashing more than a mile out. They reminded him of the waves in Puerto Escondido, and the fact that he had then not even considered riding their backs.

The decision was made to not head for shore.

Ben would spend the night on the water for the second time in three days.

He turned the bow of the kayak to face the setting sun and took a deep breath. In the final moments of the giant fireball's glory, he leaned back and took in the sights and sounds of this part of the Pacific Ocean. His feet dangled lazily in the water as he looked up at the sky, now beginning to show faint traces of orange and red from the sunset. The air was warm and brushed against his face with only the lightest kiss of a breeze. It came from the north, from over the mountains, and now and then mingled the sweet salt smell of the sea with a whiff of the jungle's decay and rebirth. This was the scent of life at its most basic and harshest, and at its sweetest to him. He listened to the waves roar as they made their way toward the beach, so boastful of their prowess. He listened and watched the pelicans and seagulls soar over head, keeping one eye on him, and the other eye on dinner. Their cries sounded far off and muffled, as Ben fell into a deep state of slumber.

After a while, he sat up and, in the last rays of the setting sun, lifted his hand and thanked God for His Majesty.

The sun disappeared completely, and a stillness fell on the water.

It was like this every night for Ben.

All creatures, man and beast alike, who look to the ocean for survival, have gone to their respective homes to rest and wait for the next day. Whether it's a fisherman's hut by the sea, or a coral cave to hide the moray eel, all have a home for the night. The ocean itself senses that its treasures have satisfied enough lives for the day and falls into a lull. The breakers ceased their loud crashing, and lapse into a more peaceful rumble.

Ben loved the ocean and its surroundings. Especially at end of day. He stretched out, his back over the deck, and closed his eyes, letting the stillness and solitude envelop his fading senses.

He rested body and soul and waited for the next day, and the challenges it would hold.

Chapter 42

Let bravery be thy choice, but not bravado.
Menander (342 BC-292 BC)

T he sea provided gentle rocking all night. Ben managed to get several hours of good sleep, awoke just before the sun, and ate a quick breakfast of dried oatmeal. This was the point in the ocean voyage where the sunrise was directly in front of the kayak, and sunset at its stern. The compass, mounted on the front of the kayak confirmed the heading – 270 degrees.

"Aye, mate! She be east by east true," as the ancient mariner spoke in days gone by.

Now, with the beginning and end of each new day for almost two weeks, Ben was able to feast eyes on the sun's imminent cycle at all hours of the day. There was truly nothing so beautiful to him as the sun reflecting its majesty across the water, giving him a golden pathway toward his destiny.

By midday, far off to his left, Ben saw what he presumed to be the city of Acajutla, El Salvador. With a population of fewer than 18,000 people, there were a few hotels and houses in a somewhat better state than those in Guatemala. Hope stirred in Ben as he sensed a change with this new country, and he hoped it was not because he was becoming used to the potential hostility of these Latin cultures.

With only one gallon of water left, he would have to stop somewhere and re-supply by tomorrow. Ben paddled along the coast, passing Acajunta and staying a few miles out from shore. The swells rose with enormous power, and he estimated some were over twenty five feet tall. He would ride up to the top of one and, from that height advantage, see for miles and miles around. Then he would plunge headlong into its trough, the dark blue and pewter waters rolling up around him and shutting the horizon from sight. All day he rode those huge swells. Never in danger, but constantly aware of the power around him.

Sunday, January 19, 1997
La Libertad, El Salvador, Central America

Ben reached the outskirts of La Libertad, just before sunset. Watching the lights shining out over the water, he chose to stop just north of the city itself. The beach curved around to form a point near the westernmost part of the city where Ben finally surfed one good wave to shore. That particular spot was best due to the calmer waters and generally smaller breakers. Just twenty yards to the south the waves broke with fury, but here the surf was diluted by a small river, and made the journey to the beach a safe one.

The battered tent was pitched next to several palm trees. Ben remembered that it was Sunday, so he broke out his Bible and diligently read the Scriptures.

The only audience he had was the gently swaying branches overhead, but it felt good to read the Bible out loud.

An occasional sand crab came over to check me out, but they must have decided that my sermon is not exciting enough.

The weather was now hot, and the air retained its humidity at night. Still using the tent to avoid mosquitoes, Ben no longer slept in the sleeping bag, but comfortably stretched out on top of it. He let his mind drift away to other times, and slowly he fell into a peaceful slumber.

Suddenly, out in the darkness, a loud *THUD* jolted Ben from his sleep.

The source was only inches from his head on the other side of the tent's flimsy wall.

He sat up, startled, his heart beating wildly.

Scrambling around, he found the broad bladed Bowie knife that faithfully lay to his right side. He grasped it tightly, and twisted around to get out of the tent.

Whatever was out there would get a shock tonight.

With a wild war cry that startled some birds roosting overhead, Ben scrambled through the door of the tent and stood up, brandishing the 12 inch blade of the deadly knife in front of his buck-naked body.

He crouched in a combat stance and swayed his upper body left and right in a stealthy scan of the darkness.

His eyes slowly allowed the dim starlit shapes around him to materialize.

With visions of pirates, he was greeted only by silence.

I knew the culprit must have crawled to the other side of the tent, so I ran around to where I was sure someone crouched close to the ground.

Stabbing and slashing the air with the large Bowie knife, and raising no enemy combatant, Ben finally realized that the only armed man on the long stretch of sand was him.

With his breathing slowing, and his heart climbing back into his chest, he now wondered whether the sound had been a dream. Slowly, placing his feet carefully, Ben walked around to the front of the tent, and peered down to where he thought he'd heard the noise. There, a small, dark, round shape was sitting in the sand.

Here his nemesis lay, burrowed in a dimple in the black sand like a golf ball in a hazard. With a chuckle Ben picked up the large coconut. The milk inside trickled out, and down the smooth outer shell, as he examined it closely.

Though this coconut was rotten, it gave him an idea.

Why I had not thought of it before? For the last four hundred miles, the shores have been covered with coconut palm trees. Almost every tree bore a dozen or so coconuts. If I reach a few each night, I will have enough milk to drink for dinner. I might even find a way to pour the excess liquid into my empty gallon jugs, and not have to stop for water ever again.

Ben sheepishly put away his combat-ready Bowie knife, thankful that he had not cut off something personally important during his ferocious naked attack on the wild coconut. Climbing back into the tent, he felt a little foolish for acting so rash. But at least something good had come out of it.

At first light Ben climbed out of his tent, and looked up at the tree that had been the source of such alarm the night before. Coconuts hung in clusters just out of his reach. He carefully piled a few rocks to make a stepladder, and twisted the green, smooth skinned, globes until they fell to the ground. He sorted them according to size and color – his choice being slightly smaller than a soccer ball and dark green - and picked four coconuts that were to his liking.

Ben set the first one on the ground and took out his knife. Slicing away the soft outer shell with a few hacks, he carefully chipped away the green skin around the top of the coconut until a small corner of the brown shell was revealed. Then he raised the knife, keeping his other hand well out of the way, and struck the nut with full force. One blow, then another, and after the third, he revealed the delicate soft white meat soaking in the sweet coconut liquor inside. Ben placed the opening to his lips, tilted his head back, and let the cool liquid run down a parched throat.

The milk was delicious and sweet, enhanced by the fact that he had obtained it from the wild himself. With a smile of self satisfaction, Ben poured the contents of the remaining three coconuts into an empty gallon jug. Then he stood, turned, and began a walk of several hundred yards down the beach to the village of La Libertad.

The small fishing village was much cleaner and nicer than the last few he'd visited. Pleased, he walked down the main street to a market and purchased four gallons of water. Back down the peaceful street, he strolled onto the hot black sand and untied the kayak. He was out on the ocean before 10:00 a.m., refreshed by the pleasantness of the town.

Perhaps El Salvador will not be so bad after all.

Ben relaxed somewhat, knowing that if he had to stop, he might be able to do so without getting into trouble.

From where he paddled Ben could still see the town's pier and the restaurants that dotted the shore.

They seem as plentiful as the grains of black sand on the beach.

He passed by a string of rocks that jutted from the mainland. He was careful not to get too close, and moved a little farther out to sea to avoid the real dangers that lurked just beneath the surface. Then, once again, Ben was in open water.

For the last week, he had not seen dolphins, whales, or sharks. Their presence was sorely missed. Clouds on the horizon warned of the possibility of a storm by nightfall. Late in the day he looked for appropriate cover, and found it in a deep lagoon, almost fifty miles southeast of where he'd started the day. He was continually amazed at the number of miles covered each day now, sometimes almost effortlessly. Gone were the days, early in the trip, filled with tides and conflicting currents that threatened to push him north, and away from his final destination.

Now, the ocean's southerly surge accommodates me as if she is happy to have this little kayak, and its wide eyed captain, paddling through her waters. She more than tolerates my presence, actually assisting me now at every turn.

Ben camped in sight of a city named Jiguilisco, (*hig-wee-lee-sco*) inside a lagoon about two miles away from the ocean. He chose a small stretch of sand that peeked out from the midst of the surrounding swamps. Large, elegantly plumed birds flew everywhere, but avoided his camp. The water, however, seemed to be void of activity, and he was not interested in attempting any further exploration. The tent was erected, and a sheet of plastic was placed over the mesh top in case rain fell later.

A southerly wind pushed the storm directly overhead, and by 7:30 p.m. the first few droplets began to fall. The storm brought a chill to the air that Ben had not felt for several weeks. He drew his body close inside the sleeping bag, and watched bemused as a few raindrops seeped into the tent.

There were no coconuts to forage for in the marshy soil, so Ben left quickly the next morning after breakfast. The rain had stopped sometime in the night and the tent was relatively dry. He folded it up, along with the bed roll and sleeping bag, and put them back into the kayak. The water that morning was as smooth as glass inside the lagoon, and Ben paddled into the ocean feeling positive about the turn the trip had taken. The rain had cooled the air down several degrees, and the new day and a good night's rest gave additional strength.

That strength, however, did not last.

The day passed by slowly and, at times, Ben felt a little weak. Surprisingly, until this point, his general health – not counting the recurring pain in his hip - had held up pretty well. At the beginning of the expedition he had feared that exposure to the elements, fatigue, and the daily grueling workouts, would take their toll on his body. For the most part he'd never felt better in all his life. Now, as the day progressed, the first symptoms of sickness came on. Suddenly, Ben realized just how fortunate he had been.

By late afternoon he headed for a long narrow stretch of land that jutted out into the ocean. He calculated that he was nearing the Gulf of Fonseca and this was the entrance to a large bay.

Ben was now utterly exhausted.

His hands shook a little as he hauled the kayak onto the sand.

A chill crept over his body and he shuddered, despite the warm air.

The chill was from deep inside him.

He gave it only a fleeting thought, but it did not bode well.

He felt his strength waning rapidly.

With deliberate, focused effort he pitched the tent, and took out several articles of clothing, food, and medicine. He knew he'd be too weak to paddle the next day and planned to make the best of it. Adding insult to injury, Ben developed a debilitating case of dysentery during the night. Waves of gripping cramps continued well through the next day, and he spent most of the time either doubled over in pain, or squatting over the sand in the thick brush behind his tent.

Sometimes it felt like his intestines were going to fall out along with everything else.

I won't go into most of the details, but let me just say that for the next week, everything I ate seemed to turn to water inside. Not accustomed to such unusual conditions, my stomach would then get rid of the waste in a pistol-like, rapid fire motion.

The intensity of the sickness during the first two days kept Ben all but totally disabled. He began to worry about the dehydration that, he knew all too well, could kill him. He forced himself to drink, even as it fought back and wounded his weakening body. Sleep helped. But it also drove the fear of maybe not waking up.

Then, gradually, his stomach and bowels relaxed their attacks, and allowed him to rest and gain on rehydration.

My flu, along with my weakened muscles, gradually recovered from the dull throbbing pain, and I felt better in a couple of days. I hope it is flu. Malaria is not a good alternative. I rested those days, and made sure that I took vitamin C pills every few hours. I am anxious to resume my travels. Most of the time I sleep, which my body no doubt relishes, making up for the last few weeks of abuse.

Chapter 43

To be exempt from the passions with which others are tormented, is the only pleasing solitude.

Joseph Addison (1672 - 1719)

On the 23rd of January, 1997, Ben felt like a new man. His stomach was retaining food, and his strength had returned. He turned his sights away from the beach to the Gulf of Fonseca, shared by El Salvador, Guatemala, and Honduras, where he would be entering Honduran waters.

As the kayak rounded the point that Ben had marked on the chart a few days prior, the Gulf was calm. The water rolled by rapidly and he made good time. In mid-afternoon he paddled past El Tigre Island, just as a pod of dolphins passed the kayak several yards to the right. Ben felt strangely welcomed to these new waters by his old friends.

He rejoiced at the return of marine life, and headed quickly to the mainland to spend the evening. Spying the deep inlet that led to the Bay of San Lorenzo, Honduras, Ben made his way along its shore to the city of the same name, founded in 1522 by Spaniards.

Passing by several handmade wooden canoes and other small vessels, he waved at the people he saw. In return, he was greeted with similar friendly gestures, smiles, and words of *hola* and *bueno*. Ben felt relieved to have passed by two unfriendly Central American countries unscathed, and to now receive a warm welcome in the third. He decided to stay in Honduras for a couple of days. Soon, he was pushing the kayak up on a small beach on the outskirts of San Lorenzo, Honduras.

The air was still and hot. There were several people in the area. Some sat on a concrete wall near the beach where he landed, and others strolled down the street on foot or on bicycles. No one seemed in a hurry.

Ben smiled at the people who were looking at the kayak.

I see admiration in their eyes.

The kayak was tied to a wooden post, perhaps part of an old pier. Ben made his way a few blocks to the immigration office. Once inside the small building, he handed the officer his passport. The officer looked a little surprised to see him, and, when Ben told him his mode of transportation, he raised his eyebrows, but stamped the page anyway. Ben paid him thirty Limperas for his service, about US$2.50, and he handed back his passport with a thirty day visa.

It was a sleepy little Spanish colonial town, and nothing seemed to bother the people much. Ben felt at ease with the locals and knew he would have no problems communicating his needs. He went back down to the beach and, as always, was relieved to see the kayak still resting near the water's edge. Ben still had ten feet of chain, a lock, and a steel eye-bolt screwed into the hull of the kayak. He secured the rig and waved to the men sitting along the concrete walkway, hoping that a show of friendliness would deter anyone from meddling with his supplies.

Ben walked through the small city and looked for a place to spend the night. It had been a long time since he'd slept in a good bed or taken a fresh shower.

Although I no longer yearn for these comforts as I had in the beginning, it will be a nice change from my usual accommodations.

A small hotel sat near the water. Ben walked into the lobby, paid for a room, and followed the lady to his quarters. The room was small with a bed in the center, dingy yellow curtains, an old blanket on the bed, and a stand-up shower in the corner. After setting his bag on the bed, he jumped eagerly into the shower. The water was cold, but, after he'd adjusted to the shock, he felt revived and clean. Soon, the salt and sand swirled away down the rusty drain.

Ben went down to the hotel lobby. Beyond the back window he saw a large deck with tables overlooking the water. He went outside, sat down at one of the tables, and ordered dinner. The view looked out over the bay, and at the green sloping hills that led out on either side of the waterway to the Gulf. Ben could not see the open ocean from where he sat, *but it was a nice view anyway.* Canoes glided by beneath the deck, and Ben rested his eyes and enjoyed the moment.

When the meal came - rice, beans, tortillas, and fried plantains - Ben attacked it with the same vigor as he had the shower. To him the simplest necessities of a modern society were extravagant and rare luxuries.

He enjoyed every morsel of the simple food.

Last year in the States, I would have complained because there was no steak.

The next morning after a quick, fresh water shower, Ben checked out of the room, and shoved off from the small beach in San Lorenzo. There were no waves coming into the bay, and the kayak slipped out into the Gulf of Fonseca with ease. The waterway was much like a river with narrow banks, a smooth surface, and protective green sloping hills on either side. Soon the water fanned out into a wide bay, and Ben was paddling into open water.

Near noon, he once again spotted the small, volcano shaped, island of El Tigre. Its lush green tropical cone contrasted with the deep blue water. A few beaches dotted its western shore, and that was where he headed. The power of the Pacific Ocean did not reach these tranquil waters because of the protecting arms of both El Salvador and Nicaragua, which shared the Gulf of Fonseca with Honduras. The jagged headlands stretched far into the Pacific, and provide the Gulf with calm waters most of the year. It was again an easy paddle to land on the island's beach. Ben climbed out of the cockpit and stretched tight muscles as he surveyed the verdant scene.

This was definitely the tropics now. Banana trees, palm trees, and other types of big leaf vegetation, densely covered the entire island. Beyond the beach the foliage left little room for the sun to reach the ground. Ben slung a hammock that he'd acquired in Puerto Escondido between two palm trees. The giant fronds leaned far out over the water's edge and provided him perfect shade from the hot sun.

Like a weary animal thirsting for a drink, the palm trees stoop over to kiss a drop of the cool waters of the Gulf.

Constant exposure to the sun had negative effects on skin, eyes, and stamina, and Ben was continually putting on lotion, even though his skin had tanned and seemed used to the abuse. He wanted to take no chances with skin cancer. Now in the rare shade, Ben relished the comfort and cool air beneath the trees. Lying in the gently swaying hammock, he closed his eyes and listened to the sounds of the jungle. Green parrots and blue and red macaws squawked from the branches. Waves brushed up against the shore, soft and reassuring with their constant swirl. Gentle winds blew the leaves in a rustling that joined the water's hypnotic rhythm. A symphony of life and motion surrounded him.

The delicate balance between nature and its surroundings was like harmonic chords, delicately written.

The island's tranquility put its soothing arms around me and lulled me to sleep. I stayed there for several days, losing track of the hour, the day, and the week.

Occasionally, Ben would walk to the other side of the island to a small village, Amapala, built into the side of the volcanic hill. There were a few tourists looking at the shops and eating in the restaurants. It was a quaint town, and most of the visitors must have thought it fairly isolated. But Ben had changed into a person who needed space, time to think, and very few distractions. Each time he visited the village, he looked forward to getting back to 'his side' of the island, and away from human contact.

It's not that I dislike other people's company. I am just learning to live on my own. Whether I'm on my side of the island, devoid of civilization, or out on the Pacific Ocean, a peace comes over me that I cannot explain. Perhaps it's the freedom I feel, being away from all of the pressures and restrictions that society placed on me.

Something has changed inside me, and I can't put a finger on when this actually occurred. Now, completely separated from all types of modern 'conveniences', I find myself at home. I'm rapidly becoming aware that I might never want to go back.

I do not feel the need for companionship.

I have nature herself and the Creator of the world.

I now believe that lonely solitude, is a figment of my imagination.

With all of this beauty at my fingertips, what more can I want?

Somewhere over the last four months, Ben had learned what it meant to survive on his own, and within himself.

Maybe it's my exposure to the ocean's majesty, I can't really tell. But time seems to have a different tempo on the water. Days seem like weeks, weeks like months, and months like years. Indeed, it's as if my existence on the water is all I have ever known.

Lying there in his hammock beneath the palm trees and looking out over the blue water, Ben could only think of the many different struggles, triumphs, and joys, he'd experienced during the expedition.

Memories from that "other world" grew dimmer, receding into the recesses of his mind.

He consciously let them go, not wishing to hold onto them any longer.

Ben was perfectly happy to live in this new world, and did not need any one or anything to tell him differently.

Heather. . .

I thought of her often in the first weeks, especially after I left San Carlos. The memory of her beautiful face and the scent of her hair lingered on. It penetrated my solitude and comforted me in the darker hours of the night. Eventually, though, she faded away into the past, and the sting of our separation has dwindled down to only a dull ache. The romance was no doubt ill fated from the beginning, plagued by bad timing. I think nothing more of it now.

I am closing another chapter in the book of my life, and it's not Heather who is to blame, it's me. Indeed, all of my friends now seem to drift off to another time and place, like the clouds floating there atop the currents of air. One moment they're there, floating by, oblivious to their surrounding, and I'm thinking they'll always be present to fill my life with joy. Then, with both clouds and friends, I am surprised when I look back at the past and see them disappear over the horizon, never to be experienced again.

The home I'd left behind seems like another world.

It has dissolved into only distant memories I can scarce recall.

This day near the end of January, as Ben sat under a palm tree and felt a refreshing breeze blow against his face; he looked back over the past few months, and could hardly believe he'd ever lived elsewhere.

The only life I've ever really lived is here on the ocean. The birds, the waves, the trees, and the beaches, are my friends. The creatures that swim beneath the surface of the waters take the place of romance.

Glimpses of the past seemed willing to surface, but another part of Ben's mind thought the wiser.

Work?

The word seems to mean something, but I can't quite place where it came from. The ocean herself is the only one who tells me what I can and can't do, and I readily enjoy this new found freedom. No longer do I have to conform to the standards of society. I am a free man, and now I feel like I can float away down this new current of life forever.

Ben's relationship with God strengthened. He tried to imagine what it would have been like in the Garden of Eden. This place where he now dwelt had to be the next best thing to that paradise. Although he knew that the end would come soon, Ben no longer looked forward to his forced entry back into the old life.

The solitude and loneliness that had at first so haunted his mind, and that threatened time and again to end the journey, now became his comforting blanket.

It surrounds me with anonymity, and I feel its warmth and security daily. I turn to God with my questions and problems, and feel that I am strengthened daily by His encouragement.

Ben was sure that he had never tasted life until now.

The pursuit of wealth no longer covers my eyes like a cloth, blinding my sight, and robbing me of true freedom and joy.

Being out here alone, stripped of what I knew as the pleasures of society, has taught me new meaning, new understanding, of who I am. In that other world, I would wake each morning and search for answers about what to wear, which car to drive, or who to call for a friendly conversation.

Out here I wake and ask, 'Will I be alive in 24 hours?

My perspectives on life have changed to the core. Time has slowed, and I've gained a primal, real-time, vivid, and cutting, drive for instinctual survival.

I've stripped my mind and thoughts to their basic components.

With this new view, it now seems so real to me that I've been on the ocean my entire life.

The pressures of traditional "success" had released their grip on Ben's soul. The vice of conformity no longer threatened to thwart his sense of self esteem and worth. Ben now wished his journey would never end. The only reason to go back, he felt, was to be close again to his mother, father, and brother. Those ties he could feel strongly at times, and he knew with conflicted emotions that the days were numbered until he would *have to go back.*

For the present, for this moment in time, though, his eyes would be open, and his soul alive. Ben had stretched his sense of values as he moved from reaching for success, to reaching for significance.

Ben wasn't clear on how he would fit in, or even if he would remain in that society. But one thing was for certain, Ben Wade would never again live life with his head down, and oblivious to the wonders life could give.

Chapter 44

B en left Isla El Tigre, Honduras on Saturday, the first of February, 1997. After days of inactivity on the quiet shores, he felt reinvigorated by the rhythm of the morning's paddling. There were a few smaller islands that he made his way around before getting out into the Pacific Ocean.

By mid afternoon I felt the surge of the open ocean beneath the kayak, and I knew I'd reached her welcoming arms.

Ben had stayed in Honduras for almost a week, and he hadn't yet applied for a visa into neighboring Nicaragua. The nearest border town to the island was a good two and a half hour journey inland. As he'd lounged comfortably on the beautiful beach in El Tigre, he could not persuade himself to take a boat back to the mainland, a bus to Ticaro, and then on to the border. Perhaps it was his self separation from the burdens of civilization that kept Ben from being concerned with minor details, such as the clearance to enter a foreign country.

Now he looked out across the long 200 mile coast of Nicaragua and wondered if that had been such a good idea.

Surely, Ben told himself confidently, *there are only a few towns along the coast and I won't have a problem traveling to the next country.*

The humidity was stifling. *As humid as a demon's breath.* Afternoon showers came and went, only temporarily thwarting the heat and its attempt to sap his strength. The coast was long and grueling without much diversion or interest. Long beaches stretched for miles, as far as the eye could see, and Ben couldn't find a cove or bay to invite him in for the night.

He was actually becoming a little bored with the monotony of paddling. No matter how close Ben came to shore there was absolutely nothing to see from where he sat at water level. He reflected on just what a beautiful part of the world he had passed during the previous months. There had been wonders at every turn, but now, the monotony of the white sandy shore dulled his sense of adventure.

That would soon change.

Two days after leaving the island, Ben landed on his first Nicaraguan beach. The surf thundered to shore, and he had a hard time catching a wave in. Finally, he saw his chance, and slid up into the face of a good wave, just as it turned radically, and suddenly broke off to his left.

Ben jammed the kayak's rudder to that same side to try to pick up the curve of the water.

The white foaming mass behind him seemed to snarl at his misfortune and, for a moment, Ben thought he would turn end over end.

The outrigger helped the kayak hold an even keel.

But, after skidding farther down the face of the wave, partially sideways, the kayak landed at the bottom with such force that Ben's head snapped forward and he lost sight of the land.

Just as the wave began to roll the kayak over, he struck out into the water with the paddle with all his strength, keeping just ahead of the giant foaming crash of the white water surging behind the little craft.

With this maneuver, he was able to skid onto the beach in one piece.

Ben felt the strength of the undertow as he leapt out of the cockpit and into the receding water. Without hesitating, he wedged the paddle between the seat and the rudder pedals, and hurried to the sand, holding the safety rope in one hand, as he crawled to safety above the reach of the surf. The broad beach where he now stood stretched monotonously out to the horizon.

Several local people surfing nearby stopped and peered at the new arrival.

They probably wonder what kind of crazy gringo would attempt to kayak through these monstrous waves.

Ben had landed near the village of Poneloya, Nicaragua; population less than 2,000 souls. It was no different from the rest of the towns he'd visited in Central America - small, dirty, and devoid of tourists.

At dusk, Ben ate a small dinner in town composed of two tortillas slathered with beans and cheese, and some type of lumpy meat. He didn't ask what it was and, frankly, he didn't care. Back at the little campsite, he went over to the kayak and found the small bottle of pills he'd purchased in Honduras, and read the label to make sure he knew the right dosage on the correct day. Ben swallowed a Chloroquinine pill and walked back over to the tent. He had enough medicine to last for two more months, ample time to get through the rest of Central America. It had cost only two dollars for the bottle of pills, a small price to pay for a drug that could prevent most strains of malaria from attacking him.

The next few days seemed to drag by at the slowest, and most lethargic, pace he had yet known. After he slipped between Isla Juan Venado and the mainland, the coast remained flat and the weather hot. Even the ocean grew still. One night Ben looked at the knifelike sliver of the moon, and realized why the elements were so calm. The tides had receded, and the pull of the moon was not as great as it had been when full. It was as if the entire earth were still. In the beginning, Ben had longed for the days when the moon would be either full or new. The ocean grew calm for four days at every change of the moon, and now, as for all eternity, she answered the moon's commands.

Once again, Ben wondered why he should ever go back home.

He had never known such peace.

I think back, especially to the first month of the journey, and realize just how much I have been through to get to this point. God has been faithful in His protection of me, and I almost feel like leaning back and allowing myself to just drift away into the ocean; far away from anything that can hurt me, change me, or command me.

This is my life, and I want no other.

February 4, 1997
El Astillero, Nicaragua

Ben landed on shore close to a fishing village named El Astillero. There were only a few men standing around when he paddled into shore. He was no longer concerned about needing a visa, so when the kayak was securely tied, he sauntered down the one dirt road into town. As usual, several of the locals gawked at the strange white man wearing only a pair of shorts and strolling calmly through their street. Ben wondered if they'd ever even seen a *gringo* in these parts.

He was to find out that they had - and these gringos were not such good people.

The town had one dirt *avenita* which cut it in half, and Ben walked down this small lane, scattering chickens and dogs wherever he stepped. He seemed to be the only one moving in the sleepy little town. The afternoon sun was still beating down unmercifully, and the people sought refuge under the shaded awnings and wooden platforms that lined the street.

A small taco stand sat temporarily unattended on one corner, a fire still burning low beneath a black iron skillet. Ben watched the coals and sniffed the smoke, detecting the essence of what it usually produced. He found his mouth beginning to water as he sat down at one of the stools and waited there by himself, figuring that someone would have to show up sooner or later. Soon enough, an old, and rather large, lady came over from out of the shadows and asked if he wanted something to eat. Ben ordered five *Carne Asada* tacos and a soda to drink. He finished his meal, as he watched the sun dip over the horizon.

In the cooler evening air the people of the town stirred. Carts appeared out of nowhere, being pushed by their owners down the narrow street, attempting to sell their wares. More taco stands appeared on the corners, and two cowboys, astride their horses, showed off their animals with obvious pride.

Ben was a little relieved that he had not walked into a ghost town. Although he was anxious to get back to the kayak, and away from people, it was nice to know that these people were still going about their simple lives. He sat back on the small wooden stool and ordered another soda.

Ben wondered if these people had ever been beyond their small corner of the world.

Do they live, breed, and die, within this small village? I Look around at the people and guess that to be true. They have remained unchanged for God only knows how long, seemingly unaffected by the evolving world they don't seem to belong to. I see no running water, no cars, and no electricity. I figure that they might be here somewhere, but on the surface, I could go back fifty years in time and not see any difference.

Not too long ago, the "ignorance" of this country, whose people had never seen a "civilized community" of prosperous, industrial, citizens, would have galled him. Now, after months of hardening to the realities of another world, and the freedom one possesses from ridding oneself of these maddening burdens, Ben admired the small village for what it had taken to resist the change of outside forces.

It was naïve though, because one cannot "resist" what one has never seen.

Ben now stood fast in his beliefs and opinions of the negative effects of society. In a way, he was almost envious, as he sensed that, although they lacked knowledge of other places, they were completely at ease with their current lifestyle.

Ben was so lost in his analysis of this lost city, that he didn't notice when an old man came over and sat beside him. Ben finally sensed him sitting there quietly, and, with a start, wondered how long he'd been there. His small frail hand tugged gently at Ben's arm until he turned his head and looked the old man in the eye.

His white beard flowed past his neck, and he seemed older that the village itself. The wrinkles on his face ran deeper than the scar that ran along his right cheek. His body was haggard, and his frame stooped from the wear and tear of many years of hard living. His eyes, though, were clear and alert, and seemed to look through Ben's gaze and into his mind.

"*Que pasa*?" Ben said after he'd had gotten through staring.

"I speak English a little," the old man said, which surprised Ben, who looked into his eyes, drawn by the wisdom he thought laid there.

"Do you have drugs?" the old man asked in almost a whisper.

Disgusted and incensed by his question, Ben pushed the old man's hand off of his arm, and quickly stood to leave.

I should have known.

"Wait, un momento, por favor, please," he said, clutching at Ben's arm again. Ben looked at his small frame, and thought that maybe he knew something that Ben should know too. No one around them took any notice. Whether by choice or habit, Ben didn't know. Reluctantly, he sat back down.

The old man spoke, his voice tight with barely controlled anger, and what he told Ben probably saved his young life.

"I don't want no drogas, *tapatho*," the old man said in a hissing, angry whisper. Then, more gently, he added, "Gringos come here from U.S. to buy drugs, like cocaine, sometimes from Colombia too. Not good you get involved."

"Okay," Ben said. "So, why are you telling me this. I don't have any drugs, I told you."

"Maybe yes, maybe no," he said, eyeing Ben again.

Was the old man some kind of policia?

"I saw you come in on your little barca. Gringos don't come here too much, not on little boats. Gringos stand out, and that is no a good thing for you."

"Well, okay, that's true", Ben muttered. "So then, why are you talking to me? And why do you speak such good English, anyhow?"

"I live en Florida for a little time. Mi Padre was deportado. Es no importante. *You*, mi amigo, look like you will find trouble."

"That's crazy, old man," Ben said, losing his patience, "I'm leaving first thing tomorrow." Again, Ben thought about getting up to leave. But something told him not to, at least not yet.

"No, señor, it is mi who gets upset with su actitud. I am look at you, *Pelon*! Scraggly beard, y un *earring*! Anybody see you, they think you one crazy hombre, or on the drogas. Here? Alone? In Nicaragua? Hah!" The old man scoffed and spat on the ground.

Ben started at the sudden act, but kept his haughty attitude up front, part defense and part style. "I don't care; I'll be out of this whole damn country in a few days."

"I am hoping so, young gringo," the old man said slowly. "If policio catch you, they make you pay. If others finds you, they think you try to take their trade. You dead, hombre. You a dead man."

His words cut Ben to the bone, and he squeezed his hands together tightly, knowing that what the old man said had a ring of truth. The old man finished the conversation with emphasis, "You better get out of my country as rapido as you can. No even to look back!"

Ben needed no further urging.

One of the cowboy's horses strutted by, and several people, including Ben, looked up to see what the commotion was about. Ben noticed the other vendors eyeing him with sidelong glances.

He felt very uncomfortable.

What is it about this town that seems so odd? Maybe the old man is right.

Ben turned back to ask him a question, but he was nowhere in sight.

Ben began a cautious walk back to the beach, feeling that every evil eye was on him. The next morning, February 5th, Ben left the small town of El Astillero, Nicaragua. Still wondering about his meeting with the old man, and his sudden disappearance, Ben paddled quickly and was soon out of sight of the city.

I should be close to Costa Rica in two days. I'll take no more chances and head straight there without stopping. If the police question me in the next town, I will probably be deported. But, if I run into any drug traffickers... well, I may not survive.

Ben swallowed hard at the thought, and tried to put it out of his mind.

Chapter 45

Don't let us make imaginary evils, when you know we have so many real ones to encounter.

Oliver Goldsmith (1730-1774)

B y that evening, Ben had traveled a good forty-five miles, and the sun had not yet dipped below the horizon. He knew he'd have to spend the night on the water, but, even with the disconcerting lecture by the old man in El Astillero, his spirits were high.

Tomorrow I will be in Costa Rica. Everything I have heard about the country is positive. Good relations with tourists, beautiful beaches, clean cities, and friendly people. I'm ready for a change!

As he casually paddled by a small point, Ben looked into the cove that housed what he presumed to be the town of San Juan Del Sur. The half moon bay that curved around to the other side was pretty and quiet in the stillness of the late twilight. It looked inviting, and he almost wanted to stop and spend the night. But, with the warnings of the old man ringing in his ears, he decided to keep pressing on.

The bright lights of the town came on one by one, winking across the water. It was definitely enticing and looked beautiful from his position on the water.

He began to think twice about his decision.

Maybe I've overreacted to the dangers of drug smugglers and the police.

But something in the back of his mind told him to be on the safe side. He shook his head, now ready to brave the night.

Across the bay, below where the hills behind the beach seemed ominously dark in the last rays of the sun, Ben spotted an impressive boat. Taking it for a pleasure cruiser, his first instinct was to turn in and pull alongside. But, as he got closer to the craft, his heart jumped to his throat, and he dug the paddle deeply into the water to stop the forward motion of his craft.

The large yacht sat still in the water, slowly bobbing up and down on its anchor. It was bright white, sleek, and well over fifty feet long from its clipper-like stem to its broad stern. The last of the setting sun glinted gold off the glass of the large windows surrounding the flying bridge with its prickly array of antennae.

On a closer look, Ben saw another, smaller, powerboat in the water, tied up to the yacht. As he sat still on the water and looked toward the boats, he saw two men on the deck of the yacht, and two more in the motor boat, busily unloading cargo from one to the other.

In a flash of unwanted realization, Ben decided he'd seen enough.

He hoped the bundles were not what he thought they were.

Turning slowly in a wide circle out to sea, trying not to act suspicious, Ben quietly, but quickly, thrust a paddle into the water. His heart was beating fast, hard, and loud, in his ears, as he glided out of the bay. When he saw the hills on the far side of the inlet drawing near, he sighed in relief.

The sun had now fully set, and the last lingering light of the day had given way to the night. Ben sat back in the cockpit and stopped paddling. He reached for a drink of water.

Then a shout erupted from the twilight darkness.

It came from behind him, and sent shivers down his spine.

Instinctively, Ben looked around.

He could barely make out the two men on the larger boat, but he could tell that one was pointing in the direction of the kayak.

He sat still and waited, hoping he could shrink back into the shadows of the shore.

Then he heard the unmistakable sound of the engine of one of the boats spring to life.

It shattered the evening's stillness – and Ben's nerves.

Without hesitating, he turned around and picked up the paddle.

More shouts criss-crossed the night air behind him.

His mind raced, and his heart sank.

The low rumbling of the boat engine increased.

Ben prayed that they were not after him, as his paddle stroke increased and his arms burned from the intense effort.

His heart pounded fiercely in his chest, and he could feel his body drench with nervous sweat.

"Not now," Ben cried out in a barely audible whisper.

"Not like this," he pleaded to the dark night.

The rumble of the engine grew louder, announcing that it was moving closer and closer.

Ben knew it would be only another moment before the boat would round the point.

There is no place to hide!

He feared the worst, and Ben knew he had only a few seconds to react.

Quickly he headed for the shore. Ben had cut the small cove in half, paddling from point to point, and was now only about fifty yards away from the surf.

He looked over his shoulder once, and saw the spotlight of the boat dancing over the dark waves, flitting back and forth.

Searching.

Are they looking for me, or just heading back home?
Dear God, I know the answer!

Heedless of the waves, and without enough time to wait for the surf, Ben leapt into the foaming white water, and dragged the kayak until he felt the sand beneath his feet.

Then he heaved himself to the shore.

I fell a few times as the surf crashed into me from behind. It hit my back and pushed me over. The kayak was more buoyant than me. It raced ahead and pulled me closer to the shore.

Knee deep in the sea, Ben ran through the shallows, and up to the palm tree covered beach. He pulled the kayak out of the water a few feet, draped a couple of dead palm fronds over the gray hull, and ran into the jungle, hiding among the massive trunks of the trees. His limbs weakened, as Ben collapsed to the ground, making sure he was well hidden.

I hope that the boat will not find my kayak, if that is what they are after. I lay flat on my stomach and peer out to the dark ocean. The engine of the boat is now loud, and I see its light again just before it races into sight.

The light sweeps the shore and briefly blinds me. I can hear the engine's roar mixed with shouts from the men on board.

They are close to the shore.

I keep as still as possible and hide in the undergrowth.

After an eternity of just a few seconds, the boat eased past Ben's hiding place without slowing or stopping. The light swept the beach once, and the twisted palm fronds over the slender kayak cast a fumbled shadow against the treeline. Then the light searched just beyond the surf, apparently not discerning the beached craft. Eventually, the boat moved out of sight, its light still flickering across the water.

Ben let out his breath with a rush of air. He was safe after all. As he stood slowly and walked back down to the kayak, Ben laughed softly, trying to relieve the tension.

What if I had just reacted without thinking? Had they really been up to no good? Were the words of the old man spooking me still?

Ben would never know. Not this time.

Although he had not planned on spending the night ashore, he figured he might as well, now that he was there. Still shaken from what had just happened, he secured the safety line to the tree that he'd just taken cover behind.

The kayak was safe for the night.

That was more than Ben could say for himself.

Too tired to pitch the tent, he rolled out a sleeping bag close to a palm tree and lay down to sleep. As he lay there tossing and turning, his mind churned with thoughts of his close brush with disaster, sleep was a long time coming.

But better days were ahead.

February 7, 1997
Costa Rica

There must have been a lingering doubt in Ben's mind somewhere. Perhaps, though, it had vanished long before. Maybe after he'd been so close to the eye of a hurricane, or when his hands were covered with sores, and his back blistered and burnt, or when his mind struggled with insanity – and, yet, with all this, continuing to press on.

Still, Ben had never fully imagined himself entering this beautiful country until it happened on that Friday morning.

The glorious coast stretched out before my eyes. Rain forests, jungles, palm trees, streams, monkeys, tapers, sloth, boa constrictors, and white pristine tropical beaches. Never before have I seen such beauty. Never before have I seen such lush vegetation, teeming with life, and abounding in spirit. Even the name itself brings about an image of adventure and wonder: Costa Rica. The rich coast. How can I dare ignore her with such promises of magnificence and splendor? I have heard of this magical place all my life. I want to step onto its shore almost as desperately as I want to step onto South America!

A mysterious and ethereal mist hung along the shore. Ben strained his eyes to make out the elusive shadow of the wonders before him. Shortly after dawn, as if to welcome his arrival, the mist slowly rose like a spectral curtain. The sun emerged, reluctantly casting forth its cheerful rays in layers of golden light. Ben was struck by the color laced vision of the coast emerging slowly into view. He began to see lush green tropical rain forests that sloped down to the indigo ocean, and stopped only a few feet from the water's edge. The seemingly infinite variety of trees were so thick that he could not make out their different kinds. He could only see a dark, thick, verdant mass, perpetually shaded by mats of lianas and branches that had no end and no beginning.

In stark contrast to the long straight coast of Nicaragua, here there were coves, and hidden beaches, beyond count. Ben didn't have to look on charts. He knew he'd arrived. Islands emerged on the horizon like soldiers cresting a hill. He felt invited to their pristine beaches. The main coast itself now jutted wildly into the ocean, confusing Ben's sense of direction.

Thinking at first that it was another island, he had turned to skirt around its eastern tip, wanting to keep the mainland in full view. But, after an hour of progress, Ben realized that it wasn't an island at all, but part of the mainland. It was a costly mistake as far as his daily progress was concerned, but one he was glad to make.

The humidity was gone and, although the temperature still flirted with ninety degrees, he felt dry and comfortable. Because he'd miscalculated the peninsula's length, and mistaken it for another island, Ben had lost several hours, and several miles. By late afternoon, he'd still not gone ashore.

Ben looked with growing interest at the mountains with their swirl of greens of every hue. He could hold back his curiosity no longer. Skirting around what he took to be the Parque Nacional Santa Rosa, Ben made sure that the kayak was far enough away from the ocean's currents to avoid being smashed against the mainland. The imagined cries of monkeys, and the roar of a jaguar, rode above the noise of the surf.

The first accessible cove would be the dash for shore.

Just as the sun was descending in its final daily plunge, two jagged rocks presented themselves, rising out of the water low on the horizon. The ocean surged mightily against the two enormous structures that prevailed against it for the moment. Seawater swirled dangerously over the lower reaches, tugging at the surface. The kayak was propelled quickly between the two rocks, about forty yards apart, and soon found the tranquil waters of the bay. The breakers that rolled to shore were only about three feet tall, as the tiny craft steered its way safely to the beach.

Ben looked up in wonder at the trees towering overhead, enshrouded with vines in a tangle like sailing ships rigged by drunken sailors. The beach was about fifty yards wide and curved gracefully into a perfect half moon bay. The forest, not as dense as Ben had thought from the water, came down to a few yards from the crashing surf.

After I landed I looked around, anxious to see signs of life. I am disappointed. I see no monkeys, no snakes, and no big cats. Maybe they're waiting for me to go to sleep.

Not funny!

The kayak was pulled a little way up the beach and tied to a nearby tree. With so many different types of vegetation, Ben couldn't begin to guess the species. A small trail cut through the forest. Whether made by animals or humans, he couldn't determine for sure. There were no other traces of civilization. Ben sat down with his back against the kayak, and relished the peace and quiet that he found there.

Just me and my kayak.
Sweet.

The sun had set, and in the twilight he took out a chart to see if he could determine where he'd landed. There were so many inlets and coves that it was impossible to be sure.

Sometimes, after a long day, I sit back on the shore and wonder about my life. Tonight, the only thing that keeps passing through my head is the fact that nobody in the world knows where I'm sleeping this day. At first, it terrified me to think that if I got into trouble no one would be there to help. But now, I truly revel in the secrecy and simplicity of it all.

My reliance on other people is no longer necessary.

It actually gives me strength and courage to know that at any moment I can be swept away, and no one will ever know.

The only person who can prevent that from happening is me!

Ben put the chart away and looked at his watch, feeling silly that he was keeping track of the time. It had ceased to be a habit long ago, but now he was just wondering if he should go to sleep or not.

At the mercy of nature, I do as she tells me, and when she tells me. I can not hope to stay up past the sun's departure. When it rains, I feel it soaking through my skin. When it is hot, I can not escape to the nearest air conditioner. And, when the animals are hungry, I can't just walk past their cage.

So unlike the security of civilization!

Yes, at times it is frightening to be alone. At times I do feel helpless. But overall, being alone now gives me a spirit of toughness, independence, and confidence. This new found will to survive, and the successes I've had these past years – whoops, make that months – are empowering!

I know I can survive!

The tent was pitched with the hope that the taped and re-taped rods would hold together one more time. Ben knew that soon he would have to leave it behind, a thought that worried him less and less each day. The only reason he pitched it that night was for some pitiful cover, in case the animals of the forest ventured too close, and to keep the mosquitoes at bay. Malaria was a lingering fear. As Ben climbed inside, lay down, and closed his eyes, the jungle came alive.

Sounds he'd been too busy to hear before now roared out. The loud cries of wild animals shattered the stillness of the night. First he heard the whining of an insect. He didn't know if they had tropical crickets here the size of a football, but that's what it sounded like to Ben. Everything was out of scale to him. Beetles the size of butterflies, and butterflies the size of birds, silently enthralled him. A few raucous birds found it easier to make themselves heard at night, and their bickering lasted long past midnight. He listened to all of this cacophony as it blended with the other, more familiar, sound that he knew so well, the ocean.

The ocean was calm, and it shared this with Ben who now fell quietly to sleep, ready for the next day to come.

Chapter 46

The first act of awe, when man was struck with the beauty or wonder of nature, was the first spiritual experience.

Henryk Skolimowski

T he morning's first light produced more mosquitoes than usual. Considering the several holes now in the outer structure, not surprisingly, they'd found a way into the tent. Ben made a note to dig out the duct tape the next night and see what he could do about patching it up. He sat for a while that morning, and looked out across the cove to the other side. He didn't know if there would be more spots as pristine as this in the days to come, and he wanted to enjoy this one as long as possible.

The oatmeal breakfast he swallowed was more of a necessity than a pleasure. He'd grown accustomed to the plain fare of dried food. Now, before shoving off, supplies were checked to see that there was enough to make it the rest of the way.

I have, perhaps, two weeks left in my travels, maybe three. There's plenty of oatmeal, but not much else. Maybe a few multigrain bars. At the next town I have to buy more food.

Ben walked knee deep into the water and slipped under the gentle surf. Today was the day to bathe and, although he had no soap, he scrubbed vigorously at his salty skin. Back on the warm sand, he took out a palm sized mirror and peered at it intently. The face that stared back did not look familiar, and the transformation of his appearance was astonishing.

Strange that I hadn't noticed it before.

Clouds formed overhead, moving fast and low, and the sun disappeared. Ben looked up, and then back at the mirror and his reflection. For a brief second he wondered what kind of man this was that stared back at him. The tough, worn, hard, weathered face that peered from the glass, looked thin and haggard. The beard, unshaven in a week, partially hid a dark tan face, with wrinkles not seen before creasing the skin around the eyes. The hair, unkempt and uncut, fanned out like a rooster's feathers. Ben noted the gray that crept around the temples.

The sun came back out, and flashed from the mirror to end Ben's contemplation. He shook his head slowly, and shrugged off any feelings at the changes in the once handsome face.

A razor was produced, shaving cream lathered across the long whiskers, and a shave was begun.

Whether I shaved to keep my self esteem from crashing to earth, or because the facial hair irritates my dry skin, I can't tell. It's a long, slow, painful process. After a few nicks and cuts, I finish. Salt water burns the new skin, and I quickly go back to the kayak to spread lotion on my face.

Once out past the two large rocks, Ben turned to head south again. By midday, the kayak entered a calmer stretch of water. The swells, smaller than they had been in several weeks, fanned out toward the shore. Normally, riding up and down the ten to twenty foot swells of the Pacific, several miles out in the open water, Ben could see land for only a few seconds before plunging down the other side. Now with the small swells, he could see to the horizon where the land continued to curve and caress the sea.

Ben took the opportunity afforded by the stillness of the water, to stop and eat some lunch. Later he grabbed the kayak's safety line and jumped into the cool water. More clouds had blown overhead, and the sun hid behind their massive forms. Still, the air was hot and he needed to cool down.

Swimming first to the front of the boat, he locked his arms around the slender hull and let his legs bob slowly to the surface. The tip of the kayak was tapered, and thin enough to let him do this. As he let himself relax and float in the water, gently bobbing up and down, he periodically, looked around for sharks.

But nothing disturbed this peaceful setting.

After I let the ocean massage my muscles with her gentle hands, I swim back over to the cockpit. I pull myself out of the water and stand up to let the wind dry my body.

Lunch was nothing too special, but it filled the hollow in his stomach, and kept hunger pangs at bay. The chart he'd unfolded ruffled in the wind, and Ben held it above his shoulders to avoid the ocean splashing over the sides. His best guess, seeing the calm water in every direction, was that he'd entered the Golfo de Papagayo. Smiling at the progress made, he figured to be near the small village of Tamarindo, some twenty miles ahead, by nightfall.

Tamarindo is in the Costa Rican province of Guanacaste on its northwest coast, and about in the middle of the Pacific coast of Central America. This part of the world was in stark contrast to the beginning of the trip, with its barren deserts and rock faced mountains. The vivid green of this world was too beautiful to describe, or even fully grasp.

The clouds spattered the ocean with a few heavy drops, but nothing more serious than that. Ben paddled quickly into the large Gulf, keeping an eye on the shoreline as it passed by. He spied several inlets and coves but didn't investigate any closer. The coast continued to be dominated by thick vegetation. Even from low in the kayak's cockpit, he could see the forests bounding up the hills and across the horizon. Once in a while, a large wooden house would break the monotony of the jungle's dominance. Ben wondered what kind of person lived in the middle of nowhere.

Maybe it's someone like me.

This far south, the sun set quickly. Because Ben had not found a suitable place to land for the night, he decided to continue on. Waves exiting the Gulf were now throwing themselves to the shore with great intensity. He dared not chance a ride to the beach, not that staying at sea for the night was safer. Also, the mosquitoes would not venture this far out into the ocean.

The air was chilly. Ben pulled out the sleeping bag, wrapped it around him, and tied himself to the frame of the kayak, as he'd done so many nights before. Sleep did not come at once, as Ben gazed up at the dark, cloud filled sky. No stars twinkled that night, and the moon crept up, *unnoticed* – as Ben surmised - *by any creature on the earth.*

A little after midnight Ben sat up, untied the ropes around his body, and climbed back into the cockpit. The sleeping bag was soaked on the edges with saltwater that he hastily wrung out. He was cold, and decided to pick up the paddle and resume. Occasionally, Ben saw a few lights over on the shore. They looked distant, and he wondered just how far he'd drifted away from the land. As long as he could see the coast's dark shadow, Ben was comforted that he was still on course. His body temperature rose with the paddling activity. The sleeping bag was now wadded up in his lap, a poor choice for storage, and soon the bag was wetter than it had been before. Ben shook his head. He knew it would be a long night.

After an hour of paddling, he couldn't keep his eyes open any longer. Paddling at an angle to get back closer to the coast, he could now vaguely see the mainland looming in the dark night. Exhausted, after having slept for only a few hours, he decided to try to get to the shore. The waves had lost much of their force, and, after twenty minutes, a large beach emerged directly to the left of the kayak's course. As he drew near the surf, which rolled forcefully to the sand, Ben was only forty or fifty feet out, and could see a good night's rest in a few minutes.

One wave broke ahead, pulling the craft with it. He paddled backwards for a moment to let it roll by. Timing was essential to be positioned between the waves, especially for a fully loaded kayak which was not as nimble as a surfer. Bad timing was trouble. Then, as soon as the wave's grasp loosened, he dug into the water and pulled vigorously with the paddle. The first wave broke in front of the kayak, and the tiny craft proceeded through its calm backwater, reaching the shore before the wave behind could pick it up in its vacuum.

Ben was too tired to pitch the tent. After pulling the kayak up the beach and tying the rope around his leg, he curled up in the still damp sleeping bag and fell asleep. His last waking thoughts were of the location, the jungle, and the overwhelming feeling of relief he felt lying on the solid ground of the beach. It was well worth the extra effort to gain a few more hours of sleep, and he was happy about reaching dry land that night, instead of staying out in the open ocean.

The tropical sun was threatening to emerge from behind the coastal hills of Costa Rica when he heard the rustling sound. It came from the direction of the gentle waves lapping the shore. Ben sat up and looked at the surf through watery eyes, wondering what it was that had made a sound.

A seal?

Then, another sound. It was a swishing of the sand, and it came from just over his left shoulder. Turning with a start, Ben marveled at the sight before him. In the sand a few yards away, and then farther on down the beach at different intervals, worked some of the biggest turtles Ben had ever seen. He watched in amazement as they pushed the sand with their legs to create large mounds across the beach. Several were already heading back to the ocean, and as their large carapaces, some over two feet long, hit the surf, the water parted with ease. With flippers thrusting into the swirling breakers, they were soon out into the open waters and out of view. One by one, the turtles finished what they were doing on the beach and left the sand for the sea.

Ben wondered if perhaps they had laid their eggs, but could not be sure. The ecosystem here was fragile, and he didn't want to disturb what they had done with the mounds of sands. Before preparing to set sail, he walked carefully up and down the beach. There were dozens of the little mounds. He looked at the evidence with a special tenderness, knowing, that whatever those large turtles had been up to, he was lucky to have witnessed it.

I make this special entry in my journal.

I look at my charts with particular thoroughness. There is a beach by the name of Playa Grande within the boundaries of the Parque Nacional Marino Las Baulas de Guanacaste that is a frequent location for large turtles to lay their eggs.

This is the place! What great luck!

With only a few bags of oatmeal, two PowerBars, and a bag of dried mash potatoes left in his larder, Ben's food supply was now almost exhausted. He had not yet found a town, and he checked the map to see how far the next one might be. Puntarenas was only a few days away and he decided that it would be the stop. He had either not seen Tamarindo, or had passed it in the night while asleep.

The days were running closer together now, and Ben had to frequently update his journal to know the day or even the month. Time was slipping from his grasp.

He thought of it less and less as the days progressed.

What is the need anyway? I do not need to conquer anything now. The light at the end of the tunnel is now a giant glare. I know it will not be long before I reach South America.

And then . . ., well, who knows?

311

Chapter 47

And now the end is near. And so I face the final curtain, I'll state my case of which I'm certain.

Paul Anka,
From the French original, Comme D'Habitude

I hold back feelings of despondency, and refuse to think about life apart from the ocean. I know that this expedition will soon be over, and then what will I do? There's a woman from home who passes through the outer reaches of my memory. What's her name? I can't recall. Wait, of course I can. Heather.

Where will I go once I'm finished? Surely, I had a home. But where was it? I only know the sand for a bed, and the open sky for my roof. Where will I go and what will I do?

Maybe it didn't have to end. Something told Ben that he must go back to the States, but he didn't have to listen to that voice inside his head.

He was a free man and able to go anywhere and do anything.

No, I don't have to go home. I can just continue to paddle around South America and live off the ocean.

She provides for me much better than I have done for myself

Ben's journal entry gave him an idea for dinner that night.

Here around me, I have all of the food I want. Fish swim in abundance around the kayak, day and night, and I am worried about how many bags of oatmeal I have left? What am I thinking?

He was still paddling off the Nicoya Peninsula, and headed toward the shore after the long day on the water came to a close. The sun was just beginning to dip behind the horizon as Ben steered the kayak safely behind a large bluff that stretched out across the water. Before he headed to the beach, he took out the fishing pole that had been strapped, unused, to the poles of the outrigger. He baited the hook with an artificial lure, one of those Gary had given to him in Punta Finál. Ben smiled and nodded his head in appreciation of Gary's generosity. *"Maybe you'll help me catch a big fish tonight, Gary!"* Ben said out loud to no one in particular, except maybe the wind that whispered through the trees on the far shore.

He had been talking to himself more frequently of late, and found he enjoyed the one way conversations; fewer arguments that way.

Sometimes, I even remark about the sky being so blue. It feels comforting to hear my strong, reassuring voice break the silence around me.

Ben grasped the rod between his knees, and let the line trail several yards behind, as he slowly made way to the shore. The beach was still fifty yards away, and Ben felt sure that he would soon have a bite on the line. And, sure enough, he felt a tug. Without hesitation he picked up the rod and set the hook. The reel shot forward, spinning rapidly on its axis. Ben waited until the line was almost out and then grabbed it with his right hand. *"This one's gonna be huge!"* he cried out excitedly. He let the fish swim in and out of the current until it tired, and Ben reeled him into the kayak.

It was a dark colored fish, most likely a Bonito. The Bonito has a "tuna-like" appearance, dark blue-gray back, darker head, and silver flanks and belly. The series of oblique stripes running along its upper back confirmed his suspicion, as Ben peered into the clear water, salivating at the catch he'd just landed.

Now he had a predicament. The fish was wildly thrashing against the side of the boat, and Ben knew he should kill it before bringing it on board. *"Should I kill you-know-who with my knife?"* Ben asked the fish who continued to try and free itself from the line. *"Or, should I try and bring you to shore and then hit you with a rock?"* Ben didn't want to attract any shark's attention with the blood. Being so close to shore, he decided to kill it in the water.

Not as messy this way.

He had no club to use, and the next best thing seemed to be the great bowie knife that lay strapped to the hull in front of the cockpit. Ben unsheathed the knife and waited until the fish lay still. It was awhile before it did, but finally, tired of its struggle for life, the fish swam close to the boat and stopped its movement completely. Ben looked into its eyes and it returned his stare. As if telling Ben it was ready to die, it rolled slightly to one side and remained still. Solemnly, he brought the knife close to its head and, as quickly as possible, brought it down with great force, splitting its skull. The Bonito struggled for only a moment and died.

Ben picked up the paddle, leaving the fish trailing behind in the water. The blood was already flowing into the water around the kayak, staining the blue sea a crimson red. There were no sharks yet, and he didn't wait to find out if they would join his feast. He was soon on the shore, and hauling the Bonito out of the water. The fish was a foot and a half long and weighed close to ten pounds.

Several pieces of driftwood lay scattered across the beach, and, after setting the fish down next to the jungle's edge, Ben gathered the wood to start a fire. After building a small pyramid with dry twigs, overlain with more ample pieces, he took out a few waterproof matches that had gone virtually unused until now. It took several tries, but eventually the fire caught hold in the smaller twigs, and climbed upwards along the wood. Small embers burned and dropped off as he stuck more wood into the coals. As the fire burned with a trail of smoke curling into the air, Ben went back down to the fish, gutted it, and washed the carcass in the waves before cutting several large fillets.

He walked back into the jungle and chose a small, fresh sapling; its branches small enough to break off, and yet sturdy enough to whittle the tip down to a sharp point. Soon, the fish fillets were cooking, three deep on the tips of the skewers. Ben roasted a total of six fillets and, as the smell wafted through the calm night air, he was almost beside himself with anticipation and delight.

I burned my fingers a little in anticipation of the feast, but I hardly noticed. I was so hungry that I pulled the first piece off while the center was still a little raw. My stomach didn't revolt, so I swallowed the half chewed piece like an animal. I actually grunted in satisfaction! I left the other pieces to cook while I went down the beach to find some coconuts. There were plenty of trees to choose from, but few that had clumps of the nuts that were low enough. Finally, twenty yards away from my fire, I found a palm tree that was only about ten feet tall. Several of the fronds hung down over the sand and hid a few coconuts. I twisted off two of the biggest, greenest ones I could find.

The sun had completely set when Ben walked back to the campsite. The dusk that now draped over the coast softened his emotions, and the harshness of the environment around him.

His bonfire rose cheerily, a stark contrast to the dark horizon.

I had a feeling so warm, so cozy, that it blanketed my soul in unison with the calm night air. I stopped in mid pace to savor it. Such a passion rose within my breast, so violent, so clean, so primal, and so pure, that I thought I might never leave this spot.

Ben was so uplifted by this little fire that he gathered more wood from the jungle and built it up to a blazing bonfire. He sat down and felt the heat. He was a happy man. He savored the rest of the fish, and threw the remains back into the ocean. It was a kind of offering for her bounty. He knew they would not last long before the scavengers cleaned up the messy feast.

Ben flopped down on the sugary sand, and brought his knees up to his chest. Looking out through the fire, and into the darkness beyond, Ben felt completely satisfied. Mesmerized by the dancing flames, he closed his eyes and felt the clean warmth on his brow. He wished somehow to slow down time. Ben looked at his watch, and realized that it had stopped at 7:29 p.m., February 10th 1997. That, he thought, would be the last time he would know the time of day, the date, or even the month.

Lost in a literal sea of his old and new memories, adventures, rain forests, and the rhythmic dance between himself and the ocean, Ben was gradually slipping into a state of absolute bliss and oblivion.

The morning sun gently kissed him awake. Ben realized that he could not remember just when he'd drifted off to sleep. The embers from the fire had long since died, as he rose slowly, stiff from the cold night. The air was already warming, though, and soon he was ready to head off again.

The ocean looked rough, and the blue waves were speckled with white spume, but Ben smiled, knowing that it wouldn't matter. This rhythm that he had danced to for so long, was now slowly coming to a halt. No matter how frantic the pace became in the end, Ben would enjoy it until he could paddle no more.

He could see a point of land jutting seaward dead ahead of his course. It was impressive in size, and he paddled away from the coast and directly toward its tip. It was mid afternoon, and it took a couple of hours to reach the giant outcropping of rock that split the sea in two, scattering gigantic waves in all directions. Ben paddled between the mainland and a tiny island to avoid the wave's ferocious pounding.

Soon he was traversing the calmer waters of the Golfo de Nicoya, Costa Rica.

By evening, Ben had covered over forty five miles. He could see the skyline of the large city of Puntarenas a couple of miles ahead. A small ferryboat passed by on his right, the steady *ker-chunk, ker-chunk* sound of its large one-cylinder engine welcoming him back to civilization. It was the first time in a week that he had seen or heard any sign of human life. Ben waved to the passengers, but doubted if they saw him. *"Hey guys! Look at me,"* he cried happily to no one in particular. *"Yeah! I am a free man!"* He smiled at the ocean around him. Soon, he spied the beach next to the city. It was incredibly long. Ben estimated it to be four miles. There were many boats plying the waters on all sides, and he continued slowly, watching their every move. Most of the sailors who passed close enough, waved to him, a gesture he happily returned.

The water passing so close beneath his elbows, didn't look too clean. Ben noticed that nobody was swimming in the gentle surf when he landed ashore. The city near the beach was not so busy as to force itself upon him, and Ben stretched on the sand before setting off to look for a pay phone.

After only a few rings, my mother answered the phone. She immediately asked, 'Ben! You remember Liz Brea don't you?

'Of course. We knew her twenty years ago,' I said.

'Well, dear, she married a man from Honduras, and I just talked to them a few weeks ago. They said if you are anywhere near them to call and see if you could arrange a visit.

'I don't know about that, Mom,' I said reluctantly. The last thing I want to do now is visit an old friend, especially if it means backtracking up the coast to Honduras – and leaving the ocean.

'I really think you should, sweetheart,' Mom said again. She loves calling me by that name, and it makes me feel loved again.

'I'll see what I can do, Mom. This will be the last time I call you. Okay?'

'Okay, dear. Are you almost done?

'Yep. It's almost over, but I don't know if I want to come back home.

'Well, I think you should, dear. Aren't you tired of the traveling?

'No, not at all,' I said with a new confidence, that I now felt whole heartedly. 'Anyway, I love you, Mom. Tell Dad too.

However pleasant the conversation was, Ben's heart still belonged to the ocean. He was afraid of the time when he would have to eventually let go of the journey.

He knew something would be missing from his soul, and he wondered how long he could stay away.

At night, I strain to hear the ocean's rumble, and yearn to feel the winds echo across the rocky cliffs and wooded hills.

How can I give this all up to go back to society? Will I be content to stay ashore in the midst of a million people, and not become restless?

It was a new question Ben now faced. One that would torture him to the end.

Back on the beach in Puntarenas, Ben knelt in the sand and gazed out to sea, his mind clearing from the conversation with 'civilization'. Looking now closer to the beach, he saw that the water was cloudier than before.

He was anxious to head back out to sea.

He was off before noon.

That night, Ben camped on a small beach thirty miles south of the city. He'd seen only one other boat that day, and knew he was miles from the nearest human. The jungle beyond the sandy shore grew thick and coarse. It was becoming more humid everyday, and the mosquitoes whined noisily around his ears as the tent was hastily set up. One of the rods broke again as it was being pounded into the ground. No surprise. Now, no matter how much tape was wrapped around the crack, it would not stand up straight. There was not much hope in prolonging the tent's life much longer.

Just feet away, the jungle was alive. Ben could hear the shrieks of monkeys and various night fowls. Insects buzzed so ferociously that he sat up several times during the night, checking to see if they had crawled inside his ears. More than once he awoke to small rustlings in the low ferns just outside the tent. Ben breathed quietly, not wishing to alarm any animal that nosed about. Soon, the sounds receded back into the forest, and he knew he was safe.

Ben awoke wondering what day it was. He had not read the Bible out loud for several days, and thought perhaps it might be Sunday. It didn't matter much, for he prayed every day as he left the shore. Ben didn't look at his journal, which would tell him the date if he counted up the last few entries. Instead, he packed everything up in the kayak and took off from shore, paddling straight into the teeth of the oncoming surf.

The ocean snarled in welcome.

The first wave crashed over his head.

Ben calmly held his breath, braced his back against the seat, and dug the paddle into the swirling water.

The dance was on.

Stroke right, stroke left, stroke right again.

Ben could feel the muscles in his arms responding with greater strength.

He broke through the first wave, and shook his head vigorously, clearing ears and eyes.

A faint smile broke across his lips as he soared up the face of the next breaker. He'd done this many times before, and relished the thrill of crashing through the face of his ocean.

Over the top of the next wave, and quickly gliding down its back, Ben yelled at the top of his lungs,

"I love this! Have you got anything else for me today?
Bring it on!"

The open waters beckoned him forth, as the kayak rolled up and down each swell. It crested high, then slid down the back of each mountain, adding an extra push to Ben's strong stroke, and increasing his momentum. Still fascinated after all these months, Ben watched as the sharp bow of the kayak cut keenly through the water, and ripples of white foam parted, leaving little waves to form and head back out away from the craft.

The sun directly overhead signaled midday. It had been four hours of non-stop paddling when Ben stopped for lunch. He'd bought a few items in Puntarenas, but only enough for the next few days. The lack of food didn't seem to bother Ben too much, as he reminded himself of the bounty all around him.

Before starting out again, he checked the chart.

I always keep it in a waterproof plastic bag. I've used the same bag for the entire journey. It once held beef jerky, and the zip lock top is perfect for my continual daily use. Everyday I fold the chart to the day's location and slip it in the bag. I sometimes look at the chart a dozen times a day, and the bag's none the worse for wear.

Sometimes I wish I could say that about me!

The kayak was only a few miles off shore, and the coast was fairly well defined. A good sized river flowed out of the hills twenty degrees north of where he took the reading. Up ahead, due east, another point cut into the horizon. Ben drew two lines that intersected in the middle of nowhere. He'd seen no cities all day, and the chart showed none he'd missed. The closest guess he had to this location was that Puerto Quepos lay ten to twelve miles ahead. Now the location of the sun said well past noon. He could reach the city by nightfall.

The day went by smoothly. The only deterrent of the past few days seemed to be the weather. There had not been rain for several days, and the sun beat down mercilessly throughout the day. The temperature must have been in the high eighties, and the fierce glare from the sun off the water caused continual squinting of eyes, and wiping of sweat from his brow. Finally, Ben dug out a hat, and pulled the wide brim down low on his forehead. At times, he closed his eyes completely to shut out the penetrating heat and glare. Ben let the ocean rock him up and down.

The direction he was headed didn't seem to matter too much.

Despite the seeming lethargy from the heat, Ben reached Puerto Quepos ahead of schedule. The sun had not begun its descent when he steered toward a small canal that led to the city. Surf broke so abruptly against the sand bars that guarded its entrance that the kayak was almost overturned, but the water in the canal was smooth and the kayak glided easily over to the shore.

As Ben pulled the craft onto the beach, he wondered if the map had misled him. He could see no city. The only thing that met his gaze was a long, tall sand dune.

Then a sound that revealed a street just beyond the sand roared forth - the revs of a car engine. Alone on the beach, Ben threw a line around one of the tall trees to secure the kayak, and climbed up the sand bank on all fours.

He reached the top of the dune, and gazed out at the modern city. Surrounded by primary rainforest, Puerto Quepos draped itself across the tropical inlet that Ben had just navigated. The village center was a delightful six-block square of restaurants, bars, hotels, bakeries, art galleries and gift shops, all fronted by the main beach.

Ben's stomach growled at the smell of roasted meat, wafting up on a small breath of wind.

I love my solitude.
And I love my steak.

He strode down the dune toward town.

Chapter 48

All animals except man know that the ultimate of life is to enjoy it.

Samuel Butler (1835-1902)

Across the street, Ben noticed a rather fancy restaurant with a brightly painted sign that announced *El Grand Escape*. That sounded promising to Ben. He crossed the street, walked in the front door, and took a seat at the nearest table. A refreshing breeze wafted through the room, and Ben sat back and relaxed. The cool temperature felt great. He doffed his broad brimmed hat with the élan of a gaucho and placed it on top of the table. There were a few waitresses in back. One smiled at Ben as she watched his theatrical gesture, and held up a finger for 'I'll be right there'. Ben smiled back and took the time to look around the place.

He noticed scores of photographs hanging on the walls. Most were of men with big fish, no doubt caught in the nearby waters. *"Hey,"* he said softly, *"there should be a picture of me up there. Too bad I didn't take one."*

He thought fondly of his fine catch the previous day and broadened his smile. First Ben checked the menu, and then his wallet. Finding over $150 dollars, he quietly thanked the few generous Mazatlan benefactors who had eased his worries about money. He knew he needed to save some for the long trip home, and was still not sure how he was going to swing that one.

That is, if he chose to go home at all.

Ben decided to be blissfully ignorant about future problems. He nonchalantly ordered the biggest steak on the menu from the waitress with the deep brown eyes and the engaging smile. After he ate the perfectly prepared beef, Ben sat back for a few minutes, sipped a cold drink, and savored the memory of every bite of his meal. He paid the tab, left a tip, and strolled contentedly back down to the beach.

In no time, the kayak was back in the canal, and moving vigorously toward the shallow breakers. Going out was, for some reason, much easier than it had been coming in, and the kayak split the waves and headed for the open ocean.

By now it was late in the day, and Ben paddled for only an hour before heading for the shore. After rounding Punta Quepos, covered with a thick rain forest, he headed south past several shady beaches. He saw a few people walking along the shores there, and decided to press on for a more isolated beach.

Several tiny islands, less than a hundred feet wide, spread out to the right. Ben paddled between them, counting a total of six before a larger point loomed in the distance. The sun was now setting rapidly, and he decided that, people or not, he'd camp there for the night.

The chart showed that he was just south of Playa Puerto Escondido, Costa Rica. The jungle was so thick that Ben could not step on the shore without lowering his head to dodge overhanging branches. The white sands, mingled with sea-rounded dark stones, penetrated the rain forest for only a few feet. Ben felt like he was conquering the Amazon jungle.

He made another bonfire that night, and curled close to its warmth on the soft sand. He took out several items that had gotten doused with saltwater over the past week, clothes, food, and sleeping bag, and laid them by the fire to dry. Finally, everything in order, he laid down, turned his back to the warmth, and was soon asleep.

A scream ripped through the silence of the night.

Ben was jarred from a deep sleep, hardly daring to breathe.

He turned over slowly to face the jungle.

It was close to midnight. There were still a few burning embers in the ashes of the fire pit on the sand.

Several branches moved overhead, giving way to some animal.

Rustling leaves caught his attention.

His heart pounded in his chest as he forced himself to lay still.

Whatever it was, Ben did not want to announce his presence.

Hoping that he could hide from view, he pressed as flat as he could against the cold, hard sand. The moon came out from behind the clouds and cast an eerie light toward the jungle.

Long shadows stretched out from the taller trees and fell silently over the campsite.

Crickets and insects of the forest stopped chirping.

A dead, silent, fearsome, calm fell over the area.

Ben lay still and waited for something to move.

Has the animal, whatever it is, seen me? Is it watching my every move, aware that my eyes too are searching?

I can't tell, but I feel its presence.

Another scream rent the air, sounding like a woman in intense agony.

Branches over Ben's head swayed in the still air, and he could tell it was where the sound had come from.

He realized that his fists were clenched tightly, and his lungs were gulping in as much air as possible.

He looked up to see if the animal that moved among the trees could be seen.

Another movement, still overhead but farther off to the left.

More now to the right.

Then, a wild flurry of voices, as several monkeys screeched at once.

Ben caught a glimpse of one, less than twenty feet away, dancing madly from one branch to the next. Other monkeys imitated the first. The ones he could see were white, and stood out against the dark background of the jungle.

Now, Ben saw that they were keenly watching the ground below them.

It was then that he realized that he wasn't the one who had disturbed their night.

Whatever it was that caused the monkeys to erupt in such violent screaming laid close to where Ben lay.

A rustle, a movement nearby in the undergrowth.

The sound of branches breaking, a crackling that sounded like paper being ripped and leaves being torn apart.

Ben's breathing stopped abruptly, caught in his throat.

Whatever moved out there was a large animal.

Taking only short breaths now, he listened.

The sound of low, heavy breathing reached his ears.

The sound was half huff, half grunt.

The only animal that hunts on the ground at night is one of the giant cats that frequent this coast.

Ben shut his eyes tightly, and tried to dissolve into the night.

A jaguar? Can I jump up and run down to the kayak in time to get away?

Then he remembered the safety line tied to a tree.

It was impossible to untie it, run to the shore, and paddle the kayak away before the predator overtook him.

Ben reached down slowly and felt the large knife that was half buried in the sand close to his leg.

Who am I kidding?
This blade, no matter how sharp, is no match for a jaguar.

The monkeys grew quiet, and Ben wondered if they'd scurried away to safety, leaving him as the only victim.

Had they deserted me in my most desperate hour?

More rustling, then silence.

Shortly, another monkey screamed into the night.

Ben started again at the intrusion into the silence.

No others joined its cry, but Ben knew they were still there in the trees.

For some reason, he felt better knowing that the little creatures shared his plight.

No. My friends are still there; as scared as I am, but still there. A sense of tension crawls up my spine. I know I'm being watched, and I know the big cat is near. I can feel his large yellow eyes boring into my skull. I try to make myself as small as possible on the jungle floor. As I wait for the jaguar to rip into my back and claw its way into my heart, the adrenaline that roars through my veins, and rings in my ears, is overpowering.

After what seemed like hours the large animal on the ground moved again. This time the noise was farther off. The monkeys continued to hop from limb to limb. Their rustlings, too, faded into the night. They would probably follow the hunter until it was definitely out of the area.

Thankful that they had alerted him to the dangers as well, Ben sat up and stoked the fire. He hoped the blaze would keep off other animals that prowled in the night. Soon the fire was roaring. Over the next several hours, Ben fed driftwood to the flames.

I can't remember that I slept anymore that night. After awhile my mind slowly shut down. I kept watch with my back to the fire. It probably wouldn't do me much good, but it felt right.

The fire caused shadows to play on the forest, a counterpoint to the shadows cast by the moon. The result was like a hand puppet theater of forest monsters playing on my mind.

I think I eventually dozed off around four a.m.

Ben awoke late the next morning, wondering if it had all been a nightmare. The fire wasn't quite out, and the events of the night returned quickly to him. Thankful that he was still in one piece, Ben ate a dull breakfast, and packed all of the now dry supplies back into the compartments.

He was standing in the waters edge, knee deep in the surf, when he looked back at the jungle. Something white moved about in the trees and caught his eye. He looked closer and saw the tiny face of a monkey. *"Hey little guy,"* Ben said, calling to the monkey. It cocked its head to one side when it heard his voice and let out a low whoop. *"Did you save my neck last night, little chango?"* Ben asked. The little spider monkey paced the limb where he perched, smiling, waving, and gesticulating.

And, of course, watching, always watching.

Ben walked back up on the beach, hauling the kayak behind, and set the paddle down on the sand high enough to be out of the reach of the waves. As he neared the jungle, the monkey moved away into the trees. Ben stopped, not wishing to frighten it. *"I'm not going to hurt you,"* he said softly. There was more movement overhead and soon, more than a dozen monkeys, all white faced and about a foot tall, hopped from tree to tree.

There was a little path that Ben had not seen the night before. He looked back at the kayak to make sure it was far enough out of the water. The monkeys still looked at him inquisitively. Ben looked around nervously and hesitated, wondering if the jaguar was still nearby, prowling, sensing an easy kill of this man. But sounder reason and curiosity stepped in as he decided to investigate the jungle for a few minutes.

He walked up the beach to the head of the trail. The dark jungle quickly enveloped him, and it took a few minutes to adjust to the change in light. Ben walked only a few feet into the jungle, as its dense vegetation left little room to move about freely. The only relief in sight was the thin trail beneath his feet, as it wound up the hill and disappeared several yards ahead in a mass of vines, ferns, and tree trunks. Insects flew around his exposed skin, and he swatted constantly at the biting animals that sought to devour his flesh. In a matter of minutes, he was covered with dozens of tiny red bumps.

Ben hoped that none of the mosquitoes carried malaria.

There were now more monkeys overhead. Ben counted a total of fifteen. He watched as they danced around in circles, looking at the trees, and then at him. He continued through the thick undergrowth, attempting to follow the winding path that disappeared, and then reappeared, every several steps. There was a movement to his left. A tapir scurried quickly away. The jungle was incredibly alive with movement. Several times Ben saw various rodents and mammals foraging for food. Some moved away frightened by the intrusion, others remained still, curious about his presence. Ben could not imagine anyone passing beneath this canopy of life, and remaining emotionally untouched.

The path climbed upward, and he looked back, hoping he could find an easier way out. Something in this jungle was calling him deeper into its grasp. Through tiny open patches in the forest Ben could just make out the blue water near the campsite. He looked for a moment, then turned to continue his exploration.

More monkeys frolicked overhead, this time playing with each other, as they chattered and jumped from limb to limb, following him down the trail. Although they kept their eyes on Ben, they seemed comfortable with his presence. The path became wider, and the trees drew back to let him pass. Overhead, they arched their branches to form a large canopy twenty feet in the air. Very little sunlight penetrated through the mass of vegetation, and the air was heavy with humidity. He heard a loud raucous *caw* several yards ahead. Cresting the hill, he scanned the branches for more signs of life. There, a brilliant flash of red quickly retreated back into the forest. Ben left the trail and listened for more signs of movement. The raspy cry of another tropical bird sang out. Behind him, Ben saw a blur of blue and yellow, and caught a brief glimpse of the vanishing parrot.

The monkeys must have been busy playing somewhere else, or maybe he had just walked out of their territory. More birds fluttered above, and Ben's head jerked back and forth, trying to catch the beauty of their movements. An enormous, bright red, macaw landed on a branch twenty feet above his shoulder. It was over a foot and a half long, with graceful tail feathers hanging down over the branch. Another macaw, possibly the first one's mate, flew over next to the branch.

I slowly took out my camera and began to take pictures. Startled by the flash, the two birds let out a few raucous cries before flying off to a safer perch.

I closed my eyes and listened to the sounds of the forest.

Far off in the distance I heard the gurgling sounds of a stream.

Continuing to follow the trail, Ben was soon lying next to the small river, and dipping hands and head in the cool water. He swung his feet into the current, and the water swirled about his ankles to form small pools and eddies. It flowed to the south, and Ben wondered where it poured out into the ocean. There were no animals drinking from the stream that he could see, but he knew that if he waited long enough there would be another glimpse of life.

A few small chinks of sunlight burst through the thick canopy of the forest and danced across the leaves and trunks of the trees. It was now quite muggy, and Ben slapped insects from legs, back, neck, face, and arms. It was time to head back to the ocean and continue on. Retracing his steps along the trail, Ben was followed by several birds and monkeys. He ducked under the last few branches that hung over the beach. Now he looked back at the wildlife that abounded there. He waved goodbye to the creatures and talked to them one by one.

"You are so pretty and red!" he called to the birds of paradise.

"Hope to see you soon on down the coast. Goodbye little friends. Thanks again for last night," he called to the monkeys.

Then Ben waved again unselfconsciously to the expanse of forest, and turned back to the ocean.

It was now close to midday, and the air was hot and still. Ben hopped into the cockpit and paddled out through the waves. Once out into open water, he stopped to jump in for a swim. The water felt refreshing and he scrubbed off the sweat, bugs, and dirt, of the forest floor in the clear blue sea.

But the call of the jungle remained in his mind, now competing with the pull of the ocean in his young mind.

Chapter 49

In all things of nature there is something of the marvelous.
Aristotle (384 BC - 322 BC)

Near dusk, the lights of a small city appeared up ahead. It was Dominical, Costa Rica. Ben rested for awhile and let the swells carry the kayak closer. The current was still going with him, and he was traveling close to fifty miles a day. Still, Ben didn't bother to look to see what day it was.

What does it matter to me anyway? I have no need for it. I sleep with the night's darkness blanketing my eyes and I wake with the sun's warming rays. What more can I ask for? What else can tell me as perfectly as the sun when I need to do things. My stomach tells me when to eat, and the heavens tell me when to sleep. Nothing can be simpler than that.

For some reason, Ben had not wanted to buy many supplies in Puntarenas or Puerto Quepos. He'd left in a rush with only a few loaves of bread, a pound of oatmeal, and some green bananas. Now he sat back with his dinner and ate banana sandwiches. *Quite good, actually, and very filling*, he thought as he threw the peels overboard and took several gulps of water.

The stars were out, covering the sky in their multitudes. Ben winked back at the ones he knew, and called out their names one by one. "*Hello, Mr. Dipper. Good to see you tonight,*" he said to his familiar friend. "*How do things look from up there. I'll bet you didn't think you'd be seeing so much of me. Well, I'm still here."* Ben looked over his shoulder and added, *"You neither, eh North Star? Can't say I blame you. Might be seeing more of me in the future. Don't know if I'm gonna stop. If I don't stop, I'll be seeing your cousin, the Southern Cross.*

Just love being out here with you guys, night after night."

He stretched out, eyes still open.
Ben was no longer alone.

My friends look out for me from above. The ocean gently caresses me with her arms and rocks me to sleep. The coast invites me to shore each day, and presents me new gifts at every turn. I talk to everything, and God smiles down on me from above. There's no need to close my eyes to pray, either. All I do is open my mouth to talk, and I know that He is right there listening to every word I say.

If this is a dream, let me never wake; and if I am awake, let me never close my eyes.

Ben nodded off to sleep, adrift on the open ocean.

A wave crashed over the bow of the kayak, and washed into the cockpit. Ben woke with a start and sat up coughing. Reflexively he picked up the paddle.

Has a storm come up in the night?

His eyes focused by the moon's pale light. The ocean was a little rough, but there was nothing extraordinary in view. The sky remained cloudless, and capped with a twinkling dome.

"Well," he said with a laugh. *"I'm awake now. Might as well start paddling again."*

Ben stood up in the narrow cockpit and stretched tired muscles. Several miles in the distance, he thought he could see the shore. He had no idea where he was, or how far out to sea he'd drifted. He was not overly concerned. The night air was warmer than it had been for several weeks. He was nearing the twentieth parallel, if not already on it, and he could feel the gradual change in the weather. It became hotter and more humid each day, and the sun rose and set with greater finality. There is little twilight as you near the Equator. More clouds formed on the horizon during the long days, but it hardly ever rained. The official ending of the wet season was December.

Ben continued to paddle through the night. Sometimes he would close his eyes and relax. With the paddle gripped firmly in both hands, he dozed off for a few minutes, then woke again and, with eyes still closed, began to paddle. It was now a habit. It happened several times, sleep, paddle, eyes barely open, eyes closed, half awake, half asleep.

The sun was already high by the time he fully opened his eyes for good. The kayak was quite close to the coast. It must have drifted back in the early hours. Ben's stomach growled impatiently, and he took out several bags of oatmeal. Without dirtying a bowl, he poured a little water in the bag and swallowed its contents. He had a gallon and a half of water left, and made a mental note to drink sparingly for the rest of the day.

All that day, Ben paddled without seeing any habitation, large or small, on the shore. He was passing through the Bahia de Coronado. The water there didn't seem any calmer than the open ocean. Swells still crested twenty feet over his head, and he leaned forward in anticipation of each new wave. He passed a small island, and, as crystal blue water danced about the kayak, he could see the rock's dark forms beneath the waves. Several boats came and went from the mainland. None passed close enough to see the small kayak.

"*There must be something on that island. Maybe a resort,*" he said aloud.

He would never know. Ben paddled on.

Later in the evening, several deep inlets appeared on the shore. They looked like some type of swamp or lagoon. The kayak angled over closer, as Ben searched for a suitable place to spend the night.

This turned out to be a mistake.

A great crash sounded in the distance, and Ben scanned the horizon to see where the turmoil came from. A hundred yards ahead of him white caps mounted their attack on the land. They extended several miles out to sea. He looked out to the open ocean to see if there was an end to the uproar.

None was in sight.

Ben stood up and braced his legs on the inside walls of the cockpit. He needed to keep his balance against the rolling sea.

Toward the mainland the cause of the ocean's rise became apparent. In an instant, just before racing down the backside of a giant wave, Ben glimpsed the Rio Sierpe flowing steadily into the ocean. It was a large river and Ben knew, if he valued his safety, that it would be best to head back out to sea.

He hoped it was not too late.

The kayak, steered by the rudder, veered, and ran straight out to sea.

The compass pointed almost due south, and Ben remembered that the coast of Costa Rica curved sharply to the east. He kept a cautious eye on the waves that crashed toward the shore, careful not to be drawn too close to their pull. His stroke quickened a little as the fear of overturning the kayak spurred him. An hour passed, and his arms were extremely tired. But now he could see the last of the whitecaps fifty yards ahead. Just to be on the safe side, Ben paddled out farther than he needed to, and headed east, parallel to the coast. From several miles out, the shore, now off in the distance, looked Lilliputian. Most of the time, unless he climbed to the top of a rolling swell, Ben couldn't see anything but the ocean around him. It moved constantly, shifting here, breaking into small waves there, and his eyes never alighted on any particular spot for long.

A few miles past the river, a tiny town appeared on the horizon. Ben steered diagonally toward the cluster of houses and huts. In an hour he was surfing the four foot tall waves to shore. He was just north of the town and dusk was falling. Once the kayak was secured, Ben donned the old white dress shirt that Carl and Gary had given him a seeming lifetime before, and walked up toward the town.

There were a few people on the beach, and none had seen his arrival. Ben felt anonymous, which is what he preferred. He looked down at his shirt, seeing some stains of blood and unknown substances, and noting that the sleeves were now tattered, and a few buttons were missing. He tugged it to proper alignment, and, with head held high, proceeded on his way.

There were several small, expensive looking, hotels at the edge of the town. The whole place was so small that Ben could have walked through it in a few minutes. He strolled through the front door of the first hotel that looked descent and sat down in the restaurant. The waiter, dressed in neatly pressed white cotton shirt and pants, came over. "Good evening, sir," he said with only a slight accent. "How are you?" Ben asked. "Fine, thank you, sir." He was middle aged, and looked as though he might be a surfer. "What's the name of this place?" Ben asked. "The Cocalito Lodge, sir," he said with an air that told Ben it was probably the nicest place in town.

"Let's see," Ben said looking down at the menu. *"Nice menu. Fish, chicken, shrimp. What shall I have? Haven't been eating a lot lately. Haven't really felt like it. The water's been pretty rough so I haven't been able to fish as often as I'd like to. Maybe I'll have some fish. Fresh here? Should be. Is that what I want?"*

"Excuse me, sir? I don't understand," the waiter asked, puzzled, and interrupting Ben's monologue. Ben looked up at him quizzically. "Oh, sorry," he said, embarrassed.

Am I crazy? He must think so. I've spent so long by myself that I forgot that I continually talk out loud. Now, without even knowing it, I let my thoughts evolve into words.

"Yes, right," Ben continued hastily. "I'll have the dorado."

I love mahi mahi.

Ben expected the waiter to leave, anxious to get out of his sight. But he just shook his head and smiled. Maybe he knew what it felt like. Ben nodded back, now feeling welcome in this tiny spot of civilization.

I barely tasted the meal. I was so ravenously hungry. I motioned for the waiter to come over. "What city is this?" I asked. There had been no clear indication on my map. "Drake, sir," he said. "How far am I from the next national park?"

"About four miles. It's a rain forest."

"Corcovado?" I asked, pleased with my progress.

"That is correct, sir," he said smiling.

"Is there a place here where I can clean up? An outdoor shower or something?"

"Um, yes," he answered, looking around before he spoke. "There is. We have facilities to rent. They are eight dollars a night, but you can use it for free if you hurry."

I smiled and left him an extra big tip.

Ben practically ran back down to the kayak. He grabbed a toothbrush, razor, and soap, and hurried back to the shower the waiter had pointed to earlier. The water felt wonderful, and Ben scrubbed vigorously at the salt that caked his body from head to toe. He stepped out, refreshed, clean, and feeling like a new man. The night air felt brisk against newly scrubbed skin. Ben breathed in deeply and felt the tingle and tightness of a clean, freshly shaven face.

He walked over to a small store and bought a few groceries. He packed bananas, six gallons of purified water, and some bread into the little backpack that he always carried with him into a town. Walking back down to the kayak, Ben watched the waves slowly lap onto the shore. A calm fell over the ocean, and he could see the moon reflecting brightly off its smooth surface. The groceries were stowed in the kayak, and a spot on the sand next to a giant palm tree was chosen for a bed. With his back to its trunk, Ben slept again under the stars.

He was still skirting the edge of the Parque Nacional Corcovado the next day, when the surface of the water suddenly broke a dozen yards to his right.

The sound made him look over in startled bewilderment.

The ocean was fairly calm, and the breeze that lifted off the shore made no sound, save a slight rippling on the water.

The air was hot, humid, and still.

He sat squarely in the small craft, the paddle laying across the cockpit. Ben was still, except for his eyes, which scanned back and forth.

So, what had made the surface move like that?

Ben would soon have his answer.

Not too far in front of the kayak, the water swirled in a great mounding, circular eddy.

Ben locked his eyes on the spot when, suddenly, a dark form replaced the mounded sea and loomed from the water, blowing an enormous jet of air and sea spray into the blue sky.

With growing excitement, his heart pounding in his chest, Ben watched a whale's back lift ponderously from the ocean's surface in a gigantic ballet, and then quickly sink to disappear beneath the surface.

He paddled toward the spot where the whale had come up for air. He passed over the spot, and could see that all around him the ocean was moving. He scanned side to side in search of any sign of the great beast.

A startling shadow passed directly underneath the tiny kayak.

Ben slowed his stroke, and glided silently through the swells.

He caught another movement out of the corner of his eye, and turned just in time to see the shadow loom and the whale head for the surface once again.

"Oh my God," Ben exclaimed, as the great whale, a humpback, emerged from the ocean a scant fifteen feet from the kayak.

Ben froze, and stared directly into the huge eye that peered knowingly back at him.

Elation overcame fear, and maybe common sense.

His was a fragile craft, and it would not take much of a close encounter with this leviathan to crush and sink what was Ben's only lifeline.

But Ben was far removed from that thought.

"Where are you going, my man? Hey, Señor Whale! I can't believe what I'm seeing. You're huge." Was I talking or just thinking? I shake my head and paddle again. The giant beast submerged itself again, but the water continues to ripple and break in all directions. I know it is still just beneath the surface, eyeing my slow, pathetic movements. "Please come up again," I cry.

The sun beat down hot, and the slight breeze that attempted to cool things off had ceased. Ben was alone on top of the little boat a few miles from the shore, with the biggest whale he had ever seen just beneath the water. His heart beat fast in anticipation and he continued to scan the horizon. For a moment, all was still, and he thought he'd seen the last of the humpback.

Then, the water boiled and churned, a dark grey shape rose, growing in size and intensity, and, with a burst of speed, the whale crashed through the surface of the sea!

Ben stopped paddling and reared back in the seat, recoiling from the violent specter.

Just twenty yards away, the whale burst from the sea in a rush of sound, and speed, and crashing strength.

Once again, Ben looked straight into its eyes, and strained to feel its emotions.

Free? Happy? Grand? Proud?
The giant black and gray speckled tail loomed out of the water, paused at the top of a great arc, and then slapped violently onto the indigo sea, driving plumes of spray high into the air.

Ben closed his eyes, as the misted brine floated over his face.

It felt like the entire ocean had lurched forward.

A gigantic ocean roll careened the kayak skyward, and, for a moment, Ben thought that the whale had swum underneath him, and was lifting him high into the air. Then, as gently as if he were an infant in a crib, the wave set Ben back down, leaving him breathless, ecstatic, and in one piece.

Ben sat stunned for a few minutes - or it might have been hours. For the next hour he looked frantically about. Sometimes, far off on the horizon, he thought he could see the spouts of more whales, but he was too far away to be certain. Lost in a daze of his own making, he paddled half heartedly for the rest of the day.

I wished with all my heart that I could see more of this gentle beast. I want to swim, to join him, to move through the water like this beautiful creature. The rush, the adrenaline, the power, the passion, that this whale has blessed me with, is something I shall never forget.

Chapter 50

The self is not something ready-made, but something in continuous formation through choice of action.

John Dewey (1859-1952)

To his left was the Peninsula de Osa that protected Drake Bay from the sea. Ben stayed well clear of the peninsula's tip, then turned east, and crossed the bay to the protected beaches of Costa Rica's Parque Nacional Piedras Blancas. Here he chose to rest.

The kayak was safe from the surf, tied to a coconut palm. Ben felt strangely calm and safe in front of the dense rain forest. Waves rumbled in the background, giving a booming basso accompaniment for all the other exotic sounds. The wind had died down to a whisper, so the sounds of the jungle rang loud and clear. Orange crickets and lace winged, red-eyed cicadas hummed and chirped their mating choruses from the trees. Birds rustled on the ground, foraging for food. Most prevalent were the howler monkeys, screaming and calling to each other from all directions. Many other sounds, indistinguishable to a first time visitor, reached Ben's ears.

He closed his eyes and felt the rhythm of his soul mesh with his surroundings.

For Ben, the jungle, like the ocean, has a living, breathing life of its own. Also like the ocean, he could feel the sense of movement all around, and he knew that every living thing was aware of his presence. The trick was not only to blend in with the animals, but to become one as well. As he moved stealthily up the narrow path, he began to call out in different voices and syllables.

337

He called to the birds, *"Caw! Caw! Caw caw!"*

He screamed at the monkeys, *"Whoop, whoop, whoooop, whoooooop, whooooooeeeeeaaa!"*

Some of the howler monkeys followed his progress, peering down as they nimbly leapt from tree to tree. Occasionally he would catch a fleeting glimpse of a white-nosed capuchin monkey among the toucans and scarlet macaws.

This place was heaven to Ben.

Ben was in a remote section of the Parque Nacionál Piedras Blancas in southern Puntarenas Province, Costa Rica. The tall dense foliage, lush and extravagantly verdant, is an evergreen primary forest of indigenous trees and plants. As he walked down the path which twisted this way and that, he always stayed aware of where his beloved ocean lay – now to the right, now behind, now to the left.

The consciousness of this living body of water was comforting, and the short distance he kept between them was always in the back of his mind.

Don't go too far. Remember how to get back. Gotta get moving soon.

Humid and hot, it was evident to Ben that this forest got lots of rain. It was also evident that it had a large population of snakes and other reptilians, and he kept alert to movement on the ground.

As he rounded a bend in the trail, Ben froze in his tracks, staring in confused disbelief.

Something unusual up ahead had caught his eye.

Something stood out from the side of the trail that did not belong.

Ben stared hard in disbelief, trying to focus on the obviously foreign object.

His reverie at becoming one with the jungle suddenly snapped back to screaming reality.

It was a telephone!

Ben was looking at a bright yellow telephone booth.

An object that earlier in his journey had given Ben hope of connections with loved ones, now stood as a stolid testament to the invasion of civilization to these primal and sacred ends of the earth.

Ben shook his head to clear the vision - but the thing remained.

Are you friggin' kidding me?
What the hell is this thing doing here in the middle of this jungle?
Do they have to penetrate every sacred place on earth?
I can't believe it!

What's wrong with these people?
The audacity of the person to violate God's natural beauty!

Ben's thoughts spiraled from incredulity, through anger, and on to the heights of rage.

And then something happened in the very core of Ben's mind; something deep, part primal, part survival, part instinct - an instinct that had been slowly wending its way to the surface for many months now; surfacing from beneath the loneliness and suffering that afflicted his sanity, and sought to drown his soul.

It was as if Ben stood outside himself, and peered back at a lone man standing in the middle of the jungle, hardened by many months at sea, steeled by the tides of strength, forged by every type of human suffering possible, and now seething with an uncontrollable rage against ... *against what ....? Against, against* ... and at that instant it became clear to Ben, as clear as anything had every been to him.

He knew what he had to do.

Ben rushed headlong, running and stumbling, over to the iconic telephone.

Hands shaking, he took a deep breath, and dialed the operator. The call was placed and, after a few rings, a familiar voice answered. "Yes I'll accept the charges... Ben is that you?" Heather asked.

Ben, now strangely calm, answered quietly, "Yeah it's me."

"What's wrong baby? Are you all right?" she asked nervously, hearing the coldness that formed around those first few words. Ben spoke slowly, and with an even tone, "I called to tell you something."

Now Heather felt the coldness. A tightness coiled its way around her heart. She new that something was wrong, seriously wrong. "What, Ben, what..."

"I'm changing, Heather. Actually I have already changed. Completely changed. I'm not the same man I was a few months ago - weeks ago for that matter."

"I know that baby. I know you are but ..."

"Just listen to me Heather. I can't say this any other way, but I don't think I'm coming back."

"What??!!!"

"You need to move on, Heather - find someone else and forget about me," Ben said stoically. Heather almost screamed into the telephone, exasperated, crushed, by what she was hearing, "But I can't! You know I can't do that. I love you."

"I love you too," Ben continued with cool, relentless, almost automaton precision. "And that's why I'm telling you to move on. *I have changed*. I don't need anyone or anything. I cannot give up this freedom that I've found. I can't give up this journey that I've become. This is love. This is life. This is complete and total peace that I've found out here on the water. And this is me. I can't come back, and I can't ask you to wait for me any longer. As much as this hurts me ... to do, to tell you this ... I know I must."

There was only silence on the other end of the phone. Ben knew that he had sent her world spinning and crashing down. When she spoke her voice was wracked with sobs or anguish. "But you, you pr-promised me you would co-come b-b-back to me. You promised!"

"I know I did. But I have to do this, and I have to do it now. I won't be calling for awhile. Don't worry, I have been to hell and back. I will survive, but I have to be on my own now. Completely. I want you to know I will always love you. No matter what happens ... I love you."

Ben hung the pathetic, ugly, yellow telephone back gently into place, not waiting for a reply. He felt a strange detachment as he walked slowly down the path. It was an odd moment, a continuance of the seeming out-of-body experience he'd felt earlier. His heart was rent by two totally different emotions.

First, was the heartbreak that he knew was pushing him toward the precipice of madness, and the feeling that he was just one step away from a complete breakdown that would send him sobbing and crying for Heather and the familiar safety of home.

Second, was the strong wave of discipline and courage that washed over his mind and heart and replaced old feelings. A sense of attaining the impossible crashed into his soul. At first he didn't know what it was, but as his pace quickened along the path toward the ocean he realized just what it was *not*.

It's not courage or strength.
It's not peace or arrogance.
I know what it is!

It's the feeling that nothing can stop me now!
Nothing is going to stand in my way.
Not loneliness, not anger, not desperation, not despair – these have fallen away like shackles from an escaping prisoner. This new freedom has pushed me forward and I finally know this new sensation that dominates my mind and body, my soul and character.
I am invincible!

Chapter 51

They are never alone that are accompanied with noble thoughts.

Sir Philip Sidney (1554-1586)

Ben set up his camp on the small beach that rimmed the jungle. He was emotionally drained, but also feeling the strength of his decision filling the void. He stood on a little dune of sand, and looked out over the water that he was to cross the next day, the Golfo Dulce. There was a twenty mile stretch between the peninsula where he stood and the mainland. He could have continued to follow the coast around to Golfito, but that would have taken two or three more days to complete. The open water should not be too rough. He'd seen several boats on the horizon passing through the Gulf earlier. Ben walked up the beach and foraged for coconuts.

Chopping the top off one in a now practiced manner, he tilted the small opening to his mouth.

The cool liquid ran down to my mouth, spilled over my chin, and dribbled down my chest. I relished several gulps before I took the sweet fruit away from my mouth. It was so good, sweet, and refreshing, that I sat down and cut a larger opening in the top of the shell, and poured several bags of dried oatmeal into the coconut bowl, mixing it with the last of the natural milk. I stirred it vigorously with the plastic spoon I carried with me, and ate the gruel without chewing. I stared about, looking for something else to eat, but there was only the coconut in my hands. Again, I took out my knife and cut several chunks of the tender white meat inside. They were also sweet, although not so much as the milk.

I ate as much as I could, and then rolled the shell down the beach until it fell gently into the surf.

Ben was feeling deeply the power of the moment. He took in a deep breath and looked down at his body, now tan, lean and strong.

As the sun set over the water, Ben noticed a small island out on the horizon. The sun dipped down behind the island, illuminating its shape, and blurring it slightly with shimmering radiance. He closed his eyes, blinded by the spectacle in front of him, and began to sing.

Softly at first, then loud and clear.

I sang a song that I wish I could now recall.

I want to write down its words.

It is of the sea, clear and blue, of the waters that leap about on all sides, and of the coast that produces such wonder and amazement.

It's for the creatures that swim so freely in the ocean.

It's about my God, who, under great and varied circumstances, has helped me every step of the way.

I sing whatever words come to my lips, and whatever notes rise from my heart. They come straight from my soul, my core, my being, and, I know in my heart, they come from the ocean.

I cry a little as I lay down to sleep, wondering why I have been so blessed. Blessed not only with safety, but also with beauty and adventure.

I feel like the luckiest man alive, and shake my head sadly, hoping that it will all not come to an end too soon. The stars, my friends, come out to check on me, but I'm already asleep. No doubt they look on me with the love of a father, and watch over me while I lay motionless on the small beach in the middle of nowhere.

One man, one boat, one purpose, and one with nature.

In my heart I know exactly where I am.

I am somewhere.

In paradise.

Ben looked once more out across the great expanse of water toward the other side of the Gulf. This time he had no one to watch out for his progress. He took a deep breath and shoved off into the water. Most of the time, he could not see the other side. He set the compass on 120 degrees east. Without much of a current, he would see land by the afternoon. Several boats passed on the horizon, both in front and in back of the kayak.

None came close enough to cause concern.

Ben crossed the Gulf on a virtually flat and calm sea. He was closer to land than he thought, and decided to land at a small beach called Esterillos; he was taking a break for some food.

After eating he took off through surf that was only two feet tall.

It was well worth my time and effort to be on dry land. I'm refreshed after my little break and I'm gaining good ground now, passing miles and miles of endless shoreline.

Approaching Panama, Central America

By nightfall, an enormous point jutted twenty miles into the ocean. It was Ben's first look at Panama. The point was called Punta Burica, and he set his gaze solidly on its massive form. He continued to paddle well past night fall.

The moon came up and lit his way. He was closer to the point than he'd thought, and, encouraged by a feeling of strength, Ben put his head down and paddled in a fury. The ocean grew calm and aided his progress.

After a few hours of this exertion, the adrenalin driven fury produced exhaustion, and Ben stopped to catch some sleep. Slipping on a wind-breaker, he huddled in the cockpit and watched the swells roll, and the moon reflect the movement of the sea.

It wasn't long before heavy-lidded eyes closed, and Ben fell into a sound sleep.

I slept until morning and woke with the sun. I am amazed at how well I have slept, and I cannot recall waking once, the first time for as long as I can remember. The morning air is cool. I jump into the water to refresh and stretch my cramped muscles. The water is invigorating, and I am soon drying off inside the cockpit.

The wind is blowing steadily from the north.

Ben was still a few miles from Punta Burica, on the very tip of Costa Rica. He adjusted the heading slightly to counteract drift during the night. Ben passed Punta Burica where the surf pounded ferociously into the bluffs, sending mountains of white water high into the air. Just beyond, the kayak slid into the calmer waters of the Golfo de Chiriqui.

There were several islands off in the distance, and Ben thought momentarily of the novelty of spending the night on one of them. The coast had flattened out a little, but still remained a dark and verdant green. Four gallons of water were still on board, two in the outrigger, and two in the cockpit, so Ben decided to pass up the city of David, Panama, that would be coming up soon.

It's the third largest city in Panama, and I know it is better if I do not clutter my mind and body with the distractions of a large city. Just the thought of the crowds, the acrid smells, and the filth, makes me cringe.

With no intention of landing, Ben headed in the city's direction. By late afternoon he could see a few buildings on the horizon. There were also several islands that repeatedly blocked the view of the city and, at times, the open waters of the Pacific as well. Ben stayed clear of the nearest island, as the ocean hurled itself violently against its rocky shore. Even standing off to sea, he could hear and feel the thunderous activity.

Still paddling in the Gulf, the water close around him was without whitecaps.

I think it strange that the surf should remain so strong against the islands, while the rest of the water rises and falls so lazily around me.

The last island passed behind by mid afternoon. The coast was now bending to the south, and the kayak skirted away from the shore to compensate for the angle it created. As the craft headed out to sea, Ben kept the shoreline in sight, as he veered off at an angle that he hoped would put him on a heading straight for Punta Jabali, Panama. It had not yet appeared, as it was still a good fifty miles away. The sun waned astern the tiny kayak.

Ben saw a black object pass within his shadow on the water.

As it emerged into the sun's path, and floated toward the kayak, Ben realized, with mixed feelings of wonder and dread, what it was that approached him. Then he recognized the danger.

A Pacific sea snake, one of the deadliest reptiles in Central America, undulated effortlessly through the dark water.

Ben shipped the paddle, and tensely waited for it to pass by.

But it isn't passing by. It's turning, turning, toward me . . .

Abeam where Ben sat, his body within inches of the water, the deadly serpent turned, raised its yellow marked head out of the water, and slithered directly toward the boat.

Ben recoiled, his body chilled in fear.

He slapped the water between them with a violent swing of the paddle.

The beady eyed sea serpent paid no attention.

As if driven to some unknown destiny, the snake lurched forward and bumped the kayak inches from Ben's exposed arm.

His blood ran cold with fear.

There is no where to go, no where to run.

The snake's forked tongue flicked the air, taking readings for an accurate strike.

I see the head bend slightly, and its muscles curve elegantly in the water, leaving small ripples behind. The body is entirely black, except for the bright yellow streak that runs across its brow. It sits there now, as if treading water and evaluating my meager worth. It seems bored with me. It's moving along the edge of my little world. I turn in my seat and let it pass, watching its head move back and forth just a few inches from the water.
This is crazy.
If I am bitten they will find me washed up on the shore.
Maybe. . .

After an eternity, and for reasons known only to God, the deadly poisonous reptile turned, and passed by Ben without hesitation or recognition.

There were no more cities along this coast. Except for a few large and ponderous cruise ships off in the distance, Ben had not seen another boat or human for the entire day. As darkness set in, he sat back to wait out the long night.

Layers of clouds rolled overhead, playing with the last rainbows of the setting sun. Ben sighed as he realized there would be no stars out that night. He would have to wait and see his friends some other time. The air was warm, and, once again, he stood up to stretch stiffened limbs. The kayak was a good seven miles out from shore, so Ben was not concerned about drifting against any rocks. He fell asleep quickly.

At the first dawn's glow, Ben awoke, and was immediately disorientated by the strange quality of the light. A low fog had rolled over the ocean and visibility was only a few yards. An eerie calm lay over the water. He rubbed rheumy eyes to clear the sleep. Waves crashed somewhere in the distance, the sound muffled by the damp air.

I begin to move slowly at first, and I shake my head several times to make sure I am not dreaming. The fog is so thick, I cannot tell which direction the sun is positioned in this sky, or the direction to land.

I still don't know the date. Is it February still? Or maybe March? I can't recall. This morning without the sun, I cannot even estimate the hour of the day.

A sharp noise sounded somewhere to his left, and Ben turned to see if anything was visible in the shadowy fog.

The sound was almost like a dolphin surfacing for a breath of air, but in this gloom he could only imagine the worst.

He quickly recovered his journal, and began to write, hoping this act would quell the uneasiness that floated toward him in the mist.

After a long stretch of sanity, my mind now begins to conjure up all kinds of ridiculous images. Another shark? A whale? Or is it possible I had come too close to the shore? Without being able to see, I feel quite helpless. It's different from the darkness of night. Now with my mind attempting to play tricks on me I see strange forms peering out of the mist, and coming menacingly toward me. My imagination is clearly enjoying torturing me with fear and doubt. I shake my head many times, and manage a wry smile.

I tell myself repeatedly that it's only the morning fog.

It will soon lift.

Please, God, it will.

Without any serious incidents, save those that played in his mind, Ben watched the sun streak through the low marine layer. At first, it was just a thin ray of sunlight that sparkled on the water. Then the air around grew brighter, and Ben could see several hundred yards around him. Sounds now reached his ears without having to pass through the moisture. They grew louder, as Ben could now hear the far off cries of seagulls near the shore, and the waves rumbling in their eternal contentment.

His demons rushed away from the light.

At the first sight of land Ben blinked in amazement. To the right, still partially enshrouded by low clouds, was a dark mass of solid ground. He quizzically looked down at both of his compasses, the one around his neck first, and then at the one on the bow.

Had I accidentally gotten turned around during the night?

At first, he thought that's what had happened.

The coast had been on his left for the last five months. Both compasses pointed a few notches above 100 degrees, slightly southeast.

Then he realized it was an island that he was looking at, but soon, the mainland itself shook off the fog shroud, and he could see both landmasses on either side of his kayak. The chart had the answer. To the right was Isla de Coiba and, to the left, Punta Jabali.

The momentary, but disconcerting, disorientation was over.

The day passed slowly. By late afternoon, Ben was ready to head to shore. He'd traveled over a hundred miles in two days, and was ecstatic at his growing strength and endurance.

The great mass of the Azuero Peninsula jutted out into the Pacific Ocean ahead, and Ben watched the water beginning to grow anxious, as if anticipating the change in the coastline. White streaks of high flung foam dotted the horizon, and the surf built to new heights against the intrusion of land. He had just passed Cebaco Island in the province of Veraguas, Panama, and decided to spend the night in a small cove that came into sight.

Punta Mariato, on the far tip of the Peninsula, took most of the Pacific's power and fury, leaving room for calmer waters beneath its protective wing. The point stuck out into the open ocean for several miles, and the kayak was steered quickly into the bay it provided. Just before the sun dipped over the western horizon, the little craft surfed the small three foot waves to the shore. The water was clear and the beach was flat. Isla Cebaco was still visible to the north as he took out the sleeping bag.

He no longer cared about the loss of the tent.

The nights are no longer windy, and the animals are now my friends and will not harm me while I sleep. The air is pleasantly warm. I am too tired to light a fire this night, and the sand beckons me to lie down on her soft chest. The wind again tousles my hair, and whispers softly into my ear.

I fell asleep quickly last night. But not before I saw the clouds roll by, and the stars peek out from beneath, winking to me.

I smiled at their return to the sky.

Ben saw no cities as he paddled past Punta Mariato the next day. His gaze continually swept the horizon, watching for anomalies in the waves. He also glanced now and then toward shore with the thought of seeing some sign of civilization. The ocean surged forward just south of the point, and he braced himself as the swells came rolling quickly toward the coast. Paddling furiously up their faces, and then holding the paddle overhead in triumph, Ben soared down the back of each new wave in elation.

With my paddle clenched tightly in both hands, I take in a deep breath each time I rush down the steep swells. It's an incredible sensation of speed and motion as I feel the wind whip across my face; the waves smack the bow, and the taste of sea salt is life itself. The ocean rises and falls, as if breathing deeply in unison with my own lungs.

This is paradise.

Once past the point, the swells evened out. They were still well over fifteen feet high, with wider troughs between them that made for many exhilarating rides. Ben watched the shoreline appear, and then disappear, several times that morning.

Turning his face to the risen sun, Ben quickened his stroke and yelled loudly into the wind, *"South America, here I come. I can almost see you there on the horizon."*

It was still over two hundred and fifty miles to the shores of Colombia. But with each passing hour, Ben could sense her coming closer into his grasp.

When I think of landing on her shores, which was often now during the day, my heart beats fast and my breath comes sharp and deep. It's hard to believe the journey is nearing its end. And when I finally do arrive, what should I expect?

What do I plan to do?

What happens next on this great adventure of mine?

Ben Wade would, unfortunately, find answers to his questions sooner or later.

They may not be the answers he wants to hear.

Unlike the beginning of my voyage, when I continually sought solace in the company of people, now I seek only isolation. I possess a deep yearning to stay free, and a burning desire to remain anonymous.

My destiny is to be alone.

Chapter 52

It made our hair stand up in panic fear.
Sophocles (496BC-406BC)
Oedipus at Colonus

That evening, Ben camped on a small beach just west of Punta Mala. Unlike the last point, this one did not stick so far out into the ocean, but only gradually projected its head to break the Pacific swells that marked the entrance to the Gulf of Panama. The waves still came into the shore with impressive force. There were several good beaches, and Ben picked one that looked like it had slightly smaller breakers.

It was hard to tell which one to pick from behind the waves.

I point to one area and say aloud, "I think I'll head for you. You look good to me." I sit still and wait just outside the reach of the powerful waves. Each pulls gently at my kayak and invites me along for the ride. I shake my head slowly and say, "No, I will wait for another one."

Soon it looks as if they are taking a short break. I turn my head to look behind me and see the position of the next wave. Its back arches several yards behind me, and, as it comes closer, I put my paddle in the water and thrust myself forward. I feel its draw and sense its power as I continue to paddle. But the strength of the wave makes me feel like I'm going backwards.

The wave's top begins to curl over.

Tiny flecks of white foam dance down the wave's face and envelope me.

I've done this many times, thousands of times in fact.
But this one is different.
Sickeningly slow, the grip of pending disaster grips my stomach.

The bow of the kayak parted the water rapidly, as he raced down the face of the wave. Several feet below, the ocean leveled out and, in a manner of seconds, the kayak was in its trough.

The rudder was jammed to the left, but once out in front of the wave, the kayak began to slowly curve to the right toward the inside of the wave.

The paddle dug hard into the water, attempting to thwart the kayak from rolling into the breaker's vacuum, but Ben was powerless to avoid what awaited him.

The strength of the ocean was much too great for his feeble attempts to save himself.

With sickening slowness, he watched in agonizing fear, as the kayak turned completely sideways into the curling vortex of the wave.

Saltwater rushed over his face as the kayak began to roll.

Ben took a last quick gulp of precious air, and felt the swirling wave engulf him.

His whole world turned upside down.

Bubbles teased his face and his lungs burned.

He vainly attempted to push off of the floorboards in the cockpit to clear himself from the boat.

It was too late.

The force of the wave pushed him down toward the bottom of the sea, head first.

No air.

Salt stings.

Lungs burn.

The undercurrent flipped Ben over, and, with a rush of motion, sound and light, he felt his body lurch forward again.

He lost touch with his boat.

Where is it?

The kayak's solid hull smashed into the back of his skull.

His head snapped violently forward, and, for a moment, everything went black.

Ben forced his eyes to open and search for the light on the surface of the water.

Up, up, on the surface.

Is that the surface?

No air! I'm drifting . . . drifting . . .
During the fall I tense my muscles, and wait for the moment of impact.
Now, I relax and let the ocean take me where it would.
Briefly, I resurface, and gulp the precious air.
I see the kayak only a few yards away, gliding toward the shore.
Somehow, it has landed on its back, and is sitting upright in the water.
Another breaker comes crashing down on top of my head.
I swim with the white water toward the shore.
Now I'm further away from where the breakers begin their descent.
Their power is lessened where I swim.
It is only a few seconds before I resurface.

Ben swam with few powerful strokes toward the kayak and reached the safety line. The cockpit was full almost to the brim, and he knew it would be useless to try and climb aboard. He grabbed the safety line and swam out in front, careful not to get too close to the nose.

The back of his head throbbed, and he touched the matted hair gingerly. Fortunately, there was no blood. After a few long minutes, Ben felt the hard sand surface under his feet and scrambled onto the shore, dragging the kayak behind.

Two of the three gallons of fresh water still clung to the outrigger poles and, although he'd lost a few supplies, Ben felt lucky. The kayak was far enough up the beach to keep out of the waves for awhile. He turned his attention back to the ocean to search for the paddle. The arm of the paddle was blue and the blades were a bright white. It only took a few frantic seconds to see it bobbing up and down fifteen feet from the shore. It was caught in the wave's rhythm and, at times, it disappeared from sight. Ben ran down the shore a few yards, closer to where it floated, and jumped in. He swam out, grasped the paddle firmly with one hand, rolled over onto his back, and caught the next wave to the beach.

Ben stood on the sand, and bounced a few times on the balls of his feet to clear his ears. He felt the dull pain again on the back of his scalp and, out of instinct, reached back and touched the welt that had begun to rise. It was about the size of a golf ball and he looked to see if there was any blood yet. There was none.

"Guess I won't be surfin' anymore waves to shore soon," Ben told himself as he shook his head and laughed.

He felt a little dizzy, and sat down on the beach to allow the dry sand to cling to different wet spots along his shorts and arms. He laid back to soak up some of the warmth radiating off the beach, closed his eyes, took in a deep breath, and sighed, allowing the adrenaline to slowly ebb away.

What a rush that was! I haven't been on a wave that size since October.

I must have dozed off. The sun is lower on the horizon. I don't remember going to sleep. The land behind me is not as dense jungle as it was in Costa Rica, but the forest still covers the hills with dark green hues. The beach is long and wide and the trees don't come so close to the sand. There are still several palm trees dotted along the fringe of the beach and I'm going now to gather their fruit.

Ben built a fire, and sat down to eat a bar of chocolate and some oatmeal. The final chart lay spread out on the sand, its corners lifting off the beach with the breeze that blew across the water. Along its edges were four coconut husks to keep the chart from blowing away. The sun had set, but Ben could make out the details by the light of the fire. He had landed near Punta Mala, and, from there, he calculated the distance to Colombia. It was roughly two hundred miles.

He now made a crucial decision to cut across the Gulf of Panama, and head in a diagonal line to South America.

There were several reasons behind the decision.

I talked them over with myself that evening, and convinced myself again of the safest and quickest route across the ocean. Well, I don't want to go near the Panama Canal, that's for sure. Too many ships. Of course, that means I have to go out in the middle of nowhere, a hundred miles from shore.

How much fresh water do I have now?"

A quick check showed two and a half gallons left. Enough for three days if he rationed it. If Ben was fortunate, and hit smooth water, and paddled fifty miles a day, it would take four gallons.

Not enough water.

Ben brushed away some of the sand that had blown across the chart, and looked hard at the map point he was near, and then at the mapped shape of the jagged coast of Colombia.

He searched for an answer to jump out and speak to him.

I can collect water out of these coconuts and use it to fill the other two empty jugs. That will give me five gallons. Plenty of liquid. Okay, that one's solved. Take several more with me for good measure.

The sky was still black. The stars had not come out yet. Ben closed his eyes and let his thoughts drift away. After relaxing for only a few minutes, he sat up and stared into the fire.

Judging from the chart, it'll take me more than two weeks to reach my destiny if I continued to hug the coast of Panama. Also, there are too many large freighters coming in and out of the canal, and I don't want to get caught in the traffic.

The coast of Colombia looked tantalizingly close when he looked again at the chart. It acknowledged his gut instinct.

Ben quickly folded it up before he could change his mind again.

I'm gonna head straight for South America.

Ben stood up, brushing the sand from his shorts. He walked over to the water's edge, and looked out into the blackness. There was nothing to be seen, except for the few waves that lapped and curled and receded at his feet.

He turned around and lay down by the fire to go to sleep.

Morning dawned. The ocean scene rolled out before his eyes as Ben stood at the edge of its great endless mass.

This was truly Ben's church.

My heart beats faster, as I anticipate the next several days on the open water without the comforting sight of land. But doubts crowd my thoughts. I wonder what might happen if I am swept up by the currents and can't reach Colombia.

Maybe, I will miss Colombia altogether.

By the time I drift down to Ecuador it will be several weeks later.

Ben pushed the thoughts aside, and turned his attention back to the water supply. The night before, he'd gathered eight coconuts, and now patiently extracted the milk from each one. After pouring the last drop from the last coconut, there was still only four gallons of liquid. It took three more of the tropical fruit to top off the last gallon.

Satisfied that he had enough liquid until land is again reached, he sliced the white coconut meat inside the shells and placed it in plastic bags. The food supply was dangerously low, but there had not been a city in sight for days, and Ben didn't want to waste the time looking for one now.

By late morning, the five gallons on the outrigger poles, the coconut meat, ten bags of oatmeal, a half eaten box of cereal, and three slices of sweet bread, were all that had been secured.

Ben turned now to the ocean and looked out past the point and into the deep blue waters that expanded before him without definition or confinement.

Chapter 53

Courage and perseverance have a magical talisman, before which difficulties disappear and obstacles vanish into air.

John Quincy Adams (1767-1848)

The waves were not as large as the night before, but they still crested over seven feet high. Holding onto the kayak, Ben swam out a little ways into the surf. His feet were still touching the sand when the first wave crashed over his head. He jumped into its face and pushed the buoyant kayak over the top. Three more waves followed in quick succession and were defeated the same way. Then a small lapse in the rhythm of the breakers appeared and Ben pushed off the bottom, jumped into the water-filled cockpit and began to paddle. He cleared the next several breakers with only a few narrow misses and crested the last wave, just a few feet before it curled over and headed for the shore.

Paddling out a hundred more yards, until he was sure he was out of the break, Ben bailed out the water that sloshed around his waist. It took several minutes, and when only a few inches remained in the bottom, Ben rested tired arms, and took a large sip of precious water.

The land drifted slowly away, as Ben thought of the fire from the previous night. It would be his last for many days. He stood up in the kayak for one last look at the coast. It was there, motionless and green, and he waved his hand high above his head in a farewell gesture. With a mild sense of sadness, he sat back down and resumed the stroke.

If all went as planned it would be the last time Ben saw land until Colombia.

I began to grow worried that first evening as I stopped and ate supper. What had I been thinking when I looked over the charts last night? True, I have enough water for several days. But my food supply is already running out. I try to limit the bags of oatmeal at lunch, but my stomach doesn't seem to allow such skimping. My muscles grow weak from lack of protein. I ate four bags of oatmeal around noon, and several handfuls of the frosted flakes.

After only two hours that morning, the coast that the kayak had left, disappeared behind. Land was nowhere in sight. The indigo blue ocean with its pewter flashes and frosty laced trim wavetops spreads out endlessly across the horizon.

There was no turning around now.

Ben ceased looking back.

Indeed, it will no longer provide shelter, stability, or safety for me. So why would it continue to peek its head over the horizon and watch my progress?

I have abandoned the coast, and it has now abandoned me.

For the first time in months, I feel alone.

The waves rolled endlessly by, and Ben grew tired of watching their monotonous shapes. The kayak rose and fell with the swells. Ben closed his eyes at times to block out the repetitious scene that surrounded the small craft. He couldn't judge progress with the coast, and wondered if he was even moving forward. The compass pointed southeast and Ben knew that eventually, whether he was alive to see it or not, his path would run into South America.

Several things bother me now as I sit here and watch the simple sunset. For one, I do not have enough food to last past tomorrow. I can not believe I have been so nearsighted. Another thing that worries me is my inefficiency to calculate the miles I travel each day. There is nothing to take my bearing from. Although my compass could still be pointed toward the coast, as far as I know I might be pushing farther south and never hit anything. If I'm pushing farther west, away from Panama and Colombia, I will never know the difference until it is too late.

The Pacific Ocean stretches out for thousands of miles in that direction and there is no telling what will happen if the currents become too strong.

Ben tried, rather unsuccessfully, to push the morbid thoughts from his mind. Muscles tired a few hours after the sun had set. A brisk wind blew from the west across the water. It was coming from behind the kayak, and Ben praised God for the extra push. For now, at least, he was drawing closer to South America.

I am cold. I put on my wind breaker. The moon is rising and the stars are slowly following. Seeing them there in their proper places provides me with an inner warmth and serenity. I smile weakly at them, and begin once again my ritual of welcoming those stars I know by name.

The moon is reflecting off the black water's surface and the heavenly white line bears down on my kayak.

It looks like I'm traveling on a quicksilver road to the moon.

The night completed its cycle and met the dawn. Ben suffered from the lack of sleep that night. He ate two more bags of oatmeal. Only three more bags, plus a little cereal, remained. It was now painfully obvious that he did not have enough food for the rest of the day, let alone the next two.

Ben would just have to catch the rest of his meals.

After disposing of the trash from breakfast, he cast a fishing line out the back of the kayak and wedged the fishing rod between the outrigger poles and the cockpit. He could only hope for the best.

The ocean swells now rose above twenty feet. Before, the kayak had always managed to ride their backs up and down, because they were pushing south or south east. Now, though, Ben felt the water rushing north into the Gulf of Panama, as he was attempting to paddle east. Instead of the bow parting through the swells, the kayak now rolled side to side. It took extra concentration to retain balance, as each new swell threatened to roll the kayak over. Ben hesitated his stroking as each new wall of water rose by his side, and lifted the paddle in the air so as not to catch it in the current.

With clear skies and the weather holding, Ben saw nothing out of the ordinary, except for the size of the ocean's swells.

Sometime around noon he took a break. The sun was directly overhead and hot, and he took off his hat and wiped the few beads of sweat that had formed on his brow.

I squint into the harsh light, and decide to go for a swim. There are no sharks around that I can see. I take off my sunglasses and dive overboard.

With my safety line clutched tightly in my right hand, I swim around for a few minutes and let the cool water soothe my tired muscles.

Ben swam back to the kayak and lifted himself up the few inches into the cockpit. He'd been careful to avoid the fishing line that lurked beneath the water, waiting for a victim, a meal. He wondered if any fish would swim up close to the surface. The nearest shore was over a hundred miles away, and Ben hoped fervently that some type of fish would pass this way. By nightfall, Ben was still unaware of how many miles had been paddled. The fishing line trolled silently behind the kayak, without so much as a nibble the entire day.

Ben drank a half gallon of coconut milk for dinner, with several pieces of the sweet white flesh. His stomach growled, but there was not much of anything he could do about it. Ben felt a chill pass through his body, grabbed his jacket, and settled down for the night. An uncomfortable night.

Dawn found a cramped, cold, wet, tired, and hungry traveler.

Why did I attempt to forsake the safety of land and head out into the open ocean?

Ben stood up in the cockpit and strained his eyes in hopes of seeing some semblance of land. There was nothing. The only thing that met his eyes was the glare of water sharply reflecting the risen sun. He had caught no fish, and ate the last of the cereal for breakfast. A few bags of oatmeal, which he would save for as long as he could, and a few chunks of raw coconut remained.

At least there are still three gallons of water left.

Half way through the tortuous day, Ben's stomach had finally resigned itself to reality and settled into a tight knot, protesting the absence of its regular amount of food. Lethargically, he continued to paddle toward the southeast, and hoped that he was still headed in the right direction.

His energy waned and Ben wondered what he would do when the oatmeal ran out. *"Come on you stupid fish,"* he yelled. *"I know you're down there. I've got something for you. Please come and eat my bait."* This foolishness was of no use.

The water rolled on, and the sun continued to beat down as the paddle dipped slowly into the waves. Hunger-dazed eyes closed. After a few hours, Ben dozed off. He had nothing to eat all day.

My head jerks back sharply each time I catch myself sleeping. At least I think I'm catching myself. There's never anything to see except the blue ocean. There are some bright, turquoise green patches here and there. Other than that, I have seen nothing spectacular for several days.

Ben shook his head to clear the drowsiness, and opened up another gallon of coconut water. His thirst quenched for the moment, he resumed the stroke.

How long did I sleep. Nothing's clear.

At one point, Ben thought he saw the dark silhouette of land ahead. But, as the kayak crested the next swell, the mirage faded back into the bright azure sky. For several minutes he continued to look in that direction. Each time he reached the top of a swell, he could see nothing but light skies and dark waters.

Hallucinations?
My muscles weaken. I feel a fever coming on. I swallow hard, and try not to think of anything but the next wave. I close my eyes and feel the weariness overtake me. I force myself to look ahead and focus on the bow of my kayak. It bounces up and down and sometimes side to side as each new wave crashes over its vee-shaped hull.
There is a splash off to my left
I look, but there is nothing there.
A sound mixes with the waves.
I looked up to see if it is the cry of a bird.
There is only the blue sky, void of anything save a few white clouds off in the distance.

The remaining bags of oatmeal, and the last few chunks of coconut, were consumed late that afternoon. It was his sixth day on the open ocean without seeing land. The eternal vastness of the ocean sea consumed him.

For all I know I've been swept past South America, and am drifting toward the Antarctic.
Dear God, how will I know?

Ben pulled out the final chart. It was something to simply pass the time, because it really did him no good now.
Ben wondered how edible it might be.

How would taste if I soak it in saltwater?

Ben laughed at the thought, but knew grimly that if he didn't catch something soon, he would be hungry enough to eat just about anything.

There was a whisper in the wind and Ben opened his eyes slowly. Then he heard it again, soft but still audible.

Groggily, he looked around.

Nothing.

His head nodded forward and he was about to doze off again when the wind picked up.

"What is that noise?" he asked out loud.

The ocean swells settle down a little, and the kayak gently rocks back and forth in their pull. The wind swirls around my head like rushing water. I stand up and breathe in deeply.

"Enjoy this creation." Was that my thought, or had I said it?

I cannot tell.

I barely dare to breathe.

I wait for something else to happen.

I feel as if a fog has rested lightly over my eyes, and I feel a peace flooding through my body.

I sit down now and close my eyes.

I feel my body relax.

My breath and my heart resume their normal rhythm.

I speak to the waves around me, "I've been on this ocean for more than five months and you have not forsaken me. I have prayed this entire time and God has not turned his back on me. Why should I not enjoy this time alone, like the rest of my journey? This is just one final obstacle."

My head is spinning and my heart beating loudly in my chest again.

I feel like I am going to faint, but despite the internal turmoil, I smile.

Ben turned in his seat to watch the last half of the sun disappear slowly beneath the waves. He shook his head in appreciation for its beauty, and watched the slow rhythm of the waves roll all around him. The wind continued to whisper across the water, and he sat back and relaxed, knowing that somehow everything would work out.

I might have slept, but I don't remember.

Did I wake up, or have my eyes been half open the entire night?

I can't tell!

It doesn't matter!

All that matters is the deep trance the ocean holds me in.

I am riveted still by its vast power, majesty, mass, and overpowering will to exist in a state of constant motion.

Am I paddling?

My hands still grip the paddle, and its blades still dip into the water.

I can't tell if they are moving or not.

I lean forward, and then sit back.

I think of going for a swim, but do not.

Or did I?

Images float through my mind.

Sometimes I think I can see the shore.

Bright flashes of light explode from the corners of my vision.

I wonder if I have taken off my glasses.

Was the sun blinding my sight?

I raise a hand to my head, but stop short as another wave rises to my right.

I turn to greet it.

A high pitched whining came from somewhere. Instinctively, Ben swatted the air behind his neck, thinking it was an insect of some sort. He opened his eyes, and half expected to see the forest draped beaches of Costa Rica nearby. All he saw was water. Still, the buzzing persisted. He looked to his right. Something was moving rapidly there, and he was going to find out what it was that was making that annoying noise. A lever of some sort was moving in a circle.

It was black, small and had a handle on its end.

That was just my fishing rod.

"Oh crap!" Ben blurted out, blinking his eyes. He shook his head and sat bolt upright in the cockpit. *"I think I've got a bite!"* Indeed he had. The line on the reel was almost out, and he fumbled with the rod. Lifting it high in the air, Ben set it in his lap and slowly tightened the reel's tension. Something was on the end of the line, and he felt lucky that it hadn't dragged the pole overboard. *"I got you now fish!"* he cried triumphantly.

My stomach rumbles again, awakened by thoughts of a meal. It reminds me that food is on top of the priority list. I have to turn around and sit on the lip of the cockpit to see which way the line moves. Several times it swerves to the left, and then back to the right. I have no patience and I

*reel in the line continually and hope that it will not break under the tug of
the fish.*

Several flashes of movement kept Ben focused as the fish swims close
to the kayak. He saw that it was a fairly good catch. Eventually, the fish
tired and he brought it close to the boat. After locking the reel so it couldn't
get away, he clutched the fishing pole in one hand, and sliced a knife into
the fish's skull. After a few quick, powerful jerks, it lay still. Blood was
everywhere. The water was quickly turning crimson around the cockpit.
Ben grabbed hold of the fish to bring it on board. He didn't have much
luck. It was extremely slippery, and must have weighed over ten pounds.
Eventually, after much pulling and grabbing and cursing, he hauled the entire thing over the rim of the kayak and onto his lap.

He cut off the head and tail and threw them overboard. Now, there was
blood all over his hands, lap, and the floor boards of the kayak. A strong
metallic smell filled his nostrils and, had he not been so hungry, Ben would
have vomited. He held the now much lighter fish over the water, and used
another knife to skewer its body. He knew his fingers were too slippery to
hold it steady. If he had dropped it back into the water, there was no telling
how he would react. Ben would probably have dived in after it.

Holding the fish over the water, Ben sliced its belly open, and emptied
its organs into the ocean. He couldn't tell what kind of fish he'd caught. It
was dark brown, almost black, over most of the body, with a few flecks of
white along its head and back. Ben dipped it back into the water, and then
set it between his legs. Without waiting to clean himself off, he picked up
the paddle and dug into the water. Now fully alert, Ben knew that the blood
would certainly attract the sharks and he wanted to be as far away from the
sight of the killing as possible.

*No telling how big the marine life is at this depth, and there are
probably some Great Whites somewhere. I look around as I paddle. My
heart beats faster. With every wave that breaks, and every stroke I splash, I
turn in fear and half expect to see a fin break the surface. None does. After
maybe half an hour, I stop and look around again. I have convinced myself
that I am at a safe distance.*

There was a small piece of plastic mesh between the outrigger and the
kayak. A few of the gallon water jugs were tied there, and constantly
bobbed in and out of the swells. Ben placed the remains of the fish there,
and then jumped into the sea to wash away the blood that still clung to his
skin and shorts. After a quick swim, he climbed back in, careful not to

upset the kayak and send the fish flying into the water. Ben placed the fish in a thick plastic wash basin. It was the same container he used to shave and it proved most useful. He splashed some water over the fish to clean off the rest of the blood, and then scrubbed the floorboards with his hands.

After a few minutes, he felt he was reasonably clean.

I now turn my full attention to the fish, and cut off five thin strips from the middle of the carcass. Quickly, I cram one into my mouth, eating it raw. I consider it delicious because I am so hungry. As I take another piece of the bloody carcass, and began to chew it, I remember something.

There is an entire book of waterproof matches left in one of the compartments. I find the box and light a small blue candle that I have saved for some reason. It is hard to keep the candle lit. The waves want to slosh over the sides and snuff it out. I balance the paddle under my forearms. The candle is in my left hand. Two pieces of fish are on the tip of my knife and I'm able to keep the fire going. The swells pitch me back and forth. I focus on the small morsels of fish that will soon satisfy my hunger, and save my life.

Both sides of the fish were blackened. Ben took a big bite from the piece on top. It tasted charred and smoky, but he'd soon swallowed both pieces whole. He hardly noticed that the middle was raw. A few drops of water landed on the candle wick, and it was awhile before he was able to light it again. Ben put the remaining three fillets on his knife and cooked the rest of the fish. He sat back and swallowed the last bite.

Then he thanked the ocean and her Creator for the provisioning. Everything would be just fine. There was still over a pound of fish that he had not eaten. He placed it in a small bag for the next day's meal. With his stomach full, and his strength returning, Ben got out the sleeping bag and curled up for the night.

The familiar faces of the stars that stretched out across the arc of the heavens seemed particularly close that night. Ben thought he could almost reach out and pluck some from the sky. Drifting off to sleep was a manner of seconds and Ben slept most of the night without disturbance.

Chapter 54

I *didn't have the faintest idea where I was or how long I'd been pad-*
dling, or even what day it was. Regardless of my ignorance, my spirits
could not have been higher.

Ben looked across the water, searching for South America. A pod of
whales broached the surface off to his right, about fifty yards away. He
waved to them, but they didn't show any interest in him. Breakfast was
cold fish. Ben's energy level had risen, and he felt like a new man. His
paddle stroke quickened with each second. As the blue water rushed by
inches below his strong arms, Ben could feel that the end was near.

The end of the journey, or the end of Ben?

Only God knew.

My ears are alert, and I hear each wave that slaps against the hull.
My eyes are sharp and focused. I scan the horizon for any sign of life or
land. I can still taste the fish on my lips and the salt on my tongue. I can
feel my muscles rippling with each stroke, and my skin is tight, and tan, and
lean. The sun beats down on my shoulders, but my hat provides plenty of
shade for my face and neck. I have never felt better in all my life!

The past few days had passed with little food or hope. The dark memory was now fading away as the morning progressed. Ben had finally shed
the exhaustion induced trance of those days.

I think I can go all day without stopping.

Sometime in the late morning a sound reached Ben's ears that made his heart jump.

Maybe it was carried on the wind. For an instance I thought I was imagining things again.

The sound came again. Not louder, but more persistent. A distant rumbling.

Was it the waves near the coast of South America?

Ben stood up in the cockpit of the kayak, braced himself, and strained to see land. With the clouds on the horizon, he couldn't tell for sure. A dark form emerged far off in the distance, and Ben hoped his eyes were not deceiving him.

Barely noticeable at first, the ocean swells changed direction. For a moment, Ben thought he'd gotten turned around. After checking the compass, and assuring himself that he was still on course, he knew for sure that the ocean was now rolling to the east. That could only mean one thing. The ocean floor, no matter how deep, was rising.

The coast of Colombia is near!

Ben tore into the water with new fury at the hope of seeing land before the day was out.

I hear a distant cry that sounds like a seagull. In the air, a hundred yards away, are several dots circling in the sky. I blink and rub my eyes, and see that it is no mistake.
My heart is leaping with joy!
I know that I am getting close to my final destination.

Ben strained his neck to see some type of outline on the horizon, but it refused to emerge. The sun was just beginning to arc down in the sky when he saw it. Twenty miles away, just barely visible, the dark form of a mountain rose above the ocean. He stopped paddling, frozen with the possibilities.

Standing up again to get a better view, he saw there was no mistaking it.

The coast of South America lay directly in front of me.

Ben let out a tremendous cry of joy, hope, and relief. He could hardly believe his eyes.

My breath is short, and my heart is pounding. This time it's from joy. My stroke has doubled in intensity. Images float by, and I shake my head as I remember all of the trials, and hopes, and fears, and obstacles that I have overcome to get to this point.
It does not seem real!
Is it a dream?
No!
It cannot be a dream.
I have already dreamt of this moment.
Now, here, it is upon me. It is real!

Ben stopped paddling and jumped out of the cockpit into the water. He swam vigorously to the front compartment, crawled on top of the kayak, opened the hatch, and took out his journal. He slid back along the slender deck to the cockpit, and opened up the journal's stained cover.

Tearing furiously at the pages, Ben looked for the last entry he'd made. He knew that this was a day to be remembered for the rest of his life.

Lately, Ben had not bothered to write down the day or the month. Now it was time that he should. The last dated entry was February 10, 1997. There were sixteen small entries since that date, some only one sentence long.

Just two days before he had simply written this:

No food. Can't go much longer.
Where is this South America?
I think I shall never find it.

Other entries were more elaborate, but that was all the information he needed. Ben knew the day and the month. He could not believe that it was almost over.

Here is what Ben wrote that day:

I cannot believe that my long struggle is almost over. Here, standing immovable in front of me is, undoubtedly, the coast of South America. It has been almost six months now since I first pushed off the sand at a small beach called San Felipe in Baja California. It seems like I have been here

on this beloved ocean called the Pacific for more than ten years.
This is my life.
This is my love.
I don't want to ever leave.
But, I have made it alive to the continent of South America.
I always believed in myself, and now it has become a reality.

With each stroke, Ben could see the land getting closer. Soon, he could see the rugged mountains that shadowed the shore, just as his water borne surroundings began to fade slowly away.

His peripheral vision grew darker, and a brilliant center-focused light shone across the waters and onto the shore.

The waves slowed down, as did his mind, and moved up and down in a trancelike state.

I am dancing slowly now, taking my partner's hand softly into my own, smiling at her beauty, and counting our final moments together.
She holds me close, gathering me up in her arms like a child.
I bow my head one last time to weep.
A sadness that I thought I could never know comes over me.
I mourn for the time, too soon, that we will not be together.

The seagulls cried louder overhead, gathering to see this new spectacle on the water. Ben could see their faint outlines above, but did not move his eyes from the ocean swells around him.

Here he had known safety, majesty, beauty, danger, death, promise, hope, failure, disaster, heartache, loneliness, comfort, devastation, suffering, pain, success, glory, loss, and pride.

He could write pages on each of these emotions.

Emotions that, through the testing of his inner strength, developed a softer, yet more chiseled man, with many newfound characteristics.

I feel much closer not only to myself, but to God.
The ocean has given me wisdom and humility at a price that has been difficult at times to pay, but well worth the cost in the end.
The land comes closer now, and my eyes are turned toward the heavens.
I cannot see clearly.
Is it because of the tears in my eyes, or the incredible feelings of awe I feel as I near this new continent?
I am completely out of touch with reality, or so it seems.

Perhaps I am now more deeply involved with the circulation of life on this planet. More than I have ever known before, and possibly anyone else has known for that matter.

There are a few white puffy clouds overhead, I think, but I am soaring higher now just off the surface of the deep blue water, and heading south.

Sounds echoed, wind whispered, and waves thundered toward shore. But the sounds barely reached Ben's ears. The ocean glistened diamond-like in the afternoon sun, and the swells continued to roll south.

Ben couldn't really focus on any one thing.

Whatever it was that stole my mind in that moment, I cannot recall the hour, or the swells of the ocean, or the view of the coast, for the remainder of that day.

Was it the lingering effects of hunger, the reality shock of facing the finality of his next landing, or the sudden crash of the adrenaline that had kept him alive these many days? Whatever it was, it played with Ben as he ricocheted from reality to fantasy, from facts to phantoms.

I look up and see Heather. She comes toward me over the water, float-ing wraithlike above the waves. Rays of sunlight are focused only on her. I see her golden hair wafting about her shoulders in the cool breezes. She wears a silken gown of the purist white that contrasts with her flawless bronze skin. I stand, arms outstretched. She is so beautiful, I begin to weep again. I have not lost her after all.

The kayak reaches the top of a wave, and then begins to glide slowly down its back.

I slip, and begin to topple over.

I catch myself, as one foot touches the cool water.

I blink in surprise.

Heather is gone.

Ben scanned the horizon for any signs of life. There were none.

The sun winks at me in amusement, and I shade my eyes to block out its scorn.

He sat down, numb from the turn of events. Picking up the paddle, Ben began to do the only thing he knew how. He closed his eyes, and let the slow rhythm of the paddle striking the ocean's surface carry him back into a trance.

Dolphins swam all around him, and Ben watched the sun set over the horizon.

People, many people, stand waving, and watching my progress. I look toward each one. White people, brown people, familiar faces, and strangers, even my family, stand there cheering me on. I smile, not at their approval, but at my own.

I have not turned back.

I have succeeded in doing what everyone had said was impossible.

In the beginning, no one had thought they would ever see me again. Most said that they had just talked to a dead man.

They had been wrong!

Although it almost cost me my life, I have overcome insurmountable odds to reach this coast, this point in time.

I almost listened to those whispers of doubt and failure, and lost sight of the eventual goal. But through the strength of God and persever-ance, I have made it six thousand miles to the coast of South America.

Also, along the way, I have learned who I am, learned to be patient, and learned the value of good character.

And so much more.

The slender, gray, eighteen foot long kayak with its torpedo-like out-rigger, slid without fanfare onto the rocky shore of Colombia, South America.

Trancelike, Ben stepped out of the kayak, and knelt on the pebbled beach. He kissed the wet ground, and let the swirling, foam flecked sea lap around his feet. Crouched there, with the sun just beginning to set, Ben lifted up his hands and cried out as loud as he could.

But, there was no response.

There was no one there - no city, no crowds, no family, no press, and no other boats.

He blinked back the hallucinations.

It was just the way he preferred to end it.

No people, but plenty of his new found friends.

The surf thunders onto the beaches along my way, and cheers loudly with its approval. Far off on the horizon the sun waves goodbye, and winks at me as if he's known all along that I would arrive here safely. The dolphins and whales, and even the sharks, swim beneath the surface, no doubt keeping an eye on me, and congratulating me for my efforts and perseverance.

Soon, the stars will be out to fill the huge amphitheater of the heavens, and sing their praises for the God who saw me through my many perils.

Even this beach lies still in awe. Although a stranger to me, I feel a shared companionship that I have known with many others along the way.

My friends all.

The wind whispers into my ears, and caresses me with her arms, and comforts my tired body. She lifts me off of the sand, and away from the coast. Finally, the ocean rolls, and waves, and thunders, and weeps great tears onto the beach. The sun is casting a magnificent orange glow across her surface, and her many sparkling eyes look to me with love. She spreads out before me and gestures slowly, beckons constantly, and I know that I will always be welcome on her breast.

It is here I belong.

It is here I call my home.

It is within her reach that I find my happiness, and the answers I have so desperately sought.

Answers about me, the world around me, and my future.

February 27, 1997.
On the Beach
Colombia, South America

Ben rose from where he knelt on the stony beach, and cleared his mind of the rush of phantoms. He looked around, walked a ways up and then down the beach, as if to test its firm reality. Finally, he went back to the kayak and recovered his journals in their protective plastic bags.

With this treasure, and his shark scarred paddle for a staff, he climbed the rocks near the cliffs at Punta Charambira, Colombia, South America. On top he closed his eyes, and lifted his arms again to the heavens. The feelings of pride and strength from what he'd just accomplished surged through him.

I took in several deep breaths, feeling the blood pound in my temples, and chills rush up my spine, and the flush of red that covers my face, and the passion for this beautiful ocean that rises in my breast and consumes my soul.

371

Then in a loud voice, Ben cried out. *"IT'S FINISHED, IT IS FINISHED!"*

He said this over and over, until the walls of rock echoed with his cries, and the seagulls, waves, wind, and breath of the ocean, joined in with his song, filling the evening sky with their voices lifted together in harmony. *"IT IS FINISHED, NOW!"* Ben cried one last time.

But it wasn't finished.

Ben watched in disbelief as a small boat approach the shore, first with curiosity, and then with fear, as it headed straight for his kayak on the beach. The men in the boat were armed and menacing, but, so far, they had not looked up and seen Ben on the cliff. Ben knelt in the rocks near the rocky edge, and hid himself while he watched the intrusion on his sacred, hard won, world.

Angrily, he watched as the men ransacked the tiny craft. There wasn't much left to steal, but Ben felt violated by the act.

Then he caught sight of another, larger boat rounding the point, and speeding toward his beach. The thieves on the beach, having raised an alarm at the other boat's appearance, moved about in initial confusion.

At first Ben resisted the urge to charge down the cliff, and confront the thieves. But now, as he looked down at his journals, and clenched his fists until the knuckles whitened, and knew what he had to do.

Between the rocks near his feet there was soil loose enough that he could dig with his hands. Ben quickly buried the trusty zip-locked plastic package, and marked the spot with the broken paddle.

Then he turned back toward the beach.

Ben Wade stood, rose to his full 6'1", raised his muscular arms over his head, palms forward and fingers spread, and stepped to the edge of the steep bluff.

With a scream drawn straight from his jungle mentors, Benjamin Wade propelled himself down the steep trail, directly toward the startled men on the beach.

Gunshots rang out, and screams pierced the solitude of this sacred place.

Chapter 55

Ben's momentum, and gravity itself, erased any thought of turning back from his mission to cleanse his sacred beach of the men who were now scattering below – or he would die trying.

The initial gunshots came from the approaching boat, a Colombian Coast Guard RIB (rigid inflatable boat), patrolling for drug runners. It had been following the group that had violated Ben's meager possessions on that Colombian beach, and, when they had seen them caught off guard, they attacked in full force.

The intruders returned fire, and tried to find cover on the beach, but cover was scarce, and the gunfight that ensued was short, and lopsided in favor of the Federales. The surf stained red as the drug smugglers lay wounded on the pebbly beach.

One lay dead.

Unable to stop his plummeting descent down the steep trail, a wild haired, half naked, salt encrusted, Ben Wade stumbled onto the beach, startling the Federal Guardsmen who quickly aimed their weapons at him. He slid to a stop, hands raised, and eyes wildly flicking back and forth around the surreal scene before him.

"Please, please, don't shoot. These men were stealing . . .!"

It didn't take long, however, to establish his innocence, when a man stepped off the RIB, and identified himself in a clear Texas drawl, as a U.S. Drug Enforcement advisor. "Relax, son. You're American?" He said.

"I am," Benjamin Wade replied, standing straight and tall.

The shock of the encounter on the beach sliced through the reverie of Ben's triumph, and hammered home the reality of life - and death - in the wild.

That day, as the boats prepared to leave the beach below the cliffs at Punta Charambira, Colombia, Ben stood and looked first out to sea, and then up to the place above him from which he had launched his quixotic defense.

My journals are buried up there, overlooking the sacred ocean.

They are my record of triumph, my written legacy, and the documenta-tion of my solo kayak record.

Is that important now?

I think I know better.

My record of triumph, my legacy, my documentation, is etched in my heart and my soul.

Etched forever under the watchful and protecting eyes of my God.

I have no need for the paper.

Ben Wade lost none of what he'd learned, during his voyage, save for the idea of sailing on forever. His growth from boy to man was etched in the places he had touched, and had touched him.

The only record left on the beach that day was the footprints that led to the water and the waiting craft.

Footprints that blended back into the sand with the first kiss of the surf.

The ocean that he loved took her last souvenir.

Chapter 56

Mississauga, Ontario, Canada
September 25, 1998

"So you've concluded that he did make it to Colombia," Marlene reflected, "but from his last entries before he landed on the beach, I'm not sure of his mental state."

"I share your concern, Ben's an amazing guy," I said. "He drove himself beyond any reasonable breaking point for months and miles."

Marlene slammed an open palm on my desk. "We've got to find out, to be sure, how it *really* ended!"

"You noticed. I wrote that last chapter based on our experience with those druggies at Punta Charambira. It made sense for at least one possibility. But, you're right; someday we'll know who Ben Wade is – and how it *really* ended."

I closed the last journal page, and idly swept the few grains of Colombian sand from the cover. I turned back to my keyboard, and began to write these last few words, "Someday, somehow, we may be blessed with knowing the end." The last page was printed and added to the manuscript.

Though I made a number of cursory searches for any information on Ben Wade, I came up short. (This was in the days before wide use of the internet.) The manuscript lapsed into a corner pile on my desk; frequently thought of, but with no fresh activity.

Janesville, Lassen County,
California, USA
Summer, 2003, Five Years Later

In March of 2000, Marlene and I had retired, and moved to the High Sierra Nevada mountain county of Lassen, in my native California. More specifically, the little village of Janesville. We built our dream home, a log lodge, in the forest at the foot of Thompson Peak, with a view of the Honey Lake Valley spread below.

The open and friendly nature of the Lassen folks, natives and new-comers alike, made getting acquainted, settling in, and getting involved almost too easy.

One example involves wine.

One of our new friends suggested that we needed to get a group together for the enjoyment of fine (or just available) wine. The Janesville Wine Guild was born, and quickly grew to include a dozen people. A fine and amicable group of new friends. Our group's format for getting together was to have a member host a dinner and feature paired wines with the food. We made all the moves of tasting and evaluating the wine, at least for as long as we could before simple wine drinking and relaxed conversation set it.

A few weeks ago we had such an event at the hilltop home of one of our group, Toni Healy. As we did the meet-and-greet preliminaries, Toni made an announcement to the group. She stood on the little balcony overlooking the living room, clapped her hands to quiet the group, and said, "As you know, I am an attorney. But you may not know, unless my dear husband, Rick, has squealed on me, that I do not cook. Since it's my obligation on this festive occasion to provide proper sustenance, I have invited a friend – who does cook, and cooks very well. He's new to town, but if you've been following the college sports you know we have a new coach for ladies soccer."

"Great, counselor, but when do we eat?" A voice came up from one of the group, followed by a chorus of chuckles.

"Completely out of order. Sit down or I'll fine you for contempt," replied Toni Healy, Esquire.

"He's already contemptible," someone offered.

This was the point that I'd stepped in from the deck where I'd been enjoying the magnificent view, and a glass of Merlot, and casually listening to the proceedings through the open door. Toni Healy turned toward the archway to her right, gestured to someone with a wave of her hand, and said, "Let me introduce our soccer coach, trumpet player extraordinaire, and our cook for tonight – no, our *chef* for tonight. Ben, come in here. Dear friends, meet Mr. Ben Wade!"

I looked up in disbelief to see a tall, broad shouldered, nicely tanned man in his early thirties. He had a shy smile, and wore his thick dark brown hair in a pony tail. Piercing brown eyes were set off by his aquiline nose, scaled to present an overall strikingly handsome visage. Below the edge of the sleeve hem of his short sleeved shirt, my stare focused in on the tattoo of a crown of thorns. I dropped my gaze to look at Marlene who stood just below the balcony, and was now staring at me with wide, questioning eyes.

"Is it *our* Ben Wade?" She mouthed.

I shrugged my shoulders, took a sip of wine, and looked back up at the young man. His presence spoke of the characteristics I had envisioned during my many hours with the journals, but I couldn't be sure. My mind swirled with unanswered questions, but I waited until after a fine meal – he *is* an accomplished cook - and the wine tasting, to seek answers.

Eventually, after the whirlwind of attention to Mr. Wade subsided to a polite roar, I stepped up to Ben and shook his hand. "Nice to meet you, Ben. Thanks for a great meal, and welcome to our little group," I said, lamely. Ben replied with more than a little shyness in his voice. "You're welcome, and I appreciate you having me here."

At this point I decided to either look silly, or brilliant. "Ben, I think I have something of yours." His expression was quizzical.

"Of mine?"

"Yes. A journal, Ben. I have a journal about a long voyage."

His eyes went wide and his jaw dropped.

I knew then, here is *our Ben Wade*.

Our guest was, in fact and truth, Benjamin Wade, *Kayak Extremist* (as he signed his note in Acapulco.)

My manuscript was, of course, resurrected. Now, though, I was blessed with a ready consultant to clarify, verify, and complete my assumptions.

Let me take you back to that fateful "last day", and, with the help of Ben himself, finish the story.

Epilogue

February 27, 1997.
On the Beach
Colombia, South America

With some help from the DEA agent, Ben convinced the Colombian Federal Officers to leave him on the beach. He promised to leave Colombia and make his way to Panama on his own.

As he watched them sail away, a weariness came over him the likes of which he'd never felt before. From his recovered belongings he pulled the sleeping bag above the tide line and collapsed into its familiar feel and smell.

The next day Ben sat there on the beach at Punta Charambira considering his options. He really was not sure what he should do. At the time he landed the day before, he was ninety percent sure that he was never going back to his old life. But now, sitting there, a little more rested and clear headed, he thought about how much his parents had suffered.

His commitment slowly changed to fifty-fifty.

Late that second day, Ben pushed off from the beach and paddled toward Panama, this time staying along the coast. He paddled for the next four days, sleeping on the water, because he didn't want to go ashore in Colombia again. Because of the drug runners, it was too dangerous. Those 4 days on the water took their toll on Ben. The ocean swells were huge, there was no breeze, and it was *hot as hell*.

By the time he approached Panama, he was only twenty five percent in favor of not going home.

As I neared the port and the Panama Canal, there were so many damn boats around that it scared the shit out of me. I thought of my options: pack it in, turn around, and go around South America. Which is stupid! How do I get around Tierra del Fuego in a kayak? No way! Or, I can go thru the Canal. Not sure how that works. One thing I know for sure, paddling north and retracing my voyage is not an option.

Ben tied his kayak to the dark, foreboding, creosote stained dock, and made his way to street level on the dingy and dangerous waterfront. For the next two days he looked for some sea captain to take his kayak as far north as possible. The caveat was that Ben had no money, and whoever took pity on him would be providing the transport gratis.

Those two days, Ben haunted the seedy little bars that stunk of stale smoke and cheap liquor. Everyone he met was drunk, or working on getting that way.

I thought really hard about just getting back on the kayak and leaving. Where? I didn't know.

Finally, Ben met a ship's officer who was able and willing to help him out. He could put the kayak on deck and take it up to Acapulco. Ben called Alonso, who readily agreed to meet the ship there. Ben gave the officer the contact information, and returned to his small craft to ready it for the voyage home.

In all honesty, I figured on never seeing my boat again.

Ben turned and walked away, straight into the arms of two Panamanian Immigration Officers who had been watching the tall gringo. Without a word the taller of the two men produced handcuffs, while the other rested his hand on the butt of a mean looking pistol jammed into his waist band.

Ben felt a chill run down his spine. He had no papers.

Yes, there were more troubles, trials and tribulations. What we know for sure is that Ben Wade made it home.

But the rest of the story must wait for another time.

Author's Note

The final chapter describes exactly how Marlene and I met Ben Wade. Since that day, Ben has become a part of our lives, a close and dear friend.

Of course, I had never seen Ben's journals until we discussed the writing of some form of book retelling his sea voyage story. We decided on the format of a novel, rather than a travelogue, so that we could give the reader a full journey with Ben. The core events, the people Ben met, and Ben's journal entry "thoughts", are all true. My and Marlene's dialogue, are fictional "connectors" for the plot.

The book delivers Ben's story on three very distinct levels: the travelogue journey along the coast, the action and adventure of his trials and tribulations, and the personal journey of Ben's mind - the psychological challenges and growth in maturity.

To this day, although I am probably the most intimately familiar with this story of anyone besides Ben Wade himself, I cannot fathom what drove this twenty four year old to persevere in his quest. He was repeatedly crushed mentally, constantly challenged physically, facing imminent death on many occasions, and yet he shook off each instance, set his eyes on the horizon, and paddled away toward Colombia. I have never met an individual who could focus on life with such laser sharp intensity.

For any more common man, it truly would have been a voyage beyond reason. But for Ben Wade, his sense of what is the limit of reason is infinitely beyond the common man.

I have included a mini biography of this remarkable soul to give you a glimpse of what I mean. The tasks that he has chosen to pursue, in music, in sports, and in life's far-out adventures, all require that laser-like focus if one is to reach the levels of success he has attained.

If I can talk him into another round of excruciating brain-tag, I hope to one day bring you the exciting details of Ben's kayak journeys down the Orinoco River in Venezuela, and the Amazon River in Brazil.

Just as with the coast of Central America, my own personal travels have introduced me to the places where Ben sought adventure. But, I can assure you, my views and experiences were from much safer, and calmer, venues than those Ben sought out and reveled in.

One last note: What happened to Heather?
We don't know, and we've actually tried to locate her.
She's been lost to history.
Heather, if you read this, please contact me.
Ben would like to say hello.

Ben Wade featured in a Honduras newspaper report

Ben Wade and his "Mazatlan" Tattoo

Life Saving Coconut Milk

Acknowledgements

The very first acknowledgment is obvious: my friend and collaborator, Benjamin Wade. Without his tenacious pursuit of the impossible dream there is no story. Sometime after we met at that wine tasting party (yes, that's true!), I asked Ben if he planned to write a book about the journey. He told me that he'd started to transcribe his journals and record his memories, but that nothing was finished. Without hesitation, I asked if he would like to collaborate on the work. If I had hesitated, I might have thought more about the immensity of the task, and chickened out right then. But, I didn't, and Ben agreed to the venture. We decided that putting the work into the form of a novel would best tell the story.

Working from the material he provided me, the true story began to reveal itself. That is, the mental struggle, the psychological dangers, and the maturity growth, that Ben Wade endured and triumphed over. I can't thank him enough for his patience as I probed and prodded him for details, and recollections of feelings that dredged up some of the not so pleasant memories of the adventure.

Benjamin, I raise my glass in admiration and gratitude to you.

Converting over 130,000 words from Ben's first person notes to the third person narrative, and then writing the story line around it, was a breeding ground for typing, tense, syntax, and other errors. Without my long suffering proof readers I would have drowned in the effort. Sheryce Long, English teacher at Southwest Baptist University, painstakingly read every word and ferreted out the tiniest details. Dr. Ray White, and his charming and vivacious wife, Denise, rose to the challenge and provided the sounding board I needed for continuity and 'read'. Also, on a daily basis, my own bride, Marlene, always kept a smile as I hollered down from my loft office, "Honey, come on up and read this paragraph...", and provided a lot of candid views.

Thanks, guys.

On another note, we are grateful to Ron and Liz Ronstadt for, first, saving Ben's skin when he ran out of potable water and nearly killed himself with dehydration, and, second, for allowing us to use their names in the book. Our thanks to Ben's friend, Christian Serino, for providing him with an "anchor back home."

Thanks, folks, on a lot of levels.

Finally, my thanks to the good people at Outskirts Press. This new age iteration of the old world of the book printing business delivers their valuable service with professional aplomb at every turn. My Author's Rep was teacher, mentor, and guide par excellence. Everyone in production, marketing, and operations, responded to my sometimes inane questions with the utmost courtesy and patience. Thank you!

Bill and Liz Ronstadt aboard _Sarafina_

Benjamin Wade

A Mini Biography

A t this writing, Ben Wade is still a young man in his late thirties. However, by any normal standards, he has managed to cram double that time into his lifetime accomplishments. I have included this biographical sketch for your information, and to better help you to understand this remarkable man.

Benjamin Wade was born on September 18, 1971, and spent his early years in Knoxville, Tennessee. At age six he moved with his family to Moscow, Russia, then part of the communist Soviet Union. For Ben this was an early eye opener of what life was like outside the 'pampered' US.

His parents were involved in the underground church, and his father taught at Moscow University. Ben saw first hand how propaganda and communism worked. They returned to Tennessee after two years.

Ben began playing the trumpet at age 8, a year before most kids start because of their two missing front teeth. His entire family are accomplished musicians. He also began playing sports at that time, including Football, Baseball, and Soccer. There was an incident in elementary school that was predictive of Ben Wade's life.

"At the end of the 5th grade, in a general assembly with 500 kids, they asked students to stand and tell what they wanted to be. Only a dozen of us stood up, but I remember vividly standing and saying, 'I will be the best trumpet player in the world'. This was a defining moment in my early life.

Of course everyone laughed at me, which fueled my focus even more."

Three years after Ben started playing, in sixth grade, he was winning every competition he entered. This streak continued for seven years, and he was never beaten, whether it was a regional, state, or national competition.

At age 12, and for two years, Ben and his family lived in Bangalore, India. This was another great eye opener to see the poverty of the world. Ben reports that they all got sick, lived without cold water or refrigerators, and with dirty food, and no air conditioning in 125 degree weather.

A pivotal moment during this time for Ben, was that he broke the barrier from being a child musician to a professional. He began to practice four hours a day on his trumpet because there was not much else to do. At first he couldn't push through, whether it was range or technique, to the higher skill level he needed. Finally one day he did, and he soared in skill and confidence. He also played hours upon hours with the family quartet, and listened to his father interpret music every day. (This gave Ben the foundation on which he can now interpret music for the Susanville Symphony Orchestra.)

At age 14, Ben and the Wade family lived in Budapest, Hungary. This was his summer 'coming of age' as a teenager. The living was cushy. He started worrying about his appearance, and his thoughts. He also discovered his strong ego, charisma, and sense of leadership.

Reflecting again on the music, a most important time in his young musical life was his junior year in school. Ben was invited to the International Trumpet Guild competition for the best trumpet player under 18. Audition tapes were submitted, and he was one of four selected from around the world. At NTSU in Denton Texas, they converged for the live competition, and Ben was named the best trumpet player in the world under 18. He was 16 years old.

When he finished high school he faced a split in the road – music or business. His choices were Oberlin Conservatory for the trumpet, and the University of Tennessee for a business degree. The family business in Southern California was an option after school. Ben finally did not major in music because he saw the life that his trumpet teacher lived, playing in 16 groups at one time, and giving 30 different lessons. Ben could see himself burning out and losing his love for music. He decided to major in business.

You've read in the story about the California experience after college, and the decision to take the sea kayak voyage, so we'll move to 1997.

After returning from the trip Ben made the celebrity rounds and then tried to settle back into a "normal" life – without much success. Then he fell back on his sports experience, and was hired to start the Simpson University women's soccer team. Simpson University is a private, evangelical

Christian, liberal arts university, founded 1921. Ben moved to Redding, California and coached there for two years. He also started the men's baseball program at Simpson, played in their Jazz band, and taught math, music, and soccer.

Adventure was still in Ben Wade's blood. In 1998 he kayaked down the Orinoco River in Venezuela, and in 1999 he added the Amazon River in Brazil to his list of adventurous feats. Both of these trips are subjects for future books!

In 1999 Ben moved to Patten University in Oakland, California and started both the men's and women's soccer programs, adding the baseball program the second year. While at Patten, Ben picked up his trumpet again, and played with the San Jose Symphony and the San Francisco Symphony orchestras.

In 2001 Ben Wade tired of the big city and moved to Lassen Community College in Susanville, California to start their women's soccer program. He had a 67-6-1 record at Lassen and is recognized as the #2 winningest active community college coach by the NSCAA.

While in Susanville, Ben played trumpet with a number of groups. Under his leadership, these groups finally coalesced into the Susanville Symphony Orchestra, which is today in its sixth successful season. During this time, Ben attended the nearby University of Nevada, Reno, and earned his Masters Degree in Conducting.

Ben continues as the resident Conductor, Composer, and Creative Director for the Susanville Symphony. Susanville, California, is the smallest city in America with a symphony orchestra, and the only one with Benjamin Wade conducting.

* * *

An amazing footnote to this book and to Ben's story:

On February 12, 2009, Ben Wade appeared in the CBS TV series, SURVIVOR – TOCANTINS: The Brazilian Highlands. We won't know if he won the competition or not before this book goes to press.

One more story for Ben to tell in the future!

Benjamin Wade
Conductor and Artistic Director
Susanville Symphony Orchestra
2008

About the Author

Tom Gauthier lives with his wife Marlene on a small, timbered ranch in Janesville, California. Tom is a retired Human Resources Development executive, having worked for one multi-national corporation for over 34 years. He holds a BS in Management, an MBA and an MS and Doctorate in Psychology. Tom and Marlene have four grown children, thirteen grandchildren and five great grandchildren.

He is a veteran of the Army and Air Force Reserve, having served in Intelligence and on a Flight Crew. Since retiring in 2000, he has consulted on communications and quality management, and serves on his school board, hospital board, and airport commission.

Tom has written commercially and for corporate education for many years, and has written and produced four musical comedy plays. This is his second novel.

Other novels by Tom Gauthier include:

Code Name: ORION'S EYE
© 2008 Tom Gauthier
Published by Outskirts Press, Collins, CO

For more on Tom's books, visit his website at: **www.tomgauthier.com**

This book has been read by:
Stan & JoAnne Walton - 2011

Printed in the United States
219147BV00005B/1/P

9 781432 712341